THE IMAGE OF THE NON-

THE LITTMAN LIBRARY OF
JEWISH CIVILIZATION

Dedicated to the memory of
LOUIS THOMAS SIDNEY LITTMAN
*who founded the Littman Library for the love of God
and as an act of charity in memory of his father*
JOSEPH AARON LITTMAN
יהא זכרם ברוך

'Get wisdom, get understanding:
Forsake her not and she shall preserve thee'
PROV. 4:5

*The Littman Library of Jewish Civilization is a registered UK charity
Registered charity no. 1000784*

THE IMAGE OF THE NON-JEW IN JUDAISM

◆

The Idea of Noahide Law

DAVID NOVAK

SECOND EDITION

Edited by
MATTHEW LAGRONE

Oxford · Portland, Oregon
The Littman Library of Jewish Civilization
2011

The Littman Library of Jewish Civilization
Chief Executive Officer: Ludo Craddock
Managing Editor: Connie Webber

PO Box 645, Oxford OX2 OUJ, UK
www.littman.co.uk

_____

Published in the United States and Canada by
The Littman Library of Jewish Civilization
c/o ISBS, 920 NE 58th Avenue, Suite 300
Portland, Oregon 97213-3786

First published by the Edwin Mellen Press 1983
Second, revised, edition published by the
Littman Library of Jewish Civilization 2011

A catalogue record for this book is available from the British Library

The Library of Congress catalogued the first edition of this book as follows:

Novak, David, 1941–
The image of the non-Jew in Judaism.
Bibliography: p.   Includes index.
1. Noahide Laws.   2. Aliens (Jewish Law).
3. Gentiles in Rabbinical Literature.
4. Judaism—Relations   5. Philosophy, Jewish.   I. Title.
BM520.73N68 296. 1'8   83-21989

ISBN 978-1-906764-07-4

Publishing co-ordinator: Janet Moth
Proof reading: Bonnie Blackburn
Index: Matthew LaGrone
Production: John Saunders
Designed and typeset by Pete Russell, Faringdon, Oxon.
Printed in Great Britain on acid-free paper by
the MPG Group, Bodmin and King's Lynn

PREFACE

THIS BOOK is an attempt to understand the role the image of the non-Jew has played in the history of Judaism. The image of the non-Jew is one that has had a profound influence on the way Jews have interacted with actual non-Jews they have encountered at various points in their history. It has also shaped the way they have understood their own identity in determining just what distinguishes them from the non-Jews around them. The image of the non-Jew in Judaism, therefore, should be of interest to those concerned with the history of Judaism itself, as well as those concerned with Jewish–Christian and Jewish–Muslim relations, comparative religion, the development of Jewish law and philosophical deliberation on Judaism.

A study such as this would be likely to have a rather episodic character were it not for a crucial factor. Since rabbinic times the concept of *sheva mitzvot bnei Noah*—the seven commandments of the sons of Noah—what we call Noahide law, has provided the conceptual framework for just about every serious Jewish treatment of the image of the non-Jew. For this reason a study of the use of this concept in both Jewish law and theology gives historical continuity to a treatment of the image of the non-Jew in Judaism. Furthermore, it enables one to lay the foundation for a systematic philosophical reflection on Judaism because a philosophy of a religion involves at the outset an idea of the human person for whom that religion is to be instructive and normative. A study of the crucial concept of Noahide law, then, enables a philosophy of Judaism to be historically rooted without being only a treatment of things past, that is, a constructive enterprise emerging out of the very object of its interest and understanding.

The most persistent characteristic of this concept throughout its development is that is has a double reference. On the one hand, it refers to that body of law that the rabbis and subsequent Jewish thinkers believed pertained to all humankind, as distinguished from the 613 commandments of the Torah that were and are the obligations of Jews alone. On the other hand, it refers to that body of law to which the Jewish people themselves were considered obligated prior to Sinai. It appeared to me that this double reference was in the mind of virtually all those Jewish thinkers who dealt with this concept. This means that the gentile world that confronted them in the present was paralleled to the pre-Sinaitic world, and that world became a model for negotiating with the contemporary gentile world. The former reference played a significant role in Jewish theology—that is, if revelation made the Jews what they are now, what does revelation presuppose? The latter reference played a significant role in Jewish law—that is, it provided a scale of values to determine the moral commonality between Jews and different gentile groups.

The historical work has been the most difficult, for it required the analysis of a vast amount of material and the supposition of a line of development, especially in rabbinic literature. Thus the first chapter attempts to assign a point of genesis for this concept. This required careful analysis of biblical, rabbinic and Hellenistic texts in order to sort out antecedents and consequents. It demanded, furthermore, polemic with several scholars who proposed different points of origin. Several of these scholars were my teachers.

My approach in the following chapters is best described as a "history of ideas" method. Although I have tried to be cognizant of modern philosophical, literary and historical treatments of specific classical texts, as the notes surely suggest, I have been principally occupied with the development of a concept. For this reason, I devoted minimal space to the construction of texts and their transmission. Indeed, the concept of Noahide law appears in so many texts in so many different expressions that I had to look for an underlying frame of reference. One might describe this approach as "topical" rather than "situational." My primary concern has been to show the recurrence of this concept with a certain set of recurrent questions. However, this synthesis does not intend to smooth away differences among individual thinkers: questions concerning meaning are, of course, to be answered.

The first seven chapters deal with the Noahide laws individually. I have attempted to accomplish two goals: first, to show the halakhic development of each law as it was discussed in the rabbinic sources, in the codes and in the responsa literature; second, to show how the concept of Noahide law and its attendant questions seem to be conceptually if not literally involved in speculative discussions of what halakhah pertained prior to Sinai, and practical discussions of what halakha pertains to non-Jews and Jewish relations with non-Jews.

Because my first concern is with the history of this concept, primary discussion has relied heavily on the analysis of the classical rabbinic texts by traditional commentators. Other, non-traditional, commentators have been cited and discussed, but the traditionalists have the advantage, conceptually speaking, in that they have attempted to deal with the living issues in the rabbinic world as equally living issues in their own world. As such, they are the primary developers of that tradition. This appeared to me to be of great significance philosophically in that philosophers can only reflect on those questions they themselves ask out of their own immediate concern.

The second part of this study, beginning with chapter 9, deals with the "theory" of Noahide law. Chapter 9 considers the role of aggadah in the rabbinic speculation regarding the transition of Jews from *bnei Noah* to *bnei Yisrael*, emphasizing revelation as the proximate cause of transition.

The final chapters—tracing the arc of the Noahide from Maimonides to Cohen—were easier to write because these thinkers negotiated the Noahide systematically in their work. In the last chapter, I outline the major points that emerge from this study. I conclude with a discussion on why Noahide law might be an appropriate starting point for Jewish philosophy today.

D.N.

I am honored that Professor Novak permitted me the opportunity to edit the second edition of *The Image of the Non-Jew in Judaism*. As his doctoral student at the University of Toronto, I urged him to consider publishing a new edition of this work. The rationale behind this edition is not so difficult to detect. "The number of Jews in the world," Milton Himmelfarb famously wrote, "is smaller than a small statistical error in the Chinese census." Consequently, how a minority religion uses its sacred literature and frames its moral and philosophical narratives to navigate and negotiate the often knotty relationships with other communities is perennially relevant, and all the more so in a globalized world. The content of the book did not require massive reworking; it largely stands as it did in 1983. Style and syntax were smoothed out, and a new Afterword was added.

We are grateful to everyone at the Littman Library for recognizing the significance of this book and bringing it to the attention of a wider circle of readers. In particular we extend our thanks to Connie Webber and Janet Moth, who shepherded this edition expertly despite working with a frightfully inexperienced editor.

University of Delaware
22 Adar II 5771

M.L.G.

ACKNOWLEDGMENTS

I AM GRATEFUL to the following scholars, who answered my specific queries, critically evaluated my ideas, and provided encouragement and guidance throughout the whole project: the late Jacob Agus, Eugene Borowitz, the late Emil Fackenheim, the late Robert Gordis, Germain Grisez, the late Milton Himmelfarb, the late Louis Jacobs, Reuven Kimelman, Ralph Lerner, the late Jakob Petuchowski, the late Steven Schwarzschild, Michael Wyschogrod and Bernard Martin. Finally, I am grateful for the assistance of the J. Richard and Dorothy Shiff Chair in Jewish Studies Research Fund of the University of Toronto.

D.N.

ACKNOWLEDGEMENTS

CONTENTS

CHAPTER SUMMARIES

MATTHEW LAGRONE

CHAPTER 1. The Origins of the Noahide Laws

This chapter begins with reflections on some previously proposed historical timeframes for the formation of Noahide law. Earlier scholars located its origins variously: in the Bible, among Hittite legal scholars and during the Maccabean era. This chapter maintains, contrary to prior scholarship, that the concept of the Noahide is absent until the first century CE; that is, it is a rabbinic creation. While theology can discover the beginnings of the Noahide laws in the Torah, their historical starting point can only be established following the social, demographic and religious dislocations of the Second Temple's destruction in 70 CE. For the rabbis, these laws originated prior to the Sinaitic revelation; they were the moral standard for the entire gentile world, and that world of course included the ancestors of those who would later accept the covenant at Sinai. Israelites before Sinai, then, were Noahides.

The Noahide laws were also considered obligatory for all time, and would be the measure by which gentiles would be judged. In order to give the Noahide laws a biblical imprimatur, the rabbis linked the Noahide (*ben noah*) to the *ger toshav*, the non-Jew who lived in the land of Israel and accepted Israelite rule. However, these laws never constituted an active body of applied social and criminal regulation, and they are not descriptive of any actual historical period. By the time that the laws received their basic formulation in the Talmud, no gentiles were living under Jewish jurisdiction, and as a consequence the rabbinic imagining of these laws as a functioning legal system was of theoretical value alone. The theoretical nature of the Noahide laws, however, was not a disadvantage but rather a benefit; it made the laws philosophically attractive, a rich source for reflection on the essential structures of Judaism itself. Because these laws were considered by the rabbis to be rational—that is, knowable even in the absence of a divine revelation—and universal—that is, it is a part of human nature across time and place—they formed a moral connection between the people of the covenant, Israel, and the gentile world.

CHAPTER 2. The Law of Adjudication

Although following the Sinaitic revelation Jews were obligated to follow the 613 commandments, prior to this experience Jews as well as gentiles were judged by the Noahide laws. This experience of living under Noahide law prepared the Israelites to accept the greater and more specific revealed law at Sinai. The former law is separate from the latter; it is general, rational and universal, applying to all people, a moral universe preceding any particularity.

The rabbinic tradition presents two divergent positions on the nature of the law of adjudication. The first position, articulated most fully by Maimonides, was that this law was to be imposed upon gentiles by Jews; that is, ideally, Jewish judges would arbitrate Noahide laws for gentiles. The second position, advocated by Nahmanides, holds that non-Jews establish and maintain their own courts separate from Jewish courts, and judge based on the general principles of Noahide law. The latter view acknowledges the moral legitimacy of gentile courts and indirectly of gentiles themselves whereas the former only allows gentiles to share in a universal aspect of Jewish law. Nahmanides' position represents a richer notion of an independent Noahide law.

This chapter also devotes considerable space to charting how the rabbis consistently moved Jewish law in the direction of Jewish and non-Jewish equality in matters of civil jurisprudence. Clearly drawing on non-Jewish models of justice, the rabbis adjusted those laws that did not pertain to ritual matters (and consequently were not immediately rational and universal, unlike ethical concerns).

Finally, the law of adjudication was used by the rabbis to justify non-Jewish political authority over Jews. Because gentile nations adhere to and are obligated by the Noahide laws Jews can affirm local authority because it is grounded in a universal law. Ultimately, this law confirms that Judaism recognizes gentile moral normativity. Also explored is the best-known rabbinic recognition of that moral and legal normativity: the principle of *dina d'malkhuta dina* (the law of the land is the law), first enunciated by Samuel, a third-century Babylonian Amora.

CHAPTER 3. The Law of Blasphemy

Blasphemy is the explicit rejection of the God of Israel, who is also the God of the whole world, as a fundamental aspect (*yesod*) of Judaism. According to the rabbis, blasphemy is forbidden not only to Jews but also to gentiles, and the prohibition for Jews and non-Jews appears to be the same in the Talmudic sources. This is because reverence for God is assumed to be universal, an attitude written into human nature. Punishment for this sin, however, varies:

gentiles are disciplined for misusing any divine name of God, whereas a more severe penalty is administered to Jews who blaspheme the Tetragrammaton.

In the Hellenistic era, the Noahide prohibition of blasphemy was re-evaluated by Josephus and Philo. The former wrote that no one, Jew or gentile, should blaspheme even the pagan gods, a tactic clearly prompted by concerns for Jewish flourishing in a wildly pluralistic environment where Jewish mono-theism was an outlier. Josephus' reasoning for this reconsideration of blas-phemy was based on a temporizing pragmatism. His contemporary, Philo, offered a more reflective response: he suggested no one ought to ridicule "the gods"—even though they were non-existent—as it would lead to contempt for the name of the true God. Behind this lies an assumption that the pagan men-tion of god or gods is really directed at the One God. For Philo, then, polythe-ism is a philosophical mistake, but behind its error is latent monotheism.

CHAPTER 4. The Law of Idolatry

This section highlights the tension between biblical and rabbinic attitudes towards gentile idolatry. The Bible consistently forbids idolatrous actions for Israelites while distinctly not excluding such behavior among gentiles. As gentiles are not participants in the Sinai covenant, they cannot be guilty of idolatry, even if their cult is consistently scorned in the Bible. Idolatry appears to be exclusive to Israel in the Bible, and consisted of either unfaithful-ness towards God or the worship of something other than God. While non-Israelites are not guilty of idolatry per se, they are condemned when they attempt to convince Israel to worship their gods. The prophets frequently par-allel these acts to adultery, the Israelites lusting after foreign deities. Contrary to the biblical permission of pagan idolatry, the rabbis forbade anyone, Jew or gentile, to practice idolatry. According to one rabbinic line of thinking, all gen-tiles are idolaters, while another distinguished between contemporary and ancient idolatry. In either case, a radical innovation was introduced: idolatry was to be removed everywhere. The rabbis had to reinterpret biblical verses that ostensibly permitted gentiles to engage in such activity, and consequently pagan idolaters were now morally culpable for their religious practice. Philo, Josephus and some Amoraim, on the other hand, attempted to prove that most pagans were in fact monotheists in their thought, even if they indulged in ancestral practices reminiscent of pure idolatry.

For medieval Jewish thinkers, idolatry was believing that something finite was in fact infinite, and worthy of worship. As Jews lived almost exclusively among Muslims and Christians, not ancient pagans, thinkers such as Saadiah Gaon, Maimonides and Menachem ha-Meiri had to reassess contemporary idolatry. For example, ha-Meiri denied that the paganism and polytheism that the rabbis encountered was alive in his day, and therefore there were no idolaters. Islam was never considered idolatrous, while the Christian case was more complicated. A consensus on the latter slowly emerged: although Christians use intermediaries in their worship—most notably, Jesus of Nazareth—they ultimately intend the God of Israel.

CHAPTER 5. The Law of Homicide

This chapter argues that the law prohibiting murder is the Noahide commandment most immediately and rationally evident. The rabbis considered its prohibition from two distinct points of view, the theological and the political. In theological terms, murder is the intentional taking of another human life, a life created in the image of God (*b'tzelem elohim/imago dei*). Although the act is directed at an innocent, God is indirectly diminished through the wanton destruction of one of his creatures. In political terms, murder wrecks social life. As human beings are social animals, they need protection from those who would disrupt the smooth functioning of life.

Regarding murder at the individual level, the rabbis differentiated criteria for the punishment of Jews and gentiles. For Jews who commit murder, the death penalty is employed only under the strict standard of "hatra'ah," or forewarning. The potential murderer is warned by two witnesses of the consequences of his action, and if he proceeds to murder, then he is liable for capital punishment. Such a dispensation was not available to non-Jews. Forewarning was a rabbinic innovation, conceived in the context of worsening Jewish–Roman relations. The Roman government regularly sentenced people to die on the thinnest evidence, something which violated the basic moral norms of justice.

The law of homicide also deals with the morally knotty issue of abortion. Rabbinic Judaism permitted abortion only when the mother's life was in danger, but for Noahides abortion was proscribed in every case. But medieval exegetes corrected this apparent double standard, eventually sanctioning the use of abortion for Noahides when the mother's life was threatened.

CHAPTER 6. The Law of Sexual Relations

Noahide law forbids several types of sexual relations, including incest, homosexuality and bestiality. Regarding attitudes towards incest, few differences can be found between Jews and non-Jews, although the rabbis recognized a significant dissimilarity toward relations between brother and sister. Noahide law was more permissive in this instance because it was also more general, whereas Jewish law knew of the specific prohibition of brother–sister relations. The rabbis were not the only Jews to reflect on prohibited relations: Philo held that sexual closeness between parents and children, or between siblings, breached the prior relationship of father and daughter, mother and son, or brother and sister. Like the rabbis (who rarely deliberated in overt philosophical language), he insisted that reason instructs us that intimacy should branch outside of the family.

This chapter also considers how the rabbis and later medieval thinkers addressed homosexuality, which was pervasive in the Greco-Roman world, and the nature of gentile family ties.

CHAPTER 7. The Law of Robbery

The prohibition of robbery is based on the principle that society is necessary for human flourishing. And a central element of the construction of any human society is property, or the relation of persons to things, especially in economic transactions.

The rabbinic tradition makes fine distinctions between Jews and gentiles regarding robbery, ultimately creating a double standard. But this double standard needs to be placed in its historical context; it was the result of a cascade effect. Due to several brutal wars between Jews and Romans (66–70 CE and 132–5 CE), some rabbis charged that gentiles were naturally cruel and devoid of compassion, and therefore, because of their lower moral standards, what constituted robbery for gentiles was subsequently reduced. However, this difference was not allowed to stand for several reasons, including the diminishing of God's name in the world (*hillul ha-shem*) and the fact that gentile monotheists were law-abiding peoples because of their (tacit) acceptance of Noahide law.

Although the practical effects of a socially unfair law were removed, the rabbis maintained that Noahide law remained stricter than Jewish law regarding robbery. Like other violations of the Noahide commandments, the penalty was assumed to be death. In atypical historical circumstances—especially times of war or oppression—the rabbinic supposition was that all gentile robbery was aggressive and occurred because of anti-Jewish attitudes and not greed. Because the crime was ideological and not practical, its intent was far more lethal and therefore any act of robbery, no matter how minor, was to be punished with death. An important twentieth-century scholar, Samuel Atlas, the chapter notes, proposes a novel theory as to why this was the case.

CHAPTER 8. The Law of the Torn Limb

The prohibition against tearing a limb from a living animal is explicit in Scripture, and the only one of the seven Noahide laws to be found immediately in the Torah. According to the rabbis, tearing a limb from a living animal was part of ancient pagan religious ritual, and thus was a species of idolatry. Clearly, such a practice was to be avoided by Israelites.

At first view, this law appears limited in scope, but this chapter argues that it has implications for Jewish–gentile relations extending beyond the immediate purpose of the law. The chapter will show again how Noahide law has directed some innovations within rabbinic law, namely, in reducing double standards in laws that pertain to both Jews and non-Jews.

The law of the torn limb also introduces the question of nature in Jewish thought. In the pre-philosophical world, this Noahide rule could be understood as tampering with nature, violating the cosmic order. As the idea of natural law enters into sustained philosophical reflection, the "nature" in natural law refers to universal human nature. And thus a thinker such as Maimonides is more concerned with what a violation of this law says about the human being per se—the law of the torn limb seeks to remove anti-rational cruelty—rather than a violation of the cosmic order.

CHAPTER 9. Aggadic Speculation

Aggadah represents Judaism's theological imagination, whereas halakhah corresponds to Judaism's legal dimension. This chapter argues that the rabbis used the creative resources of theological inference to discover how the tradition charted universal moral law.

This charting is particularly common when it comes to revelation, as the relationship of Jews and non-Jews to the Noahide law changed appreciably in the rabbinic mind. According to a famous aggadah, all people originally experienced the Noahide laws as divine directives. However, after Sinai, non-Jews no longer accepted the divine origins of these laws. The rabbis asked: are they still bound by a law they do not accept as God-given? Yes, they answered. Although gentiles no longer perceive a transcendent intention behind the laws, they are still obligated to adhere to them because of their social and political value. This powerful aggadah can be read in two ways: first, because non-Jews no longer hold to the divine origin of the Noahide laws but still observe them, the laws themselves must be rational, that is, capable of being understood and followed in the absence of direct revelation; second, if the rational element of the commandments are minimized, as they are by the medieval kabbalists, then the moral distance between Jews and non-Jews becomes abysmal. This chapter argues for the first view, which is philosophically more coherent and more in line with the developed Jewish tradition from rabbinic times to now.

CHAPTER 10. Maimonides' Theory of Noahide Law

According to Maimonides, Noahide law is binding prior to its acceptance. It is written into the human constitution and exists before any possibility of assent. Maimonides maintains that there are three potential sources for knowledge of Noahide law: (1) the Mosaic tradition, both written and oral; (2) rational investigation; and (3) the general revelation found in the Torah. For Maimonides, the latter source is primary for gentiles. Despite the theocentric partiality here, he does not rule out rational investigation as a method for acquiring knowledge of the Noahide laws. Such a method is legally permissible, making its possessor both wise and moral, although theologically this method is insufficient. Rational recognition of the laws does not require belief in their divine origins, and politically this is satisfactory; that is, Jews can flourish among gentiles who accept the law while at the same time ignoring its foundations in divine revelation. The upshot of this is that Maimonides affirms that rational discovery of the Noahide laws is possible, meaning that the laws are independent of historical revelation.

This chapter also reflects on the long-standing scholarly dispute concerning whether or not Maimonides engaged in natural law thinking. This section considers the exegesis of his *Hilchot Melachim* (8:11), which has divided scholars on its true philosophical and philological meaning.

CHAPTER 11. Albo's Theory of Noahide Law

The great fifteenth-century theologian Joseph Albo considered Noahide law to be a category of divine law. He divided law per se into three classes: natural, conventional and divine, in an ascending hierarchy. Natural law is concerned with right and wrong in the human situation; conventional law is related to what is desirable; and divine law is occupied with true good and true evil. The superiority of divine law consists in its specificity, and it is greater than either of the other two groups because it is absolute like natural law and transcendent like conventional law. Despite the superiority of divine law, this chapter argues that Albo's philosophical and theological thinking demonstrates a strong interrelationship among the three laws.

CHAPTER 12. Late Medieval Developments

Following Maimonides and Albo, several other prominent Jewish thinkers reflected on the role of Noahide law both within Judaism internally and in relation to gentiles externally. Perhaps the medieval thinker who expanded the concept of the Noahide to its greatest point was Menachem ha-Meiri. He states definitively that there are no idolaters today like the pagans of the ancient world. Non-Jews are bound by religion, and clearly function in the moral universe as Noahides. By accepting the universal moral law, one that is written into the very essence of being human, Christians (and Muslims, although Meiri did not live among them) have a point of ethical commonality with the people of revelation.

This section argues that Meiri revived the biblical institution of the *ger toshav*, though of course absent the political dimension. After the full parting of the ways with the new Christian movement towards the end of the first century CE, the idea of the *ger toshav* had fallen into desuetude as the person with such a status was a quasi-Jew, not fully integrated into the community but recognizing Jewish authority. The rabbis were concerned with preserving the integrity of Judaism following the destruction of the Temple and the rise of gentile Christianity, so they did away with categories that obscured relations between Jews and non-Jews. But by Meiri's time no one would confuse the two groups, and fear of religious syncreticism was now past. The result of this institution's philosophical revival by Meiri was that contemporary Noahides could now be considered potential Jews.

This chapter also considers the work of two nineteenth-century Italian-Jewish thinkers, Samuel David Luzzatto and Elijah Benamozegh. The latter presents a novel approach to Noahide law. He is the first—and, to this point, only—important Jewish philosopher to deem the content of this law to form a separate religion, "Noahism," a religion that Benamozegh judged distinct from Judaism's monotheistic rivals.

CHAPTER 13. Moses Mendelssohn and his School

The first truly modern Jewish philosopher, Moses Mendelssohn tendered a philosophically rich interpretation of the Noahide laws, one at great variance with the interpretations that preceded it. In *Jerusalem*, Mendelssohn held that the Noahide laws were not part of revelation, and were universally intelligible through human reason. In fact, revelation is inferior to reason because the latter is immediately and publicly available to all and the former is a snapshot in time, restricted, non-universal. Consequently, Noahide law, which is universal, is greater than revealed law. Mendelssohn is not calling for the removal of Judaism, and in fact holds that Judaism is the most rational of the revealed religions. Nonetheless, Judaism remains a component in a universal religion of reason. Mendelssohn's reversal of the traditional understanding of the respective roles of Noahide and Mosaic law was revolutionary.

CHAPTER 14. Hermann Cohen and Jewish Neo-Kantians

As with other thinkers covered in this book, Hermann Cohen's presentation of the Noahide laws is placed within its historical context. Cohen desired to show that Jews in late nineteenth-century European (and especially German) society could be and were in fact good citizens, and that their Judaism was an aid to citizenship. Judaism was not an insular religion, and Jews supported the secular state, Cohen affirmed. For instance, he maintained that the aim of the law of adjudication was "objective lawfulness," a signal starting-point for any society, secular or religious.

Cohen's view of moral law was shaped by Kantian ethics. He argues that Noahide law confirms the humanity of gentiles, and that this rabbinic construction was the first of its kind. Recognizing the humanity of others is the beginning of autonomous ethics. For Cohen, the human ethical future is best presented through Jewish universalism, leading to universal ethical monotheism in the messianic age. This last point has been central to liberal Jewish theology since Cohen's time.

CHAPTER ONE

THE ORIGINS OF THE NOAHIDE LAWS

1. Introduction

In this chapter I attempt to locate the origins of the Noahide laws in the history of Judaism. I first present the primary literary data, then I examine all of the pertinent theories in terms of the evidence they present. This evidence often seems counterfactual, and, in some cases, the philosophical assumptions that underlie them also appear counterfactual. Thereafter I present my own theory and its evidence. A detailed examination is called for because there has been so much speculation about when the concept of Noahide law emerged in Judaism. How one locates this point of origin will, to a large extent, determine how one views the essence and development of this concept. Although we should avoid the genetic fallacy of reducing a concept to its origins, the demonstration of the order of its initial manifestation in history is required for a critical understanding. History is only intelligible if one can show how the components developed.

2. Literary Data

The first explicit presentation of the Noahide laws is found in the Tosefta, a work dated to the late second century.[1] The text reads:

Seven commandments were the sons of Noah commanded: (1) concerning adjudication (*dinim*), (2) and concerning idolatry (*avodah zarah*), (3) and concerning blasphemy (*qilelat Ha-Shem*), (4) and concerning sexual immorality (*giluy arayot*), (5) and concerning bloodshed (*shefikhut damim*), (6) and concerning robbery (*ha-gezel*), (7) and concerning a limb torn from a living animal (*ever min ha-hy*).[2]

Subsequently in a Tannaitic work, *Seder Olam*, and in the Babylonian Talmud, we find virtually the same statement quoted, except that the prohibition of blasphemy precedes that of idolatry.[3] Furthermore, this text calls blasphemy *birkat Ha-Shem* (literally, "blessing the name of God"), which is a transparent example of a term used in its opposite meaning.[4] In several midrashic texts we find the order of presentation as follows: (1) idolatry, (2) blasphemy, (3) adjudication, with the last four commandments in the same order as in the three aforementioned works.[5]

In the Amoraic elaboration of this *baraita* in both the Talmud and Midrash, the sequence of these laws and their content is traced back to Gen. 2:16: "And the Lord God commanded man saying, 'from every tree of the garden you may surely eat.'" This commandment is the first explicit divine direction to a human being in the Torah's account of creation. A persistent attempt has been made to see Noahide law as biblical law. How one interprets the words in this verse determines the sequence found in the Noahide laws.

The first word is *vayitzav* ("and he commanded"). In the Gemara the Palestinian Amora, R. Johanan, connects this word with the word *yetzaveh* in Gen. 18:19 where Abraham is anticipated as commanding justice; hence for him *dinim* (adjudication) is the first law.[6] On the other hand, the Gemara presents a Tannaitic tradition quoted by R. Isaac that the first word refers to idolatry. The text links this word to Ex. 32:8 where the worshippers of the Golden Calf are described as straying from the path God commanded them (*tsziveetim*). The Midrash connects this word with the term *tzav* in Hosea 5:11, where idolatrous decrees are condemned.[7]

The third word, *elohim*, denotes God, idols or persons possessing authority. The Gemara takes it in the third sense, namely, "judges," as in Ex. 22:27, "the judges (*elohim*) you shall not curse."[8]

In both versions the fourth law is the prohibition of bloodshed, as the word *adam* (human being) is linked to Gen. 9:6, "whoever sheds human blood (*dam ha'adam*) . . ."

The fifth Noahide law concerns sexual immorality. The corresponding word in the sequence of Gen. 2:16, *l'emor* ("saying"), is taken in both versions as it is used in Jer. 3:1, ". . . saying if a man send away his wife." The context here deals with unfaithfulness, using its sexual manifestation (*zenut*) as the model.[9]

The sixth Noahide law is the prohibition of robbery. The corresponding words in Genesis are taken by the Midrash as "from every tree of the garden you may surely eat." The implication is that there is a limit to what may be eaten, and consequently what is outside this limit is stolen. In the context of this narration the act of eating from the tree of knowledge of good and evil is the sin of robbery (*gezel*).[10]

The seventh Noahide law concerns eating a limb torn from a living animal. In the Gemara this prohibition is traced back to the words, "you may surely eat (*akhol tokhel*)," which Rashi interprets as meaning, "that which is ready for food (*omed l'akhilah*)," but you shall not eat a limb torn from a living animal because a living animal is not ready for food but must grow and reproduce. The Midrash, in one passage, sees the prohibition of the torn limb as hinted at (*ramzu*) in the entire verse about eating.[11] Another midrashic command to Noah, "only flesh with its lifeblood therein (*basar be-nafsho damo*) you shall not eat" (Gen. 9:14).[12] Indeed, before Noah no flesh at all was to be eaten from either a living or slaughtered animal.[13]

These Amoraic attempts to find in the Written Torah both the source and order of presentation of a traditional prescription have parallels.[14] Indeed, one of the most important projects of Pharisaic Judaism was to show that Jewish tradition emerged from Scripture.

Several Tannaitic opinions added prohibitions such as cross-breeding (*kl'ayim*), castration (*sirus*), eating blood from a living animal (*dam min ha-hy*) and witchcraft (*kishuf*). Some of them are added to the other seven. One of them substitutes two of them for the law of adjudication and the prohibition of blasphemy.[15] Other Tannaim limit the Noahide laws to the prohibition of idolatry, or those concerning idolatry, blasphemy and adjudication.[16] What emerges from all of this discussion is that in the Tannaitic period, there was debate over the number and content of these laws. We have no record, however, that any authority in this period rejected the doctrine per se.

3. Historical Hypothesis I: The Noahide Laws are from the Biblical Period

Throughout the history of Judaism some have attempted to uncover the source and order of presentation of the Noahide laws in the Torah. For example, Meir Abulafia (d. 1244) wrote, "the Gemara derives them from Scripture (*veyaliflahu mikra'ai*)."[17] He notes that the words of Gen. 1:29, "and God said, 'behold I have given every seed-bearing plant . . . for food'," would have been sufficient to permit the consumption of all vegetation; and that the words of Gen. 2:17, "you may not eat of the tree of the knowledge of good and evil," would have been sufficient to proscribe the exception to that general rule. Therefore, the verse under discussion (Gen. 2:16), came to be the basis of a prescription (*le-drashah hu d'ata*),[18] dealing with humankind *in toto* and not just with the first two humans in the Garden of Eden.

Following this general line of thought, there were later attempts to demonstrate that the Noahide laws were accepted by its literal subjects, the "sons of Noah," that is, the peoples of the ancient Near East. With the discovery of literary remnants from these civilizations, some scholars have tried to show that their law codes bear out the original universality of the Noahide code. These attempts have not only been a continuation of the exegetical tradition enunciated by medieval commentators such as Abulafia, but have been part of the Orthodox reaction to the assertions of critical biblical scholars that the laws of the Torah are mostly unoriginal, that they are *derived* from earlier non-Israelite sources. This response endeavored to deny such claims.[19] As part of this apologetic project, some Orthodox thinkers turned the critical argument on its head, as it were, by showing that the non-Israelite law codes are derived from the Torah rather than vice versa. These laws play a central polemic role here because Jewish tradition designates them as universal in scope, unlike the remainder of Mosaic law.[20] Consequently, if a Jewish influence on ancient law is to be acknowledged as Jewishly legitimate, there must be at least a part of the Torah applicable to humankind in general. Therefore we can understand the desire of these scholars to see Noahide law as essentially Toraitic and then to see comparative jurisprudence as confirmation. Moreover, one can also see this project as part of an attempt by Jewish scholars, Orthodox and liberal, to contradict anti-Jewish claims, widespread in nineteenth-century academia, that Judaism has always regarded gentiles as little more than savages. If Judaism acknowledges the original source of both Jewish and non-Jewish law to be the same, then Judaism by extension acknowledges the essential moral personality of gentiles.[21]

Philip Biberfeld presents the most explicit treatment of this Orthodox theory. Biberfeld's approach reflects the influence of Samson Raphael Hirsch, especially the latter's belief that non-Jewish culture is relevant to Judaism.[22] In the mid-1930s, Biberfeld attempted to prove the central role of the Noahide laws in his history of law. His point is the claim that ancient history shows that the source of law was considered to be of divine origin and design. In other words, law is revealed.[23] In presenting this view, Biberfeld follows Hirsch. The latter wrote:

With this prohibition the education of Man for his moral high godly calling begins . . . It is a *prohibition*, and it is not a so-called "reasonable prohibition" (*mitzvah sikhlit*) . . . of oneself one would never come to forbid it, and even after the prohibition no other reason for it could possibly be found other than the absolute will of God.[24]

As such, Biberfeld takes the Noahide law to be the archetypal law out of which all other ancient law systems emerged. This theory, that all other legal systems are copies of the Torah, some with more and some with less fidelity, was advanced in ancient times by Hellenistic Jewish theologians as well as by several of the Church Fathers.[25] Today, of course, critical objections to this ancient theory have become more accurate with the proliferation of comparative data. Thus, Biberfeld's problem was to navigate the cognate data *consistent* with

Noahide law and the data *inconsistent* with it. This describes how he later attempted to resolve the problem in a later work:

All these traditions were the common inheritance of all of the descendants of Noah. But . . . they had become corrupted and mixed with mythical and polytheistic elements. The Hebrew traditions retained the simple, original purity which fixes them as closer to the source than the versions of the other peoples.[26]

Biberfeld here uses the method of the critics in assuming a primary source and subsequent derivations.[27] For him, of course, the primary source is the Masoretic text and the subsequent *derivations* are the cognate documents. Such a supposition, however, is not cogent. Biberfeld establishes an arbitrary standard to determine historical data rather than interpret them. In other words, those data that contradict his theory are considered derivations from the original law. As a result, this effort to confirm an ancient *consensus gentium* for Noahide law fails because it can draw the same conclusion whether the data agree with the Noahide laws or differ from them. There is great poignancy about an Orthodox Jew in the Germany of the mid-1930s arguing for the primacy of universal morality. But, in the end, Biberfeld's work reveals more about the man and his time than the ancient world. One can see his theory as a part of an Orthodox reaction to biblical criticism, a Jewish reaction to anti-Semitic charges of xenophobia, and a human reaction to the absence of international morality in the modern world.

An analysis similar to Biberfeld's was put forth by the great biblical exegete, M.M. Kasher:

These laws found in the ancient codes of Hammurabi, Assyria and the Hittites which agree with the statutes of our holy Torah confirm the notion, it seems to me, that laws were known in the world similar to those said at Sinai, except that the kings and judges in those days made the laws agree with their own outlooks and methods according to their own situation.[28]

Kasher attributes the attempt to show the derivative nature of the Mosaic law to anti-Semitism (*sonay am yisrael ve-torato*).[29] Clearly an *ad hominem* approach characterizes this theory.

4. Historical Hypothesis II: Noahide Law is Hittite Law

We have seen that efforts to present Noahide law as biblical, in both source and order, emerge originally from the Amoraim and afterward were used by medieval and modern thinkers. The modern proponents of this theory attempted to find historical corroboration for it in the law codes of other ancient peoples, especially in the law codes of other ancient Near Eastern peoples, which were only recovered in the twentieth century.

Chaim Tchernowitz (Rav Tzair, d. 1949), in attempting to bridge the classical and modern presentations of this theory, argued that the rabbis themselves may have acknowledged an ancient non-Jewish version of the Noahide laws. Tchernowitz, however, was not deducing his theory from scriptural texts like the Orthodox scholars; rather, his argument was based on historical evidence. He quotes from the *Yalkut Shimoni*, a midrashic collection edited in the Middle Ages: "Ten commandments were commanded to Israel at Marah, including the seven the *sons of Heth* accepted."[30] The version of this text found in the Gemara refers to the seven Noahide laws.[31] Tchnerowitz argues that the contemporary discovery of the Hittite code is closely paralleled to what the rabbis designated as Noahide law. Indeed, the extensive Hittite conquests in Asia made their law international in scope, as was the case later in antiquity with Roman law. Based upon this midrashic text, plus contemporary historical evidence about the Hittites and their laws, Tchernowitz saw this favorable recognition of Hittite normativity as an ancient tradition accepted by the rabbis. With the demise of the Hittite nation the reference to its law would no longer have any historical significance, and subsequently they were attributed to the sons of Noah, whose normativity is explicitly noted in Scripture.[32]

Tchernowitz's theory is clever but not convincing. First, he assumes that the text in the *Yalkut*, referring to the Hittites, is more original than the text in the Gemara that references the Noahides. However, the Gemara was edited long before the *Yalkut*, and one would have to have comparative evidence that the latter's version is prior to the Gemara's version. Tchernowitz offers no such evidence, because this is the only place that the Hittites are mentioned. One could make a stronger argument that the inclusion of the Hittites is a scribal error made in copying the original text from the Gemara. Second, it is highly unlikely that the rabbis would have deemed the Hittites as the original promulgators of international law inasmuch as they were one of the seven Canaanite nations (Gen. 15:20–21) whose very neglect of the Noahide laws resulted in God's disenfranchisement of them.[33]

Aside from general references in the Bible to a recognizable universal morality,[34] one cannot see the Noahide laws as a legal system in the biblical period on the basis of either internal textual evidence or external evidence provided by the law codes of cognate civilizations. The only two Noahide laws explicitly enunciated in the Bible are the proscriptions of bloodshed (Gen. 9:6) and the eating of flesh from a live animal (Gen. 9:4). We have already seen the inadequacy of the historical methodology used by some Orthodox scholars in order to uncover evidence of the specific Noahide laws in non-

Jewish documents from the biblical period. Moreover, already in the Middle Ages there those who did not take the Amoraic exegesis of the verses from Genesis literally. For example, Judah Halevi (d. 1142), writing about a certain type of rabbinic interpretation of Scripture, made the following point:

> ... or they use Biblical verses as a kind of fulcrum of interpretation in a method called *asmakhta*, and make them a sort of hallmark of tradition (*ke-siman le-kabbalatam*). An instance is given in the following verse: "and the Lord God commanded the man saying, of every tree of the garden thou mayest freely eat." It forms the basis of the "seven Noahide laws" ... There is a wide difference between these injunctions and the verse. The people, however, accepted these seven laws as tradition, connecting them with the verse as an aid to memory (*she-makel aleihem zikhram*).[35]

In other words, the verse is not literal; instead, it is a mnemonic device. *Asmakhta* means that the origin of these laws and their legal status is rabbinic, and they are "read back" into the Bible.[36] Indeed, if one examines the rabbinic exegesis of Gen. 2:16, one can see that it is based on the *associations* the biblical words have with full statements elsewhere in the Bible. Furthermore, these associations are nowhere designated *gezerah shavah*, that is, analogies considered bequeathed by pre-rabbinic, even Mosaic tradition.[37]

5. Historical Hypothesis III: The Maccabean Origin of Noahide Law

In a 1930 article, Louis Finkelstein attempted to prove that the Noahide laws are a product of the Maccabean period:

> The occasion for their establishment is then clear. For the first time in four centuries, the Maccabean victory had put Jews in a position of authority in their own land. But Maccabean Palestine contained a large heathen population . . . The scholars of the day were now confronted with the problem of giving these gentiles a constitutional status in a Jewish state. Were they to be compelled to observe the whole Torah, or any part of it? . . . The answer to these questions was given in the Noahide laws.[38]

The textual basis Finkelstein brings for his theory is based on a verse in Jubilees (7:20), a non-canonical work from this era. There we appear to find a variation of the doctrine of the Noahide laws:

> Noah began to enjoin to his sons to (1) observe righteousness, (2) to cover the shame of their flesh, (3) and to bless their Creator, (4) and honor father and mother, (5) and love their neighbor, (6) and guard their soul from fornication and all iniquity.[39]

Although the enumeration of commandments here differs somewhat from the rabbinic versions, this text, nevertheless, seems to be demarcating a specific number of commandments incumbent on a gentile.

However, in a study of Jubilees and its relation to Jewish law, Chanock Albeck (d. 1972) argued, quite convincingly, that the fundamental project of this book was to show that the *entire* Torah was known by the patriarchs, and even earlier by Noah and his sons, as oral tradition before its public revelation at Sinai.[40] This doctrine was later emphasized in rabbinic literature.[41] Therefore, the text does not in fact demarcate a number of specifically Noahide laws but only indicates Noahide observance of the Torah later to be revealed at Sinai. In other words, the emphasis of certain specific laws does not rule out a commitment to the Law as a whole.

This type of presentation has both biblical and rabbinic parallels. For example, Deuteronomy records that in the covenant between God and Israel, before crossing the Jordan, the people are admonished to "keep the entire commandment (*kol ha'mitzvah*) which I command you this day" (27:11). Nevertheless, eleven transgressions are specifically mentioned (27:15–25), followed by the words, "Cursed be the one who does not uphold the words of this Torah to do them" (27:26). In the Septuagint the verse reads, "who does not keep *all* the words (*en pasin tois logois*) of this law."[42] These eleven items were clearly chosen as outstanding examples of a larger class, not as members of a closed class. Furthermore, after the return from Babylonian captivity the covenant is renewed with God. The people are pledged "to observe and to do *all* the commandments of the Lord our master and His judgments and ordinances" (Neh. 10:30). Nevertheless, a number of important commandments are specified because of their immediate contemporary urgency, such as the prohibition of intermarriage (10:31). Later the Talmud indicated that a gentile could not be converted if he or she refused to accept the *whole* Torah, even if that refusal involved only one item.[43] Yet the prospective convert did not have to know the entire Torah in detail, an impossible task for anyone,[44] needing only instruction in a few (*miktzat*) major and minor commandments prior to conversion.[45] Finally, it should be noted that the Talmud occasionally indicated that the Tannaim at times only mentioned *some* examples of a larger class (*tanna ve-shiyaur*) when presenting the law.[46]

Finkelstein's historical theory about the Noahide laws being formulated to deal with gentiles living under Jewish rule after the Maccabean victories was subjected to a critique forty years later by Jacob Agus. Agus pointed out that "the historical situation called for the evolution of a theory of religious tolerance. However, Finkelstein does not refer to the forced conversions of the Idumeans in the South and the Itureans in the North."[47] Agus refers here to the forced conversions initiated by the Maccabean king, John Hyrcanus (d. 106 BCE), as recorded by Josephus.[48] The records of the Maccabean period indicate no such "tolerance" was practiced and that gentiles living under Jewish political rule were pressured to accept Jewish law by converting, with the specific requirement of male circumcision. At least in the case of the Idumeans and Itureans this pressure had practical results.

Hyrcanus was a supporter of the Sadducees.[49] This group accepted only the Written Torah as authoritative.[50] Now, as we have seen, the Bible does not provide a specific body of law for gentiles. It does, however, record that circumcision was intermittently *forced* upon those who were to live in proximity with the Jewish people.[51] The best example of this is the circumcision of the Shechemites at the insistence of Jacob's sons (Gen. 34:14).[52] Since the Sadducees were in political power, and since they looked to the Written Torah for normative precedent, it is difficult to see how Noahide law could have been operative during this period, for it is not found explicitly in the Bible. Even if it was a doctrine of the rival Pharisees, they were excluded from political power during the reign of John Hyrcanus and his son, Alexander Jannaeus.[53] Noahide law surely presupposes political authority for its enforcement.[54] It is unlikely that the doctrine of Noahide law refers to a *political reality* in Sadducee-dominated Jewish Palestine during the Maccabean period. Indeed we have no case (*ma'aseh she-hayah*) in any literary document from this period showing that these were implemented.

Following logic similar to Finkelstein, his colleague Boaz Cohen saw the Noahide laws as a version of the Roman doctrine of *ius gentium*, that is, that law the Roman government recognized as obligatory for all persons under its rule, not just for Roman citizens bound by the *ius civile*.[55] Unlike Finkelstein, however, Cohen did not attempt to actually date their promulgation. According to most scholars, though, *ius gentium* was a later designation for that class of law governing non-Romans domiciled under Roman rule. These people were known as *peregrini*. Beginning in 242 BCE, a special official, the *praetor peregrinus*, was appointed to rule in these cases (*quod plerumque inter peregrinos ius dicebat*).[56] This praetorship was set up when Rome began to acquire non-Roman provinces with large numbers of non-Roman subjects. In Jewish legal sources, both Hellenistic and rabbinic, no such official is expressly mentioned nor are any actual cases involving a special branch of Jewish law for gentiles presented.

6. Noahide Law and the Resident Alien

The rabbis themselves attempted to locate the Noahide laws in a sort of legal and historical perspective. If we understand this perspective both from the aspect of Jewish law and from that of history, we may then be able to discover the origin of the concept of Noahide law within the development of Judaism.

A *baraita* quoted in the Babylonian Talmud indicates how the rabbis placed the Noahide laws in a specific legal context:

Who is a resident alien (*ger toshav*)? Whoever, in the presence of three rabbinic fellows (*haverim*), obligates himself not worship idols. This is the opinion of R. Meir. But the sages say whoever obligates himself (*kol she-kibbel alav*) for the seven commandments for which the sons of Noah obligated themselves. Others say . . . who is a resident alien? Whoever eats non-kosher meat (*nebelot*) but who obligates himself to uphold all the commandments in the Torah except the prohibition of eating non-kosher meat.[57]

Thus we see the rabbis identifying the Noahide laws as the minimal prerequisite for naturalized citizenship in a Jewish state.[58] Following the principle of majority rule in rabbinic legal disputes, the opinion of the sages is the law.[59] Another *baraita* places the law of the resident alien in historical context:

The institution of the Hebrew bondsman (*eved ivri*) only applies when the Jubilee applies as Scripture states, "Until the Jubilee year he shall serve with you" (Lev. 25:40) . . . R. Simon b. Eleazer states that the institution of the *ger toshav* only applies when the Jubilee applies.[60]

Here we see that the institution of the *ger toshav*, a law-abiding gentile having an official status in a Jewish polity, only has legal force when the *whole* Jewish people is in full possession of its own land, for the Jubilee was only in effect during the days of the First Temple when all twelve tribes enjoyed political sovereignty in the Land of Israel.[61] It is doubtless that the rabbis saw the Noahide laws as having universal moral authority irrespective of Jewish national sovereignty. Yet it is important to note that they saw the full *legal* force of these laws as being contingent upon a fully constituted Jewish polity which, even in their time, was a matter of ancient history, although always, to be sure, part of the future messianic agenda. In situations of less than full Jewish sovereignty, the *ger toshav* did not constitute a complete political and legal status, because Noahide laws that define such status were not fully enforceable.[62]

Having established an important conceptual connection between the Noahide laws and the institution of the *ger toshav*, we must now examine the history of this later institution, for which there is considerable data. From the first *baraita* just quoted it would seem that the Noahide laws are a pre-Israelite institution used to constitute the subsequent Israelite establishment of the resident alien. Historical investigation will show, however, that the *institution* of the *ger toshav* long preceded the concept of Noahide law.

In the Bible, especially in the Pentateuch, the term *ger* is used in varying contexts. Sometimes it denotes an actual proselyte, that is, one who has adopted and been adopted by Judaism. We read:

And when a *ger* dwells with you and makes Passover for the Lord, you shall circumcise him, every male, and then he may draw near to it, and he shall be like a person native-born on the land (*k'ezrah ha'aretz*). There shall be one Torah for the native-born (*ezrah*) and for the *ger* who dwells among you (Ex. 12:48–49).[63]

Other times the term denotes a political alien, a sojourner among the Jewish people having a set of limited rights and responsibilities. As Deuteronomy notes:

You shall not abuse a needy and destitute laborer, whether a countryman (*m'aheikha*) or your *ger* who is in your land, in your cities (Deut. 24:14).[64]

Additionally, the Bible does not explain exactly *how* one became a *ger*, either in the religious or in the political sense.[65]

Because of the wide disparity in the use of the term, the rabbis saw it designating two separate statuses. When the term signaled a full participant in Jewish religious life they defined that person as a *ger tzedek*, a proselyte. On the other hand, when the term meant a quasi-citizen of the Jewish polity they defined them as a *ger toshav*, a resident alien. This contrast is brought in a rabbinic interpretation of the following biblical verse:

If a *ger* or a sojourner (*toshav*) among you has prospered, and your brother being impoverished is sold to a resident alien or to the offshoot of the family of a *ger* . . . (Lev. 25:47).

In the oldest midrash on Leviticus the preceding verse is explained:

Ger denotes a full proselyte (*ger tzedek*). *Toshav* denotes a *ger* who eats non-kosher meat (*nebelot*). The family of a *ger* denotes a gentile. The offshoot of a *ger's* family denotes one sold to an idolatrous cult.[66]

We see here four different statuses in this verse: (1) a full proselyte, (2) a resident alien, (3) an ordinary gentile, (4) a devotee of an idolatrous cult.

Ironically, Bible critics, who follow the Graf-Wellhausen hypothesis concerning the distinct sources of the Pentateuch, interpret the data similarly to the rabbis. T. J. Meek, for one, concluded:

Our study of the meaning of *ger* has accordingly led us to the conclusion that the word did not continuously retain its original significance but in the course of long usage went through three distinct stages of meaning, which can best be represented in English by the terms, "immigrant," "resident alien" and "proselyte."[67]

The only difference between these two interpretations is the dating of various texts. For the Bible critics the political meaning of *ger* reflects a pre-exilic period, whereas *ger* as *proselyte* reflects a post-exilic period. For the rabbis, both meanings were in effect since the time of Moses. Nevertheless, for both groups, the institution of the *ger toshav* only reflects a pre-exilic period of Jewish history.

This period is characterized by full Israelite sovereignty and occupation of the Land of Israel. Status in this society was determined by one's relationship to the land:

And the Lord spoke to Moses in the steppes of Moab at the Jordan near Jericho saying: Speak to the sons of Israel and say to them, "when you cross the Jordan into the land of Canaan you shall disinherit all the inhabitants of the land before you . . . And you shall cause the land to be inherited by lot for your families: with many increase their share (*nahalato*) and with few decrease their share . . . according to ancestral tribes (*le-mattot avotaihem*) they shall be apportioned (*titnehalu*)" (Num. 33:50–51, 54).

Full status in pre-exilic Israelite society presupposed landedness or official and permanent attachment to cultic shrines as in the case of the priests (*kohanim*).[68] Both the status of the tribes and that of the priests was determined by patrimony. In such a society a person without patrimony would be in essence landless, for even if he purchased real estate it would return to its original owner by *ancestral right* in the Jubilee year.[69] Such a purchase would in effect be a lease, the longest term possible being forty-nine years. Thus, when Moses implores his father-in-law, Jethro, to join the people of Israel in their journey to the promised land and to settle there with them, Jethro replies, "I will not go, only to my land and my birthplace will I go" (Num. 10:30). About this point the oldest midrash to the book of Numbers notes, "because *gerim* have no portion therein."[70] The *ger toshav*, therefore, was a non-Israelite living as a resident alien, in fact a second-class citizen, under Israelite rule. As a landless person, he was reduced to hiring out his services in most cases.[71]

Roland de Vaux describes the *ger toshav*:

Among the Arab nomads, the *jar* was the refugee or lone man who came seeking the protection of a tribe other than his own. In the same way the *ger* is essentially a foreigner who lives more or less permanently in the midst of another community, where he is accepted and enjoys certain rights.[72]

De Vaux later compares the *gerim* with the *perioikoi* of ancient Sparta, the original inhabitants of the Peloponnese who retained their freedom but had no political rights. Prior to de Vaux, Johannes Pedersen saw the *gerim* as primarily those Canaanite residents of the Land of Israel who were not exterminated but, rather, were subjugated by the Israelite conquerors.[73] Indeed, it was not until the second century CE that the rabbis recognized that the biblical restrictions against full conversion for such nations as the Moabites and the Ammonites no longer applied because these nations no longer existed as discernible ethnic groups.[74]

Throughout the ancient world, where full citizenship was determined by patrimony, provision had to be made for resident aliens, for it was neither possible nor practical to enslave them all. In Athens such resident aliens were called metoikoi;[75] in Sparta, as we have seen, perioikoi. In the Ptolemaic empire they were designated paroikoi or katoikoi.[76] All of these terms derive from the Greek oikein, "to dwell," just as the term ger comes from the Hebrew gur, having the same meaning. In the earliest period of Roman history, we find clientes, strangers who immigrated to Rome, where they obtained the protection of patrician families (gentes).[77] Later we find peregrines, discussed earlier.[78] The concept of the ger toshav, then, has many ancient parallels.

This parallelism was clearing recognized by the ancient translations of the Bible, most notably the Septuagint and the Vulgate. For example: "if a resident alien (ger ve-toshav) among you has prospered . . . " (Lev. 25:47) becomes in the Septuagint, "if a proselyte or paroikos (resident alien) among you has prospered . . . "; and the Vulgate offers this variation, "if a convert (advena) or a resident alien (peregrinus) among you has prospered . . . " In the rabbinic tradition, the proselyte is the ger tzedek (true convert) and the paroikoi is the ger toshav. Whereas the latter term refers to a long-standing institution in Israel, the term proselyte is a neologism of the Septuagint based on proselthein, "to come to." It suggests a religious newcomer as opposed to the older epelytos, which had a more secular meaning.[79] A fragment from Philo refers to the proselyte as advena legume et rituum as opposed to one who is only advena regionis.[80] The fact that new terms had to be coined in Hebrew, Greek and Latin for the concept of a full convert seems to indicate that the ger toshav is a much earlier institution. In fact, the Talmud recognizes that later criteria for conversion were more narrowly religious, whereas formerly they were political and economic:

. . . one who converted in order to eat at the king's table or to be a servant of Solomon is not a proselyte in the view of R. Nehemiah. For R. Nehemiah used to say that . . . the converts of Mordecai and Esther are not converts . . . unless they converted according to contemporary standards (ke-ba-zman ha-zeh) . . . Our rabbis taught that in messianic times converts will not be accepted. Similarly, converts were not received during the period of David and Solomon.[81]

7. Proselytes and Fearers of the Lord

The neat division of free non-Jews having some formal tie with Judaism into either proselytes or resident aliens seems to be a prescription *de jure* rather than a description *de facto*. Although for different reasons, both the rabbis and the Bible critics may have oversimplified the historical situation. Since the concern in this book is with the development of a specific institution in Judaism, it will be our task to discern why this easy division was suggested by the rabbis and how it affected their concept of Noahide law.

During the biblical and Hellenistic periods, the transition from a gentile to a Jew was more process than event. Tchernowitz saw conversion as represented in the Bible as a process of ascending degrees, resolving the seeming contradictions between the passages where the term *ger* denotes a purely political status and where they denote a religious status as well:

It is possible to maintain those commandments mentioned incidentally in the Torah regarding the *ger*, such as the prohibitions of idolatry, defilement of sacrifices ...violation of the Sabbath and Yom Kippur, and others; these were commandments which were generally accepted by all the *gerim* before they were circumcised. At first they were kept as options (*be-derekh reshut*) and with the passage of time they became obligations (*hovah*) in the sense that the *ger* slowly drew near to the worship of the Lord until he took upon himself the sign of the covenant and completely entered the community of Israel.[82]

In other words, for the later rabbis circumcision followed by immersion and the full acceptance of the commandments of the Torah was both the *terminus a quo* and the *terminus ad quem* for conversion. Conversion for them was an event.[83] During the biblical period, on the other hand, according to Tchernowitz, the *terminus a quo* of the process of absorption into Judaism was the renunciation of idolatry followed later, sometimes several generations later, by circumcision, the *terminus ad quem*. In this interpretation Tchernowitz was followed by his most famous student, Yehezkel Kaufmann. The latter wrote:

Later Judaism made a clear and exact distinction between the *ger tzedek* who accepted the commandments and is virtually like a Jew in all respects, and a *ger toshav* who accepted the seven Noahide laws . . . but in the earlier period this distinction did not exist because purely religious conversion was not yet practiced.[84]

Kaufmann, like his teacher Tchernowitz, saw purely religious conversion, namely, *a status resulting from an act of volition alone*, as a later innovation.[85] A Tannaitic text also sees the status of *ger toshav* as the beginning of a process that ends in full conversion:

Who is a *ger toshav*? Whoever has resolved to convert and has renounced idolatry but who still has not actually converted. We allow him twelve months to do so. This applies to a *ger toshav*, but as for a gentile it is forbidden for him to dwell among Jews and to work on the Sabbath lest the Jews learn from his deeds.[86]

The above appears to be the source for the later Amoraic statement that a *"ger toshav* who has not been circumcised within twelve months is considered to be a confirmed idolater (*ke-min she-ba-goyim*)."[87] Even in the Talmudic period, the absolute separation between the *ger toshav* and *ger tzedek* was not consistently held. A good case can be made that generally in the biblical period, and even in the early rabbinic period, the *ger toshav was in fact considered a potential ger tzedek.*

Among the Hellenistic Jews living outside of Palestine we encounter a group designated as the "fearers of the Lord" (*sebomenoi*). The term derives from Ps. 118, where three groups are admonished to acknowledge the everlasting mercy of the Lord, namely, the house of Israel, the house of Aaron, and the fearers of the Lord (*yirai Ha-Shem*). The Septuagint renders the last as *toi phoboumenoi ton Kyrion*. Usually this group was known as the *sebomenoi*, a term with the same meaning as *phoboumenoi*.[88] Both Jewish and non-Jewish sources acknowledge a group of gentiles who observed Jewish practices without full conversion. Unlike the Samaritans, however, they did not claim to be the true Israel in place of the Jewish people.[89]

Josephus was ambivalent about such quasi-Jews. He writes: ". . . many of them (Greeks) have agreed to adopt our laws; of whom some have remained faithful, while others, lacking the necessary endurance, have again seceded (*apestesan*)."[90] Elsewhere, he congratulates sincere gentiles attracted to Judaism, but warns that "casual visitors (*tous d'ek parergou prosiontas*)" should not be admitted to "the intimacies of our daily life (*te synetheia*)."[91] Those on the way into Judaism are often hard to distinguish from religious dilettantes.

The existence of these people is also attested to by the Roman satirist, Juvenal (d. 140 CE), who mocked the attraction of Judaism for Roman citizens:

Some who have had a father who reveres the Sabbath (*metuentem sabbata*), worship nothing but the clouds and the divinity of the heavens, and see no difference between eating swine flesh from which their father abstained and that of man; and in time they take to circumcision (*mox et praeputia ponunt*). Having been wont to flaunt the laws of Rome, they learn and practice and revere the Jewish law (*Iudaicum . . . ac metuunt ius*) . . .[92]

Here we see how this anti-Jewish Roman observed *Judaization* as a process taking more than one generation. The process was complicated by the fact that worship of local deities was prescribed in many places, only native-born

Jews being exempt from this civic duty.[93] As Joseph Klausner wrote, "But 'God-fearers' . . . were Gentiles who have ceased to worship a foreign deity and are keeping some of the Jewish observances which they find agreeable."[94] These "fearers of the Lord" were praised for their philosemitism.[95] Certain early Tannaitic sources refer to the existence of the "fearers of the Lord" as a separate group, neither full Jews nor idolaters:

And so you find four groups (kittot) who respond and say before Him-Who-spake-and-the-world-came-to-be, "I am for the Lord" (Is. 44:5) . . . (1) Israelites, (2) proselytes (gerai tzedek) . . . (3) repentant sinners . . . (4) and fearers of God (yirai Shamayim).[96]

Along these same lines one can understand the famous retort of Hillel the Elder to a non-Jew who wanted to convert while "standing on one foot." Hillel first told him that Judaism demands a universally recognized morality, namely, "what is hateful to you do not do to your fellow." Everything else is "commentary" (v'idakh peirusha).[97] In other words, acceptance of a universally valid moral standard already makes one a potential Jew.

Because these "fearers of the Lord" were in fact gentiles living as quasi-Jews, some scholars see the Noahide laws as originating in the diaspora as a regimen for these people. For all practical purposes these sebomenoi seem to be the same as the Palestinian gerai toshav, lacking only the political connotation of the latter. Their regimen was, therefore, religious and moral in the broad sense. As Jacob Agus argued:

The doctrine of the Noahide commandments was actually a legal application of the prophetic principle that the pagan nations might contribute to the advancement of the kingdom of God, even while they retained their own customs and rituals . . . The vast number of "God-fearers" on the fringe of the Jewish community in the first century of the common era attests to the wide acceptance of this doctrine.[98]

Agus is suggesting that Noahide law is co-equal with the sebomenoi movement. Sebomenoi and phoboumenoi, therefore, are taken as the diaspora equivalents of ger toshav. Earlier, Michael Guttmann argued similarly.[99] Agus' teacher, Harry Wolfson, argued that although Philo did not discuss the term ger toshav or paroikos as a legal institution, he did discuss the "fearers of the Lord" in a religious and moral sense.[100] And Wolfson claimed to be able to discern the seven Noahide laws in Philo's natural law.[101] However, I do not think that this is satisfactory.

First of all, it presupposes that the Palestinian doctrine of the seven Noahide laws was already known in the Hellenistic period. The only source for such a presupposition, however, is Jubilees 7:20, which Albeck showed is an expression of the pre-Mosaic observance of the whole Torah, not a law specifically limited to Noahides.[102]

Secondly, as regards Philo, his project was to show that the Mosaic Torah is *the* natural law in the most robust sense. The depth of the Torah law is its generality; its fullness is its attention to specifics as well:[103]

... let us postpone consideration of particular laws, which are, so to speak, copies (*eikonon*), and examine first those which are more general and may be called the originals (*archetypous*) of those copies.[104]

Philo, following Plato, held that the more general is the more real.[105] Indeed God is termed by Plato "the most general" (*to genik taton*) followed by the Divine Logos embracing the ideas of God.[106] If Philo is committed to showing that the Torah is philosophy in its deepest sense, he is not going to identify the natural laws in it with a code specifically enacted for non-Jews. If this were the case, the historical Torah would be in relation to the natural law as the written law was in relation to the unwritten law (*agraphos nomos*) in Greek thought, namely, an inferior derivation or application.[107] Although one might be able to discern parallels to the Noahide laws in Philo, even Wolfson could not identify a passage where Philo specifies these laws *for* Noahides. For the rabbis, on the other hand, the general Noahide laws were clearly inferior to the specific laws of the Mosaic Torah.[108]

Another problem with seeing the Noahide laws as the criteria for the *sebomenoi* is that if gradual conversion characterized this group, as it characterized the earlier institution of the *ger toshav*, why limit their commandments to seven? If gentiles observing laws sanctioned by Judaism are in effect potential Jews, legal limitation would hamper the *process* of Judaism. One might, for example, see the following rabbinic tradition, which ascribes many more commandments to the Noahides as rival doctrine to the doctrine of the seven commandments:

R. Huna in the name of Rab interpreted the verse, "And they weighed out my reward of thirty pieces of silver (Zech. 11:12)" to refer to the thirty commandments the Noahides will accept in the future ... R. Hiyyah b. Lulani said in the name of R. Hoshiah that the Noahides will accept all the commandments in the future. What is the basis for this view? "For then I will turn a pure speech to the peoples, for all of them to call upon the name of the Lord to serve Him with one mind" (Zeph. 3:9).[109]

The parallel text states, "these are the thirty commandments which the Noahides accepted for themselves (*she-kibblu aleihem*)."[110] Both texts report that the Noahides either have rejected or will reject these commandments. What is important, however, is that the Noahides, *if seen as potential Jews*, have many more commandments than seven. The version in the Babylonian Talmud emphasizes that the gentiles "honor the Torah," which might mean a recognition of their morality as essentially Jewish, thus making them potential Jews. The rabbinic doctrine of the Noahide laws seems to imply a precise distinction between Jews and gentiles rather than a mere difference in degree. The limit of the Noahide laws to seven was taken quite literally in the Talmud.[111] The *ger toshav* as characterized by the Talmud, an admittedly juridical status, should not be equated with the *sebomenoi*, a real historical group during the Hellenistic and Roman period.[112] Moreover, the supposed reference to the Noahide laws in the *Sibylline Oracles*, a late Hellenistic work, was shown by Samuel Krauss to be erroneous.[113]

The lumping together of the phenomenon of the *sebomenoi* with the concept of Noahide law, which has no solid historical evidence, seems to be the background for the assumption that the concept of Noahide law is already presupposed by the New Testament authors. They recognize the *sebomenoi*,[114] and the New Testament also had to deal with the question of minimal moral standards to be required of gentile converts to Christianity. Consequently, some Christian scholars, rightly eager to emphasize the conscious Judaic influence on the New Testament authors, explicitly make the connection. As W. D. Davies writes, "Now, that Paul was familiar with the Noachian commandments cannot be doubted . . ."[115]

Such a conclusion is, however, unsupportable for a number of reasons. First, no New Testament or Patristic text refers to a definite body of laws as specifically "Noahide" or even "Adamic." Second, even Paul's condemnation of gentile immorality in Romans 1:18 and following does not imply that he believed that gentiles could be moral in a way pleasing to God without accepting the Church's message (*kerygma*) of God's revelation. In other words, this is not an acknowledgment of the possibility of a body of moral principles to govern a humanity which transcends the religious community itself.[116] Finally, the four prohibitions mentioned in Acts 15:29 as applying to gentile converts to Christianity, namely, the proscriptions of articles dedicated to idolatry, the eating of blood, the eating of meat strangled, and sexual immorality (*porneia*)[117]—all these prohibitions are required for even minimal transition of gentile converts from paganism to Christianity. Polemics against idolatry and its practices became especially common in the Patristic literature written when Christian proselytizing efforts were already fully directed to pagans.[118]

Several historians have noted that after the rise of Christianity rabbinic references to the "fearers of the Lord" virtually disappear. Paul attracted many members of this group to the new religion. In his discourses in diaspora synagogues he repeatedly refers to "God-fearers" as well as to native-born Jews.[119]

As such, the rabbis had to mark out a strict demarcation between Jews and non-Jews.[120] The concept of *seven* Noahide laws (and no more) presupposes the acceptance of this strict demarcation. The essence of Noahide law is seen as negative, namely, restraint. As the Gemara puts it, ". . . concerning the seven commandments they are thought of as 'sit and do nothing' (*shev ve'al ta'aseh*)."[121] The concept of Noahide law could not very well have preceded this negative demarcation.[122] Thus, it could not have been the criterion for the *ger toshav* of biblical times, nor the *sebomenoi* of Hellenistic times. The concept seems to have arisen after such quasi-Judaism was impossible for rabbinic Judaism to recognize.

This demarcation between the rabbinic attitude towards gentile participation in Judaism before and after the destruction of the Temple can be seen in a comparison between two different groups of halakhic rulings.

A Tannaitic source states,

Why does Scripture say "any man" (*ish ish*—Lev. 22:18)?—To include gentiles who may offer vowed (*nedarim*) and freewill (*nedabot*) offerings like Jews.[123]

Although the formulation of this ruling is Tannaitic, there is no reason to believe that it does not reflect the practice in the Temple to accept a variety of non-Jewish offerings. As early as the First Temple there is a recognition of the Temple's attraction for "the strong who is not of Thy people Israel, who comes from a far off land for the sake of Thy Name" (I Kgs. 8:41). Although the gentile could not be a full participant in the Temple services, he was in effect a quasi-participant.[124]

The above passage should be compared with the following rulings made by the second-century CE Amoraim, R. Johanan b. Nappha, and his colleague and brother-in-law, R. Simeon b. Lakish.

R. Simeon b. Lakish said that a gentile who observed the Sabbath (*she-shabbat*) is deserving of death (*hayav metah*) as it is said, "Day and night they shall not cease" (Gen. 8:22) . . . R. Johanan said that a gentile who engaged in the study of Torah is deserving of death as it is said, "Moses commanded us Torah as an inheritance (*morashah*)" (Deut. 33:4)—an inheritance for us and not them.[125]

Now the Gemara finds that R. Johanan's statement contradicts that of R. Meir, a Tanna, that a "gentile who engages (*osek*) in the study of Torah is like the high priest."[126] The Gemara resolves this contradiction by restricting R. Meir's comment to gentile study of the seven Noahide laws. R. Johanan's comment, on the other hand, is interpreted as reference to the full Mosaic Torah. This answer is necessitated by the general Talmudic assumption that an Amora may not entirely oppose a Tannaitic opinion except with another Tannaitic opinion upon which to base his opposition.[127] The Amoraic and Tannaitic opinions had to be qualified so as to avoid contradiction.

However, what is relevant about R. Meir's statement is the use of the high priest as a comparison. Such statements probably reflect the Pharisaic struggle to establish Torah learning as the true seat of religious authority as opposed to the priesthood, controlled by the Sadducees.[128] R. Meir's statement, although enunciated after the destruction of the Temple, might well reflect a tendency existent before the destruction of the Temple, a tendency that encouraged quasi-Jews to proceed to full conversion.

With the Christian schism, the opposition of R. Johanan and R. Simeon b. Lakish reflects the emerging inclination after the formulation of the Noahide laws to no longer recognize quasi-Jews. Such an inclination was paralleled in the attempts of the Church Fathers to discourage "Judaizing."[129] Maimonides, though writing centuries later, captured the spirit of both of these rulings:

The essence of the matter is that we do not allow (*ein meneeheen*) them to innovate a religious law (*le-hadash dat*) and to make commandments for themselves according to their own opinion (*meda'atan*), but a gentile should either become a full convert (*ger tzedek*) and accept all the commandments, or remain with his own Torah and neither add nor subtract from it.[130]

Maimonides further plays down the tendency from Temple days, reflected in some of the earlier rulings, to allow gentile observance of Jewish religious practices. For the only examples he gives of this permission is the donation of a burnt offering (*olah*) and the contribution of charity (*tzedakah*).[131] As we will see later, a number of post-Maimonidean authorities reverted to the earlier tendency of permitting gentiles to observe almost any commandment.[132] Maimonides, on the other hand, reflects the development of the tradition in the Amoraic period, namely, the strict boundaries between Jewish and gentile obligations and the rejecting any form of quasi-Judaism.

8. A New Historical Hypothesis

After our careful examination of the historical theories concerning the origins of the Noahide laws, and the evidence of the primary sources, there is no convincing support that this doctrine was conceived earlier than the Tannaitic period in which it was enunciated, specifically after the parting of the ways with the now gentile Christianity. The doctrine presupposes a firm boundary between Jews and non-Jews, with no "potential" Jews in the middle. The same can also be said for the later rabbinic interpretation of the *ger toshav*. In earlier times, this practical institution had been the way gentiles could gradually be integrated into the Jewish community. Later, the rabbinic correlation of this ancient institution with the new theoretical concept of the Noahide laws enabled the rabbis to construct a model of *normative co-Judaic and pre-Judaic* human beings having a connection with a status described in the Bible. The *theoretical constitution* of the *ger toshav* led to the development of the halakhah of Jewish–gentile relationships. The constitution of the *ben Noah* led to the development of philosophical reflection on the pre-conditions of Judaism itself. The fact that the *ger toshav* and the *ben Noah* are now constituted identically establishes a crucial common point between halakhah and philosophical reflection in the history of Judaism.

We must ask now: is there any historically identifiable point in the early Tannaitic period with which the concept of the Noahide laws may be associated?

I would venture the speculation that the concept of a number of minimal, indispensable laws for gentiles might very well have emerged at the same time that a number of minimal, indispensable laws for Jews was conceived. The Talmud provides a significant decision regarding these laws:

R. Johanan said in the name of R. Simon b. Jehozedek that they voted and decided (*neemu ve'gamru*) in the attic of the house of Nithzeh in Lydda that for all transgressions in the Torah, if one is told "transgress and do not be killed," he may transgress and not be killed—except for idolatry, sexual immorality and bloodshed.[133]

The Hadrianic persecution is the historical context of this decision, when the public practice of Judaism was prohibited on pain of death.[134] At this time, the view of R. Akiva was accepted that made the study of the Torah more important than the practice of its specific commandments if a choice had to be made between the two in a time of danger and persecution.[135] R. Akiva died a martyr's death for practicing his opinion.[136]

The choice of these three commandments as obligatory appears to be based on the notion that they are *ratio per se*, that is, their prohibition is immediately evident and not the result solely of divine fiat, unlike the majority of the 613 commandments. The late medieval Spanish commentator, R. Joseph ibn Habib, wrote that these three particular prohibitions:

. . . are grave (*hamurot*), not only prohibited because of the desecration of God's name in public, for they are not even to be done in private (*be-tzina*), even at a time where is no persecution and thus no public desecration of God's name is entailed. One should rather die than transgress them because of their own inherent gravity (*homer atzman*).[137]

This definition is important because only Jews are required to die than dese-
crate God's name in public. The gravity of these prohibitions then transcends
the Jewish question of martyrdom.[138]

This emphasis on rationality comes out in the discussion in the Gemara of
this decision. There the prohibition of obeying an order to murder in order to
save one's own life is based on the rational principle (*sevara*), "who can say
whether your blood is redder, perhaps the blood of that man is redder (*sumak
tefai*)."[139] The Gemara earlier noted that the Written Torah itself compares
murder to rape, the paradigm of sexual crime. In speaking of the innocence of
the helpless rape victim, the Torah states, "and to the girl you shall do nothing,
the girl is not deserving of death (*het mavet*), for it is just as (*ki k'asher*) when a
man arises against his neighbor and murders him, so (*ken*) is this matter"
(Deut. 22:36). This comparison is taken to include more than just the similarity between murder and rape victims. It is also interpreted to mean that the
severity of the crimes themselves is similar, even identical.[140]

As for the irrationality of idolatry, the following Tannaitic text may be taken
as typical of the rabbinic view:

R. Simon b. Eleazar says in the name of R. Hileay b. Agra who said in the name of R.
Johanan b. Nuri, one who tears his clothes, who breaks his vessels, who squanders
his money in anger—he should be in your eyes like an idolater (*k'oved avodah zarah*).
For if his evil inclination (*yitzro*) told him to worship idols he would do so, for this is
the work (*avodato*) of the evil inclination (*yetzer hara*).[141]

What emerges from this text is that rationality and universality are co-equal
because both pertain to human beings per se. As such, a definition of what is
rationally indispensable for Jews necessarily leads to a definition of what is
rationally indispensable for gentiles. This sentiment is expressed in a *baraita*:

"And My judgments (*et mishpatai*) you shall do" (Lev. 18:4)—even if they were not
written in Scripture reason (*ba-din hayah*) would require that they be written,
specifically (*kegon*): (the prohibitions of) robbery, sexual immorality, idolatry,
blasphemy and bloodshed.[142]

These rational commandments, five of the seven Noahide laws, are contrasted
with uniquely Jewish commandments such as the dietary laws and clothing restrictions, prohibitions that "the evil inclination and the nations of the
world" ridicule as irrational.[143]

The universality of the three central prohibitions of idolatry, sexual immorality and bloodshed emerge from aggadic treatments of the misconduct of
both Ishmael and Esau. Both are presented in the Torah unfavorably. Yet from
Torah alone it is difficult to surmise just what they did to make them morally

unacceptable. In two separate texts, Ishmael and Esau, respectively, are condemned for transgressing the three prohibitions.[144] It is important to remember that both were pre-Sinaitic Noahides, and designated founders of the leading non-Jewish civilizations.[145]

Moreover, the Gemara records the opinion of the school of Rav, from the early Amoraic period, that a Noahide is only executed for three of the Noahide laws: bloodshed, sexual immorality and idolatry.[146] However, when idolatry is mentioned, the Amora, R. Sheshet, presents the opinion of the school of Rav as designating four such laws, not three. Nevertheless, if blasphemy and idolatry are two aspects of the sin of rejecting God,[147] then we see the three central prohibitions here as the core of Noahide law.

We can now see some indications of all Noahide laws in the part of the Pentateuch that deals with the pre-Sinaitic world. The difference between the pre- and post-Sinaitic world was emphasized in a number of rabbinic texts and was the basis of several significant halakhic definitions.[148] The rabbinic choice of Genesis 2:16 as the locus of all seven Noahide laws (or at least the six "Adamic" laws) is a convenient point of reference, as we have seen. However, the general notion that the seven laws (among others, to be sure) can be assumed to be pre-Sinaitic is not at all implausible.[149] This notion is best represented in an eleventh-century work, *Midrash Lekah Tov*.[150]

The law concerning adjudication (*dinim*) is implied by the words in Genesis 2:16, "And the Lord God commanded." Law by definition involves adjudication. Without adjudication it can only be what the rabbis called "good counsel" (*etzah tovah*). Moreover, Abraham is seen as commanding his house "to do righteousness and judgment" (*mishpat*—Gen. 18:19).[151]

The prohibition of idolatry (*avodah zarah*) is also implied by these same words in Genesis 2:16 because they indicate one absolute authority (*Elohim*). Indeed, when the serpent tempts Eve to break God's commandment, he tempts her with the promise of "becoming like God" (Gen. 3:5), that is, there will be a plurality of authorities.[152] Moreover, idolatry is considered the beginning of the process of moral degeneration that lead to the Flood.[153] However, the Noahide ban on idolatry, as an explicit prohibition, is post-biblical.[154]

The prohibition of blasphemy (*birkat Ha-Shem*), inferred from the use of the Tetragrammaton (YHWH) in Genesis 2:16, seems in and of itself to be most tenuous. Nevertheless, the arrogance of the builders of Babel—"let us make for ourselves a name" (Gen. 11:4)—can be seen as blasphemous.[155] Pharaoh, as well, was punished for his contempt for the Lord, a contempt initially expressed by his blasphemous utterance, "Who is the Lord (YHWH)? . . . I am not familiar with the Lord . . . " (Ex. 5:2).[156] His punishment implies that blasphemy is prohibited.[157] With this inductive approach we can see how the use of the Tetragrammaton in Genesis 2:16 alludes to blasphemy if it does not actually ground its prohibition.

The punishment for bloodshed (*shefikhat damim*) is clearly stated in Genesis 9:6—"he who sheds blood, by humans shall his blood be shed, for in the image of God He made man." The fact that "man" and "the image of God" are synonymous is clearly the basis for judging Cain guilty for the murder of his brother Abel (Gen. 4:10–11).[158] It also indicates why the Egyptian midwives were considered God-fearing when they saved the Hebrew male babies from execution (Ex. 1:17).[159] It justifies, too, Moses' killing the Egyptian aggressor (Ex. 2:11–12).[160]

The accepted punishment for sexual immorality (*gilui arayot*) is clearly expressed when Simon and Levi justify their revenge for the rape of their sister, Dinah: "and such is not done" (Gen. 34:7).[161] This universal, unqualified, prohibition should be compared with the local, qualified, prohibition of giving a younger sister in marriage before her older sister, considered by the text as something "not done in our locale" (Gen. 29:26). Indeed, the Flood was preceded by the account of the abduction of the common women (*b'not ha-adam*) by the men in power (*bnai elohim*).[162] The Flood itself is explicitly considered to be caused by the fact that "all flesh perverted (*hishhit*) its way on earth" (Gen. 6:13).[163] This incident was interpreted to be sexual perversion. Moreover, the abduction of Sarah by Pharaoh for his harem (Gen. 12:17) and also by Abimelech into his harem (Gen. 26:9) were all considered acts deserving punishment.[164] Furthermore, the Canaanites were ejected from the land of Israel because of "all these abominations (*hato'evot*) they did" (Lev. 18:27). The "abominations" mentioned in that chapter are sexual offenses.[165]

The explicit prohibition of Genesis 2:16 is "from the tree of the knowledge of good and evil you shall not eat." This verse means that taking God's property without permission is tantamount to theft (*gezel*).[166] Moreover, one can see how a prohibition of theft is presupposed in Abraham's rebuke of Abimelech for the well stolen by his servant (Gen. 21:25); in the quarrel between Isaac's shepherds and the shepherds of Gerar over water rights (Gen. 26:20); in the accusation that Jacob stole Esau's birthright and blessing (Gen. 27:35–36);[167] in Jacob's dispute with Laban, his father-in-law, over the ownership of their respective flocks (Gen. 30:33);[168] in Laban's accusation that his idols had been stolen (Gen. 31:30); in Joseph's kidnapping and being sold into slavery by his brothers (Gen. 37:26–27).[169] Finally, the enslavement of the people of Israel by the Egyptians was considered an act of theft for which the Israelites were rightly compensated by the Egyptians at the time of their departure from Egypt (Ex. 12:36).[170]

The prohibition of eating a limb torn from a living animal (*ever min ha-hy*) is the most difficult of the Noahide laws to rationally justify, yet it is the one mentioned most explicitly in Scripture and the only one directly addressed to Noah and his sons: "Surely flesh with its life-blood (*be-nafsho damo*) you shall not eat" (Gen. 9:4). The fact that this is only "Noahide" law specifically mentioned in the Torah, and that it is addressed to the sons of Noah, might explain why all of the seven laws are designated as *Noahide*.[171]

The concept of the seven Noahide laws appears to be a theological-juridical theory rather than a functioning body of law administered by Jews for gentiles actually living under their authority at any time in history. Its theoretical status, however, makes it philosophically significant. Philosophy attempts to gain insight into essential structures rather than describe empirical events, the task of history. Neither does it issue rulings, the task of law, nor describe internal religious perceptions, the task of theology.

The questions that we must now address are: (1) How was such a theory used in the development of Judaism? (2) How did such a theory become a basis of Jewish philosophy? In the following chapters we will examine each of the Noahide laws in detail and the development of the concept in general. Hopefully, as we move forward the robustness of this concept will become apparent.

CHAPTER TWO

THE LAW OF ADJUDICATION

1. Introduction

Noahide law has a double jurisdiction. It is both a system of law for which non-Jews *are* universally obligated and for which Jews *were* obligated prior to the revelation at Sinai. The correlation between these two jurisdictions is that Jews began as Noahides. Before the Sinaitic covenant all people were bound by Noahide law. After revelation, however, Jews are bound by the 613 commandments whereas non-Jews continued to live under Noahide obligations. It would seem, then, that this law continues to be relevant for gentiles but only *historically* relevant for Jews. The following Tannaitic text appears to express this sentiment:

It was taught: Just as Jews are commanded to establish courts of law (*batei din*) in every district and in every city, so are Noahides commanded to establish courts of law in every district and in every city.[1]

2. Who Enforces the Law?

Underlying Noahide law is the question of enforcement, namely, who is responsible for enforcement? Do Jews enforce it among non-Jews, or do non-Jews enforce it themselves? If it is a matter of Jewish enforcement, then Noahide law is an extension of Jewish law for non-Jews, a form of legal suzerainty. Conversely, if it is essentially a non-Jewish responsibility then Noahide law is something Jews *recognize* as obligatory for non-Jews, but are not obligated to implement. The former implies a legally constituted imperialism. Its intent is external. The latter suggests that lawfulness is not something Jews impose on non-Jews but rather is something inherent in humanity themselves. Furthermore, since Jews began as Noahides, human lawfulness is seen as a necessary prerequisite for the very emergence of Judaism.

From the perspective of the former view, Jewish interest in Noahide law is essentially prescriptive. As a matter of Jewish enforcement, it presupposes the legal constitution of the Jewish community. Jewish motivation regarding the prescriptive view is obvious: a part of Jewish law, for whose enforcement Jews are ultimately responsible, has universal scope. The motivation for the descriptive view seems to be to discover a point in common between Jews and the non-Jewish world, a world which both precedes and confronts them.

This difference can be seen in the dispute between Maimonides and Nahmanides.

In prescribing the Noahide commandment regarding *dinim* (adjudication) Maimonides employs a biblical example to illustrate his point:

How are they commanded concerning the *dinim*? They are obligated to install judges (*dayanim*) and legal authorities (*shoftim*) in every district and to judge according to these six commandments and to warn the people. And a Noahide who transgressed any of these seven commandments is executed by decapitation (*yehareg be-sayyif*). Because of this all of the Shechemites deserved death for Shechem by committing abduction (*gazal*) and they saw it and did not judge it (*ve'lo danuhu*).[2]

Maimonides is referring to the abduction and rape of Jacob's daughter by Shechem, a Canaanite prince (Gen. 34). The brothers of Dinah, Simon and Levi, executed the male Shechemites after concluding a treaty with them, however. They were seemingly guilty of both murder and deception. Maimonides, however, exonerates them inasmuch as they were enforcing Noahide law among non-Jews. Noahide law required the people of Shechem to execute their prince for his crimes. By neglecting to do so, this gave tacit approval to his actions. The sons of Israel, therefore, were justified in executing Shechem for his crime and the Shechemites for their crime of neglecting to adjudicate this matter. Thus Maimonides sees this case as a model for the Jewish obligation to enforce Noahide law among gentiles when the latter cannot or will not do so for themselves. He writes: "And so did Moses our teacher command us by Divine authority (*mi-pi ha-Gevurah*) to force (*lekof*) all humanity to accept the commandments of the sons of Noah; and whoever does not accept them is to be executed."[3]

The question is: Does the text of the Bible really exonerate Simon and Levi? If not, then this case is not a model for Jewish enforcement of Noahide law but rather a model for Jewish non-involvement in the legal affairs of gentiles. It should be remembered that Jacob disapproved of the actions of his sons (Gen. 34:30, 49:5–7). Nahmanides makes this point in his comment to Gen. 34:13, criticizing both Maimonides' exegesis and his legal theory as well:

This view is incorrect in my opinion because if it were so our father Jacob would then have been obligated to be the first to merit executing them . . . why was he angry with his sons?[4] . . . In my opinion the commandment of *dinim* which was specified (*she-manu*) for Noahides not only includes adjudication but, also, such things as the prohibitions of stealing, cheating, etc.... like the concept of laws (*k'inyan ha-dinim*) for which Jews are commanded ... However, they are not executed for failing to fulfill the positive commandment of adjudication ... In their law, not acting is not punishable by death.[5]

Nahmanides' contemporary, R. Jacob Anatoli (d. 1256), saw *dinim* as essentially the obligation of non-Jews to obey the laws of their own society.[6]

This difference of interpretation is based on a fundamental theoretical difference about the essence of Noahide law. If one holds that Noahide law is ultimately a Jewish responsibility, then it is essentially positive law. It presupposes external authority. Conversely, if Noahide law is ultimately a human responsibility both universal and perpetual, then it is essentially a law inherently binding on humanity. Its authority, then, is moral.

The first point of view sees Noahide law as a prime topic on the messianic agenda, for Jews did not have non-Jews (slaves aside) under their political and legal control. One can discuss the content of Noahide law, but its essential meaning like that of all positive law depends upon the character of the external authority who enforces it.[7] For Jews, without full religious and political sovereignty, this meaning depended on the character of the authority who *will* enforce this law in the Messianic future. Therefore, a pre-messianic Jewish interest in Noahide law *now* is basically a specification of the general messianic hope that the Torah will become the law for all humankind.

According to the second view, however, Jewish interest in Noahide law is of greater significance in the present. It establishes a model for the interrelation between a revealed and non-revealed system of law. By constituting Noahide law as essentially independent, the second view forces Judaism to understand itself in relation to something outside its actual or even potential legal control. As such the concept of *dinim* becomes the legal "border concept" (*Grenzbegriff*) between Judaism and the outside world. Nahmanides sees this independent phenomenon as a comparative standard for Jewish law. Consistency with universal standards of justice is seen as a *conditio sine qua non* of Judaism. He notes: "As the judgments of civilized society (*mishpatei yishuv ha-medinot*) ... the laws (*ha-din*) are the right and good as all who see them will recognize."[8] In another context he designates the prohibition of violence (*hamas*), the very opposite of the rule of law, as "something rational (*inyan muskal*) not requiring revelation (*eino tzerikh la-Torah*)."[9]

3.   Noahide Law and Sinaitic Revelation

The dispute between two Amoraim, R. Johanan and R. Isaac, illustrates the association of Noahide and revealed law.[10] R. Johanan argues that adjudication in Gen. 2:16 derives from "He commanded" (*vayitzav*) whereas R. Isaac derives it from "God" (*elohim*). According to R. Moses Isserles (d. 1572), their dispute was not merely exegetical, but also referenced a fundamental difference of view regarding the essence of Noahide law:

> It is clear as the noonday sun that R. Johanan . . . thinks that a Noahide is only commanded to observe the juridical procedure of society (*ha-minhag ha-medini*) and to adjudicate between persons equitably (*mishpat yosher*), but not in the way of the Jewish laws that Moses gave us from Sinai, but only by the rule of law (*hok nimusi*) . . . Jewish law is one thing and Noahide law is something else.[11]

For R. Johanan, Jewish interest in Noahide law is essentially descriptive. R. Isaac, on the other hand, is seen as advancing the prescriptive view, that Noahide law is part of Jewish law. Surely it could not be known, much less enforced, without direct Jewish involvement:

> R. Isaac is of a different mind . . . and thinks that Noahide laws are the same as the laws the Jews were commanded at Sinai and, therefore, derives them from a verse (Ex. 22:7) said at Sinai . . . except where there is direct evidence (*yadayim mokhihot*) of a difference.[12]

Although Isserles considers R. Johanan's view authoritative, an earlier Gaonic work, *She'iltot de-Rav Ahay Gaon*, judges R. Isaac's view as authoritative.[13] As an immediate rule of law (*halakhah le-ma'aseh*) the issue is not of much significance. But as a theological issue it is crucial, namely, does law presuppose revelation or does revelation presuppose law?

For R. Isaac it would seem that the ultimate responsibility for the enforcement of Noahide law is non-Jewish. Jews are not obligated, indeed they may even be prohibited from enforcing Noahide law among non-Jews. Noahide law both antedates and continues to exist independent of the law revealed to Israel at Sinai.

The question of whether *dinim* are something essentially universal and so accepted as a moral criterion by Judaism itself, or other *dinim* are an essentially Jewish concept applicable to humankind as a whole, underlies the following rabbinic dispute:

> "And Jethro Moses' father-in-law heard" (Ex. 18:1). What did he hear and then come?—He heard about the war against Amalek which is described in the preceding section (*she-hi ketubah be-tzido*) and then came—in the opinion of R. Joshua. R. Eleazar ha-Moda'i said that he heard about the giving of Torah and came.[14]

This debate, at the exegetical levels, centers on variant views of the Torah's literary structure. R. Joshua bases his view on juxtaposition (*semukhim*), namely, that the order of presentation in the Torah is not random, that passages are juxtaposed in order that they might be seen in intelligible sequence.[15] The fact that Jethro's arrival in the Israelite camp is directly preceded by the account of the war against the Amalekites indicates his hearing of this event motivated him to reunite with Moses, his son-in-law. R. Eleazar ha-Moda'i, on the other hand, interprets the passage sequentially (*ein mukdam u-me'uhar ba-Torah*), that passages should be interpreted in terms of their conceptual context rather than in terms of strict literary juxtaposition.[16]

At the exegetical level, the view that Jethro's arrival in the camp was prior to the revelation at Sinai seems more plausible, for Jethro expresses his motivation for coming as wonder at the military feats of God on behalf of the Israelites (Ex. 18:10). Why, then, does R. Eleazar insist that Jethro arrived after the Sinaitic revelation? Indeed, in the version of this debate in the Babylonian Talmud two Amoraim, R. Hiyya and R. Joshua b. Levi, see the crucial point as whether Jethro came before or after the revelation of the Torah.[17] Why would one wish to change the plain meaning of Scripture in this case? If one holds that *dinim* are essentially Jewish and only universal through enforced Jewish application, then Jethro's juridical advice could only have been acceptable if it were an expansion and application of the Torah *already* revealed.[18] Jethro sets forth a system of adjudication for the people of Israel (Ex. 18:17–26). What law is presupposed by this system of adjudication? If, however, one holds that *dinim* are essentially universal and not a purely Jewish doctrine, then one can see Jethro as laying down the normative conditions making the social acceptance of the revealed law possible.[19] Therefore, Nahmanides, in his comment to Ex. 18:1, endorses, on exegetical grounds, R. Joshua's view as most plausible, namely, Jethro came before the giving of the Torah. However, since we have just seen that Nahmanides, in contrast to Maimonides, acknowledges that *dinim* are not essentially Jewish, it is not unwarranted, I believe, to see Nahmanides' interpretation of the meaning of the Jethro story as being influenced by this very acknowledgment.

The view, however, that gentile normativity is subsequent to the revelation of the Torah finds expression in an aggadah:

R. Judah says that they wrote the Torah on the outside of the altar. They said to him, "how did the nations of the world learn the Torah?" He said to them, "God put the desire in their hearts and they sent scribes (*notarii*) and they copied the script from the stones in seventy languages. At that time the judgment (*gezar dinam*) of the nations of the world was sealed in hell.[20]

According to the elaboration of this text from the Tosefta in the Palestinian Talmud, the gentile scribes took their copies of the Torah home with them to share with their peoples.[21] In the Babylonian Talmud, the text says that gentile neglect of the law they had received was the cause for their doom—"they should have learned but they did not" (*she-hayah lahen lilmod vel'o lamdu*).[22] This seems to refer to the Septuagint, which made the teachings of the Torah available to the Hellenistic world, where there was widespread interest in Judaism.[23]

The important point of this aggadic motif is that gentiles were not obligated to observe laws that pertained to them until the Jews *published* these laws for them in the Mosaic Torah. Indeed, the Jews themselves were not obligated for the commandments of the Torah until they had been published.[24] Saul Lieberman illustrated the Greco-Roman background of this type of theological reasoning:

The Rabbi argued according to the legal practice of the Roman government. An edict had to be displayed in a public place; until then the people were not punishable for its transgression . . . In the opinion of the Rabbi it is portions of international law that were published by Joshua on the blocks of stone which he set up.[25]

According to this aggadic motif, then, revelation is the actual ground (*conditio per quam*) of normativity. The latter presupposes the former.

4. The Elimination of the Legal Double Standard

Although Jews did not have direct political control over non-Jews in the rabbinic era, they certainly had legal contacts with individual non-Jews. The question arose as to whether Jews were permitted to use Jewish law as leverage against non-Jews in Jewish self-interest, or whether non-Jewish normativity had to be both recognized in theory and honored in practice. This tension comes out in the following:

When a Jew and a Canaanite come to a legal dispute: if you can declare the Jew innocent (*lezakehu*) by Jewish law then do so and say that this is *our* law (*dinaynu*); if by Canaanite law then do so and say this is *your* law (*dinaykhem*) . . . And if this is impossible practice deceit (*akifin*). This is R. Ishmael's view . . . R. Joseph said that there is no contradiction. The former view refers to a Canaanite; the latter to a resident alien (*ger toshav*).[26]

"Canaanite" is only found in later printed Talmudic texts, as the earlier printed texts and manuscripts simply distinguish between a gentile (*nokhri*) and a resident alien.[27] Despite the fact that Christian censorship undoubtedly led to the use of the archaic "Canaanite" (it could not be misconstrued as anti-Christian), it, nevertheless, helps emphasize the difference between law-abiding gentiles and lawless ones. Just as the Canaanites of biblical times were seen as the model of lawlessness and, by extension, were denied protection under Jewish law,[28] so lawlessness leads to similar results in later times with any gentiles with whom Jews happen to come into contact. The later use of "Canaanite," therefore, was by analogy—the rabbis did not know an actual Canaanite.[29] Furthermore, *ger toshav* is also an analogy. Again, there were no resident aliens in the Talmudic era.[30] The recognition of gentile normativity, then, requires a single standard in Jewish civil law. No longer can there be a double standard when normativity is assumed on both the part of the Jews and law-abiding gentiles. Equal rights are thus determined by the moral character of the weaker party rather than by the will of the stronger. This recognition led to considerable adjustments in Jewish law. It functions as a moral *sine qua non* for a system of revealed law.

The following text indicates how such a moral standard of equality functioned in the development of Jewish law: "The ox of a Jew who gored the ox of a gentile is exempt (*patur*), but the ox of gentile whether docile (*tam*) or vicious (*mu'ad*) who gored the ox of a Jew pays full damages."[31] Surely, this is a double standard.[32] The Talmudic discussion of this text includes some historical background regarding the problems this passage caused:

Our rabbis taught that the Roman government sent two officials (*stradiyotot*) to the sages of Israel saying, "teach us your Torah." They read it two and three times. At the time of their departure they said to them, "we have examined your Torah and it is good except for this matter concerning the ox of a Jew who gored the ox of a gentile ... but we will not make this matter known to the government."[33]

Whether this incident occurred or not is unimportant, but it surely reflects the likely reaction of a contemporary Roman jurisconsult to a rule denying legal redress to an alien.[34] And, although it is emphasized that it would have been dangerous to reveal the background of this distinction to the Roman officials, the Gemara itself searches for an answer as to the reason for such inequity.

The Gemara questions the logic of the above distinction. If the law applies only to Jews, then gentiles should be exempt; if it applies to all, then Jews should be liable. The following exegetical reason is presented as an explanation for the seeming disregard of moral reasoning in the Mishnah:

R. Abbahu said that when Scripture states, "He stood and measured the land; He saw and uprooted nations" (Hab. 3:6), it means: He saw the seven commandments which the Noahides have accepted upon themselves, and because they did not uphold (*she-l'o kiyamu*) them He stood up and permitted their property to Jews.[35]

This, however, leaves us with the moral problem of contemporary people being legally penalized for the misconduct of their ancestors: "Will the fathers eat sour grapes and the teeth of the children be set on edge?" (Ez. 18:2).[36] Furthermore, it assumes there is no gentile normativity, a point belied by the legal objections of the two Roman officials. Their objections would be most typical of those committed to the system of Roman law.

The version in the Palestinian Talmud quotes two other rabbis arguing as R. Abbahu himself is quoted in the Babylonian Talmud. However, here R. Abbahu gives a more cogent explanation for the double standard in Jewish law:

> R. Abbahu said in the name of R. Johanan that this is according to their law (*ke-dinaihen*) . . . namely, a gentile's ox who gored another gentile's ox even if he agreed to be judged according to Jewish law—whether the ox was docile or vicious, he pays full damages . . . according to their law.[37]

However, if "their" law makes them responsible for the damages of their animals to *anyone else's*, why does "our" law make us responsible for the damages our animals cause to the animals of *other Jews only*, but makes us exempt from the damages our animals cause to the animals of non-Jews? R. Abbahu's reasoning only accentuates the double standard of the Mishnah, for "their" law by its very consistency appears more just than "our" law with its insurmountable inconsistency.

Maimonides, in codifying the law, took another line of interpretation. He states that since gentile law does not hold one liable for damages committed by his animals, it is clearly unjust; therefore, gentiles are fined (*kenas*) by Jewish law in order to lessen irresponsibility and financial loss to humanity (*ha-beriyot*).[38] Here again we see that Maimonides affirms the requirement of Jewish law for gentiles. Nevertheless, his logic contains a flaw. If exemption from payment for the damages of one's animals made for general irresponsibility among gentiles, would not a similar exemption make for similar irresponsibility among Jews?[39]

Moreover, the text in the Palestinian Talmud indicates that the Roman officials also found two other laws morally objectionable: that a Jewish woman may assist the delivery of a non-Jewish child, but not vice versa,[40] and a gentile is prohibited from stealing from a Jew, but not vice versa.[41] It is reported that Rabban Gamliel II ruled that it is forbidden for a Jew to steal from a gentile because it desecrates God's name (*hillul ha-Shem*); that is, it makes Judaism seem morally inferior.[42] Regarding the goring ox, however, he simply advises keeping the matter secret. The Sifre's version, on the other hand, only mentions the law permitting robbing gentiles and its abrogation.[43] Furthermore, the reason given for Rabban Gamliel's change of the law is not fear of the Roman government as in the case of the goring ox, but, rather, leaving the law as it had been would imply the moral inferiority of Judaism. Therefore, the acceptance of a moral standard among the gentiles, acknowledged by Judaism, had internal implications for the development of Jewish law. Once again the current printed text of the Babylonian Talmud refers to the lawless gentiles as "Canaanites"—a clear attempt to use a historically recognizable term of distinction between lawful and lawless gentiles. This is based on the explanation of R. Menachem Meiri (d. 1316) that the case of the goring ox is now anomalous:

This only applies to those nations not bound (she'aynam megudarim) by the ways of the revealed religions (datot) and morality (nimusim) . . . but anytime the law obligates them for the seven Noahide laws their case before us is like our case before us. We do not favor ourselves in the case. Thus it goes without saying that such applies to the nations bound by the ways of revealed religions and morality.[44]

Meiri had earlier explained the double standard in a way similar to that of Maimonides, whom he often follows, namely, gentiles do not accept responsibility for the damages caused by their animals hence they are not entitled to claim legal redress for damages to their animals.[45] At this level one could criticize the same flaw in his moral reasoning as was criticized in Maimonides', namely, exemption from responsibility will lead to irresponsibility no matter who is exempt. However, the matter does not remain here at this point because Meiri places all of this in the past. Revealed religion and its moral standards have changed the status of those gentiles, namely, Christians and Muslims, who are bound by them. Meiri does not have to offer a categorical justification for the double standard of the Mishnah because it is no longer applicable. Thus what Rabban Gamliel II partially accomplished by legislation, Meiri completely accomplished by interpretation.

The removal of the double standard in civil law is also seen in the interpretation of the procedure for redeeming a Jew sold into slavery to a gentile. Although the setting is antiquarian, as the law of the Hebrew bondman along with the Jubilee year ceased to be in effect with the destruction of the First Temple,[46] we see from the rabbinic discussion of this law how Jewish recognition of non-Jewish normativity influenced Jewish legal theory. The Torah states, "And he shall go out during the Jubilee year" (Lev. 25:54). This refers to a situation where the Jewish slave had not been redeemed by his kinsmen earlier. The Talmud specifies the gentile owner as one "under your control" (she-yeshno tahat yadekha).[47] In a crucial conceptual definition Rashi notes, "which teaches you that even with a gentile under your control . . . you are not permitted to practice deceit (akifin)."[48] Here the reference seems to be a resident alien.[49] The Tosafists expand this definition beyond the formal ger toshav:

Even when you are able to release the slave against the gentile owner's will (*b'al korho*) you must not practice deceit . . . even if the gentile is not under your control there are times when you are able to deceive him and cause him to err in law and reckoning . . . There are those who say that here the gentile trusts the Jew (*batuah alav*) . . . Scripture comes to let us know that we must be exact (*le-dekdek*).[50]

In other words, equality in civil law is something which is required irrespective of who enforces the law, of who is in political control, if there is the moral relationship of *trust* between the parties. Reciprocal trust is the moral presupposition of the rule of law as something essentially different from the rule of political force, even if it is at times benevolent. This reciprocal trust is more than *noblesse oblige*. To use the law to simply bolster political control is to declare it morally inferior.

5. Non-Jewish Law as a Standard of Positive Comparison

Even when Jews had political independence the reality of gentile *dinim* enabled them to freely acknowledge non-Jewish influence on their own juridical procedure. This is especially important to bear in mind today when historical study has shown how outwardly similar ancient Judaism was to its external environment.[51] If, on the other hand, one sees the relation of Jewish law to non-Jewish law as that of legal authority only, then the admission of any non-Jewish influence is problematic. Once again, we see the basic difference in the Jewish view of *dinim* making itself manifest in the Talmudic discussion of a certain procedural matter in the Sanhedrin. The Mishnah states, "In capital cases (*dinai nefashot*) the vote begins with the youngest members of the court (*min ha-tzad*)."[52] The Palestinian Talmud notes the following dispute regarding the historical background of this procedural rule:

R. Hilkyah said in the name of R. Simon that R. Johanan and Resh Lakish disputed about this matter. One said that our law is like their law (*dinainu ke-dinaihen*); the other said that our law is not like their law. The one who holds that our law is like their law can cite Gen. 37:27 and Est. 1:16 as proofs that this is the non-Jewish practice. The one who holds our law is not like their law could argue that these two examples are approved by Scripture.[53]

The Amora who maintains that Jewish procedure follows non-Jewish procedure cites two biblical precedents. The one from Esther deals with a clearly non-Jewish situation. The one from Genesis, however, deals with Judah answering before his older brothers about selling Joseph into slavery. The assumption here is that before the Sinaitic covenant Jews were bound by non-

Jewish law.[54] I venture to say that this Amora was R. Johanan. On the other hand, the Amora who holds that Jewish procedure does not follow from non-Jewish procedure insists that these two examples are only presented in the Bible because they confirm what is *already* basically a Jewish procedure.

6.　Non-Jewish Participation in Jewish Law

Not only did the acknowledgment of non-Jewish *dinim* enable some of the rabbis to affirm past non-Jewish precedents in Jewish law, it also enabled some rabbis to accept non-Jewish participation in present Jewish jurisprudence. The following ruling was referred to the Parthian king, Shapur I (d. 273 CE) for his opinion:

> If there are two gardens in steps, one above and the other with greens between them ... R. Simon said that whatever the owner of the upper step can reach is his and the rest belongs to the owner of the lower step.[55]

The Gemara reports that the Parthian king said, "congratulations to R. Simon."[56] Rashi notes that the king was "legally erudite" (*baki be-dinim*). In other words, in most questions of civil law (*din*), jurisprudence is a matter of reason and general experience; hence non-Jewish counsel is not ruled out by religious distinctions. This point is emphasized by Zvi Hirsch Chajes (d. 1855): "Since we hold that the words of the Torah are not to be turned over to others, how could they study Torah with King Shapur?—Because this is a matter of law for which Noahides are obligated."[57]

　　Nevertheless, the Tosafists emphasize that King Shapur was "erudite in Jewish law" (*baki be-halakhot*).[58] While this view appears to support Rashi's, there is a crucial difference between *dinim*, which are universal, and *halakhot*, which are specifically Jewish. Either the Tosafists have a text in which Rashi refers to "*halakhot*" rather than "*dinim*," or they differ from him without admitting it. The latter scenario seems more plausible: B. *Avodah Zarah* 76b refers to the king's knowledge of Jewish *ritual* law. If this is correct, then the Tosafists are attempting to demonstrate that King Shapur acknowledged not only the inherent rationality of R. Simon's ruling, but, more importantly, he respected the *civil authority* of the rabbis. The mention of the king's opinion here is an example of gentile respect for the good use Jews have made of their own internal autonomy. In Rashi's view, the mention of the king's opinion is an acknowledgment that gentiles respect the sound legal reasoning of the rabbis. The Gemara itself reports that Resh Lakish accepted the ruling of R. Simon as legally binding. The crucial point of difference in the interpretation of this text is whether King Shapur was praising R. Simon's view as an example of Jewish civil authority, or simply as the most reasonable ruling in the case. Again, the latter seems more likely because the king only praises R. Simon by name, not R. Simon's ruling as authorized by Resh Lakish.

We have now seen how Jewish interest in independent non-Jewish law is for the sake of constituting a moral standard to be used in regulated Jewish law itself. Such interest, it seems to me, led to a gradual acceptance of the validity of certain universal non-Jewish legal practices and institutions for Jewish litigation. In the area of *dinim* the question arose whether non-Jewish adjudication, as an independent legal procedure, was valid in Jewish cases:

R. Eleazar b. Azaryah said that if the gentile law is like Jewish law, may I conclude that their law is valid?—Scripture states, "And these are the ordinances (*mishpatim*) *you* shall place before *them*"—you judge *their* cases but they do not judge yours.[59]

We have here an example of the principle of legal suzerainty; that is, Jews have the right, even the obligation, to enforce the rule of law among gentiles. The *Mekhilta* see this principle as the basis for the following Mishnaic law:

A bill of divorce ordered (*get me'useh*) by Jewish authorities is valid (*kasher*), but by gentile authorities is invalid (*pasul*). But, if the gentiles beat the husband and say, "do as the Jewish authorities tell you"—it is valid.[60]

Gentile law, then, is valid for Jews only as an extension of Jewish enforcement; but Jewish law is valid wherever it applies to them and the Jews have the power to enforce it.[61]

However, in the Mishnah we also find a tacit recognition that Jewish and non-Jewish law have enough *in common* to allow non-Jewish jurisdiction to have validity in some cases involving Jews:

All documents deposited in the gentile courts (*arka'ot she-la-goyim*), even though their sealing is witnessed by gentiles, are valid (*kesherin*)—except bills of divorce and manumission of slaves.[62]

The simplest and most constricted interpretation of this text is given by R. Mordecai b. Hillel, a thirteenth-century authority. He states that this is a specific rabbinic decree concerning documents. The reason he gives is that gentiles are very careful (*makpidin*) about the signatures of documents registered in their courts.[63] He based this on the fact that the question of witnesses for documents is a matter of rabbinic law where much flexibility exists.[64] Hence, this is simply a specific concession in Jewish law. The later codes, no doubt reflecting the fears of even further erosion of Jewish autonomy in the Middle Ages, follow Mordecai in restricting non-Jewish legitimacy in Jewish legal affairs as much as possible.[65]

However, the Gemara to this Mishnah bases the ruling on the much more comprehensive principle of the third-century Babylonian Amora, Samuel, who judged "the law of the kingdom is the law" (dina de-malkhuta dina). Rashbam (d. 1174) explains:

All the levies and taxes and procedures regularly enacted by kings in their kingdoms are binding as law (dina). For all the subjects of the kingdom freely accept (mirtzonam) the statutes of the king and his enactments.[66]

Here, the legal authority of the state to make laws for its subjects—including Jewish subjects—is grounded in popular consent and acceptance of external authority. Such reasoning would later be called "social contract."[67] This principle in and of itself does not present any standard to determine whether these laws are right or wrong.

Finally, Rashi presents the broadest and deepest basis for the specific ruling of the Mishnah:

They are not subject to Divine punishment (kritut) because they are not subjects of Jewish marriage and divorce; but concerning adjudication (ha-dinim) Noahides are commanded.[68]

This explanation indicates that a non-Jewish society—in non-ritual cases, of course—can be the context for Jewish legal action, provided that that society's legal and political order is in basic conformity with the Noahide commandments. This is not only a de facto recognition of Jews as subject to a non-Jewish regime; it is a de jure recognition that the state's right to rule is grounded in a law directed to the conscience of humanity. In other words, we now have a moral grounding for the positive law of the gentile state. This goes far beyond a principle of consent. For a social contract theory itself provides no standard for judging which of the ruler's laws are morally binding,[69] indeed which of the laws the ruler himself has the moral right to enact. Consent alone can be either moral or immoral. It is even found among thieves.[70]

The recognition and affirmation of the presence of dinim among gentiles provided a theoretical model for determining the necessary minimum moral standards to which Jewish law must adhere. It also provided a morally acceptable system of civil law when Jewish law was practically inoperable. It enabled non-Jewish civil law at times to be morally obligatory for Jews, not just politically expedient. Thus, we will see that Rashi's designation of gentile jurisdiction as morally binding because of their adherence to Noahide laws not only explains the law concerning documents deposited in gentile courts, it also became the ultimate moral justification of the most comprehensive principle in this area.

However, the principle of dina de-malkhuta dina requires justification.

Rashbam justifies it on the basis of consent, namely, Jews have the right to contract the loss of civil independence in return for a degree of political sufferance. Civil rights, according to the Talmud, can be waived by stipulation.[71] In the *locus classicus* of this principle in the Gemara it is presented as contradicting another statement recorded in the name of Samuel, namely, "the possessions of gentiles are like the wilderness (*kamidbar*), whoever takes hold of them acquires them."[72] Maimonides explains that this other statement only applies in the absence of explicit political authority governing gentiles and Jews. The presence of such authority, on the other hand, with its advantages of law and order, removes the right from Jews.[73] Thus both Rashbam and Maimonides use social contract type reasoning to explain this radical principle.[74]

The Jewish version of the social contract theory escaped one of the main criticisms of the theory in later philosophy. It was argued by more historically minded thinkers that such a contract presupposes the existence of society, not vice versa.[75] However, the Jewish version did not use it to explain the origins of society per se, but merely to justify the right of Jews as a minority to contract for their political sufferance by relinquishing their civil autonomy. The theory enabled Jews to live in a society not grounded in the Sinaitic covenant.

Nevertheless, the principle does not offer a criterion for determining which non-Jewish systems of law are not only politically expedient but also morally binding on the Jewish conscience. If obedience to the laws of the state is simply political expediency, then the Jewish community has indeed not only lost its civil independence but some of its moral integrity as well. R. Solomon Adret (Rashba) expands:

I say that whoever relies on this to say that something is forbidden because "the law of the kingdom is the law" he is in error and a robber . . . and in the category of one who uproots all of the laws of the perfect Torah. What need would we have of all the holy books . . . ? They might as well teach their children the laws of the gentiles! Concerning this principle . . . I have greatly agonized (*yagati harbeh*).[76]

However, if one can see something basic in common between Jewish and non-Jewish society as a universal *sine qua non*, then the acceptance of the temporal authority of non-Jewish law does not involve a loss of Jewish moral integrity. The Noahide commandment of *dinim*, which we may interpret as the due process of law, is the *sine qua non* for any society having a moral claim upon its citizens.[77] If it is present, it has an immediate moral claim upon whomever lives in that society, including Jews. R. Hayyim Hirschensohn (d. 1935) adds:

Because they are obligated for law they are obligated for the prescriptions of the state (*be-nimusai ha-malkhut*) . . . not because of the power of the king but because of the legal obligation (*hiyuv dinim*) for which Noahides are obligated. If so their state is able to enact decrees (*le-taken takkanot*) and methods of acquisition which are also effective (*mo'ilim*) between one Jew and another.[78]

Indeed Samuel's very choice of the term *dina* might indicate that he defined non-Jewish law as valid by virtue of its adherence to the Noahide *dinim*.[79]

The question whether gentile normativity could be assumed or not is discussed in the following Talmudic text. The specific question concerns the appropriation of mortgaged property (*nekhasim she-yesh lahem aharayut*)[80] by a third party from the buyer to pay a debt incurred by the seller of that property:

> If a Jew sold a donkey to a fellow Jew (*yisrael habrayh*) and a gentile came and appropriated (*v'anees*) it from the buyer, it is right (*dina*) that the seller attempt to get it back (*demifatzai*) from the gentile.[81]

Rashbam explains that this is to be done through gentile jurisdiction (*ba-din nokhri*) because gentiles are law-abiding (*tzayeyatai dina hem*).[82] In the case of such appropriation by a Jew, on the other hand, the full procedures of Jewish law are presupposed.[83] Rashba indicates that in the case of illegal appropriation, either by a Jew or a gentile, compensation by the seller to the buyer is not required.[84] R. Joseph Karo (d. 1575) indicated that it was rational (*devarim shel ta'am*) that if Jewish and gentile law agreed in this question of appropriation, then the seller must indemnify the buyer for his loss.[85] Earlier, R. Yom Tov Ishbili argued that as a protection mortgages should stipulate that the Jewish seller accepts responsibility (*aharayut*), even according to gentile law.[86]

As the dialectic of the Gemara proceeds, however, this law is qualified by distinctions between lawful and unlawful gentile appropriations of Jewish property. Finally, the fifth-century Amora, Amemar, is reported to have ruled that the seller need not attempt to retrieve the appropriated item from the gentile for the buyer because "gentiles in general are robbers" (*stam nokhri anas hu*). As support for this statement he quotes Psalms (144:8), "for they speak falsehood and their right hand is deceitful."[87] This ruling is considered authoritative today.[88]

Nevertheless, as in other rulings, the question arises whether it is an absolute prescription or, rather, contingent on an empirical state of affairs.[89] If the latter, then the rule is not applied in a changed state of affairs among gentiles. Maimonides seems to opt for the former option, inasmuch as he rules against indemnification even if the gentile gained the item through due process of gentile law (*b'arka'ot shelahen*).[90] This ruling is followed by R. Jacob b. Asher (d. 1340) and R. Joseph Karo.[91] Meiri, as his wont, distinguishes between ancient, lawless idolaters and those with a legal system (*akra'ote-hem*).[92] In the latter case the distinction between Jewish and gentile law is no longer valid. Later, R. Joel Sirkes (Bach, d. 1640) also emphasized the empirical context of this law.[93] For if gentiles have an objective legal system, and if the rule concerning appropriation of mortgaged property is not uniquely Jewish, then it is hard to distinguish between Jewish and non-Jewish procedure since both are in essence *dina*.[94]

The acknowledgment that non-Jewish law may be authoritative for Jews in the absence of sufficient Jewish political independence is ultimately based on the acceptance of gentile normativity. As a famous Mishnah states:

R. Hanina the vice High Priest says that one should pray for the well-being of the government (*shlomah shel malkut*), for were it not for the fear of it (*mora'ah*) a man would swallow his neighbor alive.[95]

For Jews, acknowledgment of this type was like the principle in Roman law, *dura lex sed lex*, that is, a "hard" (imperfect) law is better than anarchy. In fact Jews were admonished not only for disobeying their own law but for abandoning law in general:

R. Joshua b. Levi saw a contradiction between two verses in Ezekiel: "And you did not act according to the laws of the nations which surround you" (5:7), and "You *did* act according to the laws of the nations which surround you" (11:12). He resolved it by saying: You did not act according to their good laws (*metukanim*); their bad laws (*mekulkalim*) you did act according to them.[96]

Obviously, the only criterion to determine which non-Jewish laws are good or not is Noahide law. If these laws are good per se, then they are good for all humanity, Jews included.

This does not involve the permanent abandonment of Jewish civil law. The rule of law is only the necessary condition for society to have moral authority; it is not the sufficient ground for a historical community. The identity of the people of Israel is grounded in God's revelation of the Torah.[97] Surely the hope of this covenanted community is that every aspect of human life, individual and collective, be illuminated by the light of Torah and the particular historical experience of the Jewish people. Although it is acknowledged that certain areas of interhuman relationships, specifically civil law, can function independently of the revealed law of the Torah, such independence reflects a historical alienation, an unhappy situation where the Jewish people cannot exercise the full hegemony of the Torah over their communal life. The recognition of the universality of *dinim*, however, enables Jews to see the lack of full Torah hegemony as a political privation rather than a moral compromise. Moreover, by seeing the rule of law as a universal moral requirement, it becomes a necessary condition but never its sufficient ground. This concept of *dinim*, when properly understood, does not allow the revealed law of the Torah to be reduced to an immanent moral universalism.

7. Differences Between Jewish and Non-Jewish Law

The Jewish interest in non-Jewish law is an attempt to see the necessary conditions for Jewish law as universal, because before the Sinaitic covenant Jews
were bound by these standards, and therefore the specific revelation of the
laws of the Torah presuppose human normativity in general. Thus, non-Jewish
law functions as a positive criterion of comparison. However, non-Jewish law
is used a negative standard of comparison in those cases where Jewish law demands a greater legal obligation. Non-Jewish law as a *conditio sine qua non*
only provides a minimal standard of similarity. Above this minimal level, however, Jewish law is dissimilar. Without this distinction, one will fall into the
error of reducing Jewish law to merely universal standards, a common error of
some modern interpreters. Universal standards are necessary for Jewish law
but not sufficient. This truth is brought out in a Talmudic text regarding usury,
a practice permitted between gentiles and between Jews and gentiles:[98]

R. Safra said that anything which in their law is transferred from borrower to lender,
in our law is returned from the lender to the borrower. Anything which in their law
is not transferred from the borrower to the lender, in our law is not returned from
the lender to the borrower.[99]

The discussion in the Gemara limits the difference between "our" law and
"their" law to stipulated interest (*ribbit ketzutzah*). However, since unstipulated interest prepayments and unstipulated supplements are not legal matters in the gentile system, they need not be so in Jewish law.[100] The reason here
is probably because such practices are too informal to be effectively controlled
by strict legal enforcement. But in the case of stipulated interest we see the difference between a covenanted community and a non-covenanted community.
Clearly the personal interdependence required in the former community
must be greater than that required in the latter, and the taking of interest is
counter-covenantal. Nevertheless, the fundamental point in common is that
the debt must be paid. The Torah need not legislate payment because a debt *by
definition* is money lent in order to be repaid.[101]

The Talmud later attempted to conceptualize the entire relation between
Jewish and non-Jewish law in the following principle: "There is nothing permitted to Jews which is prohibited (*asur*) to gentiles."[102] In our case, the application would be: since gentiles are required to pay their debts, so too are Jews;
but gentiles being permitted to both take and pay interest does not determine
what Jews are to do in this area. In other words, gentile moral standards are
the minimum but not the maximum in Jewish law. Although exceptions are
found to this principle, it was adhered to with remarkable consistency.[103]

CHAPTER THREE

THE LAW OF BLASPHEMY

1. Introduction

The law of blasphemy is designated in the Tosefta as *qilelat Ha-Shem*, "cursing the name." In other Tannaitic sources, however, it is usually termed euphemistically as *birkat Ha-Shem*, "blessing the Name," indicating the reluctance of ancient Jews to couple the name of God with a curse.[1] The law of blasphemy is marked by the use of Tetragrammaton (YHWH) as the second word in Gen. 2:16, "And *the* Lord God commanded . . ." Because the Tetragrammaton is the most unambiguous word in Scripture, there is no discrepancy in the rabbinic presentations of the seven Noahide laws.[2] In all of them blasphemy is the second law.

In the Pentateuch the explicit reaction to the crime of blasphemy is addressed to the people of Israel. The crime seems to include both cursing God with the Tetragrammaton as well as cursing Him with other names:

And to the people of Israel you shall speak saying: any man who curses his God shall be put to death (*mot yumat*); all the congregation shall surely stone him (Lev. 24:15–16).

In the Talmud it is debated whether cursing God in general is the legal equivalent of the use of the Tetragrammaton in such a curse:

"When he curses his God" . . . this includes the use of the substitute names in the opinion of R. Meir. But the sages say only use of the Unique Name (*Shem Ha-meyuhad*) is punishable by death; use of other names is only the transgression of a prohibition (*azharah*).[3]

The view of the sages is explicitly presented in the Mishnah: "The blasphemer (*ha-megadef*) is not liable for the death penalty until he enunciates (*she-yifaresh*) the Tetragrammaton."[4] Maimonides ruled that this applies to cursing the substitute name for the Tetragrammaton (*Shem Adnut*) as well as the literal name.[5] This position seems to be in effect a middle ground between the two Talmudic views presented above.

The crime of blasphemy is applied to non-Jews by an extension of the passage in Lev. 24:15–16:

R. Meyaysha said that a Noahide who cursed (she-birekh) the Name using substitution (be-kinuyyim) is guilty and liable for the death penalty, according to the rabbis. For what reason? When Scripture states (Lev. 24:16), "the alien (ke-ger) is like the native-born (k'ezrah)," this applies to blaspheming the Name; but a gentile is guilty even for a substitution.[6]

In this exegesis "ger" means "convert." The logic is as follows: the crime of blasphemy applies to all since it is addressed to any man (ish ish—Lev. 24:15).[7] Furthermore, blasphemy is committed when there is any curse against God (Elohim), namely, against any designation of the deity. Thereafter, the punishment, as it applies to native-born Jews and converts, is limited to the use of the Tetragrammaton, at least as regards the death penalty. The more general designation of the death penalty still applies to non-Jews who are not included in this specific exception. Elsewhere, the Talmud designates the actual prohibition as being expressed in Ex. 22:27, "you shall not curse God," where the general Elohim is used rather than the unique YHWH.[8]

In essence the prohibition of blasphemy is the same for non-Jews. The difference emerges in punishment. For non-Jews the same punishment applies no matter which name of God is used. For Jews, on the other hand, use of the Tetragrammaton results in a more serious punishment than the use of other designations of the deity.[9] Although Jewish society's reaction to gentile blasphemy, according to accepted halakhic opinion, is at least at one level different from its reaction to Jewish blasphemy, the act is essentially the same in both cases.

Philosophical reflection begins at this point because it is concerned more with the inner motivations of the acts than with external reactions to them.[10] Therefore, the search for the inner motivation behind blasphemy, both Jewish and gentile, reveals to us what aspect of Judaism itself might occasion blasphemy as a act of radical negation. It might very well indicate an awareness of paradoxes within Judaism itself which the blasphemer points to by his blasphemy. Thus, if understood, it can very well affect the internal development of Judaism. Such an indication does not exonerate the sin of blasphemy as the particular act of an individual in the legal sense. The value of such an indication is, rather, reflective.

Perhaps this approach might be alluded to in the following Amoraic statement that so puzzled subsequent generations: "R. Nahman b. Isaac said that a sin for its own sake (averah lishmah) is greater than a commandment not for its own sake."[11] The puzzlement came because this statement seemed to place greater moral value on intentional vice than unintentional virtue. It seemed to endorse intentionality regardless of consequences. However, if understood reflectively rather than reactively, it seems to be saying that there is *more to be seen* from specifically motivated rejection than unmotivated affirmation. Blasphemy, perhaps more than any other sin, is the specifically motivated rejection of God as *the foundation of Judaism*.[12] It is as revealing for Jewish thought as it is reprehensible for Jewish morality.

2. Blasphemy as Illegitimate Speech

Although the specific crime of *birkat Ha-Shem* involves actually cursing God, it can only be understood in the context of illegitimate use of speech about God in general. The theocentricity of Judaism requires the utmost seriousness when in engaging in what is now called "God-talk." Blasphemy is the most radical form of illegitimate "God-talk," but by no means its only form.

The Mishnah states that among those who lose their portion in the world-to-come includes one who "pronounces the Tetragrammaton as it is written."[13] In the Gemara this is qualified to mean if this is done outside the Temple precincts (*ba-gevulin*) and in a blasphemous manner (*leshon aga*).[14] Rashi explains that the pronunciation of the Tetragrammaton could not very well be prohibited in the Temple precincts inasmuch as the daily priestly blessing called for its use. Blasphemous use of the Name, however, was even prohibited there. Rashi offers another interpretation of the term *leshon aga* (blasphemy), namely, using the divine name in a gathering where the conversation is secular (*divrei hol*).[15]

Even in the early days of the Second Temple there was a tendency to limit use of the Tetragrammaton. The Tosefta and Gemara record that after the death of the high priest, Simon the Just (third century BCE), the Tetragrammaton was no longer pronounced so as to be audible in public.[16] The medieval commentators seem to be almost unanimous in explaining that the reason for this innovation was that the people no longer merited hearing the name; it was being misused.[17] The prevalence of Gnostic sects and their theurgic practices undoubtedly had much to do with these prohibitions.[18] We also have the testimony of R. Tarfon, who claims that as a child he went up with his uncles to the platform in the Temple used for the priestly blessing and heard the high priest "swallow" (*hivli'a*) the Name so as to be inaudible to the worshippers.[19] Maimonides emphasized the noetic dangers in the use of the divine names by persons lacking in the necessary moral and intellectual prerequisites.[20]

The Palestinian Talmud interprets the illegitimate use of the Name as similar to the practice of the Samaritans who constantly swear.[21] The tenth-

century Karaite Abu Yusef Ya'aqob Qirqasani indicates Karaites and Rabban-
ite agreement that the Samaritan version of the Torah is illegitimate and,
therefore, offensive to religion.[22] Thus he states that in effect the very practice
of Samaritan religious expression is itself an act of blasphemy. Although the
status of the Samaritans was debated in rabbinic times, it was finally decided
during the early Amoraic period, in Palestine where the Samaritans lived, that
their status was the same as gentiles.[23] Because of this the term "*kuti*" (Samaritan) was used in certain texts in place of "*nokhri*" (non-Jew) in censored editions of the Talmud.

All of this discussion indicates the Jewish recognition of the contempt for
Judaism by gentiles. Thus, even in early biblical times the Philistine warrior
Goliath began his challenge to the Israelite army with a curse.[24] In fact one
Hellenistic Jewish author refers to "blasphemous and barbarous gentiles (*eth-
nesin*)."[25] The juxtaposition of these two terms is worth noting. The Greek *barbaros* originally meant anyone who did not speak Greek. Although not having
a necessarily pejorative intention, it soon connoted, however, the superiority
of the Greek language as the matrix of Greek thought.[26] The "barbarian" was
by definition linguistically and, therefore, intellectually deprived. Coupled
now with the Jewish notion of blasphemy, this Hellenistic synthesis expresses
the Jewish observation that the gentiles profane language precisely because of
their lack of knowledge of the God of Israel.[27] The specific reference to "blasphemous and barbarous gentiles" is to the Hellenistic Syrians who had
defiled the Temple in Jerusalem and whom the Maccabees had driven out.

The prevalence of gentile blasphemy led to reinterpretation of certain
halakhic norms:

R. Hiyya said that whoever hears the Name of God (*azkarah*) in this age is not
obligated to tear his clothes, because if this were not said, one's clothes would be
nothing but tatters. From whom did you hear this? Certainly a Jew would not be so
sacrilegious, therefore it surely refers to a gentile. Since a gentile would not have
learned how to pronounce the Unique Name it refers to any designation. And we
infer from the qualification "in this age" that originally one was obligated to tear his
clothes. So indeed we infer (*shema mina*).[28]

The basis for the obligation to tear one's clothes upon hearing the names of
God blasphemously uttered by gentiles is traced to the verse that described
how King Hezekiah tore his clothes upon hearing the blasphemous remarks
of the Assyrian emissary, Rabshakeh (I Kgs 19:1).[29] In the version of the Palestinian Talmud the verse describing the Lord as the "God of all flesh" (Jer. 32:27)
is quoted, emphasizing reverence for God as a universal requirement. The
reason given for discontinuing the practice of tearing one's clothes is because

the prevalence of blasphemers (mi-she-rabbu ha-godfanin) made the rule impractical.[30] Later post-Talmudic authorities argued whether Jewish apostates were to be regarded like gentiles when one heard blasphemy from their mouths.[31]

On the surface it seems that the halakhah was simply concerned with the fact of gentile blasphemy and how Jews react to it. At this level there do not seem to be any internal effects from the recognition of this common state of affairs.

Nevertheless, the law of birkat Ha-Shem is essentially related to the concepts of Kiddush Ha-Shem—sanctification of God's Name—and its antonym, hillul Ha-Shem—the profanation of God's Name. These concepts indicate problematic areas of Jewish practice which might provide conditions for gentile blasphemy.[32] Concern for the conditions of blasphemy, over and above the fact of blasphemy, requires reflective insight over and above mere factual observation and legal inference. Such reflection led to important developments in Jewish thought and practice.

3. Sanctification and Profanation of the Name

The commandment to sanctify the Name is expressed in the following verse: "You shall not profane (ve-l'o tehellelu) my holy Name, and I will be sanctified (ve-nigdashti) in the midst of the people of Israel; I am the Lord who sanctifies you" (Lev. 22:32). The commandment involves three possible acts: (1) declaring the sanctity of the Lord liturgically (kedushah) before a Jewish congregation;[33] (2) declaring the sanctity of the Lord by martyrdom at the hands of gentiles in the presence of a quorum of Jews;[34] (3) causing the Name of God to be praised by gentiles as a response to an act done by a Jew.

The first form of Kiddush ha-Shem involves a purely internal Jewish relation. The second form involves the most radical form of Jewish resistance to the pressure of the gentile world to break Jewish fidelity to those acts that were judged unconditional. Even though these unconditional acts—idolatry, sexual immorality and murder—are themselves Noahide laws,[35] the peculiarly Jewish essence of this type of Kiddush Ha-Shem was assured by the prescription of martyrdom for Jews only when confronted by the choice of either doing these acts or suffering death.[36]

The third form, however, in essence indicates a Jewish reaction to a challenge by the gentile world regarded as legitimate. As such it stimulates an internal Jewish dialectic of which it is the sine qua non.

The classic case here is the story of Simon b. Shetah (first century BCE), whose students purchased a donkey for him from an Arab that had a precious pearl attached to it. When the sage discovered that the Arab did not know about the transfer of the pearl with the donkey, he insisted that the pearl be returned. The Palestinian Talmud points out that although robbing a gentile was prohibited by some authorities, all agreed that one was permitted to keep property lost by a gentile (she-abedato mutteret).[37] Nevertheless, Simon b. Shetah did not want to be thought of as a "barbarian" (barbarin) who would take advantage of a loophole in the law.[38] His intent was, rather, to cause the gentile to say, "blessed is the God of the Jews."[39] As one commentator noted, "he wanted the Name of God to be sanctified (she-yitkadesh Shem Shamayim) through him."[40]

As a continuation of this motif it is recorded that in a similar circumstance the later sage Abba Oshiyah stated that "the Torah commands (oraita gazart) that we return it." Finally, Maimonides rules:

It is permitted to keep the lost article of a gentile as it is written, "the lost article of your brother (ahika—Deut. 22:3) and whoever does return it had committed a transgression because he strengthens the hand of the wicked of the world. But, if he returned it to sanctify the Divine Name that Jews might be praised (she-yefa'aru yisrael) and the gentiles will know that they are trustworthy (ba'alai emunah) that is meritorious (meshubah). And where there is any possibility of the profanation of the Divine Name, then keeping gentile lost property is forbidden and one is obligated (hayyav) to return it. And in all circumstances gentiles are to be hidden away from thieves in the interest of peace (mipnei darkhei shalom).[41]

Joseph Karo, in his commentary to the Mishneh Torah, notes at this point that the reason for Maimonides' ruling regarding the return of property lost by gentiles is that in a predominantly Jewish area if this were not the case, the gentiles would say the Jews stole it.[42]

Looking at the sequence from Simon b. Shetah to Karo we see the development of a single act of piety into a general rule of Jewish law. The point that emerges is that Jewish behavior towards gentiles is supposed to lead gentiles to praise God: "You are my witnesses, says the Lord" (Is. 43:10), and "this people I have formed for Myself, My praise they declare" (Is. 42:6). How is this the case?

If Jewish law is conceived as a device to give Jews an economic advantage over non-Jews, it is likely to occasion contempt for Judaism and its foundation, either by encouraging blasphemy or contempt. In such a situation revelation is constituted as supernatural endorsement of particular Jewish national self-interest.[43] If Jewish law is an instrument of chauvinism, then it appears as a system morally inferior to the equity required by a rational system of ethics. The moral standards of the gentiles among whom a Jew lives are an indispensable condition, namely, hillul Ha-Shem becomes a consideration in cases where Jewish moral standards, if not altered, appear inferior to gentile norms. Hillel introduced a gentile to Judaism through the maxim, "what is hateful to you do not do to your fellow."[44] Reason, when there is *hillul Ha-Shem*, becomes morally more respectable than revelation. Patent inequality in the system of law grounded in revelation leads to its rejection, overtly or covertly, by moral persons. Thus even with fellow Jews, in cases where the strict letter of the law (*shurat ha-din*) would be inequitable, one is morally obligated to go beyond it (*lifnim mi-shurat ha-din*).[45]

Nevertheless, how does Jewish moral action, not taking advantage of the letter of the law, point to God? From Maimonides' presentation of the principles of the Sanctification of the Name and *in the interest of peace* it might seem that these are simply "good-will" gestures, pragmatic devices devised by a vulnerable minority to curry favor with the host society. However, *hillul Ha-Shem* is possible even when Jews have political control.[46] Consequently, the altruism of an act of *kiddush Ha-Shem* can only be inspired by charity (*middat rahamim*). Non-reciprocal acts point, it seems, to a supernatural source. Thus where the principle of "acting in the interest of peace" involves compromise with idolatry, the elimination of God by substitution, the principle is invalid.[47] Moreover, the related concept of "going beyond the letter of the law" is presented in one text as an appeal by God to Himself to act charitably with His children lest He destroy them with strict justice.[48] Later in the text the same prayer is addressed to God by R. Ishmael b. Elisha. Indeed the unique Divine Name, the Tetragrammaton, is interpreted as denoting God's unique charity.[49] Thus *kiddush Ha-Shem* is in essence *imitatio Dei*.[50] As such it inspires praise to God when performed with that original intention. Only by eliminating traces of chauvinism does the Torah inspire external praise for its Giver.

4. Blasphemy as Protest

Although blasphemy is a crime irrespective of its circumstances, nevertheless, those circumstances were an issue of reflective Jewish concern. This concern led to an examination of areas of internal moral ambiguity in Judaism itself. Such ambiguity is found in the rabbinic analysis of the first case of blasphemy presented in the Torah. The text identifies both blasphemer and the circumstances of the blasphemy:

The son of an Israelite woman and an Egyptian man came out in the midst of the people of Israel, and they fought this son of an Israelite woman with an Israelite man in the camp. And the son of the Israelite woman blasphemed (*vayikov*) the Divine Name and he cursed and they brought him to Moses. And his mother's name was Shlomit daughter of Dibri of the tribe of Dan (Lev. 24:10–11).

The oldest midrash on Leviticus emphasizes that the words "they fought in the camp" (vayyinnatzu ba-mahaneh) refer to the issue, not merely the location. They fought regarding "matters of encampment" (iskai mahaneh).[51] Earlier, the same midrash stated:

"He went out," namely, he went out from Moses' court whereto he came to establish residence (lit'a ohelo) among the tribe of Dan. They said to him, "by what right (mah tibekha)" do you establish residence among the camp of the Danites? He said to them, "I am descended from the daughters of Dan." They said to him that Scripture states, "each man by his own standard (al diglo) by the insignia (b'otot) of their ancestral clan (le-vet avotam) shall the sons of Israel camp . . . " (Num. 2:2). He entered the court of Moses and came out unexonerated (mehuyyav) and he blasphemed (vegidef).

The context here is the moral implications of the legal question of maternal versus paternal status in determining ancestral right, especially in the realm of inheritance.[52] The text not only emphasizes that the blasphemer was disenfranchised because of his Egyptian father, but, even worse, he was considered to be "like a bastard (ke-mamzer)."[53] R. Abraham b. David of Posquieres adds: "the author of this interpretation was of the opinion (kesabar) that if a gentile freeman or slave had intercourse with a Jewish woman, any resulting child is a bastard."[54] The rabbis debated the status of a child born to a gentile father and Jewish mother, finally ruling that the child is legitimate (kasher). Nevertheless, many earlier authorities ruled that the child is a bastard, following R. Akiva. In other words, the father is primary.[55]

The complaint of the blasphemer, then, is twofold: (1) a complaint that because of his gentile father he has no landed rights,[56] and (2) that because of his gentile father he is a bastard, one "who may not come into the congregation of the Lord" (Deut. 23:3), and thus disqualified from marrying a Jewish woman.[57] This status of permanent alienation within the Jewish people occasions blasphemy against God as a cry of utter desperation. Along the same lines, a late midrash cites the two rebels against Moses, Dathan and Abiram (Num. 16:27), cursing God when "the people of Israel withdrew from around them."[58] Alienation can well lead to blasphemy.

The blasphemer was suffering from an alienated status because of the sin of his parents over which he himself had no control. His mother, Shlomit bat Dibri, is portrayed as the only promiscuous woman among the Israelite slaves in Egypt.[59] His Egyptian father is represented as the man whom Moses killed (Ex. 2:11–12) because he was attempting to kill Shlomit's Israelite husband, who had caught the pair in flagrante delicto.[60] The conclusion of this issue in this midrash deals with the injustice of causing children to suffer for the sins of their parents.

Scripture states, "And I returned and I saw all the persecuted (*kol ha'ashukim*, Ecc. 4:1). Hanina the tailor interpreted this verse as referring to the bastards . . . the parents of these people have sinned and these unfortunates (*ve'ilan alubya*) . . . what sin did they commit, what difference could they make?[61]

The "oppressors" (*oshkafhem*) referenced are considered members of the Great Sanhedrin who enforce the Torah's law, in this case the biblical restrictions against the bastards. The "Comforter" (*menachem*) of these bastards is God himself, who in the world-to-come will purify them, based on the messianic vision of Israel as a candelabra made of gold (Zech. 4:2).[62]

The question of the conflict between ancestral guilt and individual responsibility is discussed as early as Jeremiah (32:28–29), and, especially, Ezekiel (18:2), where the ironic query is posed, "the fathers eat sour grapes and the teeth of the children are set on edge?"[63] Later the Talmud emphasized that "the iniquity of the fathers is visited on the children" (Ex. 20:5) only when the children themselves choose to follow in the ways of their evil ancestors (*ke-she'ohazin ma'aseh avotehem be-yadehem*).[64] Throughout rabbinic literature there are numerous aggadic passages indicating that ancestral guilt is not the automatic patrimony of descendants.[65] There are several halakhic ramifications of this emphasis of the priority of individual merit over patrimony. The most striking of these is the statement that in situations where one must choose to save one life before another, the life of a scholarly bastard (*mamzer talmid hakham*) takes precedence over that of an ignorant high priest (*kohen gadol am ha'aretz*).[66] The example is striking because the high priest's pedigree was unmatched. Nevertheless, the learned bastard, by virtue of his individual merit alone, takes precedence. There are also halakhic ramifications in the law that exonerates children from the criminal liabilities of their parents.[67]

The most important halakhic consequence of inherited disability, however, concerns the plight of the *mamzer*, a condition that, according to tradition, led to the first case of blasphemy as an act of desperation. The Talmud presents two solutions to the *mamzer's* plight: (1) R. Tarfon, a second-century Tanna, ruled that a *mamzer* may marry a female, non-Jewish slave, and that the child of this union would be a full-fledged Jew when manumitted;[68] (2) benign neglect.[69] It is stated that during the messianic era God will not discriminate against those families of questionable ancestry who have become intermingled (*she-nitma'ah*) with the rest of the Jewish people.[70] Although, on the surface, this seems to be an aggadic statement, it has direct halakhic consequences: because of the prominent families that are frequently involved, pedigree need not be examined with any great scrutiny, that those presumed to be normal Jews are indeed so.[71] The complaint of the *mamzerim* against the Great Sanhedrin, voiced by Hanina the tailor, may well be a moral challenge to

Jewish authorities to exercise the authority implicit in the halakhah itself to fully alleviate this undeserved predicament.[72] Although the biblical category of bastardy was limited as much as possible,[73] the same rabbinic category was enlarged.[74] The halakhah cannot simply be repealed because of aggadic speculation, it is true. However, the aggadic perspective can inform the halakhic process.[75]

In the case of bastardy we have two aggadic lines of thought: one concerned with genealogical purity, the other with individual merit. The former emphasizes a mystical ethnicity, the latter a rational morality. The connection of the bastard's complaint with the first manifestation of blasphemy in Judaism indicates the necessity for a rational approach to the interpretation and development of Jewish law. The paradoxes present at this point surely can stimulate philosophical reflection. Furthermore, Jewish history also plays a necessary contextual role in the interpretation of Jewish law. Surely the contemporary history of the Jewish people should suggest that an emphasis on mystical ethnicity that borders on racism brings us too near to those irrational ideologies that justified the greatest annihilation of the Jewish people of all time.[76]

5. The Hellenistic Jewish View of Blasphemy

The prohibition against blasphemy, as we have seen, is found in the verse, "you shall not curse God" (Ex. 22:27). The word for God there is the general *elohim* rather than the Tetragrammaton. *Elohim* is a general designation of deity as well as the objects of polytheistic worship (*elohim aherim*) and persons having authority such as judges.[77] Because of its multiple denotations it is, therefore, a plural noun. When applied to God's action, however, it usually takes a singular form of the verb as in the first verse in Genesis, "In the beginning God created (*bara elohim*) the heavens and the earth." The use of a singular verbal form is obviously meant to eliminate any polytheistic influences.[78] Nevertheless, in certain cases at least, *elohim* does take a plural form of the verb as in, "Surely there is a God who judges (*elohim shoftim*) on earth" (Ps. 58:12). In short, the noun *elohim* in biblical use has a fluidity that makes it difficult to define in any singular sense.[79]

However, whereas *elohim* in Ex. 22:27 refers either to God or to legitimate Jewish authorities,[80] it can hardly be taken to refer to the polytheistic gods. Is not the Bible replete with statements of ridicule and derision of these "other" gods?[81] Nevertheless, the Septuagint translation of the Pentateuch, which usually translates the plural Hebrew *elohim* with the singular Greek *theos*, in this case translates the Hebrew *elohim l'o tekallel* with the Greek *theous ou kakologesis*, namely, "*gods* you shall not curse" (literally, "speak ill of").

Along these lines Josephus writes, "Let none blaspheme the gods which other cities revere (*nomizousi*), nor rob foreign temples, nor take treasure that has been dedicated in the name of any god."[82] The apologetic motivation behind this passage has been noted.[83] Jews had to suppress the scripturally based scorn for idolatry in order to survive as a small, vulnerable minority in Hellenistic cities. As such a minority their self-interest was best served by becoming advocates of universal tolerance, a program that would certainly find non-Jewish sympathizers in the pluralistic Hellenistic society. Along these lines, Josephus elsewhere encourages mutual religious tolerance and respect in his polemic against Apion.[84] This appears to be the earliest example of liberalism as a program for Jewish survival and self-interest. This program would be repeated following European emancipation.[85]

This adjustment of the traditional Jewish attitude towards the polytheistic gods was accomplished by radically reinterpreting the specific proscription of blasphemy in the Bible itself. Blasphemy became an offense whether directed against God or "gods." Here we have a signal example of the dialectic between tradition and social reality with all its tensions.

However, theologians are rarely satisfied with such a sociological approach. Thus Philo attempted to discover a more philosophically satisfying reason for this seeming reversal of the traditional Jewish object of the prohibition of blasphemy. In so doing, as is the case with much genuine philosophical reflection on Judaism, he introduced a new synthesizing idea and consequently changed the internal development of Judaism.

Philo indicates that blaspheming the polytheistic gods is not a capital offense as is the case with blasphemy of the Name of the one God. Nevertheless, he notes:

No, clearly by "god" (*theou*), he is not here alluding to the Primal God, the Begetter of the universe, but to the gods of the different cities who are falsely so called . . . We must refrain from speaking insultingly (*tes blasphemias anechein*) of these, lest any of the disciples of Moses get into the habit of treating lightly (*alogein*) the "god" in general, for it is a title worthy of the highest respect and love.[86]

Now this type of argument based on the universal use of "god" (*theos*) could only be made after the beginning of the Hellenistic age. For it was not until the publication and wide distribution of the Septuagint among both Greek-speaking gentiles and Jews that the word *theos* now generally (*sunolos*) referred to the same reality. Philo, therefore, emphasizes that although pagans misuse *theos* by having it still refer to their ancestral gods, the word itself has sanctity because of its true denotation. Such an argument presupposes that, at least on a philosophical level, there is a recognition of *divinity* referring to the one God despite the continued misuse of the designation *theos* in popular polytheism.

In another passage, Philo makes the subjects of the Septuagint's proscription to be the proselytes who have joined (*proseleluthenai*) the new and God-loving society (*philotheopoliteia*). These people are particularly prone to blaspheme the gods they themselves formerly worshipped and whom "others acknowledge" (*hous heteroi nomizousi*). Philo argues that if blasphemy is permitted on this level, then:

> ... they on their part utter profane words against Him who truly is (*tou ontos ontos*). For they know not the difference, and since the falsehood has been taught to them as truth since childhood and has grown up with them, they will go away.[87]

What Philo has done is to introduce the idea that the gap between polytheism and monotheism is not absolute. Both the polytheist and the monotheist ultimately intend the same object by their use of the common term, *theos*. The polytheists pervert this ultimate intention by using it to denote inappropriate, false objects. Thus their religion is based more on philosophical error than on absolute rejection of the deity.[88] Polytheism, when transcended, is, however, potential monotheism. As potential monotheism it is not altogether evil. It is only evil if seen as the actual end of the quest for God. Now the experience of the transition from polytheism to monotheism is precisely that of the proselyte. Since Judaism itself begins with the conversion of Abraham from polytheism to monotheism, the insight of Philo into the internal meaning of the Septuagint's proscription of the ridicule of even polytheism suggests an awareness of the precondition for the emergence of Judaism. This notion of a gradation from polytheism to monotheism found expression in the writings of Solomon ibn Gabirol, who, like Philo, operated with a Neoplatonic metaphysics, with its emphasis on gradations in being:

> Yet is not Thy glory diminished by reason of those that worship aught beside Thee (*bil'adeyka*), for the yearning of them all is to draw nigh to Thee (*lehaggiya adeykha*). But they are like the blind, setting their faces forward on the King's highway, yet still wandering from the path (*veta'u min ha-derekh*).[89]

We will see how this idea was developed by subsequent Jewish thinkers in the following chapter, on the prohibition of idolatry.

CHAPTER FOUR

THE LAW OF IDOLATRY

1. Introduction

In the order of the seven laws of the sons of Noah found in the Tosefta, the second is the prohibition of idolatry, followed by the prohibition of blasphemy.[1] However, in the *baraita* presented in the Babylonian Talmud, the order is reversed.[2] In the Gemara the Amora R. Johanan bases this on the sequence of words in Gen. 2:16, where the third word is "God" (*elohim*).[3] This word is then compared to its use in the prohibition of idolatry in the Decalogue, namely, "there shall be no other gods in My presence" (Ex. 20:3). In the same Gemara, R. Isaac derives the prohibition of idolatry from the first word in Gen. 2:16, "And He commanded" (*vayitzav*).[4] This word is then compared with the word in Ex. 32:8 to describe how the worshippers of God had "commanded them" (*tziviytim*). The Midrash, which also accepts this order, connects the first word in Gen. 2:16 with the word *tzav* in Hosea 5:11, where idolatrous decrees are condemned.[5]

As we saw earlier, the sixteenth-century Talmudist Moses Isserles interpreted the dispute between R. Johanan and R. Isaac as more than a matter of specific textual exegesis but rather as a general theoretical dispute over the essence of the law for Noahides.[6] According to Isserles, R. Johanan thinks that Noahide law is an essentially gentile phenomenon, a matter in which Jews are interested intellectually. But R. Isaac maintains that Noahide law is the branch of Jewish law to be enforced among gentiles under Jewish authority. In other words, it is a matter of Jewish political interest. This difference in theory then leads to the exegetical difference regarding Gen. 2:16. R. Johanan interprets the first word (*vayitzav*) as referring to adjudication (*din*). Consequently, *interhuman normativity* is the beginning of the Noahide law and its foundation. For R. Isaac, on the other hand, *vayitzav* refers to the prohibition of idolatry. Therefore, for him, *God's absolute authority over humanity* is the origin of the Noahide law and its foundation. Hence, Maimonides, who follows R. Isaac, lists the prohibition of idolatry as the first Noahide law.[7] If the foundation of Noahide law is the affirmation of God's absolute sovereignty over humanity, the radical substitution of which is idolatry, then its foundation is exactly the same as the foundation of Jewish law, that is, "I am the Lord your God . . . there shall be no other gods in My presence" (Ex. 20:2–3).[8] If, conversely, the foundation of Noahide law is interhuman legal authority, then it is essentially different from Jewish law. Furthermore, along these lines, the prohibition of idolatry to gentiles is different than that same prohibition to Jews. For Jews, this prohibition is absolute. Because it presupposes another prohibition for gentiles, the prohibition of idolatry is more qualified. The history of the Noahide prohibition of idolatry vacillates between these two poles. Before the formulation of the Noahide law, as we shall see, there was no real prohibition at all.

2. Gentile Idolatry as a Threat to Judaism

As noted earlier, the *ger toshav* had a real status in the biblical period.[9] And although the seven Noahide laws were formulated long after the *ger toshav* had ceased to be a real status, they were conceived, either wholly or in part, to be the legal requisites for becoming a *ger toshav*. In the Talmudic discussion of the requisites for becoming a *ger toshav*, R. Meir is of the opinion that renunciation of idolatry (*shel'o la'avod avodah zarah*) is the only requirement.[10] His colleagues made the acceptance of all Noahide laws requisite, and others made the acceptance of all the commandments of the Torah requisite, with the exception of the prohibition of eating non-kosher meat, for which gentiles were seen as being specifically exempted by Scripture.[11]

Although the other rabbis saw more than the renunciation of idolatry involved in becoming a *ger toshav*, surely none of them disputed this renunciation as the primary requirement. In the scriptural evidence that we have, idolatry is regarded as a gentile phenomenon that is dangerous to the people of Israel if tolerated. Therefore, if gentiles wished to be domiciled in a Jewish society, they would have to agree to renounce idolatry and worship the one God, even though not like Jews.[12] This situation follows the biblical condemnations of tolerating idolatry and idolaters in the midst of Israel. And, although idolatry is itself considered to be nonsense, nowhere in the Hebrew Bible are gentiles prohibited from practicing such nonsense as long as their practices do not influence Israel.

At the first incident of idolatry in Israel, the worship of the Golden Calf, the text implies that the "mixed multitude" (*erev rav*),[13] simply referred to as the "the people," tempted Israel to idolatry by stating, "these are your gods, Israel, who brought you up from the land of Egypt" (Ex. 23:33).[14] This was also the basis of the prohibition of marriages with Canaanites (Ex. 34:16).[15] This prohibition was extended beyond the Canaanites when Solomon's downfall was attributed to his tolerance of his wives' idolatrous practices; they "turned his heart" (I Kgs 11:3–4).[16] The later rabbinic bans on social intercourse with gentiles were for the sake of preventing intermarriage, a step on the path to idolatry.[17]

The Bible repeatedly mocks gentile idolatry: "For all the gods of the nations are no-gods (*elilim*), but the Lord made heaven" (Ps. 96:5). However, mockery is not the same as moral condemnation. Israel, however, is censured for idolatry. This sin is unfaithfulness to God, with the added taunt that it is useless: "For two evils My people have done: they have forsaken Me the fount of living waters to hew for themselves broken wells, broken wells that hold no water" (Jer. 2:13). The two sins are: (1) forsaking God; (2) making new—and useless— gods for themselves. Of course, even if the new gods were "useful," idolatry would be no less severe a transgression. (In Jeremiah's simile, all wells are not necessarily broken, a third factor).[18] The fact that the new gods are useless indicates that idolatry is not only immoral for Jews, it is also stupid. For gentiles, however, it is only stupid, as the Bible does not seek to curtail gentile idolatry.[19] Jeremiah advises the Babylonian exiles regarding gentile invitations to idolatry:[20]

Thus shall you say to them: "The gods who did not make heaven and earth, these shall perish from the earth and under the heavens . . . Even man is a fool devoid of knowledge . . . His molten image is falsehood (*sheker*) . . . They are vanity (*hevel*), a work of delusion . . . Not like these is the portion of Jacob . . . " (Jer. 10:11, 14–15).[21]

The taunting of gentile idolatry is meant to discourage Jewish interest, even for practical reasons. There is simply nothing to it.

Such is the sentiment of Elijah's jeering of the cult of Baal (I Kgs 18:27). He is not concerned with idolatry per se, but rather its possible impression on Israel. He says to the Israelites at Mt. Carmel: "How long are you to hop on two feet? If the Lord is God, then go after Him; if Baal, then go after him" (I Kgs 18:21). The rabbis were troubled by Elijah's violation of the Deuteronomic proscription (12:13) to "offer your offerings wherever you deem fit," that is, sacrificing on Mt. Carmel, which is outside Jerusalem. They answered that Elijah's act was "an emergency measure" (*le-fi sha'ah*).[22] As Maimonides noted, he did this "to refute the prophets of Baal."[23] The whole purpose of this emergency measure was to turn Israel away from idolatry imported by Ahab and his gentile queen, Jezebel.

The idea that idolatry was a gentile phenomenon led to the conclusion that separation from the Jewish people, and perhaps from the land of Israel itself, amounted to idolatry. Thus, David complains to Saul of his expulsion from the land by the latter's servants: "They have banished me this day from being attached to the heritage of the Lord saying, 'go serve other gods'" (I Sam. 26:19). Although one could interpret this as David's condemnation of Saul's servants, the Tosefta interprets the verse to mean, "whoever leaves the land of Israel in peacetime and goes outside the land is like an idolator."[24] Also, when Naaman, the Aramean general, is cured by Elisha, he renounces all other gods exclusive of the God of Israel.[25] He then begs forgiveness for having to accompanying the king of Aram to pagan rites, with the words: "may the Lord forgive your servant for this matter" (I Kgs 5:18). Elisha bids him farewell, the implication being that idolatry is inevitable in a gentile environment.[26]

Lastly, it is worth noting when the prophets did condemn gentiles for their sins, they did not single out idolatry. When Amos, for example, denounces Damascus, Gaza, Tyre, Edom, Ammon and Moab (Amos 1:33ff.), the condemnation is for various treacheries against their neighbours, something they surely would have agreed was contrary to their moral principles, in particular "agreements to be kept" (pacta sunt servanda). However, idolatry as treachery towards God is not mentioned.[27]

All of this follows from the fact that idolatry is considered to be the supreme act of unfaithfulness to the covenant God made with Israel. Unfaithfulness involves the substitution of another beloved for god: "And My people substituted their Glory for someone who does not avail" (Jer. 2:11). This explains why atheism is inconceivable to the biblical authors. Even "the fool who says in his heart, 'there is no God' (ayn elohim)" (Ps. 53:2)[28] is denying providence, not the existence of God. Therefore, if the covenantal relationship between God and Israel is unique, idolatry is only a sin for Israel. The other nations of the world cannot be morally faulted for unfaithfulness to a covenant in which they are not a participant. It is hoped that gentiles will eventually declare, "let us go and ascend the mountain of the Lord to the house of the God of Jacob" (Is. 2:3), but this hope is delayed to "the end of days" (Is. 2:2) when God will make His covenant with Israel irresistible to gentiles.[29] Thus, Micah indicates that "in the end of days" many nations will seek instruction from Israel (Mic. 4:1–2). But, in pre-messianic days, as David Kimhi noted, when these nations are independent of Israel, the prophet indicates, "let all the peoples walk each one in the name of its god; but we will walk in the name of the Lord our God forever" (Mic. 4:5). In the absence of actual subjugation to Jewish authority, which is characteristic of the messianic period, even if gentiles acknowledge the God of Israel, either as individuals or peoples, this does not by extension entail an embrace of monotheism and rejection of polytheism. It means only that the acts of God have made an impression on them. These acts usually involve Israel.[30]

Yehezkel Kaufmann characterized the early biblical attitude towards gentile idolatry as follows:

This vision . . . may best be described as cosmic-national monotheism. YHWH is the one and only God, but he has chosen Israel alone of all the nations to be his people. He governs the entire world, but he has revealed his name and his Torah only to Israel; therefore, only Israel is obliged to worship him. The nations are judged for violations of the moral law, but never for idolatry . . . The Torah, thus, divides mankind into two realms: Israel, who are obliged to worship God, and the nations, who have no part in him. The idolatry of Israel is sin, but not that of the nations.[31]

Kaufmann's emphasis on the covenantal election of Israel as the foundation of the prohibition of idolatry for them alone is correct. Kaufmann's scholarship, of course, is a polemic against the biblical criticism of Wellhausen and his school. Wellhausen argued that "the early popular religion was polytheistic or monolatruistic—i.e., that [Israel] acknowledged the existence of gods besides YHWH and their rule outside Israel . . ."[32] Kaufmann characterizes this error as arising from the failure to distinguish between the essence and the manifestation of God. Nothing prevents the God who is transcendent in essence from limiting his direct manifestation to one elect people.[33] This idea is consistent with the idea of God's covenantal relationship with Israel. God's election of Israel as a free act presupposes other alternatives. Only the God who is prior to all his relationships is free to initiate them. Election is a selection. Limiting God's essence to Israel would make their relationship necessary rather than free for God. God's power is universal.[34] He has, however, chosen to limit his immediate presence.[35]

However, Kaufmann errs when he states:

While the same viewpoint underlies the doctrine of the prophets, they regard the past and present dichotomy of mankind as a passing phase. At the end of days all men shall worship YHWH. In contrast, the faith of the Torah sees no end to this division. It has no dream for the end of idolatry. The eschatological visions of the Torah lack the motif of a universal religious conversion . . . [36]

Kaufmann errs because the difference between the Torah's view of the relationship of the gentiles to Israel, and that of the prophets, is one of degree rather than of kind. In the Torah the *ger toshav* is an individual who acknowledges the God of Israel and subjects himself to Israelite authority.[37] The later prophets see whole nations collectively becoming *gerai toshav*, acknowledging the God of Israel and his relationship with humanity *through Israel*. No "universal religion"[38] is envisioned that supersedes the covenant with Israel. The rejection of idolatry, whether individual or collective, always presupposes attachment in some manner to Israel.[39]

Even the passage that states, "On that day there shall be an altar to the Lord in the midst of the land of Egypt . . . and the Lord shall be known to Egypt and Egypt shall know the Lord on that day . . ." (Is. 19:19, 21), is interpreted by some scholars, both ancient and modern, to refer to a shrine erected by Egyptian Jews, most probably the one at Elephantine.[40] Kaufmann himself argues against this view, calling the passage "the peak of universalism."[41] Nevertheless, the forecast of the building of this altar is preceded by the forecast of the five cities in Egypt that will be Hebrew speaking, "which swears to the Lord of Hosts" (Is. 19:18). The term "Lord of Hosts" (*Ha-Shem tzeba'ot*) refers to God as manifest to Israel as "The Lord of Hosts, God of the armies of Israel" (I Sam. 17:45). Indeed, in a related passage, part of this general section of the book, Isaiah says to the gentiles, "what I have heard from the Lord of Hosts, God of Israel, I have told you" (Is. 21:10).[42] Even if the altar in Egypt is not Jewish, it remains under Jewish influence. Finally, the designation of Egypt as "My people" (Is. 19:25) is consistent with the messianic vision of God's house as a "house of prayer for all peoples" (Is. 56:7). In that passage the next verse speaks of God gathering "the dispersed of Israel and more." Even here, Israel is still God's "portion." In other words, in both passages the fulfillment of God's covenant with Israel is the presupposition for gentile recognition of his full sovereignty over them as well.

One biblical passage that seems to regard gentile polytheism/idolatry as blameworthy is found in Job 31:26–27: "Have I looked up at the sun in its brightness or at the moon moving in splendour, so that my heart was secretly enticed and I kissed my hand?"[43] Both Rashi and Ibn Ezra interpret this as referring to forbidden gentile idolatry. However, what must be kept in mind is that Job is not necessarily presented as a gentile. Some rabbis insist he was a Jew.[44] This may be so because Job's theology is so Jewish. Furthermore, in Job 31:28 he claims that this sin would be his denying (*ki khihashti*) God above. Nevertheless, polytheism per se is not necessarily a denial; it may or may not be.[45] In any case, even if Job is a gentile, he is a person *sui generis*, a unique man before God (Job 1:8).

These biblical attitudes towards idolatry were extended in early rabbinic literature. The Tosefta, for example, stated:

Whoever sees idolatry should say, "blessed is the Long-Suffering One"; a place wherefrom idolatry has been extirpated, he should say, "blessed is He who has extirpated idolatry from our land. May it be Thy will O Lord our God that idolatry be extirpated from all Jewish places and that Thou wilt turn the hearts of Thy servants to serve Thee."[46]

Saul Lieberman, in his commentary to the Tosefta, remarked that the actual commandment to eliminate idolatry applies to the land of Israel alone. Nevertheless, Jews are grateful whenever and wherever it has been removed, but especially in Israel, where the Roman occupation made active Jewish attempts to remove idolatry dangerous.[47]

The Talmud expands on the Tosefta passage:

> Outside of the land of Israel one need not say "turn the hearts of Thy servants to serve Thee," because most of the people there are gentiles. R. Simon b. Eleazar said that even outside the Land one must say this because in the future they will convert (she'atidim le-hitgayyer), as it is said, "Then I will turn to the peoples a pure language" (Zeph. 3:9).[48]

Here the messianic hope is expressed that idolatry will be eradicated everywhere. However, the total removal of idolatry presupposes a universal conversion to Judaism. Whether full or partial conversion is intended, the text is not clear.[49] Even if the conversion is only partial, all agree that the minimal requirement is the repudiation of idolatry *under Jewish supervision*. Jewish authority over gentiles is therefore assumed. Maimonides, the most consistent advocate of this view, codifies the view of R. Simon b. Eleazar.[50] Although his opinion appears to be a minority one, Karo defends Maimonides against his critics by indicating, among other reasons, that this view is the "more reasonable" (de-mistaber ta'amayh).[51]

3. The Pervasiveness of Gentile Idolatry

The assumption that gentiles by definition are idolaters led to a number of important halakhic norms. And although the concept of the Noahide—the non-idolatrous gentile—changed this assumption, many of the norms based on it remained, albeit in modified form. R. Eliezer b. Hyrcanus, a first-century Tanna, expressed most fully the pervasiveness of gentile idolatry: "the thoughts of a gentile in general are idolatrous (stam mahshebet nokhri l'avodah zarah)."[52] Although others dispute this claim, R. Eliezer's opinion reflected the Jewish view of the gentile that had been accepted by Jewish thinkers since the biblical period. The Talmud, for example, presents a halakhic ruling that a Torah scroll written by a gentile is to be burned, basing this ruling on R. Eliezer's view.[53] It was assumed that the gentile would have written the scroll with idolatrous intent.

This idea found aggadic expression:

> A good thought is accounted as a deed . . . R. Assi said that even if a man thought to do a commandment and by accident could not do it, scripture considers him as if he did it. God does not account a bad thought as a deed.[54]

In the Palestinian Talmud it is noted that such is not the case with gentiles, that God does account a bad thought as a bad deed, and he does not account a good thought a good deed.[55] On the surface, this sounds like a double standard. However, if one sees the underlying rationale for this distinction in the idea that gentiles are by definition idolaters, then the distinction makes sense. In the Babylonian Talmud an exception is made in the case of idolatrous thoughts, even of Jews, by the Amora, R. Aha b. Jacob, who said that "idolatry is so grave (*hamurah*) that whoever renounces it (*ha-kofer bah*) is like one who acknowledges (*ke-modeh*) the entire Torah." He bases this on the biblical indictment of Israel for what is "in their heart" (Ez. 14:5). In other words, idolatry is an obsession for idolaters, whether Jews or gentiles. Where idolatry is the norm for gentiles, it is the exception for Israel.[56] In order for a gentile to escape this, he must abandon idolatry, that is, become a *ger toshav*.[57] Anyone whose status falls below that of a *ger toshav* is by definition an idolater. A Jewish idolater must repent to remove idolatry; a gentile idolater must convert to fully avoid the seductions of idolatry.

The area of halakhah where the assumption that all gentiles are idolaters led to the most far-reaching results regards gentile wine. The original name for forbidden wine was *yayn nesekh*, that is, wine "dedicated" to an idol.[58] However, even without specific proof, the rabbis assumed gentile wine began as an idolatrous offering.[59] Only after the rise of Christianity, and especially Islam, when it could no longer be assumed that every gentile was an idolater, did the restrictions against the commercial use of gentile wine cease. Nevertheless, the prohibition of the consumption of these wines by Jews retains its halakhic force.[60]

Finally, in the very section of the Talmud where the Noahide laws are presented, a *baraita* states:

As for idolatry a Noahide is only considered to be prohibited (*muzhar*) for those idolatrous practices for which a Jewish court would execute one, but he is not prohibited for those practices which a Jewish court would not execute one.[61]

If this is the case, then the prohibition of gentile idolatry presupposes gentile recognition of the authority of Jewish law. Only the *ger toshav* would be able to consistently obey the prohibition of idolatry. This, then, is the meaning of R. Nahman b. Isaac's statement, "their death is their prohibition (*azharah she-lahen zo hi meetatan*)."[62] This means that gentiles under Jewish authority are warned that any idolatrous act for which the Jewish courts are empowered by Jewish law to execute offenders applies to them as well.[63]

4. Tensions Caused by the New Concept of Noahide Law

The new rabbinic notion that gentiles are prohibited to practice idolatry, even among themselves, had a profound influence on the development of halakhah. No longer was the renunciation of idolatry considered to be necessarily part of an actual conversion in any form. The development of Jewish law up to this point, however, assumed that idolatry was a legitimate activity for gentiles, and only illegitimate after it had been formally renounced under Jewish supervision. This innovation called for reinterpretation of earlier sources dealing with the differences between Jewish and gentile idolatry. This is most strikingly seen in the treatment of the question of how an idolater renounces his idol.

The Tosefta states:

The sages say that a gentile can nullify (*mebatel*) his idol and that of a Jew, but a Jew cannot nullify the idol of a gentile. R. Simon b. Menasya said that the idol of a Jew can never be nullified (*ayn lah betaylah olamit*).[64]

Now on the basis of the earlier idea that idolatry is only prohibited to Jews but not to gentiles among themselves, this law is easily understood. One can only nullify something that he rightfully possesses. Nullification is a change of the status of an object, and only the rightful owner has this legal power.[65] This, then, explains why a gentile can nullify the idolatrous status of an object in his possession. He had a right to possess the object in this state because idolatry is not prohibited to gentiles. This explains a halakhah that stated that a gentile could inherit idolatrous objects in his father's estate, whereas his brother—who has renounced idolatry either as a partial or full convert—could not do so.[66] The former had a right to their use; the latter did not because the renunciation of idolatry prohibits the monotheist from deriving any monetary benefit from idolatry (*assur be-hane'ah*).[67]

A Jew, on the other hand, could not nullify that which he never rightfully possessed. This idea can be understood if we look at a parallel situation involving a Jew's relationship to leavened food before and after Passover. The night before Passover, when a Jew may still own leavened food, he or she is obligated to nullify the ownership of it while it is still in their possession.[68] Once Passover starts, they may only destroy any leaven on their property, because they can no longer nullify possession of something they do not own. In other words, without legal ownership they can only destroy an object's *real* status, not change its *legal* status.[69] Once a Jew has lost the opportunity to nullify the leaven, that loss is permanent.[70] So, also, a Jew can only destroy an object of idolatry, whether his or anyone else's.[71] As soon as the object becomes an idol it forever passes out of the legal control of the Jew.

Despite the illuminating possibilities of this analogy, none of the rabbinic sources or their commentaries use it to explain the difference between Jews and gentiles regarding the nullification of idolatrous objects. Despite the danger of *argumentum ex silentio*,[72] I think there is a historical reason for the strange absence in these sources and commentaries of a cogent rationale for this crucial legal difference in the law of nullification. The only rationale possible would be that gentiles have the legal right to practice idolatry among themselves and, therefore, have the legal right to change the status of their idols. However, once the Noahide law of idolatry was articulated, removing this right from *all* gentiles, the old reason no longer availed. The only type of rationale that could be given involved remote types of exegesis (*asmakhta*) of certain biblical verses. Thus, for example, the Amora, R. Joseph, derived this right of a gentile to change the status of his idol (*posel eluho*) from the verse, "the images of their gods (*pesilai elohehem*) you shall burn with fire" (Deut. 9:25). This is a tenuous association of the biblical meaning of *psl*—"to sculpt"—with the rabbinic meaning of *psl*—"to disqualify."[73]

The whole transition and the exegetical problems it entailed can be found in the Palestinian Talmud:

There are Tannaim who taught that a *ger toshav* is not accepted until he renounces his own idolatry (*ad she-yikhpor be'avodah zarah shelo*). The son of R. Hiyyah b. Ashi said that a *ger toshav* is not accepted until he renounces idolatry as a gentile (*ke-goy*). R. Zeira said . . . that since the gentile qua gentile is prohibited to practice idolatry, he cannot very well nullify (*l'o yivatel*) it. Are not gentiles commanded concerning idols? If so, can they nullify one?!—R. Jose said that this is the law, inasmuch as the *ger toshav* is the same as a Jew in some laws, and we want to emphasize that concerning the nullification of idolatry he is still like a gentile.[74]

As the eighteenth-century commentator David Fraenkel explains, the prohibition of idolatry should logically remove the right of nullification of an idol from a gentile as well as from a Jew. Along these lines of interpretation, therefore, the power of nullification is a subsequent measure to make sure that the *ger toshav* is not confused with a full Jew. However, this answer does not satisfy: why should a distinction be made at this level, suggesting as it does a compromise with gentile idolatry? Surely, the continued requirement for the *ger toshav* of eating non-kosher meat, which even the rabbis who require acceptance of the whole Torah by the *ger toshav* insist upon, surely this visible distinction should be sufficient to dispel any confusion between the *ger toshav* and a full Jew.[75] We may conclude that the original reason for allowing gentiles to nullify idols derives from their prior right to be idolators.[76] The Noahide ban on all gentile idolatry removed that right, and a new, inherently insufficient reason had to be invented for an old law that lost its initial rationale.

This transition is also found in the relation between "renouncing idolatry" and "nullifying an idol." This text, like others, is ambiguous in its use of *avodah zarah*, denoting both idol and its cult—that is, idolatry.[77] Earlier, if a gentile is allowed to be an idolater, then he can change (*mevatel*) a specific idol into an ordinary, non-sacred object. On the other hand, if a *ger toshav* has formally abandoned idolatry in general, then he has also renounced his former gentile privilege to change his idol into an ordinary object. However, the idea of Noahide law assumes that a gentile is prohibited to practice idolatry even if he never formally renounced it by becoming a *ger toshav*. Therefore, the formal renunciation of idolatry is not required to remove the right of nullifying an idol. The question, then, is: how can this right continue to be justified?

The above explains the Amoraic reluctance to ground the law of the nullification of idolatry in an actual, cogent reason. In the Mishnah this law is directly preceded by another distinction between Jewish and gentile idols, namely, a gentile's idol is forbidden upon manufacture whereas a Jew's idol is forbidden after worship.[78] In the Palestinian Talmud, there is a suggestion that this rationale explains the difference between Jewish and gentile nullification. The same Amora, R. Zeira, who in the other passage rejected the proposal that gentiles are permitted to practice idolatry, here rejects this proposal as well, indicating that this juxtaposition does not imply that the latter law is derived (*layt k'an le-fi-khakh*) from the former.[79] This rejection is on logical grounds, as R. Fraenkel notes in his comment—that is, the first clause in the Mishnah does not imply the second. Any proposed logical relation would be a *non sequitur*. However, in this same text the suggestion is made, based on the Tosefta, in contradiction to the Mishnah, that a Jew's idol is forbidden immediately, but gentile's idol is forbidden only after worship. This law in the Tosefta could function as a reason for the right a gentile, but not a Jew, had to nullify his idol. For if a Jew's idol is forbidden upon manufacture, then he has never had a non-idolatrous relation to it, and, consequently, it was never his. One cannot nullify what one has never owned. However, it seems that this line of reasoning was never followed in the Palestinian Talmud because it might suggest, if followed to its logical conclusion, that gentile idolatry is of a different kind than Jewish idolatry.[80] This could have compromised the Noahide ban on gentile idolatry, as R. Zeira noted previously.

The further permeation of the Noahide ban on gentile idolatry into the halakhic system led to additional reinterpretation of earlier norms. In the same text in the Palestinian Talmud it states, "a gentile may nullify his idol and that of his fellow gentile against his will, provided he knows the procedure of his idolatry."[81] The right of one idolater to nullify the idol of another derived from the fact that the idol was a *public* cultic object. As such, even if it were privately owned, any actual desecration (*bitul*) of it by any other idolater would cause it to lose its sacred status.[82] In earlier times it seems that the sole concern with the gentile nullification was to determine which gentile objects Jews could use and those they could not use.[83] The concern was with the objects not with their former gentile owners, all of whom were considered outside the pale of Torah. Consequently, the particular worry here was whether or not the gentile nullified a particular idol, not idolatry in general. Nevertheless, the Noahide ban now implied that some gentiles were not idolaters. Therefore, Maimonides, undoubtedly reinterpreting this text in light of Noahide law, ruled that if a gentile was not an idolater (*mi she'ayno oved avodah zarah*), that person did not have the right to nullify any specific form of idolatry.[84] In other words, that a gentile, as regards idolatry, is no different than a Jew. That gentile did not have to become a *ger toshav*. Any actual renunciation of idolatry, then, is simply a reconfirmation of a prohibition of idolatry, a prohibition already valid for all.[85] Moreover, following the destruction of the First Temple, there were no more *gerai toshav* in the legal sense.[86] Hence, the actual renunciation of idolatry by a gentile is only informal. It is similar to a Jew taking an oath to observe a commandment. It might add to his conviction and, therefore, it is permitted. However, it does not create the obligation. That comes from Sinaitic revelation.[87]

The tension between the old and new views of gentile idolatry led to new theological insights. This can be seen in the interpretation of the following verse, "And lest you lift up your eyes to the heaven and see the sun and the moon and the stars—all the heavenly host, and you be swept away and you worship them which the Lord your God has allotted them to all the peoples under the heaven" (Deut. 4:19). The original meaning of the verse was that God permitted gentiles to worship heavenly bodies; Israel, with its intimate covenant with God, was not allowed to worship something other than God. Rashbam, in particular, emphasizes this: "According to the essential plain meaning He let all the nations serve them because He is not concerned (*eino hoshesh*) with them."[88]

However, this verse also contradicts the Noahide prohibition of idolatry. When the Talmud relates the legend of how the Hellenistic king of Egypt, Ptolemy Philadelphus, invited the Jewish sages to Alexandria to translate the Torah into Greek, it indicates that certain verses were not translated literally because such a translation would have had erroneous implications.[89] An example of such liberty in translation is Deut. 4:19, which, according to the

Talmud, was translated into Greek to read, "which the Lord your God has allotted to them to give light to all the peoples."[90]

The present text of the Septuagint itself, however, records no such translation; rather, it is a literal translation of the Masoretic text.[91] Although there may have been another Greek reading of this particular verse, as only the present Septuagint text itself corroborates some of the emendations mentioned in the Talmud,[92] it is unlikely that the authors considered idolatry as prohibited to gentiles. Both Philo and Josephus, basing themselves on the Septuagint, prohibited Jews from ridiculing gentile idolatry.[93] Surely, then, if Jews are required to be at least respectful of gentile idolatry, idolatry itself could not have been considered prohibited to gentiles. This attitude, it seems, was the norm in Hellenistic Judaism.

Rashi explains the emendation as being required because, "if not, it could be said that a Noahide is permitted to practice idolatry."[94] In other words, the subsequent acceptance of the Noahide ban forced a reinterpretation of the Torah verse, which if accepted literally, could undermine the ban. Elsewhere in the Talmud, the scriptural word for "allotted" in Deut. 4:19—*halak*—is interpreted to mean, "He smoothed them over (*she-hihlikan*) with things in order to remove them from the world."[95] The idea here is that God allowed the other nations to become enthralled with the heavenly bodies in order to lead to their downfall. This is based on the idea that if one's propensity is to sin, God gives him regular opportunity to transgress.[96] If idolatry is essentially a person's rejection of God, and only thereafter does one substitute something else for God, idolatry then precedes its objects. God is, therefore, more concerned with challenging the idolater's sin than with removing the natural object which idolatry constitutes as divine and of which idols are built.[97] For our purposes it is important to note that these two interpretations remove the main biblical support for permitting gentile idolatry. The first interpretation does it by making the verse refer to the natural rather than the cultural role played by the heavenly bodies in human life. The second interpretation does it by seeing the universal propensity for idolatry as something to which the magnificence of the heavenly bodies lends itself, but does not necessarily cause.

Furthermore, in the version of this *baraita* in the Babylonian Talmud an emendation of Deut. 17:3 is put forth in the name of the Septuagint, although here too it is not corroborated by our text of the Septuagint. The Masoretic text reads, "And he went and served other gods and worshipped them: the sun and the moon and all the heavenly host, which I have not commanded." The emendation adds to the end of the verse, "to serve them" (*l'ovdam*). As Rashi points out, without this addition, one might think God was stating that He did not command the existence of these heavenly bodies (*l'o tziviti she-yihey*) and they were, therefore, divine entities (im ken elohot hen), not dependent on God's creative will for their existence.[98] In the emendation there is the addition of the words "to the nations to serve them" (l'ummot l'ovdam).[99] In other words, the point is made to the gentiles especially that the heavenly bodies are not to be worshipped. As R. Samuel Edels (Maharsha, d. 1631) points out, this verse was not needed by the Jews because they were prohibited to worship other beings in many other places.[100] Here again we see another example of the late rabbinic attempt to remove any possible scriptural endorsement of gentile idolatry. Consequently, the introduction of the Noahide ban on all gentile idolatry led to the reinterpretation of those earlier texts, which if left alone could be interpreted to contradict the new view.

5. The Non-Universality of Gentile Idolatry

The Noahide ban on gentile idolatry had the effect of judging certain forms of non-Jewish culture to be non-idolatrous. The ramifications of such a judgment had a tremendous effect in changing a number of important areas of halakhah governing relations between Jews and non-Jews.

The Mishnah states that an animal "slaughtered by a non-Jew is non-kosher (nebelah) and makes one impure if he carries it."[101] The Tosefta states that an animal slaughtered by a "confirmed idolater" (min) is considered tainted by idolatry.[102] The Gemara brings its interpretation of the above Mishnah by asserting that we must always be concerned (ve-nayhush) that the gentile is a confirmed idolater.[103] To this point, the Gemara is operating on the old assumption that a gentile is eo ipso an idolater. However, this assumption is challenged by the Amora, R. Nahman, who states: "there are no confirmed idolaters among the gentile nations." The Gemara then presents the empirical observation that most gentiles are not confirmed idolaters. This is seen to be according to the view of the third-century Palestinian Amora R. Johanan, who said that "gentiles outside of the Land of Israel are not idolaters but are only practicing ancestral custom (minhag avotehem be-yadehem)."[104] Although an animal slaughtered by a non-Jew is ipso facto non-kosher, it is no longer ipso facto tainted by idolatry.[105] Earlier the Tanna R. Tarfon declared Jewish sectarians (minim) to be worse than gentile idolaters, because "the former know and yet deny (she-makirin ve-kofrin), whereas the latter do not know and deny."[106] As Rashi points out, for gentiles idolatry is mere ancestral custom, a practice now devoid its original meaning.[107] Although R. Tarfon's statement may have mentioned gentiles for rhetorical reasons, nevertheless, it too, although less explicitly than the statement of R. Johanan, emphasized that gentile idolatry is more a matter of custom than actual conviction.

José Faur notes that during the period of R. Johanan there was a revival of pagan apologetics to counter Jewish and Christian polemics against idolatry. R. Johanan, according to this theory, made a sharp distinction between popular idolatry, on the one hand, whose intent was for ulterior reasons, and intellectual idolatry, on the other, whose intent was wholly idolatrous per se. Popular idolatry was found mostly in Babylonia; intellectual idolatry was found mostly in Palestine.[108] Faur connects the view of R. Johanan with that of Rava, a Babylonian Amora. The latter declared: "one who worships idols out of love or fear is exempt from the death penalty."[109] The Gemara qualifies Rava's ruling to apply only where the person involved did not accept the pagan deity as a god. Habit without conviction does not constitute idolatry. Intention, the proper direction of the heart and motivation of the mind, matters. It should be recalled that R. Johanan has consistently argued for the independence of Noahide law from Jewish authority.[110] To consistently maintain the universal ban on idolatry, one must understand it as being independent of even Judaism itself.[111]

R. Johanan's view of the waning hold of idolatry on gentile conviction can be seen in the following dispute:

Concerning an idol which broke by itself, R. Johanan says that it is still prohibited for use; but Resh Lakish says that it is permitted. R. Johanan says that it is prohibited because its idolatrous status has not been nullified (de'la batlah). Resh Lakish says that is permitted because it is assumed to have lost its idolatrous status, for an idolater would surely say, "it could not save itself, can it save me (le-didi matzlah li)?"[112]

The view of Resh Lakish assumes that if the idol had not broken by itself, then the idolater would still believe in it. Since most idols do not break by themselves, it follows that those still intact inspire the reverence of gentile idolaters. In R. Johanan's view, no such assumption is required. Nullification of an idol is now a purely formal procedure presupposing no conviction at all on the part of the gentile. For as we have already seen, nullification originally presupposed that the undeniable de facto universality of gentile idolatry led to the de jure recognition of the right of gentiles to practice or renounce idolatry. With the introduction of Noahide law, that right could no longer be assumed. Gentile nullification became "a law without reason" (hilkhata be-l'a ta'ama).[113] Thus, all R. Johanan need assert, as the most consistent advocate of Noahide law, is that nullification be a formal procedure rather than a mere assumed reaction to an event that has already happened. For if one follows Resh Lakish's reasoning, it implies the old assumption that the universal fact of gentile idolatry gives them the right to either deny or affirm it. Noahide law removed that right from gentiles; R. Johanan's empirical judgment removed this factual assumption which made the legal recognition of that right inevitable.

6. The New Status of Non-Idolatrous Gentiles

In the old theory, God made his covenant with Israel; gentiles were left to their own devices, as it were. Although Israel's covenant with God was superior to gentile idolatry, that superiority did not by extension intend moral condemnation of the latter's idolatry. Without a direct covenant with God nothing more could be expected of them. Whether Jews proselytized among gentiles or not,[114] I know of no early source, biblical or rabbinic, that claims gentiles are morally guilty for not being Jews. A consistent assertion of the religious superiority of Judaism did not thereby entail the guilt of gentiles for remaining idolaters. Noahide law, however, changed everything. Gentiles were now morally culpable for idolatry, even if they did not convert to Judaism. The universal prohibition of idolatry was now considered as historically and ontologically prior to the Sinaitic covenant. Following R. Johanan's empirical distinction between ancestral idolatry and ideological idolatry, a theological justification for the former had to be formulated.

According to R. Johanan:

[He] says that one's heavenly constellation (*mazel*) makes one wise or rich, and that Israel has its own constellation (*yesh mazal le-yisrael*). R. Johanan says that we know that Israel does not have its own constellation from the verse, "Thus says the Lord, do not learn the way of the nations, and from the heavenly signs (*u'me'otot ha-shemayim*); do not be afraid, for the nations are afraid of them" (Jer. 10:2). They are afraid of them but not Israel.[115]

At first glance, this passage suggests the old distinction of monotheism as the province of Jews and idolatry for gentiles. But the biblical verse employed in the passage is the key here. The heavenly bodies are termed "signs," namely, the nations of the world approach God through the mediation of nature, even through the symbolization of created nature in images. Israel, because of its unique historical relationship with God, must approach him directly with the revealed commandments.[116] Although developed most fully in the Middle Ages, we can see here the first stages of the collapse of the distinction that Israel is monotheistic and the nations are idolaters. The difference, instead, is that Israel's relationship with God is covenantal; the nations, who do not have a direct historical relationship (such as the liberation from Egypt) with God, are justified in approaching him through visible intermediaries.

The notion that gentile idolatry is not necessarily polytheistic in principle was common in Hellenistic Judaism. Philo and Josephus, as we have seen, forbid Jewish ridicule of pagan cults. The essence of these cults is not opposition to monotheism.[117] This view goes back to the very beginnings of Hellenistic Judaism, to the Septuagint and *Ben Sira*. When, for example, Deut. 32:8 states, "He set up the borders of the peoples according to the number of the people of Israel," the Septuagint translates this verse as, "according to the number of angels of God" (*kata arithmon angelon theou*).[118] In other words, the nations of the world are under indirect divine governance; they are under the authority of God's messengers. Ben Sira reiterates: "to every nation He set up a governor (*hegoumenon*), but Israel is the portion of the Lord" (Deut. 17:17).

Earlier, Malachi wrote: "From the rising of the sun to its setting My name is great among the nations. And in every place offerings are presented unto My name . . ." (1:11). The Talmud notes that this refers to the fact that even the gentile idolaters acknowledge one supreme God (*elaha d'elaha*).[119]

Surely, all of this reformulation was inspired by the fact that many pagans were monotheists in theory though polytheists in practice, that is, they approached God through the adoration of nature and reverence for the symbols which their culture had developed historically. Without the Sinaitic covenant, what could be expected of them? What mattered was gentile intention in worship. If monotheism was acknowledged, then idolatry becomes an accepted form of gentile worship.[120] Whether or not R. Johanan was aware of the Hellenistic precedents for his concept of gentile idolatry, it is difficult to determine. Nevertheless, even if unaware, it is worth nothing how the confrontation with idolatrous monotheists brought forth the same response based on the Bible and earlier Jewish tradition.

The historical application of the Noahide ban on idolatry depends on the concept of *symbolism* to be intelligible. Only the introduction of this term enables a consistent distinction to be maintained between customary idolatry (*minhag*) and idolatry of conviction. Now just what sort of symbolism is removed from the stigma of idolatry? Here, the insights of some modern philosophers can be helpful.

Pure idolatry is the elevation of something finite to the level of divine being; the finite being is taken to be the object of worship, something which attracts and compels everything inferior to it in power and wisdom. There is nothing symbolic at all about this type of idolatry. The idol is a representation of the god's power and wisdom. Since divine being is conceived of as finite and also accessible to human participation, the idol, as its representative, is the object of full devotion. The late Emil Fackenheim brought this out most fully:

With regard to ancient idolatry we shall fail totally if we mistake the idol for a mere religious symbol . . . it is not a "symbol" at all. The ancient idol is not a finite object that distinguished itself from the Divine Infinity even as it points to it. The idol itself is divine. The idolatrous projection . . . is such as to produce not a symbolic but rather a literal and hence *total* identification of finiteness and infinitude . . . the ancient idol was not an irrelevance but rather the demonic rival of the One of Israel, and radically intolerable.[121]

Following this definition we might say that the idol is representative of a larger class in the sense that king's statue represents the power of kingship.[122] However, representation of God himself is impossible because his transcendence does not admit of it: "To whom would you compare Me that I would be likened (*v'eshaveh*), says the Holy One" (Is. 40:25). Representation would necessarily reduce God to finitude.

　　Symbolism can only be legitimated in a monotheistic theology when something finite is not elevated to divine being, when God alone is acknowledged as absolutely transcendent and unique, the ultimate object of worship. Symbolism is the attempt to see finite reality pointing to this transcendence. This pointing means that the symbolic world and everything in it, both nature and culture, can be symbols or indicators of God's transcendence if they emphasize their own incompleteness and groundlessness, and also point beyond themselves.[123] By functioning in this paradoxical way, that is, attracting us to themselves and at the same time pointing us on, certain aspects of the world function symbolically.[124] Therefore, these symbols do not represent God because they do not resemble him. Their status is dialectical; they must be "thought through" (*dialegesthai*).[125] Karl Jaspers developed this insight most comprehensively:

Everything that is can be a cipher. It becomes a cipher through a transformation of the mode of being-an-object in an act of transcendence . . . the formal transcending occurring through a movement of thought . . . in which the concreteness, stability and definiteness of what is objective vanishes at once in the suspended objectivity which makes it possible.[126]

Jaspers emphasized that symbols cannot be created by humans at will, that to do so is to reduce them to the level of magical devices.[127] If this is the case, then culture itself is necessarily filled with symbols. Symbols of the transcendent evolve historically. Since the concept of Noahide law does not presuppose conversion to Judaism, that is, it does not require the non-Jew to renounce his particular culture to be considered a monotheist, its development had to constitute an understanding of non-Jewish culture that does not make it immediately idolatrous. This is what R. Johanan did in an exegetical and juridical way. Philosophical reflection on Noahide law must uncover the intelligible conditions of this enterprise.

7. Symbolic Intermediacy in Gentile Monotheism

The full practical effect of R. Johanan's assertion that a gentile is not *eo ipso* an idolater did not emerge until the Middle Ages. Its emergence would have been impossible to justify theologically in the absence of earlier development of the concept of the Noahide.

The *locus classicus* of this practical application is the following Talmudic text:

The father of Samuel said that it is forbidden (*asur*) for a man to set up a partnership with a gentile (*shuttfut mi-nokhri*), lest the gentile become obligated to swear an oath (*shevu'ah*) and he swears by his god. And the Torah stated, "it shall not be heard on your mouth" (Ex. 23:13).[128]

In the context of the Gemara this statement is preceded by the Tannaitic statement that quotes the first half of Ex. 23:13, "and the name of other gods (*elohim aherim*) you shall not cause to be remembered (*l'o tazkiru*)," and then it states, "this is a prohibition . . . not to cause others to vow by its name that they might fulfill the vow in its name." As Rashi points out, these "others" are gentiles.[129] The Gemara considers this statement as the precedent for the ruling of the father of the Amora, Samuel. Therefore, the interpretation of this passage is that partnership with a gentile will cause the gentile to swear by their idol.[130]

One can see four distinct steps in the development of the interpretation of this verse:

The Mekhilta expresses the first step:

"The name of other gods you shall not cause be remembered"—You shall not cause the gentile to swear by his god. "And it shall not be heard on your mouth"—You shall not swear by his god (*l'o tashb'a be-yir'ato*).[131]

At this stage a Jew is prohibited from direct participation in or causation of idolatry.[132] One cannot infer from this alone, however, that a gentile is prohibited from such an oath if the requirement were not made by a Jew.[133]

The second stage is located in the Gemara's reworking of the *baraita* in the context of the Amoraic prohibition of partnership with a gentile. There a Jew is forbidden from even being a contributing cause (*gerama*) to gentile idolatry. Whereas the language of the Mekhilta limits the prohibition to direct causation—that is, a Jew compelling a gentile to swear by their god—the language of the Gemara also forbids a Jew from being a contributing cause through entering a business partnership with a gentile that might result in a gentile making an oath in the name of a pagan deity. An oath requires a profession of conviction, a personal profession that is more than custom, which R. Johanan assumed was normal gentile religiosity outside Palestine.[134] A prohibition of this kind seems to be based on the premise that Noahides are forbidden to practice idolatry, at least with conviction. In this case the gentile is the direct cause of the transgression; the Jew is only setting up a situation where there is a probability of "aiding a transgressor."[135] Nevertheless, the Gemara understands Ex. 23:13 as prohibiting a Jew to establish the conditions that could allow a gentile to revert to idolatry with real conviction. Under normal circumstances anything short of direct causation of a prohibited act is not liable. In the case of idolatry, however, normal procedures do not apply.[136] Ex. 23:13 is consequently considered a special prohibition (*azharah*) against even indirect causation.[137]

The third stage is established by the Tosafists:

> Nevertheless, in this age they all swear by their saints (*be-kodashim she-lahen*) to whom they do not ascribe divinity (*ve'ein tofsin bahem elohut*). And even though they mention God's name along with them (*shem Shamayim imahen*), and their intent is for something else, nevertheless, this is not idolatry because their awareness (*da'atam*) is of the Maker of heaven. And even though they associate (*she-mishttattfin*) the name of God and something else, we do not find that it is forbidden to indirectly cause others to perform such association ... [138]

If gentiles are permitted to acknowledge God through mediation, then as long as God is the *ultimate* object of their concern, they may swear by these intermediaries and not be guilty of idolatry. Consequently, Jews may enter business partnerships with them where this type of swearing by a gentile partner might well be required, especially in the event of litigation. This view of the nonidolatrous status of Christians, despite their belief in the efficacy of the saints, is reiterated by the Tosafists in a number of other texts.[139]

Parallel to the above text, the twelfth-century French rabbi, Rabbenu Tam, begins his justifications of allowing gentiles to take their own oaths with the logic that this is "like saving Jewish property from gentile hands" (*ke-matzil me-yadam*).[140] Jews would be at an economic disadvantage if a gentile knew that in litigation a Jew could not require him to take an oath. We find, therefore, an economic and theological justification for the reversal of the Talmudic prohibition. The question is: which justification is essential in the thinking of the Tosafists, especially Rabbenu Tam?

Jacob Katz argues that Rabbenu Tam's reinterpretation was required to resolve the contradiction between traditional law and actual commercial practice where Jews could not be impeded in their business with gentiles. Theology comes later, according to Katz, as a subsequent rationalization.[141]

It is true that one cannot very well dispute the centrality of economic considerations in the development of Jewish law. Jewish law demonstrates deep understanding of Jewish prosperity: "the Torah is concerned (*hasah*) over Jewish property."[142] Nevertheless, idolatry is something that certainly transcends economic considerations alone. Therefore, the general leniency of Jewish monetary law could hardly in itself permit such a radical reinterpretation of the view of the gentile presented by Rabbenu Tam. "We do not infer ritual (*isurai*) from monetary law."[143] Although the economic situation may well have been the immediate reason for re-examination of the halakhic status of Christians, the essential grounding of that re-examination had to be theological.

Rabbenu Tam's reinterpretation centers on the term *shuttfut* (partnership). In the Talmudic text, a Jew is prohibited to engage in a *partnership* with a gentile because of the likelihood that the latter will take an idolatrous oath if litigation arises. Rabbenu Tam's re-reading leads to the notion that gentiles have the right to approach God *associating* him with intermediary sacred entities. This use of *shuttfut* appears in verbal form on the preceding folio of the very page where Rabbenu Tam makes his re-reading: "Whoever associates (*ha-mishttattef*) God's Name and anything else is uprooted from the world as it says, 'only to the Lord alone' (Ex. 22:19)."[144] This reading differentiates between gentile use of intermediacy in oaths (*shuttfut*), which is permitted to them, and Jewish use of intermediaries, which is forbidden.[145] Understanding this reading in light of R. Johanan's qualification of the Noahide ban on gentile idolatry makes it appear far less radical than imagined without taking this halakhic background into consideration. It is worth noting that R. Johanan, in an aggadic passage, considers association (*shittuf*) of God and something else to be less of a sin, even for Jews. *Full substitution* is worse, constituting pure idolatry.[146] This is expressed in his attempt to soften the sin of the worship of the Golden Calf, a common motif in aggadic literature.[147] The halakhah, however, follows R. Simon b. Yohai, who prohibits any *shittuf*.[148] According to one commentator such association, on the part of Jews at least, is considered worse than idolatry, perhaps because it is more devious.[149]

Rabbenu Tam radically changed the meaning of *shuttfut* in his Talmudic commentary. However, the term itself in another place in the Talmud refers to a *general* association as opposed to *shittuf*, which refers to a more specific partnership.[150] It seems to me, then, that although Rabbenu Tam did change the meaning of *shuttfut* as used in Sanhedrin (63b), he did not invent its meaning as a term of loose association. Hence the intermediacy that he is willing to permit gentiles is confined to oaths taken by Christians in the name of their saints. Faur notes that this is based on the Christian distinction between *adoratio*—devotion (*latria*) to God alone—and the *veneration* of saints, which is secondary.[151] However, Rabbenu Tam could not extend such tolerance for oaths based on the Christian doctrine of the Incarnation or the Trinity inasmuch as they posit a specific participation in the Godhead. In other words, these doctrines compromise monotheism in a way that is unlike the doctrine of the veneration of the saints. In rabbinic parlance they are examples of *shittuf* over and above *shutfut*.

Nevertheless, as halakhah developed, *shittuf* and *shutfut* were used interchangeably. As Katz points out, *shittuf* in philosophical Hebrew came to mean *any* designation of non-monotheistic divinity.[152] Whereas Rabbenu Tam actually acknowledged only the validity of the veneration of saints by Christians, his concept of *shuttfut* lost its original specific meaning and came to be identified with *shittuf*. By extension, then, it was used as a Jewish legitimization of trinitarian Christianity for Christians. Ashkenazi authorities, as a result, who considered themselves in the tradition of Rabbenu Tam, reinterpreted his own reinterpretation of the Amoraic statement concerning gentile oaths.[153] It will also be recalled that the Amoraic statement was a reinterpretation of an earlier Tannaitic statement. We have now seen four stages in the development of the halakhah in the area of Jewish involvement in gentile oaths.

The effect of this fourth and final development of the law was to consider pure idolatry to be, at least in the Christian West, a thing of the past. (Nevertheless, the uneasiness with this conclusion caused later halakhists to congratulate those Jews who voluntarily kept all the old restrictions against idolaters, including Christians.)[154] The theological grounding for this was made by emphasizing the historical connection between Judaism and Christianity, especially the explicit Christian acceptance of the Hebrew Bible and the doctrine of *creatio ex nihilo*.[155] We will examine this approach in greater detail when we analyze late medieval treatments of Noahide law.[156] Moreover, it is worth noting that Maimonides, who regarding Christianity as idolatry, had some positive regard for Christianity's historical connection with Judaism. Although he preferred Islam on philosophical grounds because of its pure monotheism,[157] he nevertheless permits teaching the Hebrew Bible to Christians who, unlike Muslims, accept its revelation literally.[158] Also, he praises both religions for helping prepare the pagan world to accept the kingship of God, a prerequisite for the universal messianic reign.[159]

8. Theological Effects of the Treatment of Gentile Idolatry

Reflection on other religions by Jews has been justified on the grounds that such reflection enables Jews to better understand the uniqueness of Judaism by contrast: "From the negative one can infer the positive."[160] For example,

when a verse in Deuteronomy states, "You shall not learn to practice according to the abominations of those nations" (18:9), a rabbinic text interprets it as
follows: "Scripture only states 'to practice' (la'asot)—to practice you may not
learn, but you may learn to render legal ruling (le-horot) and to understand
(le-havin)."[161] From encounters with other traditions truths about Judaism,
heretofore implicit, become explicit. One can see this as part of the rationale of
the biblical polemics against gentile idolatry. On the one hand, gentile idolatry
had to be shown as unattractive to dissuade Jewish interest. On the other
hand, this critical examination of idolatry led to the discovery of important
factors in the covenantal relationship between God and Israel.[162]

The concept of *shittuf*, that is, the idea that God has a "partner" who shares
his divinity, seems to be a rabbinic characterization of the Christian doctrine
of the Incarnation.

The Christians claimed, at least beginning with the fourth Gospel, that
their messiah or Christ is divine (*theos en*) who "became flesh" (*sarx egento*—
John 1:14) in the person of Jesus of Nazareth. They believed that God shares
his divinity. Jesus was even accused of making himself God's "equal" (*ison*—
John 5:18), although he himself claimed union with God in a participatory
sense, ". . . for the Father is greater than I" (John 14:28).[163] John the Baptist and
presumably others were not believed to participate in divinity but only to point
to it: "he was not the light, but he witnessed (*martyrēse*) about the light" (John
1:8). Furthermore, Jesus as a human manifestation of God is believed to be
more accessible than God: "No one has seen God; it is the only son (*monogenes
uios*) . . . who has made him known" (John 1:18). Thus, because Jesus is
believed to be the most accessible manifestation of God, he is held as an intermediary: "As you, Father, are in me and I am in you, so let them be in us" (John
17:21). Indeed, John's Gospel holds him as the only intermediary: "I am the
way and the truth and the light. No one (*oudeis*) comes to the Father except
through me (*ei me di'emou*)" (John 14:6).

With this background of traditional Christian theology, the intent of the
following rabbinic statement is clear:

"There is one and not two" (Ecc. 4:7)—this is God about whom it is written, "the
Lord is our God, the Lord is One" (Deut. 6:4). "And not two"—this means He has no
partner in his world (*shuttaf b'olamo*), neither son nor brother.[164]

This midrash seems to be directed against two forms of sectarianism, both
deemed incompatible with Jewish monotheism; The reference to "no son"
refers of course to Christianity, whereas "no brother" appears to refer to forms
of Gnosticism that posited two divine forces.[165]

Both forms of sectarianism involve *shittuf* to be sure, but the Christian
form conceived of *shittuf* as not only a metaphysical principle but also a

covenantal one—that is, God is accessible through one intermediary alone. Therefore, the reaction of this theology as being un-Jewish compelled rabbinic theologians to explicate the Jewish covenant as an *immediate* relationship with God. Because of this relationship, Jews became the associates or "adopted" children of God. The midrash above concludes:

But because God loved Israel he called them "children," as it is written, "you are children to the Lord your God" (Deut. 14:1); and he called them "brothers," as it is written, "for the sake of My brothers and My friends" (Ps. 122:8).

Parents, too, are called "partners" (*shuttfin*) of God in the creation of their children.[166] However, parents are not considered literal participants in divinity, and hence not objects of worship.[167]

The difference, then, between Jewish *shittuf* and Christian *shittuf* appears to be the following: for Christians, the Incarnation is a substantial relation within the Godhead that makes a subsequent covenantal relationship between humans and God possible. The "partner" of necessity stands *between* God and humanity. *Shittuf* is then a metaphysical precondition for their covenant. For Jews, at least as expressed by rabbinic theology, all Israel are considered God's associates due to the covenant. The covenant has no metaphysical preconditions in the Godhead itself. As such the direct covenant by definition precludes any intermediary. The midrash is stating in essence that Israel, because it is a direct associate of God historically, needs no intermediary.

Saadiah Gaon based the prohibition of *shittuf* on the verse, "Do not make with Me, gods of silver and gods of gold you shall not make for yourselves" (Ex. 20:23). Saadiah emphasized the word *itti* ("with me") to mean that nothing is to be *associated with* God in devotion to him. Elsewhere, he stresses there is no "partner" (*Shuttaf*) nor "intermediary" (*emtza'i*).[168] His interpretation is directed against Christianity and, with his reference to "intermediary," possibly to Islam as well.

Franz Rosenzweig, faced with the same claims of Jewish Christianity the rabbis faced, answered his friend Eugene Rosenstock, a Jewish convert to Christianity attempting to convert him, as follows:

. . . at the bottom of his heart any Jew will consider the Christian's relationship to God, and hence his religion, a meagre and roundabout affair. For to the Jew it is incomprehensible that one should need a teacher . . . to learn what is obvious and matter of course to him, namely, to call God our Father. Why should a third person have to be between me and my Father in heaven?[169]

To his cousin, Rudolf Ehrenburg, another convert to Christianity, Rosenzweig wrote, giving his own interpretation of John 14:6: "'No one can reach the Father': But the situation is quite different for one who does not have to reach the Father because he is already with him. And this is true of the people of Israel . . . "[170] As the Tanna, R. Jose, said, "Israel is beloved because the Torah did not require them to have an intermediary (shaliah)."[171]

With this aggadic background, one can see how shuttfut, as developed by Rabbenu Tam, became possible in Judaism. When Jewish Christianity was a direct theological challenge to Judaism, shuttfut had to be enunciated as the essential between Judaism and Christianity. By the Middle Ages, however, when the Judaism and Christianity had firmly parted ways for centuries, shittuf or shuttfut could be framed differently. Rabbenu Tam could use it to indicate that Christianity occupied a middle ground between pure Jewish monotheism and polytheism. Since only polytheism was considered pure idolatry, Christianity escaped the full stigma attached to it. By making this distinction, the unique Jewish idea of covenant can be better clarified, contributing significantly to Jewish self-understanding in the process.

9. Idolatry and Philosophical Reflection: Maimonides

As a philosopher concerned with the grounds of truth, Maimonides considered the existence of God to be its foundation and idolatry its antithesis, the epitome of falsehood.[172] On can see his philosophical reflection on idolatry as rooted in his work as a halakhist and theologian. As I have tried to show elsewhere, the philosophical problems that engaged Maimonides arose out of normative Jewish tradition.[173] His use of non-Jewish philosophical sources was based on methodological affinities. His involvement with "philosophy" was more methodological than substantial; he used the tools of the "philosophers" to clarify "the secrets of the Torah" (sitrai Torah).[174] He did not of course consider himself a "philosopher" in the specific sense that the term is used today, one whose only objects of reflection were those immediately available to the senses and the intellect of all humanity.[175] However, if one defines philosophy as a method in inquiry, applicable to historical traditions as well as to sense data and intelligibles, namely, a method to uncover the foundations of each of them respectively, then Maimonides was most certainly a philosopher, and his work admits of philosophical analysis. This approach alone enables us to engage his work: halakhic, theological and speculative, as a unified process of thought.[176]

As a halakhist, Maimonides had to face the idolatrous implications of permitting Jews to take oaths in the name of intermediary beings rather than in the name of God alone. He writes:

Therefore, one is not permitted to swear by any creature (*mikol ha-nivra'im*) like the angels or the stars, except by virtue of the contingent status (*tzad hisaron*) of that thing used. For example, one swears by the sun and he really means (*ve-hu virtzeh*) the Lord of the sun . . . But anytime the one who swears does not intend (*she-l'o yekhavven*) this and swears by one of the creatures, and he thinks that this thing is truly substantial (*amitut b'atzmuto*) so that he may swear by it, he is guilty (*abar*) of associating (*ve-shittif*) God and something else.[177]

Saul Lieberman believes that Maimonides is codifying a lost rabbinic source here.[178] The text is from *Sefer ha-Mitzvot*, a separate preface to the *Mishneh Torah*.[179] In the *Mishneh Torah*, however, Maimonides writes, "there is no one worthy for honor to be apportioned to him (*she-ra'ui le-halok lo kavod*) except the One, blessed be He."[180] Lieberman concludes, by combining both statements, that taking an oath in the name of an intermediary is permitted, but the oath itself is not legally binding.[181] Indeed, the Talmud earlier ruled that because oaths taken in the name of "heaven and earth" do not necessarily intend the Creator of these entities; they are, therefore, invalid.[182]

It would seem that Maimonides was somewhat embarrassed by the ruling permitting oaths through intermediaries and did his best to make monotheistic intent the determining factor.[183] Such an objective adheres closely to the Talmudic approach regarding oaths and vows, which allowed their nullification if the intent was judged unworthy, or, especially, inconsistent with true intent.[184] Furthermore, in the *Mishneh Torah*, Maimonides considers oaths "a form of worship" (*me-darkhai ha'avodah*), matters of "great dignity (*ve-hidur*) and sanctity (*ve-kiddush gadol*)."[185] However, if we combine this passage with the earlier one from *Sefer ha-Mitzvot*, we could justify the startling conclusion that worship via intermediaries, taken as symbolic rather than substantial, is also permitted at least *ex post facto*! Clearly, neither Maimonides, nor any other halakhist I know of, would ever draw such a conclusion.[186] In *Sefer ha-Mitzvot* the careful rationale given for this permission in the case of oaths only should be seen as functioning as a stringent halakhic qualification. Maimonides, therefore, attempted to limit as much as possible any practical intermediary in the covenantal relationship between God and Israel.

The halakhic problem of this kind of oath brought out a theological analysis from Maimonides as it did from Rabbenu Tam. The problem and theological logic used in dealing with it are virtually the same. In a responsum regarding whether Muslims count as idolaters, Maimonides writes:

These Muslims are not at all idolaters . . . they are pure monotheists (*meyahadim . . . yihud kera'ui*) without deceit . . . As for the house which they praise being an idolatrous shrine which their ancestors worshipped, what is the matter with this? They who now prostrate themselves direct their hearts to God.[187]

Maimonides' responsum is addressed to Ovadiah, a convert to Judaism from Islam, a man whose teacher held that Muslim veneration of certain shrines was idolatrous, and by extension Muslims are idolaters. Maimonides denies this charge and rebukes the teacher of Ovadiah. This Ovadiah is the same who queried Maimonides regarding whether or not he could recite the phrase "God of our fathers" in the prayers. Maimonides answered affirmatively: following his conversion, Abraham was considered his father.[188] Conversion involves a total change of personal identity.[189]

Maimonides' censure of Ovadiah's teacher for not only insulting Ovadiah but also his former faith is in keeping with the Talmudic approach that forbids reminding converts of their past.[190] But why does Maimonides defend Islam? Referring to halakhah alone, Maimonides was required only to reprove Ovadiah's teacher. Islam per se is not part of the halakhic matter here. The answer to this question begins to emerge if we look at Maimonides' response to Ovadiah and the point he made regarding Abraham as the true father of converts. He writes:

What is the reason for this? "For I have made you a father for a multitude of nations" (Gen. 17:5). Before you were father to Abraham, from now on you are father to all humanity . . . For Abraham is your father and of all the righteous who go in his ways . . .[191]

The printed text here is difficult because it seems to be saying that Abraham is his own father! A variant reading states, "father to a man," namely, at that time Abraham was only the father of one person, Ishmael, but it is now promised that he will be not only Isaac's father, but the father of all humanity.[192]

Although the *baraita* in the Palestinian Talmud that Maimonides quoted as the basis of his answer to Ovadiah refers to full converts (*gerai tzedek*) like Ovadiah, he expands it to refer to "humanity." That he means more than full converts to Judaism emerges from the following passage in the *Guide*, where Maimonides discusses the universal influence of Abraham:

. . . *and in thee shall all the families of the earth be blessed* (Gen. 12:3). And in point of fact his activity has resulted, as we see today, in the consensus (*me-haskamot*) of the greater part of the population of the earth . . . so that even those who do not belong to his progeny pretend to descend from him.[193]

The only peoples Maimonides excludes from this monotheistic *consensus gentium* are those like the Hindus who are outside the realm of Christianity and Islam.[194] His interest in defending Islam, therefore, is because he sees it as potential Judaism. In the specific cases of Ovadiah his prior tradition prepared him for Judaism. As we shall see later, Maimonides considered the Noahide law to be "completed" (ve-nishlamah) by the Torah of Moses.[195] As an Aristotelian, at least in regards to terminology and methodology,[196] Maimonides has designated Islam as potential Judaism. Furthermore, the only Noahides worthy of the bliss of the world-to-come are those who accept Noahide law as revealed.[197] For Maimonides, this category appears to be limited to Christians and Muslims.

The philosophical import of all of this becomes apparent when we see how Maimonides uses Islam to illustrate the preconditions of Judaism itself. Islam, especially, is an example of the transition from idolatry to monotheism in the *philosophical* sense, over and above being (along with Christianity) a contributing factor to the universal rejection of explicit idolatry, which is needed as a *historical* precondition of the messianic era.

If Judaism, in terms of its unique experience of prophetic revelation, is the full actualization of human consciousness, then there are steps preceding it. The charge of Jewish philosophy is to analyze the sequence of these steps in the order of religious development. Maimonides locates three steps: (1) substitution or idolatry; (2) symbolization or intermediacy; (3) direct apprehension or Mosaic prophecy.

The following passage explains the first two steps:

In the days of Enosh mankind made a great error . . . and the sages of that generation said that because God created these stars and planets to direct the world . . . they are worthy to be praised and glorified and for honor to be apportioned to them. This is the will of God to magnify and honor them who magnify and honor Him. And when this came to their mind they began to build temples to the stars . . . This is the root of idolatry.[198]

Maimonides emphasizes that this was not a denial of God's existence, but rather it was believed that this is the way God established the universe. Gradually, because all devotion was directed to these creations, the masses were informed by the sages of that time that there was no God except these objects of worship.[199] In other words, neglect of direct worship of God in favor of more approximate beings soon resulted in the total substitution for God by something else; this describes pure idolatry. Maimonides presupposes that worship is an indispensable human need. If directed away from God towards anything else, the act of substitution becomes the most radical denial of God's existence.

Abraham's appearance marks the transition from the first to the second step. Abraham recognized that the contingency of created things required a higher power to ground their reality.[200] Abraham not only destroys idols, but he also rejects their cult (idolatry).[201] It is important to remember that Maimonides' proofs for God's existence draw on observation of the heavenly spheres, the objects of idolaters' devotion. Seeing them as contingent, however, removes those objects from idolatrous worship. Following Aristotle, Maimonides considers the heavenly spheres as more exalted than sublunar beings.[202] The principle of the motion of these spheres and angels—intermediaries sent by God—have no permanent status themselves.[203] It is no accident that the idolaters chose to worship these exalted beings. This explains Maimonides' affinity for Aristotle's cosmology: it was useful in emphasizing the existence of God, an emphasis begun initially in Maimonides' halakhic works. While these works seek to *prove* the existence, they are motivated primarily to *disprove* the divinity of the heavens. In this desire, he departed from Aristotle.[204]

Maimonides places a proof for God's existence into the mouth of Abraham, a common tactic in medieval philosophy. The historical accuracy of this projection is unimportant in the context of Maimonides' presentation. Abraham is presented as the model of transition from negation to affirmation of God's existence and his accessibility to human worship.[205]

The transition from idolatry to monotheism involves looking at creation in a new way. Whereas formerly the objects of devotion were regarded as *participants* in divinity, capable of fully *representing* God, they now function *symbolically*. A symbol is *paradoxical*, that is, it draws attention to itself while simultaneously directing our attention beyond it. The attraction is self-affirmation; the direction is self-negation. Now this is usually seen as the Neoplatonic cast of Maimonides' thought. While borrowing the methodology and terminology of the "philosophers," the questions with which he engaged emerge from the Jewish tradition.[206] For he is not concerned with causality alone, but more with the proper direction of religious desire. Let us recall that Maimonides justified an oath taken through an intermediary. He only permits it when there is recognition of the "contingent status" of the created object used in the oath. If regarded as "substantial," it becomes idolatrous.[207] In other words, God can only be affirmed *through* creation if creation is regarded as paradoxical, that is, both presenting itself and absenting itself from the conscious desire to know God. A proof of God's existence, then, presupposes looking at the world symbolically. This symbolic perspective makes possible the transition from idolatry to monotheism.

This transition can also be seen in Maimonides' theory of religious language. In the *Guide*, he starts his philosophical reflection on Judaism with an analysis of biblical language. The problem with theological language, specifically the predicates used to describe God, is that if they are taken liter-ally, they are describing a finite, contingent being, no different than the objects of idolatrous worship. Of course, if nothing were said of God, there would be no vocabulary for worship. Without such language how could there be any relationship between humanity and God? The matrix of theo-logical language is the experience of worship.[208]

Maimonides offers two justifications for religious language, specifically for what we today call "God-talk":

First, he states that the attributes predicated of God describe only his acts but not his essence. If we say "God is good" we mean "His creation is good."[209] This gives us information about the world, but does what does it tell us about God? In what sense does the goodness of the world depend on God? On the pre-philosophical level it is simply enough to affirm God's creation of the world and everything in it.

However, on the philosophical level a more intelligible relation is called for. At this level Maimonides proposes his theory of negative attributes—positive statements about God are to be understood as negations of their opposites.[210] If we say "God is good," this translates to "God is not evil." Again, what does this tell us? About the world we learn that its goodness is essentially contin-gent, that it requires a causal explanation. About God we learn that he tran-scends our intellect's categories that are derived from our experience of the world.[211] His transcendence is his absolute *priority* to creation. Our desire to know God in this priority, what philosophers call "essence," motivates us to go through the world wherein our consciousness begins. It is this dialectical process, this *via negativa*, that saves the desire of all desires, the desire to know God as he is, from missing its mark by directing its infinite intent to that which is finite, that is, to succumbing to idolatry.

Although idolatry found its most intense expressions among gentiles, Jews and even Judaism are not immune to its temptations.[212] Anytime a sym-bol is taken literally, idolatrous implications are near at hand.[213] This is why Maimonides had to qualify the permission to Jews to invoke intermediaries in their oaths with the same logic he justified the permission to Muslims, as Noahides, to continue to venerate their ancestral shrines. The difference between Judaism and other monotheistic religions is one of degree rather than kind. Maimonides is only more intolerant of Jewish superstition because Jews have a longer and deeper intellectual tradition, which should make them more adverse to superstition and its attractions.[214]

This recognition of the symbolic character of religious language, that is, understanding it as the descriptive aspect of the *via negativa*, enables us to see *shittuf* as a new concept in medieval Jewish philosophy. Previously, *shittuf* meant "associating" the name of God and that of a created being in one devotional utterance. By presupposing a positive substantial relation between God and a creature, *shittuf* has idolatrous consequences and is thus prohibited, as Maimonides pointed out in his treatment of forbidden oaths.[215] However, when *shittuf* is understood paradoxically, namely, attributes predicated of God that negate their opposites, *shittuf* now becomes a term used to characterize the only legitimate type of description of God philosophically justifiable.

This new meaning is brought out by Maimonides:

... however clear it is to all those who understand the meaning of being alike that the term "existent" is predicated of Him, may He be exalted, and of everything that is other than He, in a purely equivocal sense ... Do not deem that they are used amphibolously. For when terms are used amphibolously they are predicated of two things between which there is a likeness in respect to some notion, which notion is an accident attached to both of them and not a constituent element of the essence of each one of them. Now the things attributed to Him, may He be exalted, are not accidents in the opinion of anyone among the men engaged in speculation.[216]

Although *shittuf* in philosophical Hebrew corresponds to *ishrakh* in philosophical Arabic, its usage presupposes its original halakhic and theological usage.[217] Surely Maimonides did not forget his previous use of the term when he approved Ibn Tibbon's translation.[218] The new connotation of *shittuf* designates the only way possible to speak about God without contradiction and error. Just as the attributes of God understood negatively negate their opposites and thus symbolically propel one on the *via ad Deum*, so the new meaning of *shittuf* negates the old meaning which, if accepted, would hinder one on the *via ad Deum* by directing one away from the true end. Thus the halakhic and theological rejection of the old designation of *shittuf* led to its philosophical reformulation by Maimonides.

The understanding of the symbolic character of religious institutions and religious language involves a recognition of their finitude and contingency. This had profound political consequences. In common with both Muslim and Jewish theologians in the Middle Ages, Maimonides regarded the relation between religion and politics to be essential.[219] Religion begins as a manifestation of human society and, therefore, has immediate political significance. This emerges in Maimonides' analysis of the beginnings of idolatry and true religion in his *Hilkhot Avodah Zarah*, as well in his earlier commentary to tractate Avodah Zarah.[220] In both places he emphasizes that idolatry is concerned with the *transmission* of divine power from a remote level to one more accessible. It thereby involves the concentration of human authority in the hands of those few who can convince the masses that they alone are able to transmit

and direct this power for the welfare of the whole society, that "political authority" (ha-shilton) will be preserved due to their efforts.[221]

For Maimonides, Abraham's iconoclasm is not only revolutionary in terms
of metaphysics and cult, it is politically revolutionary as well. For if God is
accessible without substitutions, or even without substantial intermediaries,
then the absolute political power of those in authority loses its grounding.
They no longer stand above the masses in a sacred hierarchy. Maimonides
writes:

When Abraham recognized his Creator and knew the truth he began . . . to contend
with the people of Ur of the Chaldees, saying that this is not the way of truth in
which to go. And he broke the idols and began to inform the people that it is not
right to serve anyone but the universal God (eloha ha'olam) . . . when he overpowered
them with his proofs the king sought to kill him.[222]

The king sought to kill him because Abraham's teaching was undermining
the basis of his absolute rule. Indeed, in his earlier discussion of this point,
Maimonides vividly described how idolatry was invented as a social myth by
those in power to cause those who they ruled to accept their authority as being
both necessary and beneficial for individuals and society.[223]

Just as Maimonides showed the essential philosophical difference between idolatrous and monotheistic theology and cult, he also showed the
essential political difference between idolatrous and monotheistic politics.
Concerning the authority of Moses he writes:

Moses our rabbi did not cause Israel to believe in him because of the signs he
performed, for one who believes because of signs, there is always the doubt (dofi) in
his mind that the sign was performed by sorcery or witchcraft . . . But what did cause
them to believe in him? By the revelation at Mt. Sinai which no eyes saw but ours
and no other ears heard.[224]

In other words, Maimonides emphasizes a central rabbinic point—the foundation of God's revelation was directly experienced by all Israel. As a result, all
subsequent leadership in Israel—even prophetic leadership—was limited
leadership subject to the norms of the covenant. The function of political language in this society, especially prophetic language, is essentially symbolic.
It must point to God and thereby limit its own power.

The transition from the second stage (symbolization or intermediacy) to
the final stage (direct apprehension, or Mosaic prophecy) of religious consciousness is the very heart of Maimonides' theory of revelation.

CHAPTER FIVE

THE LAW OF HOMICIDE

1. Introduction

The fourth Noahide law is the prohibition of bloodshed (*shefikhat damim*). The Gemara attempts to derive this law from a literal reading of two words from Gen. 2:16, a reading that the full context of the verse does not support. The verse, conventionally, reads: "And the Lord God commanded the man . . ." Although "the man" (*ha-adam*) is preceded by the preposition *al* (usually "on" or "about"), the context of the verse seems to indicate that *al* functions here accusatively, designating "the man" as the direct object of the command. Such use is common.[1] The rabbinic exegesis of these words, however, interprets the verse as: "And the Lord God commanded *about man*," taking *al* literally and *ha-adam* to refer to generic "mankind." This use of *ha-adam* is then linked to Gen. 9:16—"whosoever sheds human blood . . ."[2] This reading should be seen as part of the rabbinic attempt to prevent the prescriptions of this verse applying to Adam and Eve alone. Rather, it was normative for humanity at all times.[3]

2. The Rationality of the Prohibition

Of all the Noahide laws, the necessity of the prohibition of bloodshed was considered by many to be the most immediately evident. This was seen both in relation to the understanding of human character as a social and political being, and as humanity made in the image of God.

In the absence of this prohibition, it was usually emphasized that the possibility of social life would be ruined. Public safety demands it. As Philo writes, "you shall not murder—the second head forbids murder, and under it come the laws, all of them indispensable (*anangkaioi*) and of great public utility (*koinōpheleis*) . . ."[4] Our natural sociality, according to Philo, insists upon the proscription of murder.[5] Maimonides later indicated that it is the most immediately evident of all the laws governing human relations:

Even though there are iniquities more serious (*hamurin*) than bloodshed, they do not involve the destruction of civilization (*hashhattat yishuvo shel olam*) as does bloodshed—not even idolatry and, needless to say, incest (*arayot*) or Sabbath desecration—they are not like bloodshed. For these iniquities are transgressions of what is between man and God, but bloodshed is a transgression between man and man.[6]

Concerning humanity's character as formed in the image of God, the necessity of this prohibition was interpreted as being directly required by this fundamental characteristic. Again, Philo notes its theological function (following its social and political function):

Further, let him understand that he is guilty of sacrilege, the robbery from its sanctuary of the most sacred of God's possessions . . . But man, the best of living creatures, through that higher part of his being, namely, the soul, is most akin to heaven . . . and as most admit, also the Father of the world . . .[7]

Philo's comment that there is near-universal agreement regarding humanity's creation in the image of God has precedent in Plato, Philo's philosophic guide.[8] Plato, too, connects murder and sacrilege.[9] Philo, then, stresses the integral connection between humans as social beings and humans as *imago Dei*, the joint ground for the universally accepted prohibition of bloodshed.

In the Tannaitic sources this same idea emerges in the statement of R. Akiva that "whoever sheds blood it is accounted to him as if he diminished the divine likeness because . . . in the image of God He made man."[10] This status was "made known" to humanity.[11] R. Akiva, therefore, recognized universal agreement regarding the sanctity of the human person.

Jewish thinkers have usually stressed either the social character of humanity or the argument from *imago Dei* as the source of this prohibition.[12] Nevertheless, the rationality of this law was subject to less debate than any other Noahide law.

3. Comparative Jurisprudence

We have seen in the previous chapters that Jewish philosophical reflection on the Noahide laws usually involved analyzing their relation to Jewish law. Moreover, the analysis of this relation usually regarded it as necessary, that is, Noahide law was considered to be a condition of Jewish law. The understanding of just how this condition is constituted has an effect on how one interprets the major institutions of Jewish civil and even ritual law. Such understanding is a theoretical process of comparative jurisprudence. We will shortly consider how two basically different understandings of the relation of

Jewish law to the Noahide law of homicide had a definite effect on two different views of the Jewish institution of capital punishment. Prior to this consideration, it is helpful to examine what I believe to be a model of the rabbis'
theoretical comparative jurisprudence.

The Torah stipulates that the owner of a previously docile animal only pays
half of the damages it inflicts the first few times (Ex. 21:35–36). This law
appears to be contrary to rational jurisprudence. Either the owner of the animal should pay full damages, or the owner should be exempt, considering that
he could not have known what his animals would do. The Gemara records the
following dispute:

R. Pappa said that this is a monetary matter (*mamona*), because he was of the
opinion that ordinarily oxen are not properly guarded and reason (*u-ba-din*) requires
the payment of full damages. However, the All-Merciful-One had pity on the owner
as this ox was not fully vicious. R. Huna, the son of R. Joshua, said that it is a fine
(*kenasa*), because he was of the opinion that ordinarily oxen are properly guarded
and reason requires no payment of damages, but the All-Merciful-One fined him so
he would guard his ox.[13]

The dispute between these two Amoraim is essentially whether the Jewish law
of punishment prescribes more or less than what reason would normally
dictate.[14] Rav Pappa argues that Jewish law prescribes less because of God's
pity for Israel.[15] Rav Huna argues that Jewish law prescribes more than reason
dictates because God places greater demands on Israel.[16]

The Gemara defines Rav Pappa's interpretation as monetary. Monetary law
is one of the most flexible areas in rabbinic law, admitting of change when
required.[17] Rav Huna's interpretation is considered to be a fine. The laws of
scripturally ordained fines (*kenas*) are one of the most inflexible areas in Jewish law because there does not seem to be any evident reason for their legislation generally and the amount of money specifically prescribed for payment.[18]
It would seem, then, that the monetary dispensation defined by Rav Pappa
could be easily removed if rabbinic authorities deemed it abused. However,
the additional fine of Rav Huna could not be so easily removed because it is
an innovation of Torah law.

The crucial distinction concerning torts appears in two differing interpretations of Jewish law of capital punishment. Namely, should Jewish law be
stricter or more lenient than reason would normally require?

The rabbis recognized that although the Jewish prohibition of homicide
was essentially the same as that for Noahides, the Jewish law of capital punishment was more lenient than that of contemporary non-Jews, especially the
Romans. There were some who seemed to regard this as a dispensation that

could be removed if the rabbinic authorities judged it likely to be abused. Violation of any of the Noahide laws was punishable by death penalty.[19] This appears to be based on the notion that all transgressions of God's law deserve death, and that the Torah exempted Jews from death for *some* crimes.[20] Conversely, there were those who regarded this leniency as an innovation of the Torah system itself, an essential change brought about by the covenantal status of Israel, an advancement from the barbarism of the gentile world and its law.

4. Anti-Capital Punishment

In Jewish law one could not be explicitly opposed to capital punishment in principle inasmuch as it was positively ordained by the Torah in numerous places.[21] However, one could emphasize the worry that an innocent might be put to death. In the words of Robert Gordis, "the imposition of a death penalty by the court would be a fully conscious and completely premeditated act, it would be exceeding the guilt of the criminal if any uncertainty prevailed regarding the conscious and willful character of the crime."[22] In other words, it is recognized that society can commit crimes worse than those committed by any individual. We see, therefore, very deliberate steps to make the institution of capital punishment theoretical rather than practically operable, even long after the Roman rulers removed the power of execution from Jewish courts.[23] As the Mishnah states:

A Sanhedrin that executes once in seven years is called "murderous" (*hovblanit*). R. Eleazar b. Azaryah says once in seventy years. R. Tarfon and R. Akiva say, "were we in the Sanhedrin, no one would have ever been executed."[24]

The Amoraim indicate how R. Tarfon and R. Akiva could have accomplished this within the boundaries of the law.[25] In the case of homicide it could always be argued that the victim was already suffering from a fatal wound and the murderer would not be liable to prosecution in a human court.[26] Although this specific type of interpretation was not subsequently accepted, the statement of these two Tannaim is relevant because it is part of a tendency in the development of Jewish law that preceded them.[27] Josephus wrote that the Pharisees "did not think it right to sentence a man to death for calumny, and the Pharisees are naturally lenient in matters of punishment."[28]

The Pharisaic and rabbinic leniency in these matters might well have been a reaction to the judicial practices of the Romans, notorious for their numerous executions on weak evidence, especially of non-Romans in the provinces. R. Joshua b. Korhah, a second-century Tanna, rebuked R. Eleazar b. R. Simon for turning Jewish criminals over to the Romans. When the latter argued that he was only removing criminals from society, R. Joshua answered that this task was left to God.[29] Meiri later pointed out that the reason for this was that many Jews would have been put to death by the harsher Roman laws.[30] The rabbis in other places expressed disgust for Roman readiness to execute.[31]

R. Akiva's leniency regarding capital punishment was accomplished through a strict interpretation of the laws of evidence. The legal precision in determining the exact function of witnesses at times led R. Akiva to be more severe on capital punishment, but this is the result of legal approach, one that on the whole made capital punishment impossible to carry out.[32] His approach was objective; sentiment had no place.[33] Leniency could be accomplished by consistent exegetical means.[34] His reading of Deut. 19:15 ("by the testimony of two or by the testimony of three witnesses shall a matter be ascertained") shows this approach:

R. Akiva said that if testimony is ascertained by two, why are three mentioned? This is to make the standards applicable to two witnesses applicable to three. Just as with two witnesses, if one of them is a close relative (karov), or one disqualified from being a witness (pasul), the whole testimony is null and void (batlah), so also with three . . . Whence do we learn that this applies even one hundred witnesses? Scriptures states "witnesses" in the plural.[35]

The more witnesses, the less reliable.

5. Hatra'ah

Hatra'ah highlights most starkly the differences between Jewish and non-Jewish procedure in capital cases. It means "forewarning"—the two requisite witnesses to a capital crime (or one punished by lashes)[36] verbally forewarn the potential criminal of the prohibition and the legal consequences. The criminal acknowledges the warning, and commits the crime regardless.[37] In other areas of law involving intention, it is inferred from the action itself. It need not be announced by the actor prior to the act.[38] This appears at first to be far-fetched. However, it is recorded in Rav Huna's name that when saving the life of the would-be victim (nirdaf), one is required to kill the pursuer (rodef) if that is the only way to save the life of the potential victim, and that the potential killer need not be forewarned.[39] Giving and receiving forewarning in this instance clearly increases the likelihood of a crime. Time here is essential. In most cases if two witnesses would be close enough to forewarn the criminal, then they would likely be able to attempt to save the victim's life. Hatra'ah, therefore, would be precluded in many cases.

Hatra'ah is linked tenuously to the Torah:

It was taught that R. Simon b. Yohai said, "By the testimony of two witnesses shall a person be put to death (*yumat ha-met*)" (Deut. 17:6). Taken literally the Torah states: "the dead one is dead." However, it herewith prescribes that one is to be informed of which means of execution (*b'ayzo meetah*) he is subject.[40]

This tradition is recorded in R. Simon bar Yohai's name. He was one of R. Akiva's closest disciples, making this tradition all the more important.[41] According to a number of modern scholars, *hatra'ah* was an innovation of the Pharisees.[42] Perhaps it was the influence of R. Simon b. Shetah, whose son died because of false testimony.[43] He seems to have developed the strictest criteria for witnesses.[44] However, it is unlikely that this institution was in effect when Jews had the power to administer capital punishment.

Hatra'ah has the appearance of a precise ritualized procedure, one performed under highly controlled conditions. It seems to be in effect the acting out of the rabbinic distinction between a scriptural prohibition (*azharah*) and a scripturally ordained punishment (*onesh*). The Talmud frequently asks: "we have heard the punishment, where is the prohibition?"[45] *Azharah*, the word for prohibition, means "warning." In other words, we do not infer from the prescribed punishment that there must be a warning. It must be explicitly stated. This exegetical procedure insures that the criminal legislation of the Written Torah will be for the most part limited to what is explicitly mentioned as a prohibition in the text itself.[46]

Hatra'ah as the counterpart of *azharah* in action, as ritualized *azharah*, can be seen in the following Mishnah:

Whoever merited removing ashes from the altar, he should remove them. And the other priests say to him, "be careful" (*hizaher*) lest you touch one of the sacred vessels before sanctifying your hands and feet from the designated basin.[47]

Here we see admonition in a ritually prescribed context. Earlier the prophet Ezekiel spoke of the need to repeat "My word to the wicked one, 'you shall surely die,' and if you do not warn him (*hizharto*) . . . his blood I will seek from your hand" (Ez. 33:2). However, his teaching about *azharah* concerns warning the sinner of the consequences of what they have *already* done, and urging them to repent before their fate is sealed. The *azharah/hatra'ah* prescribed by the rabbis, on the other hand, is the warning to the sinner *before* they commit their crime. These witnesses, then, are not just spectators after the fact, but are surrogates of the people Israel who have been charged with the teaching and enforcement of the Torah from heaven.[48] Thus the biblical statement, "all Israel shall hear and fear" (Deut. 21:21), which originally refers to the witnesses of the execution of the criminal, is now actually effected by the witnesses to the crime itself, on behalf of all Israel, *before* the crime is committed.

As such they function symbolically in a ritualized performance that resembles the performance of the Temple priests, with all the symbolic significance attached to their mediating role. Seeing *hatra'ah* in this context, then, enables us to understand why the rabbis repeatedly insisted that it was an institution applying to Jews alone, having no parallel in gentile jurisprudence.

Because there was no parallel among gentiles, *hatra'ah* served as a negative standard of comparison.[49] A closer analysis of *hatra'ah* would cast light on gentile jurisprudence by negative inference. Rabbinic reflection on non-Jewish law took the form of reflection on Noahide law. The following Mishnah demonstrates such reflection: "Everyone is exiled for killing a Jew . . . except a resident alien."[50] This Mishnah refers to a killing *be-shogeg*, a negligent killing or manslaughter. A *baraita* in the Gemara states: "Therefore it is taught that a *ger* (*toshav*) and a gentile (*nokhri*) who killed are themselves executed."[51] Both passages seem to be ruling that gentiles are executed for manslaughter as well as murder; the crimes are in essence the same.[52] Rava qualifies this:

Rava said that one who says it is permitted (*muttar*) . . . is near to premeditation (*karov le-mezeed*). R. Hisda said that he is exempt (*patur*) . . . because it is accidental. Rava retorted to R. Hisda with the verse, "behold you are to die because of the woman you have taken" (Gen. 20:3) . . . from here we learn that a Noahide is executed because he should have learned (*she-hayah lo lilmod*) and he did not.[53]

Maimonides codifies the law according to Rava and quotes another Mishnah as the underlying reason, namely, "a man is always fully responsible whether carelessly committing a crime or with premediation."[54] He emphasizes that this only applies in cases of ignorance of the law where "he should have learned and did not learn."[55] In cases of ignorance of circumstances, however, Jewish law is also lenient with gentiles.[56] One of the major commentators on the *Mishneh Torah*, R. Judah Rozanis, makes the point that "we need to know that he committed the crime with premeditation and with intent, which is inferred from his act."[57] In other words, for gentiles premeditation may be inferred, whereas for Jews it must be explicitly verified in capital cases.

A crime can be negligent in two ways: either the person did not inquire into the specific circumstances of the act but was aware of the general prohibition, or the person was aware of the circumstances but not the general prohibition. Now, Rava's qualification surely refers to the latter possibility, that is, ignorance of the law. This emerges from Rashi's earlier comment that ignorance of the law is no excuse for Noahides because, as the Talmud ruled elsewhere, "their warning (*azharatan*) is their death (*mitatan*)": what constitutes a capital crime is known publicly, and as a result a Noahide should infer that such acts are prohibited.[58] This statement by the Amora, R. Nahman bar

Isaac, comes as an explanation of the anonymous *baraita* that rules, "concerning idolatry: anything for which a Jewish court executes a Noahide is thereby warned." Rashi clearly takes this explanation to be a generalization about *all* Noahide law. This parallels the Roman principle of "no punishment where there is no law (*nulla poena sine lege*)." Negatively, this is inferred from the fact that *hatra'ah* is not a requirement for Noahides. *Hatra'ah* explicates both a prohibition and the punishment for its transgression. Thus, in effect, by means of this comparison, *hatra'ah* establishes a special dispensation for Jews, namely, in capital cases we cannot assume premeditation unless there is an explicitly verifiable admission by the criminal that he indeed knew the law.

Nevertheless, this concept of culpability cannot be directly inferred from the scriptural proof-text cited by Rava. For this text refers to God's admonition to the Philistine king Abimelech regarding the abduction of Sarah. The king's argument is that he is innocent inasmuch as he had no knowledge of her married status. The rabbis infer that it was his responsibility to inquire. Now this is clearly a case of where a person was unaware of the specific circumstances of his act. Abimelech never claims that he did not know that it is wrong to abduct another man's wife. His case, therefore, is not a literal precedent for determining that *ignorance of the law* is no defense for Noahides, but rather is a parallel to the inadmissibility of ignorance per se as an excuse in Noahide law. The Tosafists appear to have recognized this: "Just as he should have learned, here he should have also inquired (*hayah lo l'ayyen*)."[59]

The notion that it is the responsibility of the Noahide to know the law leads to the question: from where does the Noahide learn that they are so punished and, therefore, so obligated? The answer may well be found in the Tosefta:

They said to R. Judah, "how did the nations of the world learn Torah?" He said to them that the Holy-One-Blessed-Be-He gave them the idea and they sent their scribes who carried away the script from off the stones in seventy languages. At that time the decree (*gezar dinam*) of the nations of the world was sealed . . .[60]

The Gemara adds: "because they should have learned and they did not learn."[61] It would seem as though it was the task of Jewish authorities to publish the law for gentiles. It would also seem from the aggadic treatment of the story of Abimelech and Sarah, that it was Abraham *qua prophet* who taught the Noahides (Abimelech included) that one is supposed to make careful inquiry about the marital status of any woman in the company of an unknown guest.[62]

If assumed knowledge of the law refers to published law, perhaps the source is this *baraita*:

It was taught in the school of R. Ishmael, "why did the sages say that if the court ruled erroneously in a matter in which even the Sadducees agree, they are exempt? Because they should have learned and did not learn.[63]

Now "a matter which even the Sadducees agree" refers to an explicit biblical law, written and read regularly in synagogue, a matter of common knowledge.[64] Ignorance of this law was considered so unlikely that a rebellious elder (*zaken mamre*) could hardly fool anybody by contradicting a written law accepted by the whole people.[65] We can now see how this notion lent itself to the interpretation that held gentiles responsible for knowledge of Noahide law, published for them by the Jews.

It appears, then, that *hatra'ah* as a special dispensation for Jews is based on the publication of the law. Individual gentiles are punished for their particular ignorance of the law *generally* known. Jews, on the other hand, require *particular* information of the law being *particularly* liable for capital punishment.

The epistemological question of *hatra'ah* is addressed in this *baraita*:

> R. Jose the son of R. Judah said that a rabbinic fellow does not require *hatra'ah* because *hatra'ah* was only given to distinguish between a crime of carelessness (*shogeg*) and a crime of premeditation (*mezeed*).[66]

This view implies that ignorance of the law can only be assumed for an ignorant Jew (*am ha'aretz*) alone. A learned Jew is not allowed this dispensation. As Rashi notes, "he cannot say, 'I thought it was permitted.'"[67] Maimonides rules differently: both require *hatra'ah*.[68] Although a learned Jew surely knows the law, writes a major commentator on the *Mishneh Torah*, he might very well have been carelessly ignorant of the specific circumstances involved in his act.[69] According to R. Elijah Benamozegh,[70] *hatra'ah* is required because it indicates that God's law, which is revealed, is beyond purely human intelligence. Noahides, on the other hand, have a rational law, therefore a knowable one.[71] By assuming that Noahide law is a set of rational norms, they can be held responsible for them, at least morally, even without the publication of explicit decrees.

On the surface, *hatra'ah* appears to be a double standard where gentiles are treated more severely than Jews. However, since we have no record of Jews having the power to execute gentiles when *hatra'ah* became an institution, the comparison becomes a theoretical attempt to express the observation that the Jewish reverence for human life was greater than that of the Roman Empire, that Jews were more cautious in the use of capital punishment.

6. Homicide and Agency

Rabbinic efforts in comparative jurisprudence, especially regarding capital punishment, are expressed most fully in this Gemara:

> R. Aha bar Jacob found written in the book of sayings of the school of Rav that a Noahide is executed after being tried before one judge, by the testimony of one

witness, without *hatra'ah*, on the testimony of a man but not a woman, even on the testimony of a near relative (*karov*).[72]

The Gemara tries to derive these provisions from the wording of Gen. 9:5. However, Adolf Schmiedl, a nineteenth-century Austrian scholar, showed that this passage describes Roman law.[73] As we have seen, the rabbinic discussion of the Noahide law of homicide was far more descriptive than prescriptive—it described the legal reality of the Roman Empire, and was used primarily as a basis of negative comparison with Jewish law.

In the *Midrash Rabbah* we find an important variant of the Gemara text above: "R. Hanina said that all of them are included in the laws of the Noahides . . . by means of an agent (*sheliah*)."[74] The addition seems to be directly related to an important early dispute:

One who says to his agent, "go out and kill a person"—the agent is liable for punishment and the sender is exempt. Shammai the Elder said in the name of Haggai the Prophet that the sender is liable, as Scripture states, "You killed him by the sword of the sons of Ammon" (II Sam. 12:9).[75]

The proof-text for the view of Shammai, and Haggai before him, is the prophet Nathan's rebuke of King David for having ordered the death of Uriah the Hittite (with whose wife, Bathsheba, David was then having an affair) through his general, Joab, that is, Joab was ordered to expose Uriah to certain death in battle. The Gemara based the opposing view of the rabbis on the principle, "there is no agency for transgression (*le-davar averah*)."[76] Normally, however, "a man's agent is like himself (*kemoto*)."[77] Also, the Gemara tried to qualify Shammai's indictment of the sender by making his liability a matter for divine rather than human judgment.

Scholars such as Isaac Hirsch Weiss and Louis Finkelstein, among others, have argued that Shammai's opinion is based on an actual historical incident, one found in the Talmud and Josephus.[78] According to the Talmud's version, a servant of the Hasmonean king, Alexander Jannaeus, committed murder. The Sanhedrin, lead by Simon b. Shetah, ordered the king to stand trial. When the king appeared in court, his very appearance so terrified many members of the Sanhedrin that they could not act. Only Simon b. Shetah accused the king of approving of his servant's crime.[79] The Talmud reports this incident as the reason for the law in the Mishnah that a "king neither judges nor is he judged."[80]

Josephus changes the cast, but in most details reports the same scene:

Herod, in violation of Jewish law, had put all this large number of people to death. If he is not a king but still a commoner, he ought to appear in court and answer for his conduct . . . Sextus Caesar, however, fearing that the young man might be isolated by adversaries and meet with misfortunate, sent express orders to Hyrcanus to clear Herod of the charge of manslaughter (*tē phonikēs dikēs*).[81]

Obviously, Herod did not himself kill these people, but ordered his underlings to do it for him. In another work, Josephus describes the trial at which Herod appeared, noting the terror of the Sanhedrin. He concludes:

While they were in this state, someone named Sammaias, an upright man and for that reason superior to fear, arose and said . . . "This fine fellow Herod . . . with his soldiers round him, in order to kill us if we condemn him as the law prescribes (*kata ton nomon*), and to save himself by outraging justice."[82]

We find that "a king neither judges nor is judged" refers to the Roman-ordered immunity for Herod, their vassal king, from judgment by Jewish authorities. This step was one of the first in limited Jewish political and legal autonomy. It seems clear that it was Shammai the Elder who had the courage to challenge Herod. Later the Gemara generalized his opposition into a ruling that the instigator of a murder is also guilty along with the actual murderer. As Boaz Cohen showed, this was Roman law.[83] The inability of Jewish authorities, however, to abide by this law, a law having a clear biblical parallel in Nathan's rebuke of David, is reflected in the rabbis' refusal to follow Shammai's opinion. Nevertheless, his opinion does become accepted in Noahide law. The general rabbinic tendency to veer away from capital punishment for Jews, as much as legally possible, probably was the reason that this opinion was confined to Noahide law, especially as it was a negative criterion of comparison for Jewish law. Here again we see Noahide law as descriptive of Roman reality in which Jews found themselves reluctantly living.

7. Pro-Capital Punishment

Because many Jewish liberals believe that capital punishment is a relic of barbarism, there has been a trend among them to emphasize the anti-capital punishment tendency among the rabbis.[84] What has received too little attention, however, is the equally prominent rabbinic and post-rabbinic tendency to regard capital punishment as a social necessity to be endorsed and encouraged by Jewish authorities.

In the very same Mishnah where R. Tarfon and R. Akiva made their famous statement that if they were in the Sanhedrin, no one would have been executed. Rabban Simon b. Gamliel retorts: "they too increase shedders of blood (*shofkhai damim*) in Israel."[85] This view found acceptance in the refusal of the Amoraim to interpret the laws of evidence as strictly as it was assumed that   R. Tarfon and R. Akiva would to legally prevent executions.[86] We should mention the *baraita* that states that when a specifically prescribed type of capital punishment was impossible to implement, any other type could be substituted.[87] Also, in the Palestinian Talmud, it is reported that the rabbis were of the opinion that when the elders of a city, wherein a murder victim was found without indication of who murdered him, are required to say: "our hands did not shed this blood (Deut. 21:7)," this means that they are insisting that their negligence did not allow a guilty criminal, one deserving of capital punishment, to go free and thereby commit a new crime.[88]

There is an important difference between the anti- and pro-capital punishment halakhists. The former attempted to accomplish their goals within the strict limits of the law itself; the latter regarded capital punishment as socially vital, necessary at times even when the law forbids it. Before looking at texts relevant to this, it is useful to consider a parallel to the whole process of removal of a Torah institution.

In a section of the Mishnah where the various radical procedures of the Pharisee authorities are recorded, we read:

When adulterers became numerous the ordeal of the bitter waters (*ha-mayim ha-marim*) was stopped. Rabban Johanan b. Zakkai stopped it according to this scriptural verse, "I will punish your daughters because they are promiscuous . . . (Hos. 4:14)."[89]

This verse indicates that women cannot very well be singled out for their promiscuity when the men are no better. Both Talmuds indicate that the words in the Written Torah, "and the man is innocent (*naki*) of iniquity" (Num. 5:31), mean that only the man who is free of sexual taint has the right to subject his wife to the ordeal of jealousy.[90] When this can no longer be *generally* assumed, then the institution loses its basic justification because it is a mockery of the law itself if there is a double standard of sexual purity.[91]

Whereas in the Written Torah it seems as though the husband's power to subject his wife to this order is *a right that the law enforces*, the rabbinic interpretation of the act of Rabban Johanan b. Zakkai sees it as a *privilege the law can remove*. Rabbenu Bahya b. Asher, a thirteenth-century Spanish exegete, wrote: "this means this great miracle (*ha-nes ha-gadol ha-zeh*) would no longer be done for them, for it was done for the glory of Israel in that they are to be a holy people, free from illegitimacy . . ."[92] Similarly the pro-capital punishment halakhists regard the peculiar requirements for valid testimony in Jewish law, and the even more peculiar institution of *hatra'ah*, as privileges granted to Jews. This is like the ordeal of jealousy granted to husbands, which could be removed if the authorities of the people judged that they were no longer deserving.

The most striking example of the removal of the privilege of a conviction based on strictly verifiable evidence and *hatra'ah* is the action of Simon b. Shetah in executing 80 women who were practicing witchcraft in Ashkelon. Simon b. Shetah's very name was closely associated with the strictest criteria in taking testimony. He was reticent to exercise the Written Torah's mandate to administer capital punishment for certain crimes. His action, nevertheless, is justified on the grounds that "the hour required (*tzerikhah*) such a measure."[93] The Talmud brings a *baraita* regarding this incident:

R. Eleazar b. Jacob said that I have received a tradition (*sham'ati*) that a court may inflict capital punishment not specifically prescribed in the Torah. This is not considered to be transgressing the words of the Torah, but is done in order to "make a fence for the Torah" . . . not because such a person is scripturally liable (*she-ra'uy le-kakh*), but because the hour requires it.[94]

In other words, an assessment of the social and political needs of the time was considered sufficient grounds for instituting capital punishment on an *ad hoc* basis.[95] Elsewhere, the Mishnah prescribes capital punishment for those who continually transgress negative commandments, and for those who committed murder in the presence of witnesses, but the testimony was deficient on some specific legal grounds.[96] The Gemara mentions absence of *hatra'ah* as a prime example.[97] Maimonides emphasizes that especially in cases of murder we take such extraordinary measures because murder is of such danger to society.[98] In discussing the responsibilities and obligations of the court, Maimonides writes:

It is forbidden for the court to take pity (*la-hus*) on the murderer, for they should not say, "One has already been killed, what purpose is there in killing this one?—And they will become derelict (*mitrashlin*) in their duty to execute him."[99]

Pity on murderers resulting in reticence to execute them is itself a form of social cruelty, both refusing to eliminate a dangerous person and to establish a deterrent to would-be murderers.[100]

Finally, Karo notes the opinion of Solomon ibn Adret:

Rashba wrote in a responsum, "it seems to me . . . that this is for the preservation of society (*mekuyyam ha'olam*), because if it bases everything on the laws collected in the Torah, and only does what the Torah prescribes as punishment in these and similar offenses, then society will be destroyed, for we require witnesses and *hatra'ah*. It is as the rabbis said that Jerusalem was destroyed only because they based their judgment on the law of the Torah."[101]

This radical interpretation is based on two rabbinic precedents. First, the Mishnah expresses the principle of the "maintenance of society" (*tikkun olam*) as a ground for changing earlier laws, which if allowed to remain unchanged would lead to social breakdown.[102] The second precedent is an aggadic passage indicating that at times the needs of society require one to go "beyond the letter of the law" (*lifnim mi-shurat ha-din*).[103] Usually, this principle is used to indicate a more lenient ruling.[104] Rashba, on the contrary, takes the destruction of Jerusalem as a model of societal collapse in general, and he attributes this to the fact that the authorities, by sticking to the letter of the law of capital punishment, contributed to that collapse. They should have recognized the danger to society in such leniency and acted accordingly.[105]

8. Abortion: Jewish and Noahide

The relation of Jewish and Noahide law is especially revealing regarding abortion.

The Babylonian Talmud records this Amoraic ruling:

R. Jacob bar Aha found it written in a book of sayings of the school of Rav . . . that a Noahide is liable for capital punishment even in the case of feticide—in the view of R. Ishmael. What are his grounds for this? It is written, "Whosoever sheds the blood of a human *within* a human (*adam ba'adam*) . . . " (Gen. 9:6). Who is a "human within a human?" This is the unborn child within its mother's womb.[106]

Maimonides codifies the law according to R. Ishmael's ruling. Since he does not quote the biblical proof-text, we can assume that he regarded the actual exegesis in the Talmud as merely descriptive of a truth known by reason alone.[107]

For Jews, feticide is not regarded by the Tannaitic sources as a capital offense, although it is prohibited in situations where the mother's life is not threatened by the fetus within her.[108] At this level, then, Jewish law is more lenient than Noahide law. Later in the Amoraic period, however, the Talmud constituted the following relations between the laws:

R. Jose b. Hanina said that any commandment given to Noahides and repeated at Mt. Sinai applies to both Noahides and Jews. If only given to Noahides but not repeated at Mt. Sinai, then it is for Jews but not for Noahides . . . It would seem that the opposite should be the case. However, *there is nothing permitted to Jews which is prohibited to non-Jews*.[109]

Jewish revealed law thus presupposes Noahide law and then goes on to demand an even stricter morality for Jews.

However, as the Noahide prohibition of abortion is unconditional, in that it does not consider threats to the mother's life, Noahide morality would appear to be stricter. The Tosafists, in an ingenious way, use the above principle thusly:

In this context one could say that abortion is permitted to Jews and prohibited to non-Jews. But some say that inasmuch as a Jewish mother can be saved from a threatening fetus, *it is possible that this is also the case with a non-Jewish mother as well.*[110]

The dispensation, therefore, in the case of a fetus threatening a mother's life (*ke-rodef ahareyha*) applies to both Jewish and non-Jewish mothers, just as any other abortion is prohibited to both.

Actually, two opposite options are possible: either to make Jewish abortion law as unconditional as Noahide law appears to be, or to make Noahide abortion law admit the Jewish dispensation. The Tosafists opted for the latter. The reason for this, it seems, stems from the Mishnaic principle, "one life is not destroyed for another" (*ein dohin nefesh mipnei nafesh*), a principle Maimonides declared rational.[111] Now if Jewish law refuses to declare the priority of one independent life over another, then how can it possibly rule that a dependent life (the fetus) has the priority over the independent life upon which it depends (the mother)? Where a fetus threatens the mother's life it is considered as part of her body and may be amputated as one would amputate a gangrenous limb.[112] In other situations, however, the unborn child cannot be regarded as a "limb" of its mother. Feticide in such a situation would certainly be, minimally, mutilation, which is prohibited.[113]

The new interpretation of the Tosafists deepens the Noahide definition of feticide put forth by R. Ishmael, on the basis of the halakhah subsequently developed by the Amoraim. Thus, in its relation to Jewish law, Noahide law adopts a more adequate view of abortion by including the dispensation in the case of the "pursuing fetus."

Just as specifically Jewish law in the area of abortion affected Noahide law, so Noahide law affected Jewish law.

The seventeenth-century German halakhist R. Yair Hayim Bachrach was petitioned by an adulterous woman, carrying her lover's child, requesting permission to abort the offspring of this union. Although he was tempted to grant her request because of certain legal technicalities, he nevertheless refused such permission because "of the clear and evident consensus between us and them (Christians) against abortion in the interest of curbing promiscuity and immorality."[114] In other words, general moral standards, universally accepted, take precedence over legal technicalities.

Later, the eighteenth-century Bohemian halakhist R. Ezekiel Landau warned against inferring any permission of abortion (where the life of the mother was not endangered) from the fact that abortion is not technically murder in halakhah. R. Landau emphasized that the Noahide designation of abortion as destruction of "a human within a human" applies to Jews as well.[115]

CHAPTER SIX

THE LAW OF SEXUAL RELATIONS

1. Introduction

Noahide law also prohibits certain sexual relations, in particular, incest, adultery, homosexuality and bestiality. In the *baraita* in the Talmud this prohibition is associated with the word "saying" (*l'emor*) which is taken in the sense of its use in Jer. 3:1, "*saying* if a man send away his wife." The implication is that this "sending away" is for sexual misconduct.[1] The association is mnemonic, and nothing more is made of it.

The general name for this legal grouping is *gilui arayot*, derived from the list of forbidden sexual relations in Lev. 18. In Leviticus, these relations are referred to euphemistically as "uncovering nakedness" (*galoh ervah*). This term is, for the most part, used in connection with forbidden consanguineous relations, primarily incest.

2. Incest

Philo presents two reasons for the prohibition of incest. First, he discusses it regarding parent–child relations:

What form of unholiness (*anosiourgēma*) could be more impious than this: that a father's bed, which should be kept untouched as something sacred (*hōs hieran*), should be brought to shame: that no respect should be shown for a mother's aging years ... Even among the Greeks these things were done in the old days in Thebes in the case of Oedipus the son of Laius. They were done in ignorance, not by deliberate intention (*ouch hekousiōgnōme*), and yet the marriage produced such a harvest of ills that nothing was wanting that could lead to such misery.[2]

Secondly, he discusses sibling incest:

Why hamper fellow-feeling (*koinōnias*) and intercommunion of men with men (*pro tous allous anthrōpous*) by compressing within the narrow space of each separate house the great and goodly plant which might extend and spread itself over continents and islands and the whole inhabited world? For intermarriages with outsiders creates new kinships.[3]

Philo is not advocating marriages between Jews and gentiles, a practice he explicitly condemns,[4] but rather advocating each generation breaking out of the consanguineous circle of the immediate family when marrying.

Philo's twofold discussion of incest offers two different reasons for the prohibition. Incest between parents and children (vertical or transgenerational incest) is prohibited because it violates the respect children owe their parents. Sexual intimacy contradicts their prior relationship. Restraint is necessary. Incest between siblings (horizontal or intergenerational incest), on the other hand, is forbidden because sexual intimacy should be extended outward. Sibling incest, then, contradicts this. Thus, in the same legal category, incest, we see two reasons for its prohibition: restraint as a centripetal moral motive and extension as a centrifugal moral motive.

This duality of motivation stems from Philo's Platonic metaphysics. Plato emphasizes that God is both the cause of a process of plenitude and a cause of a process of elimination.[5] However, one can also see Philo's discussion as dealing with two very different phenomena that must be dealt with differently. At this level, we can see how Philo's succinct examination provides an introduction to the rabbinic dialogue regarding incest.

With regard to the Noahide prohibition of incest, we find two opposing views, one inclusive, the other exclusive. The Tosefta provides the *locus classicus* of the Noahide law:

Every forbidden sexual union (*ervah*) for which a Jewish court executes one, Noahides are considered forewarned (*muzharin*). This is the view of R. Meir. The sages say that there are many forbidden sexual unions for which a Jewish court does not execute one but for which Noahides are considered forewarned. In these cases gentiles are judged according to gentile law; however, the one such case concerns the betrothed girl (*na'arah ha-me'usrasah*).[6]

In this dispute, R. Meir and the sages differ as to the extent of the applicability of the death penalty for forbidden sexual relations among gentiles. R. Meir makes it co-extensive with the applicability of the death penalty for Jews in similar cases. The sages, on the other hand, make an exception in the case of the betrothed girl since gentiles only regard a marriage as being valid after cohabitation.[7] Among Jews, at least *de jure*, there was no cohabitation during the betrothal period.[8] Nevertheless, both R. Meir and the sages agree that there is no difference between Jewish and Noahide law in terms of the extent of the prohibition of incest.

Another *baraita* attempts to derive this legal unanimity as follows: "our rabbis taught: . . . why does Scripture say, 'a man, a man' (*ish ish*) (Lev. 18:6)? To include gentiles who are prohibited to engage in forbidden sexual relations as are Jews."[9]

Another *baraita* presents the converse:

> It was taught: "Therefore a man shall leave his father and his mother" (Gen. 2:24) . . . R. Akiva says "his father" refers to his father's wife; "his mother" refers to his own mother (*imo mamash*); "he shall cleave" means not to a male; "unto to his wife" means not to his fellow's wife; "they shall be one flesh," namely, with whom he can become "one flesh," thus excluding domesticated and wild animals with whom he cannot become "one flesh."[10]

Maimonides quotes this *baraita* as presenting the Noahide law of incest and, then, based on the elaboration in the Gemara, lists six prohibitions: mother; stepmother; married woman; maternal sister; male; animal.[11]

We can see that whereas in other areas of forbidden sexuality there is hardly any difference between the two laws, in terms of incest difference exists at the sibling level. This difference led to two separate kinds of reflection by the rabbis. First, they were forced to realize that although the gentiles did have standards of sexual morality, they were not as precise as Jewish law. This type of reflection was in keeping with the notion that Noahide law is more general than Jewish law.[12] Second, recognition of difference between the two laws regarding sexuality led the rabbis to consider differences between sexuality inside and outside of a covenantal context.

In the area of strict halakhah regarding conversion, the question of the precise delineation of gentile incest becomes a practical problem. For what if a convert had already been married while a gentile, which marriage could be sanctioned when he became a Jew and which could not, because it was considered incestuous even on the Noahide level? Even though the legal fiction that "a convert by virtue of conversion is like a newborn child (*ke-katan she-nolad dami*)"[13] was given as the rationale for the convert's change of status, this principle was not used to totally sever prior biological ties lest conversion be used for legalized incest, whereby it could be said that "they came down from a stricter level of sanctity to a more lenient one!":

> A gentile must divorce both his paternal and his maternal sister. This is the view of R. Meir. R. Judah says he must divorce his maternal sister but may remain married to his paternal sister.[14]

Here the all-inclusive view of R. Meir is based on the verse "because of these abominations (*ha-to 'evot*) is the Lord your God disinheriting them before you" (Deut. 18:12), namely, for the very "abominations" that Israel has been forewarned (Lev. 18:26) the gentiles are being punished. We must, therefore, assume that they too have been forewarned.

In the parallel in the *Midrash Rabbah* this dispute is placed in the context of conversion, that is, "a convert who converted and was married to his sister . . . "[15] There the reason for R. Judah's view that a marriage with a paternal sister is valid is that "there is no fatherhood among the gentiles." This statement reflects the fact that the rabbis assumed that the gentiles among them took for granted only the maternal tie.

The greater tolerance for sibling incest than parental incest comes out in the following aggadah:

Scripture states, "If a man takes his sister the daughter of his father or the daughter of his mother and she sees his nakedness it is a reproach (*hesed*)" (Lev. 20:17). R. Abin said that one should not say that Cain's marrying his own sister and Abel's marrying his own sister are a reproach. Rather, I did a kindness (*hesed*) with the first ones so that the world might be built from them. "I said that the world is built by kindness" (Ps. 89:3).[16]

Here in the passage from Leviticus we see the word *hesed*, which usually translates as "kindness," used here as "reproach."[17] This aggadah plays on this opposite meaning and states that what is now a reproach was at the dawn of humanity a social necessity, namely, the outward extension of the human family, beginning with siblings. In the Babylonian Talmud, in a parallel text, we read:

R. Huna said that a gentile is permitted to marry his daughter. If you say, "why did not Adam marry his daughter?" The answer is in order that Cain might marry his sister so that "the world is built by kindness."[18]

These discussions are based on the older legend that Cain and Abel were each born with a twin sister, which explains how the Bible states, "and Cain knew his wife" (Gen. 4:17).[19] The assumption behind all of these discussions seems to be that sibling incest at a very primitive level might well be motivated by a desire to build a world, a motive itself considered good.[20] In one aggadic passage even the daughters of Lot, who committed incest with their father (Gen. 19:31–38), are considered "righteous" (*tzaddikim*) whereas Lot, whose motives were lustful only, is considered one of the "sinners" (*posh'im*).[21]

Incest between parents and children was rarely mentioned by the rabbis. When it was discussed, it was as the most sinful behavior possible.

In a halakhic context the Talmud states that the rabbis ruled that even though a convert is "born again," and therefore the ties of biology are severed, "direct incest" (*ervah gufah*) was prohibited so that the convert might not say, "one comes down from a stricter level of sanctity to a more lenient one."[22] Maimonides paraphrases:

According to Scriptural law (din Torah) a gentile is permitted to marry his mother or his maternal sister *when they have all converted*, but the sages forbade this . . . for yesterday she was forbidden to him and today she is permitted.[23]

In other words, incest with one's mother is taken as the most radical result possible if the rule that a convert is "born again" is not qualified. The important thing to remember is that no halakhic cases (ma'aseh) are brought dealing with mother–son marriages.

In an aggadic context, we read the following:

Ahaz permitted incest (hiteer ha'ervah). Manasseh had sexual relations with his sister. Ammon had sexual relations with his mother and Scripture states, "For he, Ammon, was exceedingly guilty" (II Chron. 33:23) . . . His mother said to him, "Do you have pleasure from the place whence you came out?" He said to her, "I am only doing this to anger my Creator (le-hakh'ees et Bor'i)"![24]

Here we see that the motivation for Ammon's incest with his mother was not sexual pleasure per se, but rather he chose it as the most extreme act of rebellion against God.

3. Sexuality as a Natural Right

Incest is seen as a misdirection of sexuality. The rabbinic tendency, especially in aggadic passages, emphasizes sublimation rather than repression or license. A famous aggadah relates how in the early days of the Second Temple the prayer of the people was answered that there no longer be any desire for idolatry.[25] Emboldened by answered prayer, they soon asked that sexual sin (yitzra d'abayrah) be eliminated. But an unintended consequence occurred: the loss of libido caused even the hens to cease laying eggs. To pray that sexuality be only directed to licit objects was considered impossible. Finally, it is related that they "blinded the eye" of incest, that is, they were able to sublimate their desire for incest but not for adultery.[26] In other words, sexuality is to be considered a biological and social necessity. Incest can only be dealt with on the secondary not the primary level of human consciousness.

The recognition that sexuality is a natural right comes out in the following halakhic dispute:

One who is half slave and half freeman is to serve his master one day and himself the other, in the opinion of the School of Hillel. The School of Shammai said to them . . . he may not marry a slave woman (shifhah) because he is already half a freeman; and

he may not marry a freewoman because he is still half a slave. Shall he do nothing?!
Was not the world created for reproduction as Scripture states, "He did not create it
as a void but formed it for dwelling" (Is. 45:18).[27]

The case here seems to involve a slave owned by two partners when only one
of them emancipated the slave.[28] The Mishnah goes on to indicate that both
schools finally agreed that he be fully emancipated and that he sign a note for
his emancipation price. Concerning this Mishnah, Boaz Cohen notes:

The phrase *nivra ha'olam* (the world was created) is the nearest the rabbis came to
the term *Natura*, which literally means to be born. Since the Beth Shammai invoke
natural law as their reason, they cite Is. 45:18 to which they find an allusion, and not
Gen. 1:28, which lays down the religious law from which the slave was exempt . . . [29]

Sexuality is a natural right precisely because its legitimacy is based on a
descriptive state of affairs rather than on a specific precept or admonition.
This is based on the biological connection between sexuality and procreation.
This also comes out in the Amoraic treatment of a dispute between the
schools of Hillel and Shammai regarding the commandment of "being fruitful and multiply" (Gen. 1:28, 9:1). The followers of Shammai require that one
have at least two sons; the followers of Hillel require a son and a daughter, as
the Torah states, "male and female he created them" (Gen. 5:2).[30] The Gemara
states that the reasoning of the Hillelites is based on "the creation of the
world" (*me-briyyato shel olam*).[31] This is important because the apparent admonition "being fruitful and multiply" is taken in the descriptive rather than the
prescriptive sense. Procreation is inferred then in imitation of nature.

4.   The Primacy of the Family

The prohibition of incest is not to be taken as anti-sexual, but as pro-sexual in
that it is seen as directing sexual drives to proper and satisfactory objects.
Therefore, the familial tie has to be considered the most basic inter-human
relationship. The question arises, however, whether the general human familial tie is one that Judaism presupposes, or does Judaism consider the Jewish
familial tie to be an essential break with the Noahide past? Conversion, in the
following dispute, again highlights differences between Jewish and Noahide
law:

It has been stated that if one had children while a gentile and then converted: R.
Johanan said that he has fulfilled the commandment of procreation; and Resh
Lakish said that he had not . . . R. Johanan said . . . because he has children (*de-ha-
havu layh*); and R. Lakish said . . . that a convert is like a newborn child.[32]

THE LAW OF SEXUAL RELATIONS

Does conversion sever prior biological and social ties of a Noahide? For Resh Lakish, the convert's break with the Noahide past is total; for R. Johanan, it is not. In the Babylonian Talmud it is assumed that even for Resh Lakish gentile familial ties *for gentiles* are recognized.[33] Here only slaves are denied these ties (*she'ein lo hayyas*), a point certainly having empirical validity at the time.[34] In the Palestinian Talmud, conversely, the debates centers not on conversion but whether gentiles have family ties at all:

Concerning a gentile man who had sexual relations with a gentile woman and she gave birth: R. Johanan said that gentiles do not have familial ties (*yahasim*); R. Simon b. Lakish said that they do.[35]

This issue is of course crucial for the Noahide law of sexual relations. If there are no familial bonds, then there is neither incest nor adultery.[36] I suspect that it was because of these implications that later Amoraim, who had accepted fully the concept of Noahide law, did not wish to deal with, that the editors of the Babylonian Talmud transposed the earlier debate between R. Johanan and Resh Lakish and framed it around the retroactive effects of conversion.

Although Maimonides codifies the law according to R. Johanan, he does attempt to mediate between the two views by qualifying the ruling of R. Johanan to apply only when the children of the convert also converted.[37] This is a remarkable concession to Resh Lakish that gentile family ties are not acknowledged after conversion, that "be fruitful and multiply" in effect means "be fruitful and multiply *as Jews*." According to one Talmudic passage, because this commandment was not repeated at Mount Sinai, it applies to Jews alone.[38] Maimonides' qualification appears to be based on his own opinion, as Alfasi, whom he usually follows, has no such qualification.[39]

All of this follows Maimonides' position regarding Noahide law, which he regards as a branch of Jewish law to be enforced by Jews.[40] The revelation at Mount Sinai, therefore, is the source for both laws. In the area of sexual relations, Maimonides writes:

Before the giving of the Torah a man would run into a woman in the marketplace. If they both desired that he take her, he would bring her into his house and copulate with her.[41]

Hence, for Maimonides, the Torah is the ultimate standard for universal sexual morality. The recognition of any law prior to Sinai is, then, only meaningful when retroactively viewed from Sinaitic law. Maimonides considers, along these lines, anything less than the covenantal marital bond (*kiddushin*) to be fornication.[42] His contemporary and critic, R. Abraham b. David of Posquieres (Rabad), pointed out that the Torah accepted the institution of concubinage, a common practice in the ancient world.[43] Maimonides, on the other hand, with his usual consistency, could not admit any real, religiously acceptable, institutions not rooted in divine law. As such, pre- or extra-Sinaitic familial bonds cannot be recognized, at least by Jews, in any tangible way.

This issue comes out in the Palestinian Talmud:

We have learned that the gentiles do not have marriage (*kiddushin*); do they then have divorce (*gayrushin*)? R. Judah b. Pazi and R. Hanin in the name of R. Honeh the Elder of Sepphoris: either they have no divorce, or both of them divorce each other.[44]

The assumption is that there is no marriage among gentiles at all. If this were the case, there would no point in asking about gentile divorce. Rather, the text assumes that Jewish marriage is not the same as gentile marriage, which is a sort of civil contract. As such, one cannot expect gentiles to regard divorce as Jews do, that is, as the dissolution of a covenantal bond. Therefore, the question is whether there is any formal divorce process at all, or whether the contract must be formally dissolved by both parties. In the Gemara (referring to Mal. 2:16), divorce is regarded as the breaking of a covenant. It is emphasized that the term "God of Israel" is used there. As covenantal dissolution, divorce is regarded as something for which Jews require a specific divine sanction. Considering the context of this text—following the rise of Christianity in Roman Palestine—it might very well be a polemic against Christian claims that covenantal marriage is essentially indissoluble.[45] However, for our purposes, the text clearly reflects an acknowledgment of gentile family bond, but also a recognition that revelation has elevated Jewish family bonds from the biologically and socially necessary to the level of the sacred.

The issue of whether the non-Jewish familial tie, specifically the non-Jewish marital tie, has any real significance in Jewish law came to the fore in recent halakhic discussion. The discussion centers on civil marriage between Jews. Is civil marriage a "Jewish marriage"? If so, divorce would require a *get* (formal Jewish divorce document); if not, then a civil divorce would suffice. The question is relevant because civil marriages are often, if not always, entered into by Jews of the most minimal religious commitment. Usually they have been civilly divorced long before the question of a Jewish divorce ever occurs to them. More often than not a contemplated remarriage to an observant Jew, or a turn to traditional practice, presents the question of whether the previous civil marriage was indeed properly dissolved or not. In many cases, the former spouse is either unwilling to participate in a Jewish divorce procedure, or cannot be found.

Many modern halakhists have dealt with this question, offering variant opinions either requiring or not a Jewish divorce over and above the civil divorce.[46] Although he stopped short of putting his view into practice, R. Jehiel J. Weinberg (d. 1966) did argue against the requirement of a Jewish divorce in such cases.[47] In a responsum to this question, Weinberg introduced the issue of Noahide law.[48] He argued that the halakhah recognizes marriages and that Maimonides ruled that such marriages are terminated when "the woman is sent forth on her own from the man's domain."[49] Weinberg concludes from this that any union, even between two Jews, falls into the category of such a Noahide marriage and a civil divorce suffices to terminate it.

R. Weinberg's attempt to include the modern institution of civil marriage under the rubric of Noahide law is part of a process that recognizes the validity of non-Jewish institutions when there is no direct conflict with Jewish law. His own modern recognition of the civil character of Noahide law can be traced back to Moses Mendelssohn.[50] But as an Orthodox halakhist, he could not use Mendelssohn's views as precedent.[51] The only authority he could employ was Maimonides. Weinberg's use of Maimonides' ruling, I have argued elsewhere, is problematic precisely because Maimonides does not appear to recognize any *real* validity of Noahide law for Jews.[52] Weinberg would have been better served by Rabad's use of concubinage.[53] Nevertheless, for our purposes, we can see how the relation between Noahide and Jewish law can provide a basis for dealing with problems raised by the fact that most Jews live as individual citizens under secular governments. Because this is a modern institution, halakhah does not have any ready precedents.[54]

On the more philosophical level, the acknowledgment of gentile familial ties comes out in the attempt to uncover a rationale for the commandments to honor one's parents. Saadiah Gaon writes:

> . . . in order that men might not become like beasts with the result that no one would know his father so as to show him reverence in return for having raised him . . . A further reason was that a human being might know the rest of his relations . . . and show them whatever tenderness he was capable of.[55]

In other words, the integrity of the family requires both the positive respect due to parents as well as the negative restraint from incest—both points first presented by Philo. Other medieval theologians presented similar views.[56] The fact that honor and reverence of parents are not included among the Noahide laws is because, as the doctrine was expanded in the Babylonian Talmud, only negative commandments are included in this list.[57] Nevertheless, the model of familial respect was considered to be the gentile Dama b. Netinah.[58] Even Esau, the assumed progenitor of Rome, about whom the rabbis usually had little good to say, is credited with honoring his mother and father and receiving reward from God for it.[59]

From all of these treatments of the relation between Noahide and Jewish law in this area, the following question emerges: is the Torah to be viewed as an antidote for the evils of the world bereft of revelation, or is it the fulfillment of humanity's deepest potential? If the latter, then revelation has a positive precondition, one that can be used as a positive criterion of judgment. In the former, however, then revelation has only a negative precondition, with the Torah filling a moral void.[60] However, both views cannot dispense with what precedes the giving of the Torah and what remains beyond its range. The "border concept" (*Grenzbegriff*) of the Noahide is indispensable for both points of view in their formulation of a cogent philosophical position.[61]

5. Homosexuality and Bestiality

The universal ban of homosexuality must be understood within the context of the emphasis of heterosexuality, procreation and the family as the natural state of humanity. We have seen that the rabbis understood the Noahide bans on incest and adultery as being rooted in this natural state. The ban on homosexuality follows from this in that it contradicts heterosexuality, procreation and the family.

In the aggadah heterosexuality is seen as rooted in the essentially bisexual nature of humanity: "R. Jeremiah b. Eleazar said that the first man had two faces . . . as it is written, 'male and female He created *them*'" (Gen. 5:2).[62] This theme appears in other rabbinic texts: "R. Eliezer said that they were created as a hermaphrodite (*androgynos*) . . . R. Samuel said He created him with two faces front and back and split him and sawed in two."[63] This notion of the original bisexuality of humanity, confirmed by modern embryology, was prevalent in the ancient world.[64] Its most famous enunciation came from Plato.[65] The idea here is that humanity's experience of itself as lacking the "other side" is the source of heterosexuality.[66] Thus incest, and, especially, homosexuality, are regressions in that they do not seek the "other side." Only the successful consummation of this quest for the other side leads to the recognizable family unit and the possibility of procreation.

Concerning R. Akiva's exegesis of "he shall cleave" (unto his wife—Gen. 2:24) as meaning "not to a male," Rashi comments:

For there is no cleaving (*dibbuk*), because the passive partner (*ha-noshkav*) not receiving pleasure does not cleave with him (*immo*). It is from the seed which goes forth from the mother and the father that "one flesh" is made.[67]

Here Rashi makes two important points. First, homosexual intercourse *per anum* is not the same as heterosexual vaginal intercourse.[68] It is not that the passive homosexual partner does not receive pleasure—homosexuals would surely dispute that—but rather the pleasure of *male–female union* is precluded. Secondly, such homosexual pairings preclude procreation.[69] In other words, Rashi understands "one flesh *(basar ehad)*" on two levels: one, the level of the union of the male and female bodies; two, the possibility of a new body emerging from this union in conception and then in birth.

Homosexuality as a manifestation of total gentile sinfulness emerges from an interpretation of the following verse: "And they called to Lot and they said to him, 'where are the men who came to you? Bring them out to us that we might know them *(ve-ned'ah otam)*'" (Gen. 19:5). In *Targum Pseudo-Jonathan* the last phrase is interpreted to mean "that we might have intercourse with them." Other aggadic texts present the same point.[70] Obviously, the aggadists took the verb "to know" *(yado'a)* in the sense of "carnal knowledge" as in, for example, "and the man knew *(yada)* Eve, his wife, and she conceived . . . " (Gen. 4:1). Since the Torah designates the Sodomites to be "exceedingly wicked and sinful unto the Lord" (Gen. 13:13),[71] the designation of their most explicit sin as homosexual rape indicates the rabbis' view of this as an essentially gentile problem, perhaps in the same way that the French once referred to homosexuality as *le vice anglais*.

In halakhah the assumption of the prevalence of gentile homosexuality can be seen in this passage:

One is not to place an animal in the inns of the gentiles because they are suspected of bestiality *(she-hashudin al he-rebiyah)*; nor is a woman to be alone with them because they are suspected of sexual immorality *(ha'arayot)* . . . [72]

To this Mishnaic list, the Tosefta adds, "a child is not to be turned over to him (a gentile) either for book learning or to learn a trade, nor to be alone with him."[73] Here again, in terms of actual practice the reality of one's particular society would have to be taken into consideration. This text, no doubt, represents a response to the reality of the Greco-Roman world.

That homosexuality is considered contrary to natural heterosexuality and procreation is brought out in the following text: "Bar Kappara said to R. Judah the Prince, 'what does abomination (Lev. 20:13) mean?' . . . Thus said the Merciful One, 'abomination,' that is 'something in which you go astray *(to'eh attah bah)*.'"[74] Rabbenu Nissim indicates that this refers to "one who puts aside intercourse with a woman and goes to a man." The twentieth-century exegete R. Baruch Ha-Levi Epstein wrote similarly: "It seems as though the intent of this is that he goes astray from the ways of the foundations of creation to lie with a man."[75]

Whereas there are numerous allusions to the prevalence of homosexuality among the gentiles, it was assumed that this was not a Jewish problem. Thus when the Tanna, R. Judah, ruled that two bachelors should not sleep under one blanket, it is recorded that the other rabbis stated that such a ruling was not needed because "Jews are not suspected (*l'o nehshedu*) of male homosexual intercourse."[76] In the later sources there is discussion of whether Jewish homosexuality is not conditioned by the type of society in which Jews live. R. Joel Sirkes, a sixteenth-century authority, noted that Karo suggested that the strict ruling of R. Judah concerning avoidance of close physical contact between males be again followed because homosexuality was a problem in his society (Muslim Turkey and Palestine). Sirkes observes that in his society (Christian Poland), however, homosexuality was not a real problem and, therefore, such strictures were not required.[77]

Concerning lesbianism, the rabbinic sources state:

R. Huna said that women who roll together (*ha-mesolelot*) are unfit (*pesulot*) to marry priests. Does this follow the view of R. Eliezer, who said that a single man (*panui*) who has intercourse with a single woman (*penuyah*), not for the sake of marriage, makes her a prostitute (*zonah*)? These words refer to a man, but with a woman it is just general lewdness (*peritzuta b'alma*).[78]

According to Rashi these women are engaging in genital contact.[79]

Now the question becomes: we have heard the penalty for this activity, where is the prohibition? Maimonides writes:

It is forbidden for women to engage in sexual relations with each other. We are prohibited to do this by Scripture which states, "according to the practice of the land of Egypt you shall not do" (Lev. 18:3). The sages said, "what were they doing?" A man married a man and a woman married a woman and a woman was married to two men . . . And a man should be concerned about this matter with his wife and prevent (*u'mone'a*) women who are known to do this from associating with his women and they with him.[80]

As common in the *Mishneh Torah*, Maimonides does not cite his rabbinic source.

In the *Sifra*, commenting on Lev. 18:3, we read: "And some say that Egypt is steeped in immorality (*shetufim*). Just as the Canaanites are steeped in idolatry, incest, bloodshed, male homosexuality and bestiality, so indeed is the practice of Egypt."[81] In the *Midrash Rabbah*, the following elaboration is offered:

R. Hiyya taught why is "I am the Lord" repeated twice (Lev. 18:3 and 4)? I am He who punished the generation of the Flood and Sodom and Egypt; I will in the future punish whoever does according to their deeds. The generation of the Flood was blotted out from the world because they were steeped in immorality (*shetufin be-zenut*) . . . R. Huna said in the name of R. Jose that the generation of the Flood was only blotted out from the world because they wrote marriage contracts (*gomasiyot*) for males and for females (*u-la-nekevah*).[82]

Although there is some question whether the correct reading of this may not actually be "they wrote marriage contracts . . . for animals (*le-vehemah*),"[83] it seems as though Maimonides derived the prohibition of lesbianism from the version in the *Midrash Rabbah* plus the designation of the Babylonian Talmud of lesbianism as "general lewdness." Also, Maimonides' experience as a court physician in Egypt, where lesbianism was no doubt a problem in the royal harem among females sequestered alone, may well have influenced his awareness of this issue.

The accusation that the generation of the Flood actually wrote marriage contracts for homosexual unions has a parallel in the Babylonian Talmud:

Ulla said there are thirty commandments which the Noahides accepted upon themselves, but they only uphold three of them. One, they do not write a marriage contract for males . . . [84]

Rashi makes a crucial distinction between private practice and public policy:

Even though they are suspected of homosexuality and sequester themselves with males for intercourse, nevertheless, they are not so irresponsible about this commandment that they would write a marriage contract for them.

There is an essential difference, then, between a society where homosexuality is prevalent and one that gives it official sanction. There is also an interesting parallel in the writings of Suetonius, the Roman historian. He reports that Nero wrote a marriage contract for one of his favorite lovers.[85] Whether or not this text in the Babylonian Talmud was influenced by this instance is impossible to say. However, although the text is Babylonian, its author, Ulla, emigrated from Roman Palestine.[86] Perhaps even in the Greco-Roman world where individual homosexuality was quite common, Nero's elevation of a homosexual relationship to the level of marriage was considered a breach of societal norms, an incident of moral decadence. If the text in the *Midrash Rabbah* and the Babylonian Talmud did have this instance in mind, it was considered atypical even in a society whose customs were generally regarded as morally inferior to Jewish standards.

The prohibition of bestiality is derived by R. Akiva from the words of Gen. 2:24, "and they shall become one flesh," which excludes animals with whom humans do not share "one flesh."[87] Bestiality is not only contrary to heterosexuality, procreation and the family, but it even excludes the human mutuality present in homosexual relationships. Because of this, bestiality was considered to be the epitome of depravity. For example, in the rabbinic attempt to diminish any possible virtue of Balaam, he was depicted as guilty of bestiality. When his she-ass speaks to him—"I am your she-ass upon whom you have ridden" (Num. 22:30)—one aggadic passage interprets it as "me upon whom you ride during the day and engage in sexual relations (*ishut*) at night."[88]

Nevertheless, the rabbis did recognize that at the level of what psychoanalysts call "primary process," bestiality is a human possibility. Thus when the Torah states about animals, "He brought them unto the man to see what he would call them" (Gen. 2:19), the Talmud adds:

R. Eleazar said that why did Scripture state, "this time it is bone from my bones and flesh from my flesh" (Gen. 2:23)? It teaches that Adam had sexual relations with every animal and beast, but was not satisfied until he had sexual relations with Eve.[89]

Eve satisfied him because with her he could once again—following the motif of humanity's primordial bisexuality—"become one flesh" and, also, because with her alone could he speak.[90] In this aggadic reading we see that bestiality is only ruled out after humanity has risen to the level of full consciousness. Like the treatment of sibling incest, the rabbis seem to have recognized that the overcoming of those types of sexuality, which they recognized as less than fully human, may be, nevertheless, necessary steps in the development of human consciousness as a sexual being.

CHAPTER SEVEN

THE LAW OF ROBBERY

1. Introduction

The prohibition of robbery (*ha-gezel*) is the sixth Noahide law. In the rabbinic attempt to derive these laws from Gen. 2:16, this prohibition is found in the words, "from every tree of the garden you may surely eat, but from the tree of knowledge of good and evil you may not eat." The transgression of the command was considered to be tantamount to robbing God.[1] By extension, then, robbing humans was considered prohibited. On the level of plain meaning, this prohibition makes the most evident sense from the wording of the verse than the other prohibitions.

The prohibition of robbery requires the concept of property. If society is a human necessity, then most would agree that at the minimal level it functions as medium for economic exchange, of things between persons. There is division of labor, because exchange presupposes that different persons are related to different things in different ways. This relation of people to things is what we call *property*. Society prescribes the rules whereby these relations change.

The necessary prohibition of robbery, if there is to be a consistent system of division of labor, is brought out with great cogency by Saadiah Gaon:

Theft was forbidden by [divine] Wisdom because, if it were permitted, some men would rely on stealing others' wealth, and they would neither till the soil nor engage in any other occupation. And if all were to rely on this source of livelihood, even stealing would become impossible, with the disappearance of all property, there would be absolutely nothing in existence that might be stolen.[2]

2. The Double Standard of Robbery

As noted previously, there are a number of distinctions between Jewish and Noahide law concerning robbery.[3] We are dealing with four possible relations: a gentile robbing another gentile; a gentile robbing a Jew; a Jew robbing a gentile; and a Jew robbing another Jew.

In a *baraita* we learn that concerning robbery, whether stealing or robbing or taking a war-bride (*yefat to'ar*) or the like: (1) a gentile robbing a gentile; (2) a gentile robbing a Jew—this is prohibited (*asur*); (3) a Jew robbing a gentile—this is permitted (*muttar*).[4]

The fourth prohibition—a Jew robbing another Jew—is explicitly presented in the Torah.[5]

In the chapters on adjudication and blasphemy we saw how this law developed. Although, as some scholars have noted, this double standard may well have been part of legislation put forth at the time of extreme persecution of the Jews by the Romans, where a *de facto* state of war between Jews and gentiles required the formulation of laws designed to protect Jewish economic survival, nevertheless, less bellicose circumstances required considerable redefinition.[6] Rabban Gamliel II ruled that if the practice of this law led to *hillul ha-Shem*, that is, the appearance of the moral inferiority of Judaism, then it was not to be followed.[7] This innovation presupposes that under normal circumstances of generally peaceful social interaction between Jews and gentiles, robbery is something anti-social. In the Middle Ages, Meiri indicated that Christians and Muslims, adherents of law-abiding monotheisms, were exempt from the double standard; it applied to the lawless only.[8]

These three criteria—*hillul ha-Shem*, the anti-social nature of robbery and whether gentiles abide by law—are logically related. For *if robbery is inherently anti-social, then this will only be recognized by people who are committed to lawfulness, and only these people could have moral contempt for another people and their religion which are seemingly devoid of this elementary lawfulness.*

3. Greater Noahide Strictures

Despite the consistent and successful rabbinic efforts to do away with the moral scandal of the double standard, there was no attempt to do away with the fact that the Noahide law was stricter in terms of the prescribed definition of what was considered robbery, and the prescribed punishment for the crime.

The punishment for robbery, and as we have seen for transgressions of all the other Noahide laws, is death.[9] Whether the rabbis meant that every such transgression entailed capital punishment, or theoretically deserved capital punishment, is difficult to ascertain.[10] However, considering the evidence that suggests Noahide law was more theoretical than actually a legal practice, I suspect that the latter interpretation of the requirement of capital punishment is correct.

Regarding the exact definition of robbery, we read:

There is nothing permitted to Jews which is prohibited to gentiles. What about the war-bride? There we have learned that the gentiles are not entitled to the victor's spoils (*de-l'av bnai kibbush*). What about robbery less than a *perutah*'s worth? There we have learned because they are not forgiving (*de-l'av bnai meheelah*).[11]

In other words, whereas a Jew is only legally culpable for theft of a *perutah*'s worth or more, a gentile is legally responsible for theft of any amount no matter how small the sum. In Talmud times, a *perutah* or its equivalent in goods was considered the minimum amount acceptable for any full transaction.[12]

This text in the Babylonian Talmud must be analyzed in order to see some of the problems entailed by the differences in legal culpability between Jews and non-Jews regarding robbery.

The Gemara quotes another text as seemingly contradicting the principle that "nothing permitted to Jews is prohibited to gentiles." The other text states that "they [the gentiles] are not forgiving."[13] The generalization about Jewish law being stricter than non-Jewish law, but not vice versa, seems to be a later principle. Thus, this later principle seemed to contradict an earlier one.[14] Because of this, the earlier principle concerning a Noahide's stealing less than a *perutah*'s worth, required further clarification. On the surface, it simply means that Jewish law is more lenient with Jews than with gentiles. The coupling of this law of the war-bride, namely, the right of a Jewish soldier to take any gentile woman he so chose for a wife as his victor's spoils,[15] indicates that this was no doubt the original meaning of this difference in the definition of what legally constituted robbery.

Furthermore, another question arises about the phrase, "they are not forgiving." The words literally mean, "they are not children of forgiveness." We must now inquire whether these words are meant as a *de facto* description, namely, the empirical generalization that gentiles, unlike Jews, are not forgiving even of thefts of less than a *perutah*; or whether these words are meant as a *de jure* prescription, namely, there is something in Noahide law that excludes this type of forgiveness. The former involves the whole area of historical comparison and comparative jurisprudence; the latter involves philosophical reflection on the conceptual relation between Noahide law and the full Torah.

4. An Aggadic View

As noted earlier, the greater stringency of Noahide law can be either a criterion of positive or negative comparison.[16] As a negative comparison, it functions as a historical observation of the prevalent cruelty of the non-Jewish world, no doubt the rabbinic reaction to the Greco-Roman world. When the rabbis judged that the gentile environment had changed (e.g., Christian or Muslim society as opposed to the pagan society), they reinterpreted the law accordingly.[17] As a positive comparison, the rabbis saw Noahide law as the minimal social standard that the Torah presupposes. Changes in Jewish law, which make it more lenient, occur because of the special covenantal status of Israel. However, Noahide law may be reintroduced even among Jews if there is a fall into moral anarchy.

The following passage from the Palestinian Talmud reflects the view that punishing robbery of less than a *perutah*'s worth in Noahide law is a reaction to the low moral state of the gentiles:

R. Aha said that it is written in Scripture, "for the land was filled with violence (*hamas*) from before them" (Gen. 6:13). What did the violent one (*hamsan*) do? A person would go out bearing a basket filled with some lupine. They plotted to take them from him in amounts less than a *perutah*'s worth: something which cannot be adjudicated (*she'eino yotz'e ba-dayyanim*) . . . So it was also with Sodom and Gomorrah.[18]

In a later elaboration, we read:

What is "violence" and what is "robbery"? R. Hanina said that "violence concerns at least a *perutah*'s worth; "robbery" less than that . . . So the Holy One Blessed be He said, "you have not done fairly (*keshurah*), so I will not do fairly with you."[19]

From these two accounts the following theory emerges. Under normal circumstance of social good-will and interaction, theft of less than *perutah*'s worth is ignored. However, under abnormal conditions, where is there is no social good-will and interaction, society becomes a state of war, then every act of robbery, no matter how small the amount, becomes an act of aggression. As such, society must legislate harsher and more precise punishments. The Noahide law of robbery is thus interpreted in this manner.

The notion that gentile robbery is an act of aggression, both against fellow gentiles and Jews, emerges from a discussion where R. Pappa introduces the concept of gentiles "not being forgiving."[20] The Gemara raises the question, that if Jews are indeed "forgiving," then why can it not be assumed that a Jew would forgive a gentile who robbed him of less than a *perutah*'s worth? The Gemara answers by stating that even were the Jew to do this, the fact that the gentile troubled him at the time of the robbery (*tza'ara be-sha'atayh*) cannot be ignored. This answer appears to be based on the notion that gentile robbery, especially of a Jew, is taken as an act motivated more by anti-Jewish hostility than greed. Therefore Jewish law is dealing more with the actual protection of Jewish rights than with punishing and preventing the crime of robbery per se.

Another example of how the rabbis viewed gentile cruelty can be seen in the Mishnah:

He who kidnaps a Jewish person (*nefesh me-yisrael*) is not legally liable for punishment (*hayyab*) until he brings him into his domain (*le-reshuto*). R. Judah says until he brings him into his domain and uses him, as Scripture states, "And he shall enslave him (*ve-hit'amer bo*) and sell him . . . " (Deut. 24:4).[21]

The Babylonian Talmud interprets the first opinion in the Mishnah as ruling that even if the use of the kidnap victim were worth less than a *perutah*'s worth, the kidnapper is still liable for punishment.[22] Now since concern over even less than a *perutah* is considered to be a sign of the character of gentiles but not of Jews, the Gemara's exegesis appears to be saying that the heinousness of the crime of kidnapping is precisely because it is an act where one Jew treats another as a gentile treats others. Here again we see that robbery of this sort is taken to be motivated not by greed but by aggression.

R. Hanokh Zundel, a nineteenth-century commentator to the *Midrash Rabbah*, notes: "According to strict justice (*middat ha-din he-yesharah le-gamrai*) one should not steal less than a *perutah*'s worth."[23] In other words, in principle no one should steal anything at all. However, the moral climate of a society will determine at what point actual punishment is called for. Along these lines of the morality of theft, Philo earlier wrote:

Let a man then learn from his earliest years to filch nothing by stealth that belongs to another, however small it shall be, because custom (*ethos*) in the course of time is stronger than nature, and little things (*ta mikra*) if not checked grow and thrive till they attain to great dimensions.[24]

Rabbinic sources emphasize the greater compassion and forgiving attitudes of Jews as opposed to gentiles. They considered compassion, modesty and kindness central Jewish character traits.[25] Maimonides adds:

It is forbidden for one to be cruel (*akhzari*) . . . but he should be easy to please and hard to anger . . . and this is the way of the Jewish people (*zer'a yisrael*) and their mind is firm, but the gentiles, the uncircumcised of heart, are not so.[26]

5. Rashi

Rashi appears to follow the above aggadic view, that is, that the more stringent Noahide law is a result of the lower moral standards of gentiles. He writes:

Israel too is commanded concerning robbery, but less than a *perutah*'s worth is not considered robbery in their eyes, because they are not punctilious (*she'ovreen al middatan*). They are compassionate and forgiving in minor matters (*davar kal*), but Noahides are cruel (*akhzareem*).[27]

Elsewhere Rashi stresses the above even more strongly. The context is the

Amoraic rationale for the Tannaitic requirement that a prospective convert be told, among other things, about the specific laws regarding various leavings of agricultural produce for the poor (leket, etc.).[28] The Gemara sets the rationale: "R. Hiyya bar Abba said in the name of R. Johanan that a Noahide is executed for stealing less than a perutah's worth and is not exonerated by returning the lost article (ve-lo neettan le-heshavon)."[29] Rashi comments:

So that they not say that these poor are robbers (gazlanim) and stand against them and execute them according to their laws (be-dinayhem). For Noahides are prohibited concerning robbery . . . therefore, a Noahide is executed for robbing less than a perutah's worth, because a gentile is scrupulous (kapeed) about a minor thing concerning which Jews are forgiving.[30]

That is to say, he sees the more stringent Noahide law as being an example of the absence of compassion among gentiles. The aggadah indicated that it is in response to this gentile cruelty that the Torah made the Noahide law of robbery stricter. Rashi is not always consistent on whether this is an example of gentile cruelty or the Torah's response to it. The above quote would appear to suggest the former. But elsewhere Rashi implies the latter:

It is not to be returned but he is executed for it. It is concerning Israel that it is written, "he shall return (ve-hesheev) the stolen thing which he stole" (Lev. 5:23). Concerning Noahides, however, we say that their death penalty is their prohibition. Because he has transgressed one of the seven commandments he is executed.[31]

Rashi in another passage suggests that the verse, "you shall not cheat (lo ta'ashok) your neighbor (Lev. 19:13)" refers to Jews alone.[32] Gentile robbery, then, is more than mere robbery. This is in contrast to Jewish law.

In sum, then, Rashi reiterates the aggadic view that the death penalty for robbery is the Torah's reaction to the viciousness of gentile society. However, we can also see him suggesting that excessive capital punishment in their law is the result of their basic cruelty.[33] Thus the halakhah's de jure requirement of capital punishment in these cases is in effect a confirmation of de facto gentile practices. We have already seen how there was a tendency among the rabbis to be repelled by the prevalence of capital punishment.

6. Samuel Atlas

Samuel Atlas offers a modern interpretation of the Noahide law of robbery. He argued that the distinction between Noahide and Jewish law of robbery was the rabbis' way of making a distinction between natural and covenantal law.

Atlas indicates that on the level of natural law (ba-mishpat ha-tiv'i), robbery is prohibited regardless of amount.[34] He bases his argument on Maimonides' assertion that "specifications (ha-she'urin) were only given to Israel."[35] Now although Maimonides made this statement in the context of the law of the torn limb, Atlas nevertheless takes it as a characterization of all of Jewish law in contrast to Noahide law. Noahide law, then, is more general; Jewish law is marked by its greater specificity.[36] He therefore insists that "they are not forgiving" refers not to a de facto observation about gentile morality, but instead means that gentiles are not subject to the laws of waiving rights (de-l'av bnei dinei meheelah), laws particular to Jewish law. Whatever other specifications they might have for gentiles are to be determined by the authorities in their own societies.[37] Atlas also takes issue with Rashi's observation that "gentiles are cruel." This a posteriori generalization is too broad to be useful, and there are too many exceptions for it to be rationally and legally convincing.[38]

Finally, Atlas emphasizes the following:

A Jew is obligated for commandments in the category of positive acts (kum v'aseh) such as the laws concerning various leavings of agricultural produce for the poor and positive commandments (mitzvoth aseh), which do not pertain to a Noahide . . . It follows from this that one who comes to convert . . . has a change in status (shinui ma'amado) as a Jew, a member of the witnessing community of Israel, from that of a Noahide, who is only a social creature (ke-yetzeer hevrati bilvad).[39]

In other words, the greater privileges of Jewish law are due to the covenantal status of the Jewish people, a status that requires greater solidarity and, consequently, a de-emphasis on privacy and individual rights. Atlas' theory, then, does not constitute a de facto comparison between Jewish and gentile legal practice. Rather, it represents a de jure comparison between Noahide law, as the general background of Jewish law, and Jewish law as its higher specification. The relation is formal not material, a priori and not a posteriori.

Although I do not accept Atlas' neo-Kantian view of natural law,[40] I do find his theory of Noahide law, especially in reference to the law of robbery, to be of great philosophical value. Moreover, one can find examples in the rabbinic sources that add further credence to this theory.

The notion that Jews have the right of waiver (meheelah) for certain lost or stolen items, and that we assume that such is the case even without a specific stipulation, is the essence of the concept of ye'ush, that is, the act of disclaiming one's property.[41] The Talmud discusses many cases and attempts to determine whether or not ye'ush can be assumed. The question here is: how much of the law of ye'ush is based on an assessment of the de facto state of affairs in any society, and how much of it is based on theoretical definitions of who does and does not have this legal right?

Concerning orphans it is stated that they are not "children of forgiving," that is, we do not assume ye'ush in connection with their property.[42] This assumption is not based on what they do or do not do, but rather on the lack of their legal power to do so. Rashi states that as "minors (*ketanim*) they do not have the power to make their property ownerless (*hefker*)."[43] Now the concept of *ye'ush* presupposes *hefker*, that is, in order to assume a disclaimer on another's property, it must be assumed that one has the legal power to disown that property.[44] Thus the foundation of *ye'ush* and *meheelah* is the legal question of ownership and the exercise of nullification. The relation between minors and things is not as extensive in terms of rights as that between adults and things.

The legal relation between the laws of *me'ush* and *meheelah* is recounted in the Tosefta:

One who purchases an animal from his fellow and found on it an item worth a *perutah*, he is obligated to announce (*le-hakhreez*) it, as Scripture states, "a garment" (*salmah*—Ex. 22:8). Just as a garment (*simlah*) is distinguished by being worth a *perutah* and one is obligated to announce it, so is one obligated to announce any item (*kol davar*) which is worth a *perutah*, but not less.[45]

The verse that this exegesis is based on is compared with the following one, " . . . and you shall do this [that is, announce the finding of a neighbor's lost article] for his garment and so shall you do for every lost article of your brother which shall be lost from him . . . " (Deut. 22:3). The Mishnah comments:

Surely a garment is in the category of all these things. Why was it singled out (*lamah yatz'at*)? To use it as a basis of comparison, namely, just as a garment is distinguished by having identifying marks (*seemanim*) and claimants (*tob'im*), so one is obligated to announce any lost article having identifying marks and claimants.[46]

To this the Babylonian Talmud adds the following *baraita*: "'which shall be lost': this excludes something worth less than a *perutah*."[47] Here we see that the law of *ye'ush* applies both in cases of robbery and loss. Concerning robbery of less than a *perutah*'s worth we use the term *meheelah* rather than *ye'ush*. What emerges from all of this is that the concepts of *ye'ush* and *meheelah* stem more from juridical definitions of rights than from simple observations of what is customarily done in any society. Therefore, when applied to Noahide law, it is far more theoretical than reflective of actual historical states of affairs; we see the validity of Atlas' attempt to show that the Noahide law of robbery is indicative of rabbinic reflections on the relation between Jewish law and its general preconditions.

CHAPTER EIGHT

THE LAW OF THE
TORN LIMB

1. Introduction

The final Noahide law is the prohibition of eating a limb torn from a living animal (*ever min ha-hai*). This law is expressly addressed to Noah and his descendants: "Surely flesh with its life-blood (*be-nafsho damo*) you shall not eat" (Gen. 9:4). Rashi paraphrases: "all the time the animal is alive you shall not eat the flesh." Although some interpret this as referring to a prohibition against eating the blood from a living animal,[1] the former interpretation is equally close to the plain meaning of the text.

Interestingly enough, in the Amoraic attempt to ground all of the Noahide laws as actual commands to Adam and his descendants, the Gemara presents the view of R. Johanan that the prohibition is from Gen. 2:16: "'[from every tree of the Garden] you may surely eat (*akhol t'okhal*) . . . —but not from the limb of a living animal."[2] There Rashi elaborates: only what is "ready for eating" (*ha'omed l'akheelah*) may be eaten, whereas a living animal is ready to grow and reproduce. The Tosafists say more: before Noah the prohibition of eating meat applied only to slaughtered meat, but not to meat from an animal that died without human intervention. The prohibition also applies to a limb that fell off by itself, that is, without human intervention. Because this law is derived from an earlier verse, Gen. 9:4 is interpreted more specifically to refute any supposition that because slaughtering meat was now permitted to Noah and his descendants,[3] the prohibition of eating the torn limb no longer applies;[4] and to exclude reptiles from the prohibition.[5] Only the School of Manasseh, which had a variant list of Noahide laws, is judged by the Gemara as endorsing the prohibition itself in Gen. 9:4.[6]

This law has more technical halakhic ramifications than the other Noahide laws. This is because it has the most specific exegetical base in Genesis, and because it involves comparison with Jewish laws of slaughter, an especially knotty area of halakhah. Finally, one can discern three different philosophical approaches and one possible historical source for this prohibition.

2. Idolatry

The prohibition of the practice of eating a limb torn from a living animal might reflect pagan rites that the rabbis saw as prohibited to Noahides over and above the prohibition of idolatry in general. Regarding the paraphernalia of idolatry, the Mishnah rules:

These are the things of gentiles which are forbidden and from which benefit the forbidden (*isur ha-ne'ah*) . . . hides perforated at the place of the heart. Rabban Simon b. Gamliel says this applies only when the perforation is round.[7]

Both Talmuds suggest that the law follows the qualification of Rabban Simon b. Gamliel.[8] However, the Palestinian Talmud grounds this law in a more precise context:

How was this done? One would tear the animal open (*kor'ah*) while it was still alive and remove the heart for idolatry. How does one know that this has been done? R. Huna said that when the animal was torn open while still alive the perforation is neatly round. If this were done after slaughtering, this perforation would be extended (*nimshakh*).

Apparently in Palestine, at least, there was a gentile practice of offering the heart of a living animal to a deity. The original Jewish concern with gentile idolatry was to make sure that Jews had nothing to do with it or its paraphernalia in any way. Later, the acceptance of the Noahide ban on gentile idolatry led to definitions of how far this ban was to extend into the culture of non-Jews.[9] In the text above we see more of the original concern with gentile idolatry, namely, identifying its practices so that Jews will be fully aware of what they must consistently avoid. Nevertheless, this text also suggests how the law of the torn limb may be a reaction to this gentile practice and the rabbinic judgment of it as a prohibition for gentiles. Since the heart is considered the most important organ of the body, offering it to a pagan deity would probably not be considered offering something defective. Saul Lieberman notes that a point of unanimity between the rabbis and cultic standards of the contemporary pagans, especially in Palestine, was that defective sacrificial animals were not to be offered.[10]

3. Implications for the Jewish Law of Slaughtering

Originally, this prohibition highlighted a deep difference between Jewish and Noahide law. Jews were permitted to eat meat after slaughtering, that is, after the cutting of the windpipe and the jugular vein with a very sharp knife free from any nicks. Therefore, a Jew could, for example, eat meat from an animal still kicking,[11] whereas a gentile had to wait until the animal was completely inanimate (u-be-meetah taly'a milt'a).[12] Moreover, whereas a Jew could eat the fetus of an animal that had been slaughtered, a gentile could not because the fetus was not dead.[13] Furthermore, even if a gentile slaughtered a kosher animal by the standards of halakhah, if meat had been taken from the animal before it had fully expired (koden she-tetz'e nafshah), the meat was considered to be from a torn limb and, therefore, forbidden to gentiles. The same was true if a Jew slaughtered a non-kosher animal for a gentile (or a gentile had done so for himself).[14]

Nevertheless, R. Pappa, a fifth-century Babylonian Amora, raised the question that this disparity indicates that Jewish law is more lenient that Noahide law; the opposite, of course, should be the case.[15] This later principle had the effect of modifying a number of earlier norms that were based on the assumption that Jewish law should favor Jews. A baraita bolsters this view:

If a person wants to eat meat from an animal before it had fully expired, he should cut a piece from the place where it has been slaughtered (me-bet ha-shehitah), thoroughly salt it and thoroughly soak it and then eat it. The law is the same: it is permitted to both Jews and gentiles.

Actually, the law could have developed in four directions: First, it could permit Jews to eat meat from such an animal immediately following proper slaughter, but prohibit gentiles from eating it even after the animal expired. However, this option was ruled out because of Lev. 19:26: "You shall not eat anything with its blood."[16] Second, it could prohibit Jews from eating such meat even after the animal had expired just as Noahides are so prohibited from doing. However, no one to my knowledge suggested that this be the new law. Third, it could prohibit Jews from eating such meat until the animal had fully expired, and prohibit gentiles from eating it at all. This opinion is found in the Gaonic work, She'iltot de-Rav Ahai Gaon.[17] It is also the opinion of the Tosafits[18] and Maimonides,[19] who, elsewhere, points out that the granular specifications of the law (she'urin) are for Jews alone.[20] This is consistent with his view that Jewish law in relation to Noahide law is a more specific law over and above a more general law.[21] Finally, the law could allow Jews to eat meat from such an animal after it had fully expired and extend this permission to Noahides as well. This option was accepted by Rashba, the Tur and the Shulhan Arukh.[22]

The last opinion demonstrates clearly an interaction between the two laws, an interaction leading to development in both. Noahide law had the effect of eliminating the permission to Jews to eat meat from an animal properly slaughtered but which had not fully expired. Although this prohibition is based on Lev. 19:26, R. Joseph Karo noted that it was only a general inference from the text,[23] and Meiri earlier suggested that the prohibition is not Toraitic but rabbinic.[24] This fits into the theory that Noahide law as a whole is a rabbinic institution.[25] Furthermore, Jewish law had the effect of loosening the Noahide prohibition of ever eating meat taken from an animal slaughtered according to Jewish procedures.

The effect of this option would also be to reduce the chances of Noahides violating the law of the torn limb when buying meat from Jews, which may have been a common practice inasmuch as meat that proved after slaughter to be unfit for Jews (treifah) could be sold to gentiles.[26] The earlier law whereby a gentile could be in violation of this prohibition when buying meat from a Jew placed the following burden on Jews:

R. Nathan said, "Wherefrom do we derive the prohibition that one is not to extend . . . a torn limb to a Noahide?" Scripture states, "You shall not place a stumbling-block before the blind" (Lev. 19:14).[27]

This new option makes the likelihood of the above much more probable.

Although this notion of the unanimity of Noahide and Jewish law on the question of the torn limb is an Amoraic discussion, we see the origins of it in the locus classicus of the Noahide law in the Tosefta:

. . . the torn limb: what is it specifically? A limb dangling from an animal which could not heal (y'ein bo la'a lot arukah) is prohibited to Noahides, and it goes without saying to Jews. And if it could heal, then it is permitted [after slaughter] to Jews, and it goes without saying to gentiles.[28]

Here we see the notion that in those areas of law pertaining to both Jews and non-Jews, there should not be a double standard. The Amoraic treatment of this question clearly formulated this notion into a distinct principle.[29] By doing so, it enabled this notion qua principle to be applied in a much broader context. Here we have a model of development within a legal system, a model empirically perceived and not the product of much abstract speculation.

The interaction between Jewish and Noahide law suggests how the latter can be a conditio sine qua non of the former and how Jewish law can be a development from Noahide law, a development having a retroactive effect on it. The formality of this type of discussion has importance for the logic of the relationship of these two laws within the overarching genus of law. However, logic deals only with the minimal outline of relations; it does not provide reasons for why certain norms rule the way they do.[30] As such we must now attempt to examine some of the philosophical reasons put forth by theologians for the law of the torn limb.

4. The Torn Limb and the Order of Nature

The question of whether Noahide law is "natural law" has been a central concern of Jewish theologians. We will see more of this debate later as well.[31] The solution to the question depends, to a large extent, on one's definition of "nature."

An early concept of nature, one that may be termed "pre-philosophic," looks at nature as the non-human created order that is fully complete prior to the emergence of humanity. Humans are, therefore, always in danger of becoming intruders in this already existent order. Human integration into the cosmos, then, requires their understanding of its patterns and avoidance of any disturbance of them. Positively, humanity's *modus vivendi* is to live in imitation of this order. Henry Frankfort explains:

The ancient . . . saw man always as part of society, and society as embedded in nature and dependent upon cosmic forces. For them nature and man . . . did not, therefore, have to be apprehended by different modes of cognition . . . Man also arranged his own life, or at least the life of the society to which he belonged, in such a manner that a harmony with nature, a co-ordination of natural and social forces, gave added impetus to his undertakings and increased his chances for success.[32]

This view of nature, one that permeated the ancient world, especially the ancient Near East, appears to lie behind the presentations of Noahide law that move from the prohibition of the torn limb to the prohibitions of castration, witchcraft and cross-breeding of animals and of trees. All of these acts are considered to be illicit tampering with the natural created order. The connection of these further prohibitions with the prohibition of the torn limb comes out in the text of the Tosefta and again in its quotation in the Gemara:

R. Hanina b. Gamliel says also blood from a living animal is prohibited. R. Hidka says also castration (*sirus*) is prohibited. R. Simon b. Gamliel says also witchcraft (*kishufin*) is prohibited . . . R. Eleazar says also . . . it is prohibited to cross-breed animals (*leharbi'a*) and to graft trees.[33]

Of course it is plausible to interpret these statements as simply meaning that these other laws are also Noahide laws along with the rest. However, considering the sequence in the text, it is more plausible, it seems to me, to see the addition of these other laws as part of the specific context of the more biblically explicit law of the torn limb.

The prohibition of eating blood from a living animal is explicitly connected by the Gemara with the law of the torn limb by a close reading of the verse, "Surely flesh with its life-blood you shall not eat" (Gen. 9:4).[34]

The prohibition of castration is seen as being derived from the verse, "You shall reproduce (*shirtzu*) in the land and multiply (*u-rebu*) in it" (Gen. 9:7). The Gemara states that the view that accepts only seven Noahide laws, excluding this one, would interpret this verse as a general blessing (*li-verakha b'alm'a*) rather than a specific precept.[35]

The prohibition of cross-breeding is seen as being derived from the words, "according to its species (*le-minayhu*)" (Gen. 7:14). Again, the view that accepts only seven Noahide laws, excluding this one, would interpret these words as merely indicating that usually "birds of a feather flock together."[36]

Later the Gemara discusses these additional views, presenting a more thorough foundation. The foundation is specifically for cross-breeding. But the reasoning employed is characterized by the pre-philosophic concept of nature:

R. Eleazar says that cross-breeding (*kl'ayim*) is also prohibited. Wherefrom do we derive this? Samuel said that Scripture states, "My statutes (*et hukkotai*) you shall observe" (Lev. 19:19), namely, statutes I have already made for you . . . "My statutes you shall observe": statutes which you were to originally (*m'ikkar'a*) observe.[37]

There are two ways to interpret this text. The first is enunciated by Rashi:

When He admonished Israel at Sinai not to cross-breed animals, He began with "My statutes you shall observe"—a manner of introduction not used elsewhere. From this we infer that what He was really saying to them (*hakhee k'amar lehu*) was to observe My statutes which I already made for the Noahides.[38]

Rashi's point is that the text refers to a few specific laws already given to Noahides and repeated at Sinai.

We see a second line of interpretation in the writings of R. Meir Abulafia: "Statutes which I have already created My world by them, that you not change the order of creation (*sidrei bereshit*)."[39] These statutes are not just random decrees given to an earlier generation; instead, they are "natural laws," understood in the pre-philosophic sense of *nature*. Violation of these laws constitutes an unwarranted intrusion into the natural created order of the cosmos. Precedent for this view can be found in the Palestinian Talmud.[40] Even earlier, Philo wrote:

Now it just to join together things which can associate, and the homogeneous are made for association just as the heterogeneous on the other hand cannot be blended or associated, and one who plans to bring them into abnormal companionship (*ek thesmous*) is unjust because he upsets a law of nature (*nomon physeōs*).[41]

Philo concludes: "order (*taxei*) is akin to seemliness (*kosmos*), and disorder to unseemliness (*to akosmon*)."[42]

Finally, this view of nature, seen as underlying the prohibitions of the torn limb, castration, witchcraft and cross-breeding, finds its most systematic expression in the theology of Nahmanides. He writes:

Rashi states that these are decrees (*gezerot*) of the King for which there is no reason (*ta'am*). However, the rabbis did not say that the reason was hidden concerning . . . the cross-breeding of animals . . . Furthermore, no decree anywhere of the King of Kings is without reason . . . For the laws of the Holy One, Blessed be He, are cosmic mysteries (*ha-sodot*) . . . all having correct reason and teleologically complete (*ve-to'elet shelamah*) . . . and He commanded the generative powers to bring forth their own species and that they should never change . . . so one who cross-breeds is denying (*u-makheesh*) the work of creation as if he thinks that the Holy One, Blessed be He, did not perfectly provide for every need in His world. He wants to help (*la'azor*) in the creation of the world by adding creatures in it . . .[43]

This line of argument applies to this prohibition and to the additional prohibitions we have been discussing. Indeed, in another context Nahmanides connects the statutes (*hukkim/hukkot*) of the torn limb with those of cross-breeding both animals and trees.[44] All of this is based on the notion that it is inherently wrong to upset (*le-hakheesh*) the cosmic order. This is summarized by R. Johanan, a Palestinian Amora, who explains the prohibition of witchcraft in Ex. 22:18 as being because those who practice it "contradict the heavenly family."[45] We see this paralleled in modern times with Albert Schweitzer's notion of "reverence for all life."[46] The burden of proof, for all who subscribe to this view of nature, always lies with *homo faber*. He is always the intruder who must justify his intrusion.

5. Maimonides and Natural Law

In Maimonides' treatment of the law of the torn limb we clearly see the difference between a pre-philosophic concept of nature and a philosophic one. This difference sheds light on a number of other rulings and interpretations of Maimonides in opposition to many of his non-philosophical predecessors, contemporaries and successors.

The reason for the prohibition against eating *a limb* [cut off from] *a living animal* is because this would make one acquire the habit of cruelty. Such things were done in those times by the kings of the Gentiles; this was also an action used in *idolatry* . . .[47]

Maimonides here is presenting a natural law argument even though he does not explicitly use the term "nature."

The connection of this type of practice with idolatry was already made in the Palestinian Talmud, as we have seen.[48] It should be recalled that for Maimonides the prohibition of idolatry per se is immediately evident to reason and the Torah came to eradicate it and its specific historical manifestations from the world.[49]

The designation of this practice as "cruel" (azkzariyut) is based on a certain pre-rational affinity between humans as sentient beings and, at least, the higher animals. Maimonides writes: ". . . animals feel very great pain, there being no difference regarding this pain between man and the other animals."[50] Thus, the prohibition of tearing a limb from a living animal is due to its human implications. Those who torture animals are likely to have little regard for their fellow humans. Positive fellow-feeling is a requirement of a rational and well-ordered society, one of the two main purposes of the Torah.[51]

When Maimonides uses the term "nature" (teva) it can have two different meanings.[52] On the one hand, it designates the subhuman realm characterized by the inertia of matter and by unconscious animal instinct. On the other hand, nature designates the superhuman intelligible realm with God as its apex, but also the heavenly spheres. Humans, living between these two realms, are masters of the lower one and servants of the upper one. Only what humanity can discern of the intelligible is normative for them. The lower realm is to be subordinated to the intelligibility of the higher realm. The lower realm in and of itself has no authority precisely because it lacks its own intelligibility. The rationale for the law of the torn limb, therefore, is not because it is a violation of this lower realm of physical nature per se, for this realm has no metaphysically prior authority. Rather, the law's purpose is to remove anti-rational cruelty that disrupts human life, inhibiting humanity's relationship with the intelligible realm. Moreover, although Maimonides does not follow the rabbinic opinion that considers cross-breeding of animals to be one of the Noahide laws, again in his discussion of the reasons for this prohibition he stresses its adverse effect on *human* morals—it requires human intervention in animal sexual intercourse, a practice that stimulates lewdness in thought, word and deed.[53]

The difference between these two views of nature, which we have seen differentiates Maimonides' treatment of the law of the torn limb from that of most other Jewish theologians, can be seen in his approach to the question of the commandment to heal the sick.

The following *baraita* is brought in the Talmud:

It was taught in the School of R. Ishmael that Scripture states, "he shall surely heal (ve-rapp'o yirapp'e—Ex. 21:19)." From here we derive permission (reshut) for the physician to heal.[54]

The Tosafists were quick to pick up the implication of this text that it comes to counter the possible religious assumption that healing a disease not human-caused (*bi-yedai shamayim*) must be a denial of a divine decree of illness.[55] Nahmanides, too, indicates that God's supernatural protection of Israel makes reliance on physicians a compromise of faith.[56] He refers to the above text as being merely permission only for those whose faith is not great.

Maimonides, conversely, does not codify the text at all. He instead bases the *obligation* to heal on the Deuteronomic obligation to return lost property (Deut. 22:1) and, *a fortiori*, one's health.[57] Intervention in the processes of physical nature is not in any way considered to be a possible affront to divinely created nature. Finally, Maimonides interprets the Mishnah's praise for King Hezekiah's removing the ancient "Book of Cures" (*Sefer Refu'ot*) from circulation as being because the book was an idolatrous treatise, not because of its medical subject matter. Indeed Maimonides emphasizes that the book has no scientific merit.[58]

CHAPTER NINE

AGGADIC SPECULATION

1. The Offering of the Torah

We have documented that the development of the Noahide laws can be seen in two perspectives: (1) as the pre-Sinaitic law for all humanity including Israel; (2) as the post-Sinaitic law for all humanity excluding Israel. The first provided a standard for understanding the precondition for the Torah's revelation; the second offered criteria for understanding what Jews could respect, even obey, in the non-Jewish world. This second perspective developed principally along legal lines, aiding Jews in negotiating with gentile authority and gentile religion without capitulation or complete condemnation. The first perspective matured, on the other hand, through theological categories, making it more speculative than normative. This speculation was concerned with the relevance of universal law for the understanding of Judaism itself.

This view emerges in the following aggadah:

"And he said that the Lord came forth from Sinai . . . " (Deut. 33:2). When the Holy One, Blessed be He, appeared (ke-she-nigleh) to give the Torah to Israel, He did not appear to Israel alone but to all the nations.[1]

The text continues and states that the descendants of Esau refused the Torah because of the prohibition of murder; the Ammonites and Moabites because of prohibition of incest; and the Ishmaelites due to the prohibition of robbery. In each of these cases verses from Genesis are brought to show that these nations rejected the Torah because it contradicts behavior that characterizes them and for which the Torah had condemned them. (The prohibition of idolatry, however, is not mentioned, but of course one would be pressed to find explicit condemnation of gentile idolatry in the Bible.[2]) The text concludes:

Not only did they not accept (shel l'o sham'u) it, but even the seven commandments which the Noahides accepted upon themselves (she-kibblu aleihem) they were unable to persevere in them, finally casting them off (ad she-parkum). When the Holy One, Blessed be He, saw this, He, therefore, gave them to Israel . . . so Israel accepted the Torah with all its ramifications (be-fayrusheyha) and details,[3] plus those seven commandments which the Noahides were unable to preserve and which they cast off. Israel came and accepted them.[4]

In another Tannaitic version, the view of R. Simon b. Eleazar is reported, stating that "if the seven laws which the Noahides were commanded and accepted upon themselves, they were unable to persevere in them, then all the more so (*kal va-homer*) could they not persevere in the commandments of the Torah."[5]

The central points of this aggadah are: (1) originally the Noahides accepted seven laws commanded by God (pre-Sinaitic Israel is part of this covenant and thus obligated); (2) when God offered the Torah to the nations, he addressed it to them in terms of the specific Noahide law their way of life had already rejected *de facto*; (3) each of the nations formally rejected the Torah *de jure*, a *rejection of the Torah manifested as Noahide law*;[6] (4) Israel unconditionally accepted the Torah in its entirety *and* with it the seven Noahide laws rejected by the nations. What emerges is that since the Sinaitic revelation, neither the nations nor Israel relate to the Noahide law as all humanity did, at least *de jure*, prior to Sinai. This had profound implications for the theological development of Noahide law.

2. Gentiles after Sinai

If one looks upon acceptance as the basic factor in the authority of law, then one could see this aggadah as implying that the rejection of God's law by gentiles at Sinai, on Noahide terms, leads to the conclusion that these laws are no longer binding on them. In the Amoraic development of this aggadah this notion is suggested and rejected:

R. Joseph taught, "He stood and measured the earth; He saw and He uprooted nations" (Hab. 3:6)—what did he see? The seven commandments which the Noahides took upon themselves, which they did not uphold, these He stood up and released (*ve-hiteer*) from them. Are they so rewarded?! If so the sinner is rewarded! Mar b. Rabina said that it means that even if they do observe them they do not receive reward.[7]

Clearly the Noahide laws were persistently invoked as a criterion in the Jewish judgment of the moral status of any gentile society. The fact that some societies passed this test and others failed indicates that Noahide law was considered to be still binding and that gentiles were morally capable of living up to it.

Moreover, the term "acceptance" (*kabbalah*) was first used in the case of the *ger toshav* who *elected* to accept certain minimal Jewish standards in order to live in the land of Israel.[8] In this case the binding character of the law was rooted in the acceptance by the *ger toshav* of the minimal Jewish norms

prescribed for them, and his *being accepted* by Jewish authorities. Such fundamental acceptance involves alternatives, that is, gentiles had the right not to
accept these standards, forfeiting domicile in Israel. For example, an aggadah
suggests that Joshua gave the nations of Canaan the option to accept Jewish authority and its law *for them*, or to flee or to fight. The Girgashites, the
aggadah concluded, fled,[9] wanting neither the law nor its rewards.[10] The
Gibeonites, conversely, accepted.

Nevertheless, the Noahide was judged bound by Noahide law regardless of
formal acceptance. Their formal acceptance does not create the obligation; it is
only a personal confirmation of an already existing obligation. The law is not
the result of a contract. The Noahide rejection of Noahide law at any time is
regarded as a sin deserving punishment. Such rejection is not a legitimate
option. Unlike the Mosaic Torah, the mutuality of the giving and the accepting
of the law is not emphasized with the Noahide commandments.[11]

We now see that this aggadah and its subsequent theological development
emphasizes that although Noahide law has changed for gentiles since Sinai,
that change has not been in terms of legal obligation. Rather, the change has
been in terms of the transcendent status of the Noahide laws as observed by
gentiles. Prior to the rejection at Sinai, the laws were accepted as direct commandments, and as such were immediately involved in human responses to
God's authority, a response having cosmic consequences. After Sinai, the laws
are simply prescriptions, having only social and political consequences in
those societies that adhere to them.

Since Noahide law prior to Sinai was conceived as something for which
gentiles (and Jews) were "commanded and practiced (*metzuveh v'osheh*)," we
might examine the concept in its origin and application.

The concept of "commanded and practiced" is expressed in the name of R.
Hanina, "greater is one who is commanded and practices than one who is not
commanded and practices."[12] There are two ways to see this idea. First, one
can say it means that if one has not been commanded to practice a certain law,
he or she may practice it as a legitimate option, but he or she does not receive
the reward in the world-to-come that one who is so commanded does when
fulfilling it. The Tosafists explain that whereas the latter must practice the law
with seriousness, because reward in the world-to-come implies punishment
for disobedience, the former can practice (or not) the particular law on subjective grounds.[13] Rabbenu Tam permitted women to observe commandments
for which they were not obligated and even to recite the prescribed blessing.[14]
(His views were not accepted by Sephardic authorities.[15]) This appears to be
the meaning of this concept in its original Talmudic context. However, this
meaning does not apply to post-Sinaitic gentiles because they do not have the

"take it or leave it" option women have, for example, regarding positive commandments limited to specific times, for which they are considered exempt.[16] Therefore, the use of this concept in the context of dealing with post-Sinaitic gentiles is by analogy, not direct application. The analogy suggests that although Noahide law is divine law, gentiles do not practice it as such and, consequently, in the sense of "measure for measure (*middah keneged middah*),"[17] they are not related to it in terms of its cosmic consequences. This would be quite similar to a Jew who observed a commandment of the Torah as a law or folkway, but not with the intention that it is a divine commandment per se. Such a person had definitely done something, but not as a mitzvah.[18] No reward (*sekhar*), therefore, is attached. In short, what once was a divinely commanded act is now experienced as a humanly motivated act.[19] Noahide rejection of the seven commandments changed them from mitzvot to mere "laws."

This descent of gentiles from an original condition of consciously living under divine law to a present condition of merely living under law as a human institution has had two implications. First, it implies that Noahide law is capable of being perceived rationally, that is, it can be observed, however inadequately on the level of the sacred, by human beings enlightened by their own reason. If this is the case, then Noahide law can, at least initially, be understood rationally. The separation of the Noahides from the directly divine character of Noahide law now enables it to be constituted by rational criteria. For if Noahide law is no longer observed as divine law, then human reason is the only other means universal enough to make it binding on all humanity.[20] If one views the rational component in Judaism to be central, then the fact that rational law is found among gentiles will enable Jews to intellectually, at least, interact with gentiles on the basis of a real, enduring, common moral ground. On the other hand, if one considers reason as peripheral in Judaism, then they will regard gentile rejection of the *divine* Noahide law as making for a fundamental separation between Jews and non-Jews because they essentially have nothing in common.[21] I believe that the development of the rationalist and mystical tradition in Judaism has been determined in part by how they view the post-Sinaitic relationship of Jews and gentiles in terms of normative status.

The distinction between these two views manifests itself in the dispute between R. Eliezer b. Hyrcanus and R. Joshua b. Hananiah:

R. Eliezer said that none of the gentiles has a portion in the world-to-come, as Scripture states, "The wicked (*resh'ayim*) will return to Sheol, all the nations who have forgotten God" (Ps. 9:18). "The wicked will return to Sheol": these are the wicked of Israel. R. Joshua said that if Scripture had stated, "The wicked will return to Sheol, namely, all the gentiles" and was thereafter silent, it would agree with your interpretation. However, since Scripture stated, "who have forgotten God," it teaches that there are righteous (*yesh tzaddikim*) among the nations and they do have a portion in the world-to-come.[22]

R. Eliezer takes the first clause of the verse to refer to the wicked of Israel, and the second clause to refer to gentiles who, because they are gentiles, forget God.[23] R. Joshua takes the second clause to be a qualification, that is, "all gentiles *who forget God*," thereby implying that there are gentiles who indeed remember God and thus merit a place in the world-to-come along with the righteous of Israel.[24]

According to R. Eliezer there is an ontological difference between Jews and gentiles. Therefore, the more Jews are described as the people of God, the recipients of the Torah at Sinai, the more the gentiles are described as separated from God and without virtue. Conversely, according to R. Joshua, gentiles are as capable of righteousness as Jews. The criterion of Jewish righteousness is the Torah. What is the criterion for gentiles? With the disappearance of biblical quasi-Jews,[25] the standard could no long be *some* of the Torah's 613 commandments. A new standard had to be found. It seems as though the affirmation of the possibility of gentile righteousness by R. Joshua laid the theological foundation for the constitution of the Noahide laws a generation or so later.[26]

3. Noahide Law and Reason

In the aggadah that dealt with God's offering the Torah to the nations, Israel accepts the Torah "with its ramifications and its details." The implication of this important phrase is that the Mosaic Torah is essentially a further specification of the Noahide Torah, not in the sense that it can simply be deduced from it, but rather that its general outlines can be seen there. For just as the Noahide laws concern humanity's relationship with God, fellow humans and the phenomenal world, so it is with the Mosaic Torah.[27] This greater generality of Noahide law makes it more rational because general categories are more evidently intelligible than specific norms, which inevitably involve historically contingent factors. Greater rationality, however, does not mean that Noahide law is superior. On the contrary, the greatness of the Mosaic Torah is precisely its specificity, a specificity that speaks to the greater insight of the divine author into the existential particularities of the Torah's recipients. Such insight is not as evident in the Noahide law because of its generality. The following aggadah brings this out:

R. Eleazar said that it is like a king who went to war and his legions were with him.

When he slaughtered an animal or beast he apportioned a part to everyone which suited him (*she-yagi'ah bah*). His son noticed and said to him, "What are you going to give me?" He said to him, "From what I have prepared for myself." Therefore God gave the gentiles unspecific commandments (*miztvot golamot*).[28]

Hanokh Zundel, a nineteenth-century commentator, adds:

According to this opinion there is a difference between the laws commanded to Israel and those commanded to Noahides—not only a difference in number, but a difference in how (*b'aykhut*) they were commanded. To the latter He gave commandments which are unfinished, like a vessel without its finishing touches (*bli tikkun*).[29]

This difference between the laws comes out in the Talmudic rule that the violation of a general prohibition (*l'av shebekhlalut*) is not subject to corporal punishment, which is the case when a specific prohibition has been violated.[30] For such general prohibitions come to provide a context for the more specifically enunciated prohibitions. Only these can be the subject of a specific forewarning (*hatra'ah*).[31] However, such is not the case with Noahide law since by virtue of its very generality all its prohibitions are general.

The revelation at Sinai of the complete Torah changed the status of the Noahide laws for Jews as well. In the purely legal sense the seven Noahide laws were superseded by the 613 laws of the Mosaic Torah. Thus, for Jews, every one of seven laws requires repetition in the Torah from Sinai in order to be binding.[32] Nevertheless, the aggadah about the universal rejection of the Torah except by Israel indicates that the people of Israel accepted the Noahide laws *as well* as the Torah. Why, then, mention the Noahide laws if the Torah repeats them? The answer, it seems to me, is that the Noahide laws have now become the *general outline* of the Mosaic Torah. They are considered the general standards of civilization (*derekh eretz*) that preceded the giving of the Torah and are considered the pre-conditions for the Torah's giving and acceptance.[33] As a general outline, they no longer function as specific prohibitions, but rather as *formal criteria* of judgment. In other words, one can see them as rational guidelines for the interpretation of the specific laws of the Torah. In this sense, then, the Noahide laws function for Jews in much the same way they function for gentiles. For both, they are no longer positive laws. As such they can be a basis for comparative jurisprudence and common moral discourse between Jews and non-Jews.

4. Gentile Rejection of the Torah

The gentile rejection of the Noahide laws as direct commandments enabled them to be viewed as general rational outlines of positive law. However, such a development of the legend of gentile rejection presupposes that one believes reason can discover such guidelines. However, if one does not believe that reason has any such moral relevance, then the gentile rejection of the Torah as Noahide law becomes the basis for regarding gentiles as less than fully human. This view emerges in a medieval treatment of the Amoraic elaboration of the legend of gentile rejection. The Gemara states:

Mar b. Rabina said, "How can it be said that even if the Noahides observe the Noahide laws they do not receive a reward? For is it not taught in a *baraita* that R. Meir used to say, "How do we know that even if a gentile engages in the study of the Torah that he is like the high priest? Scripture states, 'whichever man does them and lives by them'" (Lev. 18:5).[34]

The Tosafists ask:

It is surprising. Are the gentiles called "man" (*adam*)? Is there not a *baraita* which states that R. Simon bar Yohai said that the graves of the gentiles do not ritually contaminate (*metam'in*) if one is under an enclosure with them. For Scripture states, "when a man (*adam*) dies in a tent" (Num. 19:14)—you are called "man" but the gentiles are not called "man."[35]

Now the Tosafists are not conclusive about the counterexample brought by the Gemara. First, it is explained that this is a private opinion of R. Simon bar Yohai and that the rabbis reject his view in favor of the more inclusive view of R. Meir.[36] Second, Rabbenu Tam attempts to show that Scripture uses the term *adam* and *ha'adam* in different ways, some of which clearly include gentiles. In terms of strict halakhah the question of who is designated by the term *adam* seems to be mostly confined to questions of ritual, the widest area of difference between Jews and gentiles.[37] Michael Guttmann explained this radical principle of exclusion as being occasioned by the large number of unmarked graves during the political upheavals in post-destruction Palestine. Since the Jews were very careful to bury their dead and mark their graves,[38] it was not impossible to avoid them and thus maintain one's ritual purity. However, since the gentiles were not nearly so fastidious in marking their graves, it would be nearly impossible to travel freely without the doubt that one had come into contact with an unmarked grave. Therefore, according to Guttmann, R. Simon bar Yohai ruled that gentile graves do not ritually contaminate precisely to avoid this situation.[39]

This might very well be the halakhic intent of this doctrine. However, in the aggadah it had much broader results.[40] R. Simon bar Yohai was anti-Roman and wished for maximum separation between Jews and gentiles.[41] When his colleague R. Judah praised the Romans for their political accomplishments from which even the Jews were benefiting, R. Simon bar Yohai retorted:

Everything they have established they only established (*takknu*) for their own needs; they established marketplaces to set up prostitutes, bathhouses to enjoy themselves, bridges to collect tribute.[42]

R. Simon's disdain for gentiles is due to their rejection of the Torah. We read:

R. Johanan said in the name of R. Simon bar Yohai that all the good of the wicked is bad for the righteous as Scripture states, "Be careful that you do not speak with Jacob either good or bad" (Gen. 31:24) . . . here what is the evil? Because pollution (*zohama*) has been cast into him. It is as R. Johanan said that when the serpent approached Eve he cast pollution on her. Israel, when she stood at Mount Sinai, had the pollution removed (*paskah*). The gentiles who did not stand at Mount Sinai did not have the pollution removed from them.[43]

R. Simon's view was extended by the kabbalists. (Tradition, of course, holds that R. Simon bar Yohai authored the Zohar).[44] In the kabbalistic literature the distinction between Israel and the nations was elevated to an ontological principle. As such, the rabbinic notion that the difference between Israel and the gentiles was historical, that is, at Sinai the nations freely rejected the Torah and Israel accepted it, was altered by the kabbalists. For them, it was in the *very nature* of Israel to accept God's law as it was in the *very nature* of the nations to reject it. At this point the question of Noahide law becomes irrelevant since the acceptance or rejection of God's law is no longer a moral question, but rather an inevitable cosmic process. The assumption of the kabbalists is that gentiles are incapable of receiving the Torah. When the story of the gentile rejection of the Torah is told in the Zohar, no mention of the moral reasons why the gentiles rejected it are mentioned.[45] Following this line, Judah Loewe of Prague (Maharal), the sixteenth-century kabbalist, noted that "it is impossible to say that the people lacking in preparation would receive divine things . . . for if there were no need for preparation it would also be possible to say that a donkey could receive human intelligence."[46] Earlier, Meir ibn Gabbai, asked that if the very nature of gentiles prevented them from accepting the Torah, then why did God offer it to them at all? His answer is that it was to double the reward of Israel who did accept it![47] Already, the Zohar reiterated and embellished the notion of R. Simon bar Yohai that the term *adam* only applied to Jews, the people to whom the Torah was destined.[48]

In the light of these theological assumptions it followed that Noahide law was only regarded as a *diminished Torah*, which itself became meaningless once the full Torah was revealed.[49] Thus Meir ibn Gabbai asked why the seven laws were revealed to the sons of Noah when, according to rabbinic tradition, the whole Torah was already being taught in the School of Shem?[50] He answers:

When the Flood came to the world and they entered the ark the Torah was forgotten because of their great anxiety. However, the Holy One, Blessed be He, said, "If I tell them that they will cast off the yoke like the others who say, 'we do not want your ways' (Job 21:14), so I will give them a few things that they might observe them until the one who will observe them all will come." And this was Abraham.[51]

Since Noahide law is the most rationally evident aspect of the Torah, by minimizing its importance the kabbalists thereby diminished the importance of universal human reason in Judaism. For them the whole subject of Noahide law was essentially a dead-end. For the rationalists, the subject of Noahide law became the cornerstone of the constitution of a rational Jewish jurisprudence as well as the only means based on the rabbinic tradition for a consistent and realistic standard for judging and dealing with the non-Jewish world.

CHAPTER TEN

MAIMONIDES' THEORY OF NOAHIDE LAW

1. Introduction

The fullest philosophical reflection on the Noahide law emerges in the thought of Maimonides. Before turning to Maimonides, let us quickly recount the development of Noahide law to this point.

The rabbinic treatment of the Noahide laws eventually led to the assumption of their *a priori* universal status. We have seen that the *ger toshav* long preceded that of the Noahide. The latter implied that a gentile's obligation to obey a certain number of Torah laws was based on one's humanity per se, irrespective of whether one accepted Jewish legal authority. The earlier concept seems to presuppose some form of conversion as the basis of gentile obligation. The later concept saw the obligation as universal. Thus it required a definition of universal human obligation not required by the earlier concept.

As regards the earlier concept, the question, "when is there gentile obligation for Noahide law?" is easily answered: "the obligation is subsequent to the acceptance of Jewish political rule." However, if the gentile's obligation is conceived of as based on his human status, then the question about obligation is not so easily answered. For it is easier to *point to* a particular agreement than to *define* a universal status. Clearly, then, the later concept leads to philosophical reflection more immediately than the earlier concept.

The difference in philosophical significance between the two can be seen when we ask the second fundamental question about Noahide law, "how do gentiles know their obligation?" Again, the earlier concept admits an easy answer: "gentiles know their obligation when they accept Jewish political rule and its legal authority." However, the later concept does not admit such an easy answer. Here one must *discover* an obligation that already obliges everyone prior to its acceptance by any individual. Thus, here again, the development of Jewish law and theology immediately leads us to the type of questions with which philosophers deal.

2. The *Locus Classicus* of Maimonides' Philosophy of Law

Maimonides contends directly with two questions: (1) Why is there gentile obligation? And (2) How do gentiles know their obligation? His treatment of these questions presupposes the point developed in rabbinic tradition, namely, that Noahide law is universally binding even before its acceptance by any particular gentile.

In answer to the first question, Maimonides writes:

Concerning six things was the first man commanded . . . Even though they are all traditional (*kabbalah*) coming from Moses our master to our hands, and reason inclines to them (*ye-ha-da'at noteh lahen*), from Scripture it is generally evident (*me-khlal*) that he was commanded concerning them. The prohibition of eating a limb torn from a living animal was added for Noah . . .[1]

There are, then, three possible sources for Noahide law: (1) Mosaic tradition; (2) rational inclination;[2] (3) general divine revelation in the Torah. Maimonides indicates that the third source is primary. However, he does not remove the other two; they do not contradict the true source. Indeed he mentions that in addition to being divinely revealed, these laws are *also* traditional and rational.

To the second question, Maimonides replies:

Any gentile who does not accept the commandments of which the Noahides were commanded: we are to execute him if he is under our political control . . . whoever accepts the seven commandments and is obligated to do them . . . because God commanded them in the Torah and made us aware through Moses our master that the Noahides were previously commanded concerning them. But if he did them because of rational conclusion (*hekhr'e ha-da'at*) . . .[3]

Here again, there are three possibilities: (1) Noahide law is known because it is promulgated by Jewish authorities to gentiles living under their political rule; (2) Noahide law is known due to the acceptance of divine revelation by gentiles; (3) Noahide law is known because it is rationally convincing. Maimonides indicates that the second possibility alone is fully adequate to the ultimate source of Noahide law. As such, only the person who consciously confirms this true source of law qualifies as "one of the saints of the nations of the world" (*me-hasidai ummot ha-olam*) and is assured a place in the "world-to-come" (*olam ha-ba*). However, just as revelation as the source of the law did not necessarily remove either Mosaic tradition or reason, so the conscious acceptance of revelation does not necessarily remove acceptance based on compliance with Jewish political rule, nor acceptance due to rational conclusions.

In the pre-messianic era there is no Jewish authority capable of enforcing Noahide law among gentiles. This reality explains why the *ger toshav* is no longer a possibility.[4] Maimonides' allusion, therefore, to the *tradition of Moses* may well be referring to the Sanhedrin, which functioned and issued rulings with *Mosaic* political authority.[5] In this era, then, Noahide law can only be acknowledged as rational or revealed law. Although Maimonides stresses that those who accept the Noahide law because of rational conclusion alone are participants in the transcendent realm of the world-to-come, he does not state that they have not fulfilled the *legal* requirements of this law. That is to say, even if one did not regard these laws as divine commandments, this does by extension suggest that they are a transgressor. Fulfillment of the Noahide laws on the positive legal level simply implies recognition of their legal authority, not necessarily a belief about their true origins. However theologically inadequate such an approach might be, it is legally acceptable.[6] This superficial approach, moreover, does not contravene the theological foundation of the law as long as it does not constitute itself as wholly sufficient. Such an interpretation is, furthermore, consistent with the rabbinic view that religious intention (*kavanah*) is not a legal prerequisite for those commandments involving external action alone. None of the Noahide laws specifically prescribe an "inner" attitude.[7]

The Noahide laws involve three assertions: (1) they were promulgated by God to the sons of Noah, as described in the Torah; (2) they are obligatory for all people; (3) they enable one to achieve the bliss of the world-to-come. The third assertion is contingent on belief in the first, that is, *if* one believes that God commanded these laws to the sons of Noah, *then* one is assured of heavenly bliss.[8] However, the second assertion can stand alone. Maimonides admits the possibility, though not the desirability, of rational discovery of the Noahide laws. Additionally, rational discovery does not automatically eliminate recognition of the transcendent origins of these laws. Legally, they are independent. Only theologically is the specific rationality of the Noahide laws an insufficient explanation for their full human meaning. As we shall see later, Maimonides does not deem "rational conclusion" to be the only or even the highest form of ratiocination.[9] Consequently, the insufficiency of "rational conclusion" might well be that it insufficiently reasons about the deeper significance of these laws. As such, Maimonides is not making reason and revelation exclusive, but rather is rejecting a certain kind of non-theological reasoning as philosophically shallow, unable to apprehend the rational intention of divine law.[10]

This same rejection can also be observed in Maimonides' treatment of "rational commandments," a doctrine elaborated by Saadiah.[11] He writes:

But all of them are true and there is no dispute among them at all in that what the philosophers designate as vices are vices . . . and they are universally held (ha-mefursamim) to be vices: bloodshed, stealing, robbery, cheating, harming someone who has done no wrong, doing evil to one's benefactor, contempt for parents, etc. These are the laws about which the Sages, peace be upon them, said, "if they were not written (in the Torah) they should have been written (r'uyyim hayu le-kotvan)." And some of the later Sages, who are infected with the disease of the Mutakallumin, call them "rational commandments."[12]

Since Maimonides judges these commandments as evidently true, and also of universal assent, why does he sneer at those who term them "rational commandments"? The answer is that Maimonides considered rational thinking without a robust theological perspective as inappropriate to explain the commandments of the Torah or the nature of the universe. His rejection of the methods of the Mutakallumin, for example, stemmed from their inadequate, arbitrary reasoning.[13] Saadiah's rationale for the commandments of the Torah was based on an anthropocentric teleology.[14] For Maimonides the rationale of the Torah's commandments emerges out of a theocentric teleology, designed to bring one supreme good to humanity—knowledge of God.[15] We can therefore perceive that he is certainly not rejecting the evident rationality of some of the Torah's commandments. Rather, he is dismissing the Kalam's method of understanding that rationality.[16] He is rejecting the theological presuppositions that led to this term, not denying the rationality of the commandments. This fact is significant: Maimonides argues for the rationality of the Noahide laws in both the Mishneh Torah and the Guide. Already in his commentary on the Mishnah, he is laying the ground for subsequent theological effort.

Concerning the relation between proper and improper motivations in the observance of the law, the Talmud commented:

Let a man always engage in the study of the Torah and the performance of the commandments even for ulterior motives (shel'o lishmah), because even from out of such motives he will indeed come to do them for their own sake (lishmah).[17]

Since, then, reason and revealed law are not presented as exclusive, we will have to see how Maimonides constitutes their relation in the Mishneh Torah, the Guide and responsum.

3. Noahide and Torah Law

In the same section of the Mishneh Torah we have been examining, Maimonides posits a relation between Noahide and Torah law. Maimonides sees a process of revelation starting with Adam and concluding with Moses, "by means of whom the Torah was completed" (ve-nishlamah torah al yado).[18] Now this "completion" does not refer to the numerical completion of the Torah's commandments, beginning with seven and finishing with 613, because the seven Noahide commandments per se are not counted as part of the 613.[19] "Completion," perhaps due to Maimonides' Aristotelian leanings, might very well mean that this full Torah can be seen in potentia in the Noahide law.[20] If this interpretation of Maimonides' use of the term "completion" is correct, then his treatment of Torah law in general has its simplest application in his understanding of Noahide law. Noahide and Torah law are therefore members of the same genus—divine law—differing only in that the latter is a more complex development of the former. As such, Maimonides' treatment of divine law in the Guide has immediate significance for his concept of Noahide law.

Since Maimonides assigns Noahide law (and a fortiori the law of the Torah) as divine law, we must now examine his definition of divine law and its differences from human law.

Law is categorized in terms of its source and final cause, the origin of its promulgation and the goal of its legislation.[21] Ultimately, the source and the final cause must be correlated.

The source of divine law for Maimonides is the revealed will of God. In the Guide, he is more specific regarding the definition of revelation. He defines prophecy, the presupposition of the revelation of the Torah, as follows:

Know that the true reality and quiddity of prophecy consist in its being an overflow overflowing from God . . . through the intermediation of the Active Intellect, in the first place and therefore toward the imaginative faculty. This is the highest degree of man and the ultimate term of perfection that can exist for his species . . . [22]

For Maimonides, revelation is understood in terms of the human faculties to which it is addressed. The "rational faculty" is concerned with the unchanging objects of intellection (muskalot), that is, the heavenly bodies and the principles of metaphysics. Judgments in this area are "true and false" (emet ve-sheker). The "imaginative faculty" is occupied with changing political opinions through which human beings order society, framed in terms of "good and bad" (tov ve-r'a).[23] However, if the prophet is a person who combines intellectual and political excellence to the highest degree,[24] then there must be a correlation between the intellectual and political spheres to which the combined excellence of the prophet corresponds. The question is: how does revelation correlate these two spheres? By answering this question, we can see how Maimonides constitutes an inherent relation between revelation, reason and human experience. For him, one cannot ultimately exclude the other.

Earlier Maimonides designated as *clear and manifest* "primary intelligibles" (*muskalim rishonim*) and "things perceived by the senses" (*murgashim*).[25] Now the difference between primary intelligibles and sensibles, such as motion, is that the former are abstract and the latter are concrete. However, there is a relation between them over and above their both being "clear and manifest." The relation between them is that the abstraction of intelligibles from concrete sensibles presupposes an intimate awareness of sensibles. For it is reflection of the paradoxes of the senses, especially the paradox of motion, which stimulates the intellect to discover such abstract notions as causality.[26] Therefore, awareness of the objects of sense is the means to knowledge of the intelligibles to which they point.

The existence of human ability to act (*ha-yekholet l'adam*), namely, human freedom, which Maimonides names as the presupposition of all law, is also a primary sensible such as motion.[27] At this level we can begin to see the correlation of the sensible and the intellectual spheres as a political issue, because human freedom to act can never be denied if the notion of law as *commandment* be valid. Maimonides makes this point most fully in his discussion of repentance:

If God were to decree that man is to be righteous or wicked . . . like the view the astrologers (*hovrai ha-shamayim*) invent from their own minds, how could He command us by means of prophets "do this" and "do not do that" . . . what role (*makom*) would there be for the entire Torah?[28]

He goes on to say that God included human freedom in the created order just as he included all other natural phenomena. God does not change the general natural structure of the created universe.[29] Even miracles are only particularly unusual occurrences. They are too part of the natural order of creation.[30]

Nevertheless, Maimonides' understanding of the meaning of human freedom to act can be misunderstood if we read into it modern views that see freedom as a value. For Maimonides, freedom is a fact and not a value, something that humanity has more in common with animals than angels.[31] It is not considered as a human excellence, but rather as an element of necessity in human nature. The denial, therefore, of human freedom to act would imply that humanity had achieved their rational perfection like the heavenly beings. Experience surely indicates that this is not the case. The denial of human freedom to act is, then, an overestimation rather than an underestimation of human nature. He describes it:

It is our fundamental principle of the law of Moses our master . . . that man has an absolute ability to act; I mean to say that in virtue of his nature, his choice and his will, he may do everything that is within the capacity of man to do . . . Similarly all the species of animals move in virtue of their own will.[32]

Human differentiation from animals, in terms of their freedom to act, is one of degree and not kind. Ibn Shem Tov, a fifteenth-century commentator on the *Guide*, points out that "choice" (*behirah*) is a more "rational" (*sikhlit*) thing than mere will (*ratzon*) and that Maimonides uses it in regard to human beings but not in regard to animals.[33] Nevertheless, the underlying general similarities are far greater than this specific difference. Humans share with other sublunar beings *desire* that determines automatic locomotion. Desire is attracted by what it perceives as good and is repulsed by what it perceives as bad.[34] Originally, a human was a being, like the heavenly beings, beyond mundane considerations, a being only concerned with matters of truth and falsehood. The "fall" in Eden removed humanity from this pristine level.[35] Thus human freedom is humanity's awareness of their incomplete status in this world.

Like all other sensibles, human freedom to act must be explained in terms of its proper end. Just as motion can be explained in terms of the ultimate direction of its goal, so too it is with humanity's ability to act. For Maimonides, the ultimate destination of all human action is God's direct presence. God's knowability as the cosmic *telos* is a primary intelligible.[36] Therefore, the relation between sensibles and intelligibles is teleological: the latter are the ultimate ends of the former.

The fact that this ultimate end exists prior to humanity's attainment of it means that it is *discovered* not constructed. As such God, through the Active Intellect, makes this ultimate knowledge move from a state of potentiality to actuality in the human mind. For Maimonides follows Aristotle in assuming that nothing can move from a potential to an actual state without an external efficient cause.[37] This is why the knowability of the divine law requires revelation to a prophet. The Neoplatonic motif of "overflowing" or "emanation" expresses the relation between the intelligible and sensible realms viewed from the perspective of the intelligible realm.[38] It is from this vantage point that the source of revelation is considered to be the will of God. It does not mean, however, as with created beings, that God wills *because* of criteria external to himself.[39] Rather, it means that God's essence must be viewed as the ultimate source of everything. Just as Maimonides used this same emanationist logic to explain God's creative relation to the universe in general,[40] so he used it to explain the etiology of prophecy as the highest noetic creation.

Nevertheless, one can at best view something from God's perspective by means of a very tenuous inference. One cannot presume to understand the workings of the divine essence. However, viewed from the bottom up, so to speak, the relation between the sensible and intellectual realms can be grasped in far greater detail. Here, as sentient and political beings, we can speak from our own experience. Our concern, in other words, with the end of the Torah is primary and itself determines how we view its source.

The question of perspective is best seen in Maimonides' understanding of when it is appropriate to speak of the "will" of God and when to speak of his "wisdom." In terms of God's essence itself, however, his absolute unity (*yihud*) precludes any real distinction between the two faculties:

> . . . the order of all ends is ultimately due to His will and wisdom . . . they are identical with His essence: His will and His volition or His wisdom not being things extraneous to His essence . . . His is an efficient cause, a form and an end. For this reason the philosophers designated Him as a cause and not only a Maker.[41]

When we know the proper end of any created entity, and the Torah is a created entity,[42] we then can speak of divine wisdom. When we only know the presence of any entity, but are ignorant of its proper end, then we speak of divine will. Existence, in other words, as *ens creatum* continually transcends our limited intellect. That is why Maimonides emphasizes that Aristotelian teleology, and the knowledge of specific ends *within* the universe, does not fully explain why there is a universe at all. This philosophical insufficiency is what enables the doctrine of *creatio ex nihilo* to be a valid, even superior, point of view in the context of a teleological metaphysics.[43]

For Maimonides, it is always preferable to view creation from the perspective of divine wisdom. To insist on divine volition to the exclusion of immanent ends is to eliminate intelligibility from creation. Thus such a point of view reduces the divine will to divine caprice. Ultimately there is wisdom in everything that God does. Despite the fact that we are unable to discover that wisdom in *everything* does not mean that we are unable to discover it in *anything*.[44] As regards the Torah's commandments, Maimonides stresses that even though there is a general reason for every commandment that we can discern, frequently we do not know why the particulars of many of the commandments are the way they are. Concerning the *essential* structure of the Torah and its institutions we are knowledgeable to a great extent and can see the divine wisdom in them.[45] Concerning the *existential* details, we are frequently unable to detect the divine wisdom. Here, then, we defer to divine will.[46] Due to our limited intellectual powers the divine will transcends divine wisdom in that we do not understand the full rationality of the Torah. When we do understand it, however, we also perceive the essential identity of divine wisdom and will. Reason and revelation are in the end the same.

4. Law as the Correlation of Politics and Metaphysics

The correlation of the sensible and intellectual spheres in human experience is first manifest in law as the initial correlation of politics and metaphysics.

Viewed in itself the political arena appears turbulent and disordered. It seems to be nothing more than the scene of struggle, ambition, greed and danger. However, the very fact that humanity is so disappointed in this disorder suggests that people have an awareness of something more ordered, which contradicts the prima facie divisiveness of political life. Maimonides writes:

It has been explained with utmost clarity that man is political by nature and that it is his nature to live in a society . . . Because of the manifold composition of this species . . . there are many differences between the individuals belonging to it . . . the nature of the human species requires that there be those differences among the individuals belonging to it . . . in addition society is a necessity for this nature . . .[47]

Maimonides then suggests that the political nature of humanity, which strives for political unity, leads to the emergence of a leader who attempts to narrow the differences between persons by the introduction of law, that is, uniform rules of conduct applying equally to everyone.[48] If this is the sole aim of the leader, namely, to bring about political cohesiveness, without regard for the discovery of truth with which the rational faculty is concerned, then he is simply an imaginative, inventive personality. His laws are considered manmade (*nimusim*).[49] The intent of the law, then, indicates its true source:

If on the other hand, you find a Law all of whose ordinances are due to attention being paid . . . to the soundness of the circumstances pertaining to the body and also to the soundness of belief—a Law that takes pain to inculcate correct opinions with regard to God . . . and that desires to make man wise, to give him understanding, and to awaken his attention, so that he should know the whole of that which exists in its true form—you must know that this guidance comes from Him . . . and that this Law is divine.[50]

The relation between the intelligible and the political realms is that the political nature of human beings aspires to achieve perpetual unity (*hok ehad tamid*) and order (*seder*). These ideals are finally grounded in the intelligible realm. The prophet observes this essential connection, seeing the solution to society's dilemma in the encouragement of and preparation for "speculative matters" (*inyanim iyyunim*), the apex of which is knowledge of God.[51] The inventive political leader, on the other hand, only sees immediately prudent solutions to political problems. He is not interested in the theological foundation of law. Maimonides, however, does not consider this type of limited insight to be immoral. It is only theologically unsatisfying. The treatment of this type of leader and type of society he leads is described in the *Mishneh Torah* as one observing Noahide law because of "rational conclusion." Such rational conclusion, unaware of the divine source and end of law, is a conventional sort of prudence. It is most keen in those leaders whose highly developed imaginations enable their rhetoric to appeal to the less developed imaginations of their followers.

The initial motivation of any political leader, statesman or prophet is to bring unity out of diversity, harmony out of chaos. Therefore, the legislation of any political leader is given in universal norms. From the point of view of individuals, law seems to be inherently inadequate, because it cannot possibly address itself to their particular differences. However, it is their very differences, with their resultant strife and misery, which are the source of the fundamental problem with human society. The universality of law is, then, not its weakness but instead its strength:

... the Law does not pay attention to the isolated. The Law was not given with a view to things that are rare ... For the Law is a divine thing; and it is your business to reflect on the natural things in which the general utility (*ha-to'elet ha-kollelet*) which is included in them nonetheless produces damages to individuals ... [52]

The question: How can the divine immutable Torah produce damaging results for some individuals?[53] The answer to this seems to be that it depends on how individuals participate in the community constituted by divine law. If their participation is basically a tacit contract, where they give up *unlimited* freedom in return for political protection, namely, society's sanction to pursue *limited* individual freedoms, then it is very likely that in some cases this will be a bad bargain. Some individuals will in the end give away more than they receive. If, on the other hand, social participation is motivated by a desire to imitate nature, to participate in a realm of greater unity and order, then the sacrifice of unlimited human prerogatives cannot ultimately harm anyone who has risen to this level of wisdom. For understanding the true ends of human society enables one to experience divine providence (*hashgahah*), which functions on the specific rather than the individual level.[54] When one lives within the perspective of proper human teleology, one then participates in a realm that is now not only ideal but to a certain extent real. This is the difference between the political leadership of an ordinary statesman and a prophet. The former is occupied with only the prudential value of political unity and order. He does not grasp their theological grounding. The prophet, conversely, transcends the statesman in his vision of this theological grounding.[55] The difference in perspective is between "intellection" and "estimation."[56] Maimonides' refusal to include among the gentile saints who merit the world-to-come, those who practice the Noahide laws because of rational conviction alone, is based upon a distinction between prudential and theological reasoning, the former dealing with human matters only. Such prudential reasoning appears to refer to the "bringer of the *nomos*" (*meniyah ha-nimus*) he contrasts with the prophet.[57] This also explains why Maimonides was so reluctant to acknowledge a real, morally sufficient social order outside the Torah, even though he does admit a rational ethics, at least formally.

5. Moral Wisdom

By understanding the important distinction between the prophet and the statesman, we can perhaps resolve a critical textual issue in the *Mishneh Torah*.

It will be recalled that Maimonides stipulates that only gentiles who accept the Noahide law as revealed qualify as "saints" (*hasidim*) who merit the bliss of the world-to-come. Those gentiles who in the past accepted Noahide law due to Jewish political rule qualified for the status of *ger toshav* earning the right of domicile in the Land of Israel and protection through the law. For what category do those gentiles, who accept Noahide law out of considerations of practical wisdom, qualify?

At this point the respective manuscripts of *Hilkhot Melakim* present two variants. Some manuscripts, followed by the subsequent printed editions of the text, read:

But if he did them because of rational conclusion, he is not (*ein zeh*) a *ger toshav*, nor (*v'eino*) one of the saints of the nations of the world, and is not one of their sages (*ve-l'o me-hakhmaihem*).[58]

Other manuscripts present the last clause as: "but (*ela*) he is one of their sages."[59] With the manuscript evidence so divided it is difficult to draw a conclusive reading from it alone. It is easy to see how *ve-lo* ("and not") could be a copyist's error for *ela* ("but") and vice versa. The change of only one letter is involved. Therefore, it seems that the more conclusive method will have to be an internal examination of the structure of the passage in its immediate context and within the wider context of Maimonides' other remarks on the nature of law.

In terms of the immediate context the positive inclusion of those who consent to Noahide law through non-theological reasoning, in the category of gentile "sages," can be argued for on the basis of symmetry. Maimonides designates three ways of accepting Noahide law: (1) political subservience; (2) religious submission; (3) rational conclusion. The first method of acceptance is the *ger toshav*; the second one is the status of "saints." Maimonides' establishment of this correspondence between acts of acceptance and their respective categories would indicate that there is a category corresponding to the acceptance of Noahide law due to rational conclusion. The second manuscript reading we noted completes the symmetry by placing this person in the category of gentile *hakhamim*. Finally, it can be argued that it would have been awkward for Maimonides to use the negative *v'eino* twice: to eliminate this prudential person from the category of *ger toshav* and *hasid*, and then to use another negative, *ve-l'o*, to remove him from the status of *hakham* as well.[60] Such an awkward change would be atypical in the *Mishneh Torah*, known for its simple Hebrew.

A number of passages in the *Mishneh Torah* suggest that Maimonides used *hakhamim* to designate persons possessing practical wisdom, Jewish or gentile. In assigning prophecy the status of "a foundation of the religion" (*me-yesodai ha-dat*) he presents a brief description of the experience of prophecy. In presenting the prophet's self-consciousness, he notes, "and he understands in his mind that he is not like he was, but that he is exalted above other human sages."[61] In explaining prudence as the "median measure" (*middah baynonit*) Maimonides states, "and this way is the way of the sages. Every man whose moral character is medianly average is called a 'sage'."[62] These two passages suggest that *anyone* categorized as a *hakham* is a person of ordinary morality, one who is usually blind to the theological grounding of his morality.

In the *Guide*, Maimonides shows that *hakham* can be used for either a person possessing the "rational virtues" (*ma'alot ha-sikhliyot*) or the "moral virtues" (*ma'alot ha-middot*).[63] This corresponds to the ambiguity in the use of "wisdom" (*hokmah*) in the Bible. Now it is clear that if in the *Mishneh Torah* Maimonides designated gentiles whose morality is based on practical wisdom as *hakhamim*, he means that they have moral virtue though not rational virtue. They understand "conventions" (*mefursamot*) not "intelligibles" (*muskalot*). In addition, Maimonides indicates that even the *hakham* who has achieved the highest level of intellectual wisdom, namely, "the apprehension of Him, may He be exalted," has not reached the most complete state of human perfection. Rather, it is the person who also "imitates the Lord's actions" of kindness, justice and righteousness. What Maimonides is suggesting, then, is that a *hakham*, in neither the rational nor the moral sense, is the complete human being. He is the person who fully synthesizes both rational and moral virtues into one.[64] Being a *hakham* in the moral sense or the rational sense respectively is the *conditio sine qua non* for this state, but it is not the *conditio per quam*. It does not guarantee it.[65]

Returning to the case of the gentile who consents to live under Noahide law due to practical wisdom, we find a *hakham* morally adequate but theologically lacking. Therefore, it seems to me, based on contextual evidence and hermeneutical analysis, that Maimonides designated such a person as a *hakham*. This status has a material recognition, but is not endorsed as exemplary.

6. Divine and Natural Law

Regarding the origins of law, Maimonides concludes:

Therefore I say that the Law, although it is not natural, enters into what is natural. It is part of the wisdom of the deity with regard to permanence of this species of which He willed the existence, that He put into its nature that individuals belonging to it should have the faculty of ruling.[66]

In order to understand this passage we must first consider what Maimonides intends by "nature."

In the *Guide*, Maimonides uses "nature" or "natural" in two senses. On the one hand, he emphasizes nature as the intelligent guiding principle within the created order:

This meaning of "nature," which is said to be wise, having governance, caring for the bringing into existence of animals by means of an art of a craftsman, and also caring for their preservation and permanence . . . what is intended hereby is the divine thing.[67]

Elsewhere he draws an analogy between nature as this conscious ordering function in the universe and nature as this same function in the human person.[68] On the other hand, he uses "nature" to indicate necessity within the created order, that is, material that requires intelligent order:

For the Law always tends to assimilate itself to nature, perfecting the natural matters in a certain respect. For nature is not endowed with thought and understanding, whereas the Law is the determining ruling of the deity, who grants the intellect of all its possessors.[69]

We have a contradiction. However, we would do well to remember that Maimonides warned his readers in the introduction to the *Guide* that there would be contradictions (*steerah*), advising them to discover the essential meaning of his words by picking up his clues.

Nature is used ambiguously when describing humanity because humans themselves are fundamentally ambiguous. Humans are rational, capable of intellection as are the heavens, the intelligible realm in miniature.[70] We are also physical beings, motivated by desires like the animals.[71] *Nature* is a term expressing the state whereby any created being has reached the fullest perfection possible for it. It is used, therefore, to describe the conscious principle of the ordered heavens and the self-sufficient behavior of individual animals. Nature at this level is unconscious, instinctual:

None of the individual animals requires for its continued existence reflection, perspicacity, governance of conduct. For it goes about and runs in accordance with its nature . . . Consequently the individual remains in existence during the time in which it exists, and the existence of the species continues . . . [72]

Maimonides continues: those who live at the instinctual level alone perish quickly. They require governance of their conduct, governance developed by intelligent political unity and order.

Therefore, I believe the contradiction in Maimonides' use of *nature* can be resolved if we specify what he means in any particular context. When he speaks of nature as a human ideal, he intends rational nature, that principle of governance that functions in humans, the *microcosm*, or the universe, the *macrocosm*. When, conversely, he writes of nature as something requiring human improvement or development, then he intends animal nature. In animals themselves nature requires no improvement, but in human beings, being ambiguous, their animal nature must be *morally subordinated* to their rational nature. This moral subordination does not extinguish the natural functioning of anything physical in human existence.[73] It only limits the capacity of any physical drive to turn human attention from reason to sensuousness. This emerges in Maimonides' rationale for circumcision:

Similarly with regard to *circumcision*, one of the reasons for it is, in my opinion, the wish to bring a decrease in sexual intercourse and a weakening of the organ in question . . . It has been thought that circumcision perfects what is defective congenitally. This gave the possibility to everyone to raise an objection and to say: How can natural things be defective so that they need to be perfected from the outside? . . . In fact this *commandment* has not been prescribed with a view to perfecting what is defective congenitally, but to perfect what is defective morally . . . None of the activities necessary for the preservation of the individual is harmed thereby, nor is procreation rendered impossible, but violent concupiscence and lust that goes beyond what is needed is diminished.[74]

In other words, sex, when it is not a sensuous rival to the rational quest, is not attacked. In itself it is good and necessary. But it limits conscious preoccupation with sex. The Torah corrects, or tries to correct, this moral defect. Maimonides is clear in indicating that nature needs improvement only in terms of its moral relation to human life and activity. In itself, on the animal level per se, it is self-sufficient. Moral improvement is that "certain respect" (*tzad ehad*) of the improvement of nature that Maimonides mentioned earlier.[75]

This affects our free choice. As we have seen, freedom of choice is underpinned by uncertainty. But we desire to overcome uncertainty. However, now that we understand the dual meaning of nature in Maimonides' system, what he might call "nature above" and "nature below," we can see why he contrasts freedom and nature. Freedom lies between these two natures. It attempts, when morally guided, to improve nature below by aspiring to the nature above.[76]

This explains why Maimonides contrasts things "natural" to things "divine."[77] Physics is "natural wisdom," and metaphysics represents "divine wisdom."[78] Moral law is what correlates these two realms, for it causes humans, being in the lower realm, to aspire to the intelligibility of the higher realm. Furthermore, the complete morality of the prophet unifies this correlation by bringing the intelligibility of the higher to the lower realm. Consequently, Maimonides' contrast between the divine and political realms corresponds to his contrast between the natural or physical realm and the divine.[79] With this understood, we can now understand his characterization of the Torah as "entering into what is natural." It means that the Torah, as the correlation of the divine and human realms, has relevance for physical nature but cannot be reduced to it.[80] If it were so reduced, then it could not guide it morally. The Torah, then, transcends physical nature in terms of source and end.[81] The Torah itself is intelligible, even if not fully grasped by human intellect. Physical nature is itself unintelligible. Therefore, the Torah is closer to divine wisdom that willed the creation of the universe. The Torah also prescribes the ends of human striving: first, our physical end, which is a stable, unified society; second, our intellectual end, which is true knowledge of God.[82] In terms of the first end the Torah can be considered natural; in terms of the second it is divine.[83] As a result, Maimonides refers to the physical end of the Torah as being "prior in nature and time."[84]

7. Noahide and Natural Law

The Torah is most evidently natural when its political function is most manifest. It is least evidently natural when its political function is least evidently manifest and, also, when the reasons for its particular details are most obscure. Understanding Maimonides' concept of nature enables us to designate his concept of Noahide law as a "natural law" theory, for the political function of Noahide law is more evidently manifest than any other group of laws presented in the Bible or tradition.

Maimonides lists the Noahide laws in an order different from any known rabbinic text. He is unimpressed with the type of exegesis that bases its content and sequence on Gen. 2:16. Although he regards them as biblically revealed, he emphasizes that this revelation is general (*me-khlal divrei torah*) rather than specific.[85]

Maimonides explains the reasons for the Noahide laws as follows:

He first lists the prohibition of idolatry (*avodah zarah*). We have already seen Maimonides' treatment of the subject.[86] What we need to add is that Maimonides considers the affirmation of the existence of God and the negation of idolatry to be the two intelligible foundations of the whole Torah:

For these two principles, I mean the existence of the deity and His being one, are knowable by human speculation alone . . . by demonstration . . . As for the other *commandments* they belong to the class of generally accepted opinions and those adopted in virtue of tradition, not to the class of the intellects.[87]

Maimonides supports this with the Talmudic view that the first two commandments of the Decalogue were heard by the whole people.[88] The rest of the commandments were transmitted through Moses. Maimonides interprets this distinction in the promulgation of the commandments as a distinction between the commandments themselves. Moreover, the second commandment is the prohibition of idolatry, not the affirmation of the oneness of God. However, Maimonides equates idolatry with polytheism.[89] Since God's oneness is only known negatively, as is the case with all the essential attributes of God, the prohibition of polytheism is an adequate expression to humans of God's unity. This is corroborated in *Sefer ha-Mitzvot*. In this work, the first positive commandment, the affirmation of God's existence, is based on "I am the Lord your God." The first negative commandment, the rejection of polytheism, is based on "there shall be no other gods." The second positive commandment is to affirm the unity of God.

In making the distinction between "intellecta" and "conventions," Maimonides does not intend that only the affirmation of the existence of God and the oneness of God is intelligible and the remainder of the commandments, therefore, are unintelligible.[90] Such an interpretation is clearly belied by Maimonides' persistent treatment of the "reasons of the commandments" (*ta'amei ha-mitzvot*), wherein he went further than his predecessors.[91] What Maimonides does intend, I think, is that only these two commandments are *immediately intelligible per se* because they deal with the essence of God that is the unchanging foundation of all intelligibility.[92] The intelligibility of these two commandments, then, requires no external point of reference. They are ends in themselves.[93] The other commandments, conversely, all have a political context. They refer to various human actions. Their intelligibility is not immediate because politics, with which they deal, is not an end in itself. They are conceived of, therefore, as means to other ends. The commandments have to be viewed as serving either a political purpose, or as serving to eradicate idolatry. These other commandments, then, either serve to improve the body or the soul. As such they need to be both conventional and traditional. Society has both a horizontal and a vertical dimension. The former is ordered by present conventions, the latter by tradition. We have seen that Maimonides considered prophecy as the full human correlation of the divine and political realms. The Torah, the product of Mosaic prophecy, correlates the intellecta and the conventions and traditions in one normative structure. Sometimes that correlation is more evident, at other times less so. In the case of the Noahide laws it is most evident precisely because they are most general, containing few if any obscure details.

He lists second the prohibition of blasphemy. This follows naturally from the prohibition of idolatry. Whereas idolatry is the substitution of something else in place of God, blasphemy is the denial of God's centrality. It begins in illegitimate speech about God.[94] Maimonides rules, then, that blasphemy involves any designation of the deity that is irreverent.[95] He avoids regarding blasphemy, however, as only an affront to the specifically Jewish designations of God.[96] By avoiding this view, Maimonides is better able to connect the universal prohibitions of blasphemy and idolatry. He considers as barred from the world-to-come those who make flawed statements about God such as stating that he has a body.[97] Polytheists fall into the same category. Although he does not designate this as blasphemy per se, it nevertheless closely parallels the relation between idolatry and blasphemy.

The next law is the prohibition of bloodshed, involving inter-human political relations. It will be recalled that Maimonides saw the origins of the political realm in the striving for intelligent order and unity out of instinctual strife and disunity. The greatest threat, then, is violence, especially murder. Maimonides writes:

Even though there are transgressions graver than bloodshed, none of them, even idolatry, involves the destruction of civilization (*yishuvo shel olam*) . . . whoever has personally committed this transgression is wholly evil.[98]

Clearly, then, the prohibition of murder is intelligible in terms of its relation to society, a human necessity. The end of the commandment is evident. In the *Guide*, he notes:

Consequently there is . . . a cause for all the *commandments*: I mean to say that any particular commandment or prohibition has a useful end. In the cause of some of them, it is clear to us in what way they are useful—as in the case of the prohibition of killing and stealing.[99]

Now this commandment, although evidently rational, is not one of the "intellecta" for two reasons: first, its intelligibility is based on being a means to an end, the need for protection from violence; second, the commandment deals with human sociability that is not necessarily perpetual as are the intelligible objects dealt with in metaphysical speculation. However, the point clearly emerges that because a commandment is not directly concerned with intellecta does not *ipso facto* render it unintelligible, that is, not evidently based on nature.

The next law concerns forbidden sexual relations.[100] Maimonides is occupied with its political significance. He writes:

Before the giving of the Torah a man would run into a woman in the marketplace. If they both desired that he take her, he would bring her into his house and copulate with her . . . Before the giving of the Torah a man would run into a woman in the marketplace. If they both desired it he would give her her price and copulate with her in public and go his way. She is what is called a harlot.[101]

Maimonides' point is that before the Law was promulgated, sexual relations were informal and virtually unlimited. Also, they were not a matter of public control. The law was meant to limit their frequency. In the *Guide* he develops the rationale of this position more explicitly:

Accordingly, a single tribe that is united through a common ancestor . . . love one another, help one another, and have pity on one another; and the attainment of these things is the greatest purpose of the Law. Hence harlots are prohibited, because through them lines of ancestry are destroyed . . . Another important consideration . . . is the prevention of an intense lust for sexual intercourse and for constant preoccupation with it . . . if harlots are permitted, a number of men might happen to betake themselves at one and the same time to one woman, they would inevitably quarrel and in most cases they would kill one another or kill the woman . . .[102]

Maimonides, therefore, see the normative limitation of sexuality based on three reasons: (1) it contributes to strengthening the bonds of kinship, which is the foundation of social cohesiveness and continuity; (2) it mitigates violence, a chief cause of which is sexual jealousy; (3) it contributes to human rationality by containing excessive lust. All of this is accomplished by the public institution of marriage, and by extension making adultery socially unacceptable because it destroys the bond of marital fidelity.

Maimonides, in the same chapter of the *Guide*, excludes homosexuality and bestiality from the area of permitted sexual relations, because even if those types of sexuality that are physically natural (*ha-unyan ha-tivi'i*) are permitted only for reasons of physical necessity (*le-tzorekh*), and even so are limited, then that which is unnatural should be prohibited altogether because it serves no purpose. What Maimonides means, I think, is that heterosexuality is the physical basis of the family, and the family is the foundation of society. Homosexuality and bestiality serve no similar purpose, pleasure being the only end. For Maimonides they are unjustifiable precisely because they do not contribute to a higher end. Marital heterosexuality, on the other hand, can be justified both in terms of its positive and necessary contribution to society, and its making room for intellectual pursuit.

This double rationale, namely, that a law contributes to both physical and political well-being (*tikkun ha-guf*) is not a double-effect theory.[103] It does not posit two essentially different effects from one act. Rather, political well-being leads to intellectual well-being and, on the other hand, an anti-intellectual, sensuous life leads to anti-political activity. Although Maimonides follows Aristotle in distinguishing between moral and intellectual excellence, and in making the former the stepping stone to the latter,[104] he is much closer to Plato in his close correlation of these two ends. This passage from the *Guide* demonstrates this:

> ... the lusts and licentiousness of the multitude ... This is what destroys man's last perfection, what harms him also in his first perfection, and what corrupts most of the circumstances of the citizens and of the people engaged in domestic governance. For when only the desires are done, as is done by the ignorant, the longing for speculation is abolished, the body is corrupted ... thus cares and sorrows multiply, mutual envy, hatred, and strife aiming at taking away what the other has, multiply. All this is brought about by the fact that the ignoramus regards pleasure alone as the end to be sought for its own sake.[105]

As Maimonides emphasized earlier, humanity's "first perfection" is political, their "last perfection" is intellectual. Just as one cannot hope to achieve the last perfection without achieving the first, so without striving for the final intellectual happiness one cannot even attain the earlier political happiness. The Torah comes to fully synthesize these two strivings.[106]

The next law in Maimonides' enumeration is prohibition of robbery. He devotes little space to this law, for "the utility of this class is manifest."[107] Its cause is the same as that of murder and lust—excessive concentration on physical pleasure. Here the idea is that seeing such pleasure as an end in itself is essentially unsatisfying. He writes: "it is already known that *coveting* is prohibited because it leads to *desire*, and *desire* is prohibited because it leads to robbery."[108]

The law of adjudication, listed next, is the last of the six commandments given to Adam. Maimonides judges it as the enforcement of the preceding five laws and, hence, it follows them because it presupposes them. He sees, for example, the violation of this law in the refusal of the Shechemites to judge their prince for the sexual abduction of Dinah.[109] This, then, presupposes the law concerning prohibited sexual relations.

The final law in Maimonides' order of the Noahide laws is the prohibition of eating a limb torn from a living animal. The rationale here is the most obscure, although it is the only one explicitly stated and addressed to Noahides.[110] Maimonides give a double rationale:

> The reason for the prohibition against eating a *limb of a living animal* is because this would make one acquire the habit of cruelty. Such things were done in those times by the kings of the *Gentiles*; this was also an action used in *idolatry* . . .[111]

Thus we see in one commandment the prohibition of a practice both politically and intellectually dangerous, a definite correlation between cruelty to other sentient beings and the denial of the true God, namely, the denial of the integrity of creation is part of the denial of the integrity of the Creator. At the level of physical pain, Maimonides reasons that there is "no difference regarding this pain between man and the other animals."[112] Sadism is abhorrent whether the victim is human or not.

In conclusion, for Maimonides the rationale for all the Noahide laws is clearly evident, either in terms of humanity's lower physical nature, or in terms of humanity's higher intellectual nature. Noahide law is natural law in its most immediately evident manifestation. Its generality enables us to see full correlation of divine wisdom and will. It is both knowable itself (*ratio per se*) and known by all rationally moral persons (*ratio quod nos*).

8.   Noahide Law and Historical Revelation

Scholars have long debated the connection in Maimonides' thought of Noahide law and historical revelation. This hermeneutical problem has significant philosophical implications. If Maimonides makes the acceptance of the historical Mosaic revelation the *sine qua non* for gentiles to attain the world-to-come, then it would seem that *only* Christians and Muslims would qualify. As Louis Jacobs wrote: "if this were to be accepted it would certainly exclude many good men of other faiths."[113] Earlier, Mendelssohn complained to Jacob Emden, a leading German halakhist.[114] Mendelssohn argued that it would be ascribing cruel caprice to God if we believe that the only gentiles meriting a portion in the world-to-come are those whose morality is consciously based not only on revelation, but on revelation in Jewish terms. Emden responded his assent to Maimonides' opinion, sprinkling in some additional Talmudic precedents to strengthen Maimonides' case.

This apparent stance of Maimonides seems non-universalistic. It has generally been emphasized for two different motives.

First, Spinoza stresses the reading of the printed text that removes Noahide who observe the law due to reason (*a ratione ductus*) from "saints" (*nec ex piis*), and from the category of the "sages of the nations" (*nec ex scientibus Nationum*).[115] Spinoza, of course, was making a polemic against religious particularism, and holding Judaism as the most particularistic of all. A religion based on historical/particular revelation, for Spinoza, is inferior to a religion based on reason, which is universal:[116]

. . . the Divine law, which renders man truly blessed, and teaches them the true life, is universal to all men; nay, we have so intimately deduced it from human nature that it must be esteemed innate, and as it were, ingrained in the human mind.[117]

Second, some traditionalists, wishing to demonstrates that Maimonides affirmed the superiority of revelation over reason, use the same interpretation as the decidedly non-traditionalist Spinoza. Marvin Fox, for example, writes:

But Maimonides denies to such a man all claims to special merit and in the process denies that there is or can be any natural moral law . . . This extreme position of Maimonides with respect to natural law is a reflection of the normative attitude of the classical Jewish tradition.[118]

Both views are erroneous for three reasons: (1) they read the text in the *Mishneh Torah* too literally; (2) they fail to take into the consideration Maimonides' philosophical view of the relation of reason and revelation; and (3) they overlook, or are unaware of, Maimonides' explicit interpretation of the text in the *Mishneh Torah* concerning the conditions for eternal bliss for gentiles.

We saw earlier that Noahide law, for Maimonides, was accessible through practical wisdom, although it is theologically insufficient. Therefore, he leaves open the question of whether a person who combined practical and theoretical wisdom in a harmonious synthesis could merit eternal bliss if he accepted the equivalent of Noahide law from this perspective, without actually affirming its historical revelation in the specifically Jewish sense.

Such a person would, however, be a prophet. Prophecy is a universal phenomenon, found among Jews and non-Jews. It is not the result of a particular historical experience. The objective truth that all prophets experience is part of the created natural order. When and where they happen to experience this truth is of subjective importance only. For Maimonides, prophecy is not miraculous. Revelation is simply an apprehension that all those of moral and intellectual excellences are at least potentially capable.[119] Prophetic revelation is the highest manifestation of divine wisdom, and thus Maimonides judges the final authority of the Mosaic Torah as due to its greater rationality (understood theologically, of course), not to its more spectacular historical revelation. The historical revelation of the Bible, although prophetic apprehension at its apex, does not preclude prophecy outside Israel, or even outside of Abrahamic faiths.[120]

All of this can be inferred from Maimonides' concept of prophecy, especially as expressed in the *Guide*. Earlier, in the *Mishneh Torah*, he wrote:

. . . but anyone in the world (*me-kol ba'ay olam*) whose spirit moves him and he understands by his own intellect (*mada'o*) to stand apart before the Lord to minister to Him and to serve Him, to know the Lord and to walk straight as God made him . . . such a person is sanctified with greatest sanctity and his inheritance forever and ever, and he will merit what he deserves in the world-to-come . . . [121]

However, in a responsum written to Hasdai the Spaniard, a responsum composed after both of his great works, Maimonides presents a manifestly non-dogmatic view of the possibility of gentile apprehension of the way of God, independent of historical revelation:

You should know that God desires the heart . . . thus the nations of the world have a portion in the world-to-come if they apprehend what is capable of being apprehended in terms of knowledge of the Creator, blessed be He, and ordering their souls with good morals. There is no doubt that whoever orders his soul with correct morals and correct wisdom regarding belief in the Creator, blessed be He, surely such a person is one of the members of the world-to-come . . . Indeed the philosophers call him a godly man (*ish elohi*) . . . [122]

In other words, the proper correlation of moral virtue and intellectual excellence can enable one to observe the *equivalent* of Noahide law and achieve eternal bliss. Even the philosophers who reason independently, without historical revelation, acknowledge this possibility. Being part of a historical community, one that itself acknowledges the authority of historical revelation, preserving and interpreting it, makes this achievement easier by providing a traditional body of law and theology consistent with true knowledge of God.[123] That is why Maimonides assigns to the Jewish authorities the task of enforcing Noahide law among the gentiles whenever they have the political power to do so, as we have already seen.[124] However, what emerges from Maimonides' overall treatment of the question of universal law is that being part of such a historical community, however morally and intellectually advantageous that may be, is not the *sine qua non* for the achievement of eternal bliss.

In conclusion, we thus see that Maimonides' theory of law, especially Noahide law, constitutes it as rational, revealed and universal. The scope and coherence of this theory attest to a theologian of extraordinary learning and even more extraordinary philosophical insight.

CHAPTER ELEVEN

ALBO'S THEORY OF NOAHIDE LAW

1. Introduction

In the writings of Joseph Albo, a fifteenth-century Spanish exegete, we find the most explicit theory of law attempted by a Jewish thinker up to that time. In his *Sefer ha-Ikkarim* (Book of Roots) Albo carefully defines the various kinds of law and their interrelations. Noahide law, of course, is introduced into his overall theory of law. In order to understand Noahide law in Albo's thought, we must first consider his general approach to law, then the relationship of Noahide law to that approach and finally how Noahide law is related to other types of law.

Albo defines law in general as follows: "The name law (*dat*) applies to any direction (*ha-yesharah*) or rule of conduct (*hanhagah*) which includes a large group of men."[1] Then he divides law into three distinct classes: natural (*tiv'it*), conventional (*nimusit*) and divine (*elohit*). This theoretical division is based on a real division between the respective purposes these types of law intend. The source of natural law is human nature, intending a just society. Conventional law's source is a sovereign ruler who creates a desirable society. The source of divine law is God, aiming at the eternal happiness for human beings. Noahide law is included as a group within the third class of law. However, it is not so much Albo's classification of law that stimulates philosophical reflection as it is his analysis of the content of each class, its relation to its source and its purpose, and the interrelations among the classes themselves. Here we find some of Albo's most significant contributions to the development of Jewish thought.

2. Natural Law

Albo starts his analysis of law with a discussion of natural law: "Grouping and association (*ve-ha-hitavrut*) being necessary for the existence and maintenance of the species, the wise have stated that man is political by nature (*medina be-teva*)."² The phrase "political by nature" has its origins, of course, in Aristotle's designation of human beings as *politikon zoōn*, "a political animal."³ Nevertheless, Albo means here something more limited. Whereas Aristotle designated the human capacity for rational speech (*logos*) as the essence of this political nature, Albo limits it to the human need for material sustenance, whose satisfaction usually requires sustained association between human beings. Such a need leads to the requirement of some system of order which will maintain society. The most evident aspect of this system of order will be protection from such acts of violence and disorder as murder, theft and robbery. The very materialist orientation of this definition of natural law prompted Ralph Lerner to note, "it reminds one less of Aquinas than of Hobbes . . . Albo's natural law is, in fact, utterly devoid of anything that would direct men's attention to anything higher than the most elemental bodily wants."⁴

Taken in and of itself such a characterization of Albo's concept of natural law is certainly correct. However, when we examine Albo's definition more precisely some intriguing insights emerge.

Following his paraphrase of Aristotle, Albo continues: "They mean by this that it is almost necessary for man, by virtue of his nature (*mi-tzad tiv'o*), that he live in a city (*medinah*) with a large group of men in order that he be able to find what is needed for life and maintenance."⁵ Here Albo uses two different terms for "necessity." For the need for material things, he uses *tzorekh*; for political needs, he uses *hekrekh*. The use of two different terms is surely not a mere stylistic device in such a carefully constructed work.

Regarding material things "necessity" indicates what is *absolutely* needed for human life to exist, namely, those things that satisfy elemental bodily wants. Regarding society, however, "necessity" suggests what is *usually* needed for human flourishing. This second necessity is not absolute because there is always the possibility of an apolitical, solitary life. Later, when Albo writes about human nature's political nature, he indicates this possibility, noting, "for if a man dwelled alone (*yehidi*) in the wilderness, not being part of a city, he would not need this perfection."⁶ Although for most people, living in a political community is as inevitable as the satisfaction of bodily needs, nevertheless, the possibility of a solitary life suggests our political nature is not in essence the same as our bodily nature. This difference corresponds to the two terms: "life" (*hayut*) and "maintenance" (*hitkayyamut*). Whereas life's needs (*tzorekh*) are absolute, maintenance's needs (*hekhreh*) are usual. In other words, our psychic need for security, for the probable assurance that our needs will be provided for in the future, is the essence of our political nature, one that requires society. Our psychic need for security, then, mediates between our bodily needs and society. Therefore, when we share bodily needs with other living creatures, our political needs are unique to our self-awareness. Indeed, when Albo designates society as a necessity for some creatures, for whose life and maintenance it is impossible to do without, the human species is the only example he provides. While a lone individual may not require society, the species itself is political. A completely solitary individual lives on a non-human level.[7] Sociality is thus rooted in our psychic need for security.[8]

The difference between simple bodily needs, present in all living creatures, and bodily needs as experienced by human beings emerges in Albo's exegesis of a famous Talmudic text that recounts the virtues that can be learned from other animals:

... this is not to say that the animals and birds are wiser and more understanding than the human species ... but man by virtue of his intelligence and general faculties learns from all the animals all their particular instincts and apprehensions (kol ha-tahbulot ve-ha-hasagot ha-pratiyot) and gathers them all and they become general in him ...[9]

Here Albo indicates that human reason has the capacity to generalize from particular needs. It is not that human beings experience these particular tendencies outside themselves, but rather humans experience them inside themselves and subsequently see them exemplified in the behavior of certain animals. The human capacity for universalization makes this generalization possible. Indeed, elsewhere Albo notes that an overly abundant instinctual life actually weakens humanity's intellectual ability.[10] It is not so much involvement with the senses as it is one's ability to be critical in learning from them that enables humanity to intend a political order.

Concerning the elemental constitution of society, Albo writes:

Because of this it is evident (mevo'ar) that it is fitting that there exist for the whole group ... a certain order (siddur mah) whereby they conduct themselves (bo yitahagu) ... and this order includes protection from murder, theft, robbery and the like ...[11]

Here Albo has introduced a third term for necessity, ra'ui—that which is "fitting." Thus we now have three terms corresponding to humanity's three specific needs: (1) tzorekh—the need for vitality (hayut); (2) hekhreh—the psychic need for security (hitkayyamut) in society; (3) ra'ui—the political need for legal order (siddur) within society. It is impossible to understand, therefore, what Albo means by "natural law" unless we see the correlation of these three needs and the states of being they intend.

Finally, Albo reintroduces the term he used in the beginning of his discussion to describe physical necessity—tzorekh: "The wise called this order natural law (*dat tiv'it*), meaning that it is necessary (*mi-tzad tiv'o*)." Here again, I believe Albo's choice of vocabulary is deliberate. What he appears to be saying is that law is as necessary for humanity's political existence as certain material substances are necessary for their bodily existence. Thus, humanity's political need for law is discovered and fulfilled by the same process of generalization as is their bodily need for food, clothing and shelter. Each is part of human nature. The specific difference between these two types of necessity is that the former is material and the latter psychic. Also, the former concerns humanity's present existence, the latter concerns the conscious extension of that existence into the future.

Albo concludes his discussion of natural law here by noting that the fundamental prohibitions of natural law, such as those of murder and robbery, are considered natural law "whether it be ordered by a wise man or by a prophet." This concluding remark is significant and without it Albo's theory of natural law would be incomplete and liable to misinterpretation.

As we will see, a system of law ordered or promulgated by a wise man is conventional or positive law, and a system of law ordered or promulgated by a prophet is divine law. What we see here is that natural law does not promulgate itself. It is either transmitted through convention or through revelation. If this is the case, then how is natural law different from conventional and divine law?

To begin to answer this question we must first keep in mind that law in all its forms is defined politically. However, whereas there are three types of law, there are only two kinds of historical societies, societies constituted by convention and these constituted by revelation. In a modern idiom, we would say "secular" or "religious." If both are historically real, that is, are objects of experience, then both are seen *a posteriori*. If, on the other hand, it is possible for natural law to be presented in either or both of these kinds of societies without at the same time constituting a third kind of society, then it can only be seen *a priori*. In other words, natural law does not denote the real constitution of a historical society, but rather is the formal condition of any human society. Natural law, then, for Albo, is the order that makes any society morally coherent and consequently deserving of human commitment.

The moral coherence provided by natural law is justice. Albo notes that "the intent (*kavvanat*) of the natural law is to remove wrong (*ha'avel*) and to bring about right (*ha-yosher*) . . . in a way that society may endure and be maintained among men . . . "[12] The political order intended by natural law is one in which rights are protected. The original motivation for the constitution of any society is the psychic need for security in the pursuit of bodily wants. These wants are experienced by individuals who are conscious and rational.

Therefore, if society merits loyalty, then it must never ignore the rights of these individuals which *their* security requires. Moral standards are rooted in the unilateral relation between individuals and society.[13]

Although the constitution of both secular and religious societies intends more than this elementary political order, nevertheless, it is always to be included in any morally respectable society. As such the "orderers" of these societies presuppose a formal order that makes their activity, in the most general way, possible.

3. Conventional Law

Although natural law is the formal condition necessary for the constitution of any truly human society, it is not sufficient to establish that society itself. It is only a *conditio sine qua non* not a *conditio per quam*. Whereas the concrete act of ordering presupposes an abstract order as its formal condition, an abstract order presupposes a concrete act of ordering by a real person or persons as its substantial ground. Albo writes: "But this law is not sufficient (*ein . . . maspeket*) to arrange the needs of men and their life and maintenance with each other . . . "[14] The reason for this insufficiency is that the political effectiveness of natural law (that is, rational justice) depends on the constitution of a particular society by the unified consent (*haskamah kolelet*) of its members. Natural law has to become convention (*nimus*) in order to become an accepted standard of justice. Furthermore, the effectiveness of this standard of justice requires coercion:

And this order or convention is impossible to be maintained unless there be found one man: a ruler or judge or king over that group or city, forcing men to remove wrong and to maintain convention in order to complete the arrangement of that group. For this reason the establishment of the king or leader or judge is as if necessary (*k'ilu hekhrahei*) for the maintenance of the human species in that man is political by nature . . .[15]

In other words, human beings do not need society in general, but rather a particular society to help assure the fulfillment of their elemental bodily wants.

Albo's introduction of the concept of coercion is the key to understanding the transition from natural to conventional law in his overall theory. Once again, the choice of terms is crucial. It will be noted that he uses the same term—*hekhreh*—to denote both the political coercion exercised by a leader and the political necessity for such a leader. Therefore, he indicates that the essence of political leadership is coercion, that this function defines the status of the leader.

Nevertheless, the presence of the leader does not in any way transcend the formal necessity for natural law. Albo is not advocating a Hegelian-style transformation from an earlier to a later level where the latter completely subsumes the former (*Aufhebung*).[16] Therefore, since natural law remains as a basic condition for any society, the concrete coercion required in any particular society cannot contradict the basic human rights known through natural law. It remains the *sine qua non* of politics. As such, political coercion involves "forcing men to remove wrong (*ve-kiyyum ha'avel*) and to maintain convention (*ve-kiyyum ha-nimus*) . . ." The maintenance of convention must always function in concert with the removal of wrong, the basic standard of natural law.

Political coercion connects two central principles of conventional society: choice and purpose:

The fundamental principles of conventional law and its derivatives are choice (*ha-behirah*) and purpose (*ve-ha-takhlit*). This is evident and clear. For why should a lawgiver fix punishments for lawbreakers if the violator is not within his domain (*bi-reshut atzmo*) to do what he wants . . . Similarly purpose . . . is a fundamental principle of all human acts done voluntarily (*be-ratzon*) . . . for everyone who acts with knowledge and volition does so because he intends a certain purpose . . .[17]

Political coercion, morally defined, manifests itself in the ruler's commandment and in his warning to his subjects. One can only command and warn persons who have free choice, for commandments and warnings presuppose the capacity for choice on the part of those commanded and warned.[18] Political coercion means making the law explicit and creating definite consequences for both adherence to it and deviation from it, respectively. The inherent justice of the law is determined by the criteria of natural law. However, for Albo, this is merely a *via negativa*, namely, removing violence and legal inequality.

Because of its negative nature, fulfillment of the criteria of natural justice does not in any way suggest positive human flourishing. Albo makes the point elsewhere that "in their observance of them there is not the acquisition of any spiritual perfection (*shlemut le-nefesh*), for if a man dwelled alone, not being part of a city, he would not meet this perfection."[19] The observance to which Albo is referring is "the removal of wrong and the perpetuation of right," namely, the function of natural justice. Albo stresses that this only has meaning within a concrete society. And we will soon see that inside such a society the positive goals, the political teleology, are provided by historical culture not by nature. Natural justice, then, only has meaning when functioning negatively within such a society. To overestimate its function is to make natural law historically irrelevant—an all too common deficiency in much natural law theory both before and after Albo.

Only a real political community enables us to affirm human freedom and purposiveness. Human freedom is inferred from the fact of law as particular commandment to a real concrete subject. Human purposiveness is surmised from the fact of law as a particular commandment intending a concrete state of affairs as its object. Human freedom is our positive capacity for action and human purposiveness is our positive intention of fulfillment. Conventional law includes the negative pole of natural law ("removal of injustice") and the positive pole of "maintaining convention."

It is important to understand why Albo considers freedom and purposiveness fundamental principles of conventional law and not of natural law.

For Albo, fundamental principles are those ideas without which a system of law cannot be conceived to exist.[20] He states that conventional law cannot exist in the absence of human freedom and purposiveness. However, natural law can be conceived to exist without freedom and purposiveness because natural law is not essentially a commandment. Rather, it is an order that humans require for their psychic security. As such it is too close to the instinctual level to presuppose either a subject who transcends physical nature in freedom, or to intend an end that transcends mere physical gratification. Both the subject and the end of conventional law are concrete non-physical realities: persons and states of affairs. The subject and the end of natural law are much more circumscribed. Conventional law is not grounded in natural law but is only limited by it.

At this point we begin to see that the leader of a conventional society is someone who is more than an implementer of the negative criteria of natural justice. Convention is a positive entity in and of itself.[21] What is convention? This definition emerges when we look at its intent:

The intent of conventional law is to remove the undesirable (*ha-meguneh*) and to bring about the desirable (*ha-na'eh*) in order that men may be removed from what is undesirable according to human opinion. In this it is superior to natural law because conventional law also arranges the conduct of men and orders their affairs in a desirable way (*b'ofan na'ot*), arranging the political group like natural law (*ke-tiv'it*).[22]

Conventional law, by virtue of its concrete positive intent, deals with what are desiderata and what are not. Now these desiderata are in essence *cultural goals*. This is what Albo means, I think, by *mefursam*, "human opinion."[23] These goals are those affirmed by particular societies in the course of their historical tradition. We see that we move from the physical nature of human beings to their political nature and now to their cultural nature.

In contrasting natural law which "is the same for all humans at all times and at all places" with conventional law, Albo notes that "conventional law is that which is ordered . . . in consideration of the place and the time and the nature of the people governed by it."[24] Conventional law, then, is historically constituted. By distinguishing between natural law as the negative pole of human sociality, and culture as its positive pole, and by refusing to reduce one to the mere function of the other, Albo has worked out a system of law wherein there is truly a harmonious relation between formal and substantial aspects.

Albo indicates that even in animals we not only find what is necessary (*hekhrahi*) for them to exist, but also a certain super-abundance that appears to be striving for what is beneficial and complete.[25] In humanity this striving for final perfection (*shlemuto ve-takhlito*) is itself a necessity, albeit of a more subtle kind than raw physical necessity. In his development of this teleological notion Albo sees conventional good as something more particular than the more abstract natural justice.

This striving for final completion establishes a definite hierarchy in human society, a hierarchy not involved in natural justice with its emphasis on the abstract equality of all:

Although all men are equal in humanness (*shavim b'enoshut*), human perfection reaches some by means (*b'emtza'ut*) of others . . . from the wise man the order, which arranges affairs so as to attain human perfection, reaches men. This order is called convention.[26]

If there were only equality, there would be no authority in human society.[27] Therefore, equality becomes an abstract legal standard, applicable in a juridical context, but not applicable to the implementation of the concrete goals of any society. Only the realization of such concrete goals suffices for human purposiveness.

4. Divine Law

Albo argues that conventional law must be added to natural law as both its promulgation and also its positive supplement.[28] His argument was based on the criterion of sufficiency, that is, natural law is too abstract to be able to constitute by itself a real society. Conventional law, therefore, presupposes natural law but cannot be reduced to it.

Albo uses the same criterion to indicate the insufficiency of conventional law in relation to divine law. He lists a number of points where divine law is superior to conventional law:

Furthermore, conventional law is inferior (*tekatzer*) to Divine law in that it is unable to distinguish the desirable from the undesirable in all cases, because something may seem desirable or undesirable per se (*b'atzmo*).[29]

Conventional law is relative, and this is its major deficiency, making it inferior to both divine and natural law. Albo does not explicitly make this latter point but it is certainly implied by his line of argument. For if conventional law were nothing but the promulgation and enforcement of natural law, then it would share the absolute status of natural law's elementary standards of political right and wrong. However, it should be remembered that conventional law is not only concerned with right and wrong but, moreover, with what is desirable and undesirable. Because of the universal *a priori* status of natural law its elementary standards are not relative to time and place and historical circumstances. But this is not the case with conventional law which, by definition, is historically and geographically varied. Therefore, although conventional law is concretely superior to natural law, the former is abstractly inferior to the latter by virtue of its uncertainty and impermanence. If divine law is to be the supreme manifestation of law, it must combine the excellences of both natural and conventional law. In other words, divine law must be both concrete and absolute. Therefore: "its level in relation to the other laws and conventions is that of the architectonic art (*ha-melakhah ha-r'oshit*) in relation to the other arts which serve it."[30] He adds:

The intent of Divine law is to direct men to the attainment of true happiness (*ha-hatzalah ha'amitit*), which is the happiness of the soul and immortality. It shows them the ways wherein they should go to attain it, and makes known to them the true good which they should try to reach, and the true evil from which they should guard themselves . . . [31]

We now have three concerns corresponding to the three types of law: (1) natural law is concerned with what is right and wrong; (2) conventional law is concerned with the desirable and the undesirable; and (3) divine law is concerned with true good and evil. The difference between the concern of conventional law and that of divine law is essentially the difference between *apparent* and *real* good, a distinction first made by Plato.[32] Now the true good includes the excellences of both justice and the desiderata, that is, divine law includes the excellences of both natural and conventional law. Albo concludes:

. . . it also lays down the ways of right (*darkhei ha-yosher*) in order that the political group will be arranged in a desirable and complete fashion (*b'ofan na'ot ve-shalem*) so that the bad order (*ro'a siddur*) of their society will not prevent (*she-l'o yatridem*) from attaining true happiness nor burden them (*y'ikem*) so they will not strive to attain happiness and the final end of the human species. This is the purpose of the Divine law (*magamat ha-dat ha'Elohit*) and in this it is superior to conventional law . . .

The superiority of divine law lies in its certainty. He points out that even the greatest human lawgivers, unaided by revelation, made grave errors in matters of moral judgment. The example he brings is Plato's abolition of the exclusiveness of the marital relationship in his Republic.[33] Albo indicates that divine law, in both its Mosaic and Noahide manifestations, prohibited community marriage.[34] Even Aristotle censured his teacher.[35] That is to say, revealed law initially states with certainty what philosophers subsequently discover to be true.[36]

The objective certainty of divine law as intending real good is alone sufficient to assure subjective human confidence:

Furthermore, conventional law is inferior to Divine law because it is unable to make the heart of those who conduct themselves by it happy. For whoever doubts (mesuppak) something he does (po'el) whether it suffices (masik) to attain its intended end, he is not happy in his act.[37]

Once more, Albo's choice of vocabulary is significant. His use of the root spk, which suggests objective sufficiency (sippuk) on the one hand, and subjective insufficiency (safek) on the other, indicates that divine law is adequate both to real good and humanity's certainty of acting in relation to it. This is how divine law can be judged as overcoming the relativity of conventional law. Albo here emphasizes the permanence of divine law as opposed to the impermanence of conventional law, determined as it is by opinion (mefursam).

Albo also underscores that conventional law (and natural law) are only concerned with human action, that is, with standards for manifest behavior (ha-middot). However, it is not concerned with ideas (ha-de'ot). By "ideas" Albo means such notions as the world-to-come and the immortality of the soul. Since such ideas are not present in the understanding of our political nature, which is the subject of natural and conventional law, they seem to require a presentation through divine law, that is, through revelation. Unlike Maimonides, who regarded a system of law divine if it presented standards of moral and intellectual excellence,[38] Albo insisted that in addition to such a combination the system of law had to have been revealed in a particular historical event. Although one can certainly reason about revelation, reason itself is inadequate to independently discover the content of revelation.[39]

Because of the inability of human reason to uncover the details of revelation, revelation cannot be reduced to an especially vivid form of ratiocination: " . . . because of this God in His wisdom verified (l'amet) the fundamental principles (hatchalot) of the Torah by experience so that there would be no doubt about them."[40] Revelation, then, is the primary experience of the presentation of God's word. Tradition is what extends its content to those who have not directly experienced that primary event.[41] The truth of tradition emerges from the believer's trust in the character of those who have bequeathed the tradition to them.

Belief (ha'emunah) also applies to anything which has not reached the believer through the senses but is apprehended by a man worthy and acceptable (ratzui u-mekubbal) or to many prominent men (gedolai ha-pirsum) . . . and comes down as a continuous tradition to the believer . . . even though reason cannot verify it.[42]

Again, Albo's vocabulary is significant. In designating the bearers of the tradition as gedolai ha-pirsum he is using the same root—prsm—that forms the basis of "opinions"—mefursamot, that is, the content of conventional law.[43] He thus appears to suggest that "tradition" and "convention" both are prima facie manifestations of human political authority. However, what essentially distinguishes them is that religious tradition is divine law because it is grounded in a revelatory event. Ordinary convention, on the other hand, is only grounded in imperfect human notions of what is desirable and what is undesirable for a particular society.

We have seen that in many ways divine law is to conventional law what conventional law is to natural law. Conventional law transcends natural law, namely, the intent of what is good surpasses what is right. We have also seen that Albo considers divine law as intending real good whereas conventional law only intends apparent good. He emphasizes that the real good desired by all is the perfection of the soul and the attainment of the world-to-come. Only divine law provides the means for this end:

. . . why was the Divine law ordered? If it is to arrange the order and conduct of men and their vision so as to perfect the political community, conventional law suffices (taspik) for this. But it seems without a doubt that Divine law exists to lead men to perfection (shlemut) which conventional law is unable to do, and this is the human perfection contingent on the perfection of the soul.[44]

Conventional law (and, even more so, natural law) is inadequate to this exalted end, not only because its lack of ideational certitude, but also because it is not specific enough in its precepts:

Furthermore, conventional law is inferior to Divine law because it is unable to delimit the individual acts (pratai he-pe'ulot) which are to be practiced in each moral excellence, for it only informs about generalities (ha-kolelim), just as definitions (ha-gedarim) are only for generalities. The individuals have no definition. So, also, concerning the individual acts, it is impossible for conventional law to delimit them.[45]

Here we see Albo as a theologian, contrasting religious with philosophical ethics.

For the philosopher, generality is a strength. It is precisely general definitions of what is good and what evil that enables human actions to be rationally constructed in one coherent system. We see this as early as Socrates' dispute with Euthyphro. Socrates' criticism of the latter's ethical approach is that it is not based on a coherent definition of the right or the good.[46] As Socrates' disciple, Plato, developed his ethical system, especially the constitution of his ideal Republic, he was not concerned with individual acts, but rather with general ideas in which individual acts participated.[47] Moreover, ethical judgment was concerned with the overall trend of these acts, not with their results.[48]

One can contrast this approach with Judah Halevi's. In the *Kuzari*, Halevi begins with a story about a pagan king:

To the king of the Khazars came a dream, and it appeared as if an angel addressed him saying: "Thy way of thinking (*kavvanatekha*) is indeed pleasing to the Creator but not thy way of acting (*ma'asekha*)."[49]

It would seem that the king is himself a philosopher whose thinking intends a higher realm.[50] However, philosophy lacks a detailed system of human action consistent with true ideas regarding God and the world-to-come.

This critique of philosophical ethics presupposes revelation. Revelation indicates that God's primary concern in His relationship with humanity is our individual actions. Therefore, the relation between actions and ideas in divine law must be constituted on this basis. This would not be the case if our ideas about God and the world-to-come could be fully apprehended by reason. If this were so, the very generality of a metaphysically discovered system of ideas would constitute the ideal for an ethical system grounded in it. Albo, consequently, demonstrated theological consistency in grounding both the ideational and practical content of divine law in Sinaitic revelation. It will be recalled that conventional law's greater particularity was a point of superiority over natural law. So here we see divine law is more particular than conventional law, and therefore superior. Further, the greater detail of divine law is an indication of its greater truth, as it reflects divine immutable insight, as opposed to the relativity of human estimation as reflected in conventional law.

A central argument of Albo's claim for the superiority of divine law, because of the unlimited insight of God, is that it is able to adequately reward the righteous and punish the wicked. This insight enables divine law to provide rewards and punishments adequate to the individual person: "furthermore, conventional law cannot mete out punishment equal to the crime . . . but Divine law punishes each according to his crime, no less and no more."[51] Here Albo seems to be stressing that divine law is the most just form of law. Since justice is the criterion of natural law, it would seem that Albo is indicating the superiority of divine law over natural law based on the latter's own criterion. However, he writes later:

And we say that according to true equality and justice it is fitting that reward and punishment correspond to and be estimated by the act for which the reward and punishment are received.[52]

Albo then suggests that in conventional justice (ha-yosher ha-medini), that is, justice according to human consent (le-fi haskamat anashim), reward and punishment correspond to the value of the person in relation to whom the act is done, not to the value of the act itself. He indicates that "religionists" (ba'alai ha-datot) accept this conventional notion of justice. In divine law, however, the punishment for a crime corresponds not to the status of the other person in relation to whom the act is done, but rather it corresponds to the status of the actor. Therefore, we now have three kinds of reward and punishment corresponding to the three kinds of law: (1) for natural law reward and punishment are determined by the act itself; (2) for conventional law they are decided by the status of the person in relation to whom the act is done; and (3) for divine law reward and punishment are decided by the status of the actor.

Now one could infer that only natural law is in accord with what is true, that is, objective equality and justice, and that conventional law and even divine law are diluted by subjective considerations of who the actor is, or in relation to whom he is acting.[53] However, do these subjective considerations really diminish true equality and justice? If we look at Albo's examples we find that the opposite is in fact the case. In discussing true justice and equality, he writes: "for one who strikes his fellow and blinds his eye or breaks his arm, it is fitting that they should blind his eye or break his arm." This passage, of course, restates the lex talionis. However, any educated Jewish reader of Albo's book would know the rabbinic interpretation of this law, an interpretation that ruled in favor of monetary compensation for injury. One of the major rabbinic arguments against interpreting the lex talionis literally was that the eye of one person has a different value in relation to his whole life. The example used concerns the case where a one-eyed man blinds the eye of a two-eyed man.[54] If this law were literally applied, it would mean that the original victim would still have sight, whereas his attacker would be deprived of sight. Justice itself, therefore, taken out of the purely abstract realm of the a priori and examined in the light of concrete realities, requires that subjective factors be taken into consideration.

Conventional law's first principles, it will be recalled, are human freedom and purposiveness. These fundamental principles transcend order, the driving concern of natural law. Human freedom, especially, introduces a subjective factor into the institution of law. Indeed purposiveness presupposes subjective freedom just as subjective freedom intends purposes. Both are necessary principles of intelligent human action. The introduction of this factor was considered by Albo to be an improvement over natural law. By inference we concluded that conventional law is inferior to natural law because of its relativity. It is not inferior, however, because of its subjective features. Therefore, we may conclude here that the "true" justice and equality of which Albo speaks is by no means the *best* justice and the most *adequate* equality in the human world. It is only the most abstract, the simplest theory of justice.

Furthermore, whereas in conventional law justice is determined by the *outward* status of the person in relation to whom the act is done, in divine law the *inner* status of the actor is the essential criterion for reward and punishment.[55] In this sense, divine law reflects the highest justice because it comprehends the full human situation of the act, the person in relation to whom the act is done, and the inner intent (*kavvanah*) of the actor. Such a full comprehension, for Albo, could emerge only from divine wisdom. The elementary criteria of natural law would only be contradicted if the relation between act and reaction were constituted capriciously. The fact that the rationale of the system of reward and punishment in divine law can be explained suggest that this is not the case.

5. Noahide Law

As noted, Albo sees Noahide law as a branch of divine law. Since the only other system of law which, according to Albo's criteria, qualifies as divine law is Mosaic law,[56] it would surely be useful to compare these two species of divine law. Now at first glance it would seem that there is only a quantitative distinction between these two systems of law. On the one hand, the numerical quantity of Noahide law is much smaller than that of Mosaic law: seven commandments against 613. On the other hand, the number of subjects of Noahide law far exceeds the number of subjects of Mosaic law: all of humanity against the small number of Jews in the world.

Nevertheless, although Noahide law is explicitly designated as a branch of divine law, its very generality plus its universal range of subjects gives it some important points in common with natural law. Furthermore, since Noahide law was promulgated before Mosaic law, it would seem that Noahide law like natural law is co-extensive and co-temporal with humanity itself. Therefore, it might very well be helpful to examine Noahide law both from the perspective of Mosaic and natural law.

Noahide law is not only considered divine law because its means of promulgation were prophetic but, also, because its subject matter concerns God:

For through the Torah by which Adam was commanded the existence of God who spoke with him was verified (*nit'amet*), also prophecy, Divine revelation and reward and punishment. And this is because God revealed Himself (*nigleh*) to him concerning the Torah . . .[57]

The existence of God and humanity's relationship with him are certified through revelation. However, we must now ask whether or not Albo limits all knowledge about God to revelation.

It would seem that Albo does admit the possibility of some general philosophical knowledge about God. In his work, the existence of God is the first of the three roots of divine law, and Albo adduces two proofs for God's existence.[58] Moreover, he indicates that the Torah confirms proofs that are philosophical. He writes:

Because of this the Torah begins with the account of creation (*parshat bereshit*) to teach (*lehorot*) about the existence of the Maker of all that exists . . . and in this sense the existence of God is posited as a root of the Torah . . .[59]

Later:

This is the proof (*mofet*) of the existence of God . . . and it is a Torah proof which agrees with intellection (*maskim im ha'iyyun*) in the account of creation . . .[60]

From his choice of words, it is clear that the Torah promulgates what is actually known by philosophy. A "proof" (*mofet*) is logically more compelling than a "teaching" (*Torah*) or an "allusion" (*remez*). Indeed, in his presentation of the argument from design, Albo mentioned the Psalmist and the rabbis as endorsing the view of Aristotle.[61] Elsewhere, he commends the Aristotelian, Maimonidean and Averroist argument that the transition from a potential to an actual state requires an external cause.[62] Although he states that it is "first (*rish'on*) Toraitic also agreeing with intellection," this is more a concession to the greater sanctity of the Torah as a historical source than the views of the philosophers. It is clear, nevertheless, that the philosophers conceptualized these proofs more precisely that the Torah.

Additionally, not only is God's existence apprehensible through philosophical reasoning, philosophical reasoning can also constitute some sort of relationship with God. Albo states: "it is fitting for every man to acknowledge his Creator (*she-yakir et Bor'o*), and this is because it is fitting for every rational being (*ba'al sekhel*) to recognize his Creator."[63] This also follows Albo's insistence that we only know God as he is knowable to us.[64] For Albo, God is knowable by inference from the order of creation, that is, the argument from design. Therefore, God's knowability as the first cause of phenomena, but not as he exists in and of himself, indicates that a relationship based on inferential reasoning is possible between humanity and God.

Earlier, Albo appeared to acknowledge not only the possibility but the reality of some sort of natural religion:

Conventional law is that which is ordered by some wise man or men in consideration of the place and the time and the nature of the people governed by it, like the laws and statues which were ordered in some of the cities, among the ancients who were idolaters or who worshipped God by virtue of the rational order required by human reason without Divine enlightenment (he'areh ha'Elohit).[65]

From these explicit sources we learn that unaided human reason can know the existence of God, and this knowledge has the moral corollaries of acknowledging and worshipping God. If this is the case, then why did Albo not include obligations to God in his delineation of natural law? And, if he had done this, then natural and Noahide law would be more closely identical since both would include the prohibitions of anarchy, murder, robbery, idolatry and blasphemy. This would make five out of the seven Noahide laws natural laws, excluding the prohibitions of sexual immorality and eating a limb torn from a living animal.[66]

Regarding the prohibition of sexual immorality, specifically adultery, Albo certainly presents a natural law rationale. In discussing the Decalogue he states that the second table contains general laws (ha-devarim ha-kilelim) that are necessary because of humanity's political life and continuity.[67] Thus he argues that the commandments of the second table follow a logical order. First, the prohibition of murder appears, followed by adultery and stealing. He states the prohibition of adultery is midpoint between those of murder and theft, because a man's relationship with his wife is midpoint between his relationship with his own body and his own property. Since the prohibition of theft is considered part of natural law, should not the prohibition of adultery be a part as well? Moreover, Albo designates uncontrolled lust (ha-shetifah be-ni'uf) as befitting animals rather than human beings.[68]

Only the prohibition of eating a limb torn from a living animal remains outside of natural law. This law is the only law actually given to Noah: "Only you shall not eat flesh with its life" (Gen. 9:4).[69] Nevertheless, Albo follows the Talmudic view that all seven Noahide laws are actually "Adamic" laws, and these laws are known to human reason (with the exception of the seventh) outside of revelation.[70] Why then does he not identify these six laws with natural law?

Albo does not provide an explicit answer. Any answer supplied here is based on inference and conjecture. But like Maimonides before, not everything in Albo's work is explicit.[71]

In any comparison between divine and natural law it must be recognized that certain similar regulations are found in both systems. Since natural law is logically prior to divine law, we must understand why repetition is required. Albo's answer to this question is that a moral law fulfilled for its own sake alone intends the maintenance of the general political community. The same moral law, however, performed with the intention (*kavvanah*) to fulfill God's will brings about the more individual result of supernatural human happiness.[72] Moral law per se, then, is only concerned with outer acts, whereas divine law is concerned with outer acts and inner motivations.

Now Albo admits that at least the outer manifestation of moral law between human beings is generally constituted before revelation. He is not willing to admit, however, that the outward manifestation of moral law between God and humanity is generally constituted prior to revelation. Why such reluctance?

I think the answer is as follows: Albo saw the political manifestation of natural law as beginning with the general consent that founds any real society.[73] Now consent involves the explicit enunciation of a plurality of wills and their coming together into some sort of common consensus. We have, then, a public, accessible source of law. At least at the initial level of natural law, moreover, there is political equality between the several wills (*shavim b'enoshut*).[74] In the relationship with God, however, both of these conditions are absent. God's will is only accessible by revelation, an event not occasioned by human inquiry. Also, there is no equality between Creator and created. Therefore, this relationship is not just improved and elevated by revelation—like inter-human relations regulated by natural law—it is, rather, initially constituted by revelation.

Without revelation there is no guarantee that a human-initiated relation with God will not be idolatrous. That is why Albo made no distinction at all between idolaters and those who worship God "by virtue of the rational order required by human reason."[75] It would appear that Albo followed Maimonides, who did not posit idolatry as a *substitution* of something else as the object of human worship, but rather the worship of some other being *intermediate* between God and humanity.[76] Therefore, someone like Aristotle could have a true understanding of the nature of God and universal causality and still be an idolater. This is why, I believe, Albo did not include the Noahide prohibitions of idolatry and blasphemy within natural law. Humans have a natural desire to do what pleases God, but in the absence of revelation they are unable to do it.

Albo emphasizes the need for revelation as being for information about what is *individually* pleasing to God:

Moreover, even if investigative knowledge (*ha-yedi'ah ha-mekhkarit*) suffices to delimit good acts according to human nature, it is surely impossible that it is sufficient to know the things acceptable (*ha-nirtzim*) to God . . . for God is absolutely hidden (*ne'elam*), for it is impossible for us to know all the things which are good in His eyes . . . all that is possible is that one knows them generally (*al tzad ha-klalut*) such as that evil is despised in the eyes of God.[77]

Noahide law, then, is the first step in the process of divine revelation:

For this reason you will find that the Noahide Torah and the Mosaic Torah, although differing in individual matters (*b'inyanim pratiyim*) . . . nevertheless agree in general matters by the virtue of the Giver . . . the differences are geographical . . . and historical. There is no doubt that the other nations attained human happiness by means of the Noahide Torah because it is Divine, even though it is not the level of happiness achieved by Israel by virtue of the Torah.[78]

The question is: Why is the Noahide Torah less efficacious in achieving the world-to-come than the Mosaic Torah?

The answer may well rest in the particularity of revelation. It is clear that Albo emphasizes the greater particularity of divine law over conventional and natural law as its very point of superiority. However, there seem to be gradations within divine law itself. It appears that the point of inferiority of Noahide to Mosaic law is its greater generality.[79] Concerning the revelation of Noahide law, he notes:

For God revealed Himself and spoke with him and commanded him concerning the Torah which He said, "And the Lord God commanded man saying, etc." (Gen. 2:16). And the rabbis explain that in this verse all the commandments about which man was commanded are alluded to (*nirmezu*).[80]

Here again Albo's vocabulary is significant. By stating that the Noahide laws are "alluded to" in Gen. 2:16, Albo is taking sides in an earlier rabbinic dispute about the halakhic status of the Noahide laws.[81] Judah Halevi argued that the verse is only an indirect foundation for the Noahide laws. Abulafia, on the contrary, maintained that the verse is the direct foundation. Albo's use of "allusion" implies an acceptance of Halevi's interpretation. In this context the theory of an indirect source means that from God's particular commandment to Adam in the Garden of Eden there are *inferred* certain *general* human norms.[82] These norms themselves are not immediately revealed.

Such is not the case, however, with Mosaic law. Indeed precisely because of the more direct prophecy of Moses, Mosaic law can even change the less direct Noahide law:

Because of this Israel believed in the words of Moses even though there were in his words those which disputed (*holkim*) the Noahide Torah . . . And this was because it was truly evident (*berur amiti*) that God wanted to give a Torah through Moses. For if this were not the case, Israel would not be permitted to budge from their tradition and from the Torah which they received from Adam and from Noah through their fathers as a continuous tradition.[83]

This is further emphasized by Albo's distinction between a prophet (*navi*) and an agent (*shaliach*) of God.[84] Only Moses qualifies as such an agent who brings a direct, unequivocal, normative message from God. Prophets are less direct in terms of the content of their revelation.[85] Therefore, Mosaic law is not only a greater development of divine law because it comes later and contains more commandments. Rather, it is greater because its very commandments are more particular.

This too, I think, explains why Albo refused to equate Noahide law with natural law. Natural law as an *a priori* formal standard, for both societies ruled by conventional law or by divine law, is unchangeable.[86] Noahide law as an *a posteriori* political and religious phenomenon admits the possibility of change. Since his project is to show how Judaism superseded earlier forms of religion, he could not very well grant Noahide law an unchangeable status.

To date, no Jewish thinker has presented a theological theory of law as completely developed as that of Albo. An examination of this theory would, I think, do much to reverse the rather low estimate of Albo's theological facility.[87]

CHAPTER TWELVE

LATE MEDIEVAL DEVELOPMENTS

1. Meiri

Maimonides' interpretation of the Noahide laws had considerable influence on subsequent generations. His authority on this matter, however, drew more on halakhic definitions rather than philosophical reflection. He defined the Noahide laws as divine law, assigning the prohibition of idolatry as the opening law. Later halakhists took this definition to mean that if a gentile society was not idolatrous, then it could be assumed that its acceptance of the other Noahide laws followed from this *religious* fact. Maimonides' definition was commonly employed by halakhists in Christian countries. Such positive assessments were most often made when Jews were left alone by their hosts. The fact that a number of significant European halakhists made such an assessment suggests that medieval Jewish life was not merely a "vale of tears."

This approach emerges in Menachem ha-Meiri's work. This fourteenth-century Provençal rabbi insisted, to a degree unmatched by halakhists prior to him, that Noahides were no longer idolaters:

Every Noahide whom we see, who accepts upon himself the seven commandments, is one of the saints of the nations of the world and is in the category of the righteous and he has a portion in the world-to-come.[1]

By acceptance (*kabbalah*) Meiri means the acceptance of the Noahide laws as divine commandments. However, lacking Maimonides' philosophical depth, Meiri did not endeavor to constitute an essential relation between theology and moral law. Rather, he simply identifies a historical relation between the two, that is, the Christian affirmation of Noahide morality appears to be accompanied by a denial of idolatry. In separating contemporary Christians from pagan idolaters, Meiri refers to them as "the nations who are bound by religious laws (*ha-gedurot be-darkhei ha-datot*) and who have renounced polytheism (*u-shemudot b'elohut*)."[2] If we take the sequence of his presentation literally, the renunciation of idolatry is secondary to the normativity of "the nations." His interest here is with moral law, not the particulars of Christian theology.[3] In recognizing the Christian affirmation of Noahide morality, Meiri was willing to designate their theology (and associated ritual) as non-idolatrous. This emerges from his definition of *dat*, denoting "law" and connoting "religion."[4]

And the other Torahs of the ancient nations and their laws (*ve-dataihem*): their subject matter is only concerned with political conduct (*hanhagot ha-medinah*) and human statutes (*ve-nimusim*) set down by men . . . and according to their law this is totally sufficient (*haspakah shelamah*) . . .[5]

It is this aspect of human legality that Meiri emphasizes in speaking of contemporary gentiles whom he considered "bound by religious laws and statutes."[6] Such a position encouraged him to redefine broad stretches of Jewish civil law that had previously disadvantaged gentiles.[7] He made a fundamental distinction between contemporary law-abiding non-idolatrous gentiles and the gentiles of the Talmudic period.

Meiri accomplishes more, however, than to simply designate Noahide religious affirmation as a mere accompaniment to an essentially human morality. This emerges in his remarks on the *locus classicus* of Noahide law in the Talmud. He writes:

And, nevertheless, anyone who engages in the essentials and the seven commandments and in their details and what is derived from them, even though most of the substance of the Torah is not included therein, we honor him . . . All the more so if his investigation (*hagirato*) for knowledge leads him to come to the final perfection of our Torah, until he finds it perfect and converts (*yahzor ve-yitgayyer*).[8]

What we see here is nothing less than a return to the early notion that the *ger toshav* is essentially a convert *in potentia*. Once again, gentile acceptance of a part of Judaism is regarded as the beginning of a process whose conclusion, optimally at least, can be nothing less than full integration into Judaism. This comes out in Meiri's discussion of conversion. Following the Talmud and Maimonides, Meiri indicates that the *ger toshav* no longer exists as a Jewish institution because such a status assumes Jewish sovereignty in the land of Israel. The *ger toshav*, following rabbinic tradition, is designated by Meiri as a "half-way convert" (*ger lehatz'ain*). He also indicates that "relying on our understanding we would accept such a half-convert were it not for the law eliminating the *ger toshav* in our day."[9] Nevertheless, Meiri only considers this as a removal of a political status. In religious terms, quasi- or potential Jews are possible if their moral standards include the Noahide laws but are not necessarily limited to them. Obviously Christianity, with its acceptance of the moral law of the "Old Testament," fulfills this requirement.[10] In short, Christians are regarded as potential Jews. By naming such persons as "saints of the nations of the world," Meiri has in effect revived the old status of the "fearers of the Lord," a religious description rather than a political one and, as such, not removed by the rabbinic deletion of the category of the *ger toshav*.[11]

Although this has precedent in Maimonides, Meiri goes further in his halakhic position. First, Maimonides' use of "saints of the nations of the world" differs from the rabbinic designation of such persons as "righteous (*tzaddikim*)." In rabbinic parlance a *tzaddik* identifies a law-abiding person, whereas a *hasid* names a "saint," a person whose relationship with God is reflected in a life of unusual consecration.[12] Secondly, Maimonides terms all who accept the Noahide commandments to be "like a resident alien (*ke-ger toshav*)" although not literally inasmuch as the political preconditions for it are absent.[13] The term "acceptance" is important because it signals personal commitment. Since political commitment is no longer possible, the type of acceptance Maimonides suggests is religious, that is, an acknowledgement of the Noahide laws as divinely revealed.

However, Maimonides could not fully equate Christianity with this religious status because he refused to separate its theology and ritual from idolatry. This refusal was no doubt based on his philosophical standards for pure monotheism, standards that Islam, for instance, did fulfill. On the other hand, he did have a high regard for Christian acceptance of the Hebrew Bible.[14] Maimonides' assessment of Christianity, then, is ambiguous. Meiri had no such reservations. Undoubtedly reflecting the influence of Ashkenazic halakhists, who had removed the stain of idolatry from Christians,[15] he could use Maimonides' category of "like a *ger toshav*" and apply it to them.

Earlier, in examining the rabbinic sources, we noticed that in the aggadah there was a tradition that the Noahides rejected divine law at Sinai—divine law manifest in the Noahide precepts. Although this did not exonerate them of their moral obligation to obey these precepts, it did put them in the category of those who "are not commanded and practice," that is, the transcendental dimension of their observance is now lost.[16] Meiri's theory of Noahide law as embodied in Christianity (and Islam) changes this assessment of the Noahides. Through their acceptance of the Noahide laws as divinely revealed commandments, these gentiles are restored, as it were, to their pre-Sinaitic status. They are now practicing because they were indeed commanded and accept this as a faith commitment. This notion can be found in Meiri's treatment of the *locus classicus* of the doctrine of "commanded and practices." There Meiri discusses the ruling of the eleventh-century Ashkenazi halakhist Rabbenu Tam, who, basing himself on this Talmudic source, allows women to take upon themselves religious obligations designated by rabbinic definition as obligatory for men only and, also, allows them to recite the appropriate blessings for such obligations. However, Meiri does more than just paraphrase Rabbenu Tam. He adds: "For, after all, such a person is in the category of religious law (biklal ha-dat) as, for example, women."[17] Although women are the case in point in Rabbenu Tam's ruling, Meiri considers them as only one example of the halakhic application of this principle. His use of the term dat indicates that the applicability of this principle is not limited to women, and not even to Jews alone. It applies to all who accept divine law.

Meiri's constitution of this new status of ba'al dat, what we might call a "religious lawkeeper," prompted him to rethink certain Talmudic precedents that were inconsistent with his innovation.

In our examination of the development of the rabbinic concept of Noahide law we noted that the limitation of these precepts to seven was the result of the tendency of the rabbis, after the Christian schism and the destruction of the Temple, to define the boundary between Jews and non-Jews. Anything suggesting a quasi-Judaism was removed. R. Simon b. Lakish, a third-century Palestinian Amora, ruled, for instance, that a gentile who observed the Sabbath merited death. Similarly, his teacher and brother-in-law, R. Johanan b. Nappaha, declared that a gentile who studied Torah deserved to die.[18] These rulings were aimed at eliminating religious syncretism.[19] Meiri paraphrases Maimonides' codification of these rulings and then adds a reason of his own: gentiles are prohibited from observing the Sabbath because they might appear "to be from our people and others will learn from them."[20] He then adds that they may observe other commandments of the Torah because their offerings and donations were accepted at the Temple when it was functioning.[21] Here Meiri reverts to a certain type of reasoning that indicated that gentiles observing Jewish law should not be confused with Jews.[22] He then permits Torah study for non-Jews if their study of the Noahide laws likely will led them to conversion. Here too Meiri follows Maimonides, who permits gentiles to observe Jewish commandments and receive reward from God.[23]

A question arises: What is the difference between religious syncretism, which both Maimonides and Meiri judge as the basis for the prohibition of gentile observance of the Sabbath and Torah study, and electing to observe some Jewish commandments? The answer appears to be that the latter, which is permitted, is based on an acceptance of Jewish revelation without attempting to impersonate the Jewish people.[24] This was the rabbinic image of the ger toshav. Maimonides constitutes the non-political type of quasi-Judaism for individual non-Jews. Because Meiri, however, did not regard Christianity as idolatrous, he could apply all of this to Christendom in general. Christians, apparently, affirmed the Jewish source of their morality, without creating any confusion between themselves and Jews. Meiri's view was no doubt shaped by his experience in the relatively open environment of fourteenth-century Provence, at least in regards to intellectual exchange.[25]

If, on the other hand, a gentile attempted to found a new religion, not based on Jewish revelation but only incorporating Jewish practices, then this would be prohibited, based on the rabbinic rulings of R. Johanan and Resh Lakish. The intriguing thing about Meiri's reworking of the rulings of the Talmud is that these rulings were originally directed at Judaizing elements in the early Church.[26] At this point in history it was imperative to differentiate Judaism from Christianity. By the time of Meiri, however, the schism was a *fait accompli*.[27] Nevertheless, in its rejection of Marcionism with its attempted severance of Christianity from its Jewish sources, the Christian Church reaffirmed Judaism as a foundation of its life and theology.[28] However, unlike the *sebomenoi* of the Hellenistic period, they certainly did not regard themselves as subordinate to the Jews or Judaism. Meiri gave this Christian reaffirmation a halakhic sanction, and by doing so he used originally anti-Christian rulings to give Christianity a respectable status in the view of Judaism.

2. Further Legitimization of Christianity

The revival of the category of the *ger toshav* as a voluntary religious status rather than as a political status no longer possible in Judaism, and the virtual identification of this status with Christianity by many European halakhists, had significant consequences for the development of halakhah. It meant a return to the Hellenistic and early rabbinic view that God-fearing gentiles were, in essence, potential Jews. Such a view, noted earlier, is not consistent with a doctrine that limits gentile obligations to the Noahide laws alone.

This willingness to return to the earlier position—though not a historically aware return—also entailed a rejection of the limiting number seven taken so seriously in the late Tannaitic and Amoraic times. R. Israel Kogan (Chofetz Chaim, d. 1932), one of the foremost halakhists of the twentieth century, judged the Noahide laws as the *terminus a quo* rather than the *terminus ad quem* of gentile observance of the law of God. He writes:

In essence (*gufa*) if the *ger toshav* wants to accept upon himself at the inception of his "conversion" (*gayruto*) more commandments than just seven, then from then on he is obligated (*she-mehuyyav*) to uphold them.[29]

The Choftez Chaim goes so far as to say that such an act overrides the Talmudic prohibition of gentile Sabbath observance. As a Talmudic basis for his position he refers to the Tannaitic opinion, one not accepted by Maimonides in his code, that a *ger toshav* is one who has accepted *all* of the commandments of the Torah exclusive of the prohibition of meat not slaughtered according to Jewish standards.[30] Whether or not he had in mind certain East European Christian groups that had adopted many Jewish practices, this is difficult to ascertain.[31]

There are precedents for this approach. In the Talmud we learn that Rabban Simon b. Gamliel, a Tanna, recognized the legitimacy of Samaritan observance of many of the commandments of the Torah.[32] Later, a number of halakhic authorities favorably recognized Muslim observance of circumcision.[33] In both of these precedents these non-Jewish observances of Jewish precepts were considered to be acceptable for Jews. In the earlier example, Samaritan *matzah* was considered fit for Jewish use at Passover; in the latter, Muslim circumcision of a Jew was considered acceptable.

This whole process in the development of the halakhah on non-Jewish obligation can be seen as a direct recognition of Christian biblicism. The process, it seems to me, is largely determined by the development of Christianity from an essentially hostile threat from within Judaism to, at least at times, an appreciative derivative from *outside* Judaism.

In Talmudic times non-Jewish, especially Christian, appropriation of the Hebrew Bible was regarded as an act of theft. The third-century Palestinian Amora, R. Johanan bar Nappaha, justified his prohibition of gentile study of Torah by insisting that the Torah of Moses is "our inheritance (*lanu morashah*) and not theirs."[34] Such sentiment manifests itself most striking in this aggadah:

R. Judah ha-Levi son of R. Shalom said that Moses requested that the Mishnah too be given in writing, but the Holy One blessed be He foresaw that in the future the nations of the world would translate the Torah and read it in Greek and they would say, "we too are Israel." The Holy One blessed be He said to him that, "Were I to write most of My Torahs," if so, "they would be considered by strangers (*kemo zar nehshavu*)"—Hosea 8:12).[35]

This aggadah emphasizes the centrality of the Oral Torah remaining unwritten precisely because the Written Torah is available in Greek translation to gentiles. Clearly the reference is to Christian appropriation of the Septuagint and their use of it to justify their being the "true Israel."[36] At this point in history Christian biblicism was indeed a threat.

However, after the full parting of the ways, such biblicism could be regarded positively, with Jews flattered by the Church's rejection of Marcionism (whether or not they were aware of it) as it caused it to reinforce its Jewish roots, especially its veneration of the "Old Testament." Although he did not deem Christians to be fully monotheistic, Maimonides permitted Jews to teach Torah to Christians because "they say and acknowledge this Torah of ours was given from Heaven to us by Moses . . . and its full text is their possession, even though at times they interpret it contrary to Halakhah."[37] Here Maimonides makes a clear distinction between the Written and Oral Torah. We have also seen earlier that he recognized Christianity had performed a providential service by making the Torah known to pagans.[38] Most important in terms of subsequent developments, although Maimonides preferred Muslim monotheism on more theoretical grounds, on more practical grounds he preferred Christian acceptance of the Hebrew Bible. In the development of Jewish law, Maimonides' practical side had the greatest influence on his successors.

Maimonides also notes that Christian exegesis, at times, contradicts Jewish teaching. The implication is that at "other times" it does not. A number of later halakhic authorities chose to highlight those moments. Jacob Emden, an eighteenth-century halakhist, wrote as part of a long pro-Christian statement, "Know and see that the insightful Christian sages not only examine and research the Written Torah and proclaim its glory throughout the world . . . but they are also a shield and protection for the Oral Torah . . . "[39] Emden refers to Christian protection of the Talmud in the face of the opposition of some Jews, likely Karaites. He then enumerates various Christian scholars who revered Judaism and learned much from it. This apparent reference to the Karaites is significant because to deny Christian scholars access to the Oral Torah as preserved in rabbinic literature would in effect make Judaism *for them* a form of Karaism.[40] A recognition and acceptance of Christian biblicism by rabbinic authorities had to take this position since the other alternative would in effect deny the rabbinic dogma that in essence the Written and Oral Torahs are one.[41]

3. Samuel David Luzzatto

The view of Meiri regarding the lawfulness of Christianity, based on an analysis of its morality rather than its theology, was reiterated by later Jewish thinkers. There was no doubt a sociological factor in this type of thinking: it usually arose in those times and places when and where Jews were not being actively persecuted. Thus, the Italian theologian S.D. Luzzatto (Shadal, d. 1865), although familiar with Mendelssohn and other haskalah thinkers, developed the line of thought beginning with the Tosafists and coming through Meiri that stressed the notion of Christian lawfulness based on the Noahide laws. Following Maimonides he also emphasized the Christian acceptance of the

Hebrew Bible as the word of God and the foundation of morality. By accepting that Christians are fully monotheist (a view held by the Tosafists, but not Maimonides), Luzzatto could be unambiguously positive in his endorsement of Christian lawfulness for non-Jews. In fact, he praises Christian believers in the Torah as being superior to Jewish monotheists who deny the divine origin of the Torah.[42] This sentiment was no doubt directed at nineteenth-century liberal Judaism.[43]

Luzzatto developed his own form of "ethical monotheism," accentuating the necessity of the belief in one God and also the necessity for a revealed law. In a comment on the first commandments of the Decalogue, he declares:

Belief in many gods causes a division of heart between different nations. For the people of this nation who worship a certain god will hate another nation who worship another god. They will believe they have nothing in common with them, that it is as if they were not human like them. Only believers in monotheism know that we have one Father who created us and all men are beloved to Him.[44]

He then goes on to emphasize that this monotheism is not only for Jews, but gradually extends from them to all humanity. The Jews, by virtue of their being the children of Abraham, were able to accept the strict monotheism of the Torah.[45] The other nations, because they were so steeped in polytheism, could not possibly accept such a revolutionary doctrine. Therefore, revelation was vouchsafed to Jews with its eventual acceptance by humanity as its ultimate goal. Here we witness a significant reworking of the legend of the offering of the Torah, its rejection by gentiles and its acceptance by Jews. In its original Tannaitic version, gentiles rejected the Torah because it was presented to them on the basis of the various Noahide laws they had already rejected.[46] Their rejection, then, was morally blameworthy. In the Amoraic version, the notion was introduced that the gentiles could observe Noahide laws, but not as divine commandments entailing transcendent consequences. In the Middle Ages the potential for the gentiles to *reaccept* the Noahide law as divine commandment was judged by rationalists such as Meiri as being actualized by their Christianization. The kabbalists, on the other hand, saw the gentile rejection of the Torah as Noahide law as inevitable and the event that sealed their separation from God. Although Luzzatto does not refer to this legend explicitly, he clearly has it in mind. Now the gentiles are considered as *not having been* ready to accept the Torah, but clearly the Jewish influence on Christianity has begun to better prepare them for the acceptance of the Torah. In another important passage, Luzzatto judges the numerous Torah commandments as a way of shaping compassion (*rahamim*).[47] Luzzatto sees the social ordinances of the Torah as the institutionalization of this basic human trait.[48]

In a polemical passage, Luzzatto highlights the superiority of ethics over metaphysics in the Torah. Unlike Maimonides he rejects the notion that ethics is ultimately grounded in metaphysical theology. He argues, citing several biblical passages, that the only relationship possible with God is an ethical one.[49] Thus, if the Christians have a basically Jewish ethics, then their theology, exclusive of its metaphysics, cannot be basically objectionable.

4. Elijah Benamozegh

Many of the same concerns of Luzzatto are repeated in the work of his younger Italian contemporary, Elijah Benamozegh (d. 1900). Like Luzzatto, Benamozegh stresses the Noahide laws as the foundation of gentile morality. However, unlike previous or later theologians, he attempted to constitute "Noahism" as a historical possibility apart from any other religion. He refers to this religion as "the religion of the gentiles" and as the "true universal religion."[50] His use of the word *catholique* for *universal* is a deliberate indication that "Noahism" is distinct from Christianity.

For Benamozegh God has revealed a double law. One part is for humanity as a whole, the other for Israel as the priestly people. Benamozegh sees the relation between Noahides and Jews as parallel to that between Israelites and the Aaronide priests (*kohanim*) and the Levites, namely, the smaller more specialized group, because of its sacerdotal function, has a body of specific laws over and above those it shares with the larger more general group.[51]

Benamozegh breaks with the long tradition that endeavored to see Christianity as an acceptable historical manifestation of Noahism. In his view, Christianity has made true Noahism impossible. He explains this in an ingenious way. Noahism is in reality the periphery of Judaism as Judaism is the inner core of Noahism. Each only fully exists in relation to the other. Christianity disrupted this connection by reducing Judaism to Noahism, that is, it has seen the sole remaining value of Judaism for Christianity in the preservation of natural law in the "Old Testament."[52] By doing this it has taken the sacerdotal role of Israel as its own and reduced Judaism to its own pre-history. Christianity, then, has reversed the roles originally established by Torah and tradition. Noahism is essentially perverted if Israel is not deemed as playing the primary role in divine scheme in the universe. For Benamozegh this reversal of essential roles is accomplished by the introduction of pagan elements into the early Church.[53] Misplaced sacerdotal function can only be pagan. Here we have a return of sorts to the position of Maimonides regarding Christianity—its diluted monotheism, plus its clear cultic compromise with pagan imagery, makes its status for Judaism questionable, irrespective of the fact that it adopted the Hebrew Bible and adheres to the Noahide laws. Ben-amozegh was prompted to return to this view precisely because the main work in which he discussed his theory of Noahism was theological rather than halakhic, reflective rather than normative.

Benamozegh takes seriously the notion of a tradition of Noahism, accept-ing quite literally the rabbinic position that Noah's second son, Shem, the pro-genitor of Abraham, was a teacher of universal morality prior to the revelation of the Torah.[54] Benamozegh considers Noahism as having been preserved in Judaism but, nevertheless, having universal relevance. He appears to have believed that the revelation of Noahism would be sufficient to constitute a real universal moral order. Although he was realistic enough not to hold that his Noahism is itself a complete system, he insists nonetheless that it is capable of being the basis of a rational moral order, that it contains "general truths, the seeds of future progress."[55]

Benamozegh's "Noahism" had little if any direct influence of Jewish life and thought. However, he did make an important disciple in the French author, Aimé Pallière (d. 1949). Born into a pious Catholic home, Pallière moved away from the religion of his youth, searching for a more satisfying relationship with God. He met Benamozegh in Italy during the last few years of the latter's life. Pallière, following his master's advice, never converted to Judaism in the legal sense, but practiced a quasi-Judaism similar to Noahism. He was active in Paris' Liberal synagogue. Benamozegh convinced Pallière that Noahism was the explication of an oral tradition preserved since an-tiquity. Pallière in his autobiography relates an answer Benamozegh gave to several of his questions:

Know that the primitive form of all revelation which continues even after the introduction of the Mosaic law, and which still exists in our own day in the heart of the Jewish people . . . comes from oral tradition . . . Nevertheless, this code existed, and the existence of a religious law constituting the statute to which the gentiles were bound to conform cannot be contested.[56]

By making Noahism a matter of oral tradition, Benamozegh did not get involved in the obscure biblical exegesis used by those attempting to make the Noahide laws biblical.[57] Moreover, he could not be accused of being unable to supply any literary data to back up his theory. In making Noahism an esoteric tradition he might well have been influenced by the esotericism of the kabbal-ists, with whom he was quite sympathetic.[58] This theory, though, is open to a number of criticisms. First, there is the question of whether Noahism is sufficient to create religious life. S.H. Bergman writes:

Nor does "Noachism" fulfill the expectations which Benamozegh attached to it, as

the merest glance at the content of the seven Noachide provisions will make clear . . .
as viewed from the strictly religious angle, the seven commandments lack both life
and substance . . . would not a universal religion, such as that to which Benamozegh
aspired, if constructed round so meager a framework as this, be but a travesty, or
rather a crying scandal?[59]

Furthermore, enlightening as Benamozegh's understanding of the relation
between Noahide law and Mosaic law is on the conceptual level, he could not
constitute the relation historically, especially because his philosophical astute-
ness would not permit him to fall back on the tradition of Meiri and those
after him, which essentially equated Noahism and Christianity. However, his
insight regarding a connection between the Noahide laws and their underlying concept, and Judaism, can be employed fruitfully, I think, if we see a
tradition of Jewish philosophical reflection that identified the Noahide laws as
the *general formal introduction* to Judaism, a formal standard playing a crucial
role in the shaping of Jewish law at the level of jurisprudence, and as being the
halakhic and aggadic point of reference for a Jewish anthropology. His error
was to attempt to externalize and substantiate what is an internal and formal
condition of Judaism.

CHAPTER THIRTEEN

MOSES MENDELSSOHN AND HIS SCHOOL

1. Mendelssohn and Jacob Emden

It is commonly held that distinctively modern Jewish thought begins with Mendelssohn.[1] His biography reflects the situation of Judaism in Western Europe, especially in Germany, during the later eighteenth century. Mendelssohn's childhood in Dessau as the student of David Fraenkel, a great Talmudist, was spent in the cultural isolation typical of most of Ashkenazic Jewry. His move to Berlin reflects the transition from isolation to cultural interaction with the non-Jewish world. His subsequent position as a leading German-Jewish philosopher reflects Judaism's direct confrontation with the non-Jewish world, a world no longer thoroughly Christian in outlook.

Mendelssohn was keenly interested in the question of universal law, and the new cultural situation in which late eighteenth-century German Jewry found itself required that he interpret the meaning of the Noahide law in a novel way. The inadequacy of restating older meanings becomes evident in an exchange of letters in 1773 between Mendelssohn and the leading halakhist of his day, Jacob Emden. Emden had developed a lenient position towards Christianity, a position originally formulated by medievals such as Rabbenu Tam and Meiri.[2] His correspondence with Mendelssohn is of great historical significance because Emden presents the medieval Ashkenazic view of Noahide law whereas Mendelssohn insists on a kind of secular morality, a possibility rarely countenanced (except, perhaps, for a lone philosopher).[3] The fact that Mendelssohn composed his thoughts as halakhic-style inquiries to Emden— a concession to Emden's rabbinic authority—indicates that he must have believed that the resources of tradition could have provided the material to expand the universal Noahide law in new directions to account for changed circumstances. He writes to Emden:

And to me these matters are difficult (*kashim*) . . . that all the inhabitants of the earth from the rising to the setting of the sun are doomed, except us (*zulatynu*) . . . unless they believe in the Torah which was given us as an inheritance to the congregation of

Jacob alone, especially concerning a matter not at all explicit in the Torah . . . Concerning this we only have ancestral tradition, but what will those nations do upon whom the light of the Torah has not shined at all . . . [4]

Emden's answer does not deal with this fundamental philosophical problem at all. Rather, he attempts to support Maimonides' view on Noahide law. He does this by showing, contrary to Karo, that Maimonides' position has Talmudic precedent and is consistent with his halakhic approach.[5] His most significant argument is that Maimonides was a proponent of the halakhic opinion that the proper observance of the commandments requires the conscious recognition and personal acceptance of their historical revelation.[6] Since the Noahide laws are commandments, this requirement pertains to both Jews and non-Jews. In short, one cannot attain the world-to-come unless one is a traditional believer.

The tone of Emden's reply reflects a certain impatience with the kind of question Mendelssohn raised. His impatience with Mendelssohn's "modernism" was expressed elsewhere as well.[7] It is evident, then, that he was unwilling to address Mendelssohn's philosophical question. The latter would have to devise his own answer.

Before examining Mendelssohn's answer to his own question, we must first understand the consequences of this question and why the tradition represented by Emden could not possibly answer it.

Mendelssohn's question reflects the increasing interest, beginning with Descartes, with epistemology. Mendelssohn does not question the content of the Noahide laws, nor does he even dispute whether they are divine laws. Instead, he asks how they are known. He questions the justice of holding all humanity responsible for the observance of laws as divine precepts when most of humanity is unaware of this situation. He argues against those who insist on the necessity of a particular historical revelation:

God . . . was, in their opinion, good enough to reveal to mankind the truths on which their happiness depends; but he was neither omnipotent nor good enough to grant to them the faculties of discovering them themselves. Besides, by this assertion, they make the necessity of a supernatural revelation more universal than revelation itself. For if without revelation the human race cannot but be depraved and miserable, why have by far the greater portion thereof been living without true revelation from the beginning, or why must both the Indies wait until the Europeans are pleased to send them some comforters, to bring them tidings . . . [8]

One must appreciate that the explication of the Noahide laws by Maimonides can be interpreted so as to avoid Mendelssohn's concern. His assumption that reason and revelation are exclusive in Maimonides is based a misunderstanding of Maimonides' epistemology and, ultimately, his meta-physical theology.[9] However, this was not central to his dispute with Emden. Therefore, the force of Mendelssohn's dissatisfaction with Maimonides on the one hand, and Emden's attempt to show the sound Talmudic basis for it on the other hand, suggests how Mendelssohn was preparing to introduce his new view. Moreover, even at this earlier stage of his treatment of Noahide law, he does not try to reinterpret Maimonides' basic position to make it consistent with his own. Only in a letter to Lavater did Mendelssohn attempt to soften Maimonides' position by arguing—in opposition to Spinoza—for the read-ing of the text in the *Mishneh Torah* that states that gentiles who observe the Noahide laws without belief are not saints "but (*ela*) sages."[10] Nevertheless, this is a minor point in terms of Mendelssohn's philosophical outlook in-asmuch as even this reading of Maimonides' text suggests the superiority of revelation over human reason. Mendelssohn, as we will see, could not possibly agree with this.

The dispute between Mendelssohn and Emden, although ostensibly over the meaning of Maimonides' theory of Noahide law, is only localized there. Rather, it is about the definition of human morality that is the basic philosoph-ical question surrounding Noahide law.

For Emden, humanity is essentially divided into Jews and Christians. Only Jews and Christians have any real morality in common, that is, the moral teachings of the Hebrew Bible that both communities accept. Non-Jews and non-Christians might be human, but they are outside the pale of any civiliz-ation that Jews could recognize as valid by Jewish criteria. Maimonides, too, seemed to regard civilization as defined by Jewish, Christian and Muslim recognition of the God of Abraham.[11] For this reason Mendelssohn's episte-mological dilemma does not trouble Emden. The Noahide laws are not eso-teric. In the case of Christianity we can see them as part of the moral authority of the "Old Testament." Since Christians confirm that this morality is revealed by God and is, therefore, divine law, they can fully satisfy Maimonides' re-quirement that their other-worldly salvation as well as that of Jews, depends upon this conviction. Faith, not reason, is the vehicle for knowing and doing God's will. For Judaism (and Christianity) such faith proceeds from historical revelatory events and consequently requires recognition of sacred history.

Mendelssohn could not accept this definition of humanity because it mili-tates against universal tolerance and the equality such tolerance requires. The "fideism" of Emden and others like him appears to be based on the identifica-tion of a common theological point between Judaism and Christianity. How-ever, this common point involves neither tolerance nor equality, either from Jews or Christians.[12] From the view of Judaism Christianity is observing Jew-

ish morality in its most *minimal and general* manifestation. The very specificity of Jewish law makes Judaism superior. Theologians from Albo forward
make this point.[13] On the other hand, Christianity regards the Jewish "Old
Testament" to be the preparation for the New Testament, which is superior
because salvation is through the saving life and death of Jesus of Nazareth and
not "the Law."[14] Therefore, although the moral heritage of Judaism is retained
by Christians, that heritage is secondary to the Gospel. Consequently, the
acknowledgement of a basic morality in common is arrived at by the two communities from opposite perspectives. Neither community supports the view
of the other. Thus, the Jewish approval of Christian morality is really recognition of the spiritual *influence* of Judaism beyond its own people. This kind of
approval only has meaning for Jews. The same could be said for Christians as
well. Such perspectives do not make for tolerance or social equality.
Mendelssohn believed both possible in late eighteenth-century Berlin. That
non-Jewish thinkers such as Lessing were similarly convinced suggests that
Mendelssohn's philosophical treatment of Noahide law was in response to a
real historical situation and not just an exercise in speculation.[15] His debt to
the deism of the day is obvious. The spirit of this age can be captured in
Schiller's poem, "To Joy":

> Your magic binds again
> What tradition severely divided.
> All men will be brothers
> Where your gentle wing lingers.[16]

2. Mendelssohn's New Theory

Mendelssohn's *Jerusalem* deals with Noahide law on his terms. He especially
argues for the universal intelligibility of moral law in general. Although he
does not specifically mention the Noahide commandments he clearly had
them in mind as the "tenets of authentic Judaism" he writes about:

According to the tenets of Judaism, all inhabitants of the earth have claim to
salvation, and the means to attain it are as widespread as mankind itself, as liberally
dispensed as the means of satisfying one's hunger and other natural needs.[17]

Mendelssohn's argument for the immediate, universally knowable, rationality of the Noahide laws is not in itself novel. Saadiah Gaon previous suggested
the rationality of pre-Sinaitic law.[18] Saadiah, it should be remembered, regarded tradition to be a source of truth not subordinate to reason.[19] He
endeavored to show that reason is justified by tradition as it demonstrates that
tradition is consistent with reason. Truths, for him, are not all apparent and

therefore cannot be assumed to be universal.[20] For Mendelssohn, to the contrary, revelation is subordinate to reason because the former is particular and often esoteric. Reason is general and public, more democratic. Mendelssohn attempts to philosophically constitute a relation between reason and revelation as follows:

It seems to me that only with regard to historical truths did God, in His supreme wisdom, have to instruct mankind either by human means—through the spoken or written word—or through extraordinary events and miracles, if they were required to confirm the authority and credibility of the event. But the eternal truths that are necessary for a man's happiness and salvation are taught by God in a manner that is more fitting for His dignity . . . through creation itself in all its inter-relatedness, which is legible and intelligible to all men.[21]

For Mendelssohn, there are three types of truth: necessary, contingent and historical. Necessary truth is mathematical or logically manifest; it cannot be other than what it is. Contingent truth occurs in a given set of conditions from which a certain set of conclusions can be derived. God can change empirical conditions and conclusions. Miracles are possible.[22] Historical truth manifests itself culturally, in the particular events of a people.[23]

For Mendelssohn, the Noahide laws pertain only to necessary and contingent truths. The prohibitions of idolatry and blasphemy, for instance, presuppose a belief in God, and this is a metaphysical necessity.[24] These laws, therefore, relate to necessary truth. The rest of the Noahide laws, concerning as they do empirical relations in the created order, pertain to contingent truth; they are required by virtue of the fact that the world is the way it is. None of the laws refer to particular events; they are universal.

When one looks at Judaism, on the other hand, at least that aspect of it that is unique, it can only be justified on the level of historical truth. Thus, Mendelssohn sums up his view:

I believe Judaism knows nothing of a revealed religion in the sense in which Christians define this term. The Israelites possess a divine legislation—laws, commandments, statutes . . . Moses in a miraculous and supernatural way, revealed to them these laws and commandments, but not dogmas, propositions concerning salvation, or self-evident principles of reason . . . These the Lord reveals to us as well as to other men at all times through nature and events but never through the spoken and written word . . .[25]

What Mendelssohn has done was to make Noahide law *superior* to the Mosaic law in all its ramifications.[26] He never intended to diminish the necessity of Judaism for Jews. Mendelssohn, however, aspired for Judaism to be "a kind of Platonic reality."[27] Nevertheless, an abstract philosopher is not necessarily blind to history. Indeed, Mendelssohn regarded Judaism as being perfectly consistent with necessary and contingent truth, although not identical with it, as no historical tradition could be. Therefore, Judaism retains historical validity in that the world has not yet fully accepted the necessary and contingent truth it has so excellently preserved. Moreover, better than Christianity, it distinguishes between reason and revelation, and does not attempt to ground the former in the latter. It was on these grounds that Mendelssohn argued for the tolerance and respect of Judaism and Jews by the proponents of a new quasi-secular civilization in eighteenth-century Europe. Nathan Rotenstreich adds: "Mendelssohn, a child of the Enlightenment, is not concerned with demonstrating the *superiority* but the singular *right* of Judaism, which he ascribes to its particularistic elements."[28] Whereas formerly the doctrine of Noahide law was *subordinated* to the full Torah and, therefore, functioned as a universal element *within* Judaism, for Mendelssohn now Judaism becomes an element *within* a universal religion of metaphysics. The doctrine of Noahide law is reinterpreted by Mendelssohn to affirm just that, using traditional precedent.

3. Naftali Hartwig Wessely

Mendelssohn's interest in universal moral law was more than academic. It was part of his overall project to justify Judaism as consistent with the goals of the Enlightenment. Wessely (d. 1805), his disciple, carried on this work. In response to the education reforms of Austrian emperor Joseph II, he published a pamphlet (*Shalom v'Emet*) that outlined how Jews could partake of the new opportunities offered, especially in secular education.[29] His treatment of Noahide law is more thorough than Mendelssohn's. (A historical note: Wessely's pamphlet appeared in 1782, the same year that Mendelssohn published his introduction to Manasseh b. Israel's seventeenth-century *Vindicae Judaeorum*, which emphasized Jewish tolerance of non-Jews. Manasseh b. Israel attempted to convince Cromwell to permit Jews to make residence in England. Mendelssohn believed that these same arguments needed repeating well over one hundred years later.[30])

Wessely, following his master, distinguishes between reason and revelation. The former is termed the "law of man" and the latter the "law of the Lord."[31] He conceives of the relation between reason and revelation to be the relation between Noahide and Mosaic law. Wessely's identification of Noahide law with universal rational law is more explicit than Mendelssohn's:

Behold the law of man precedes in time the higher laws of God . . . and based on them one should prepare his heart to learn the laws of God . . . the law of man consists of the seven commandments and their specifies to which the opinion of most of the wise inclines . . . And the place where the law of man concludes, there the Divine law begins . . .[32]

So far, it seems, Wessely is not saying anything new when compared to the medieval rationalists. However, he declares the Noahide laws, which he subsumes under the rabbinic category of "the way of the world,"[33] were completely sufficient prior to Sinai.[34] Two new points are introduced: (1) reason is sufficient to constitute moral society; (2) reason, by preceding revelation, is independent of it. Even though he acknowledges the superiority of divine law, he does not constitute that superiority but merely stipulates it.[35] His choice of law of man (*Torat ha-adam*) is significant in what he does with it in his work. The term comes from II Sam. 7:19: "Is this the manner of treating an ordinary man, Lord God?" Here King David is awed by God's choice of his dynasty to build the Temple. The term here used refers to humanity's insignificance before God. Later, Nahmanides titles a halakhic work *Torat ha-Adam*, a work that focused on rituals for mourning. His choice of title was perhaps an emphasis on humanity's mortality in contrast to God's eternity. Wessely's use of the term, on the other hand, is for the sake of emphasizing the sufficiency of human reason. In the change of the term's connotation we see the influence of the Enlightenment's basic secularity.

Furthermore, Wessely indicates that although the knowledge of the speculative aspect of the law of man is not a religious requirement, it is a religious requirement to know the ethical aspects of the law.[36] Ethics, therefore, is the bridge between human law and divine law in that the general ethics of the former provide not only the prelude but the actual foundation for the more specific ethics of the latter.

There is little doubt that both Mendelssohn and Wessely regarded their view of the relation between universal rational law and Jewish revelation to be within Jewish tradition. Both of them were deeply rooted in that tradition and at home in its sources. Neither were assimilationists, as some later portrayed them.[37] Their main deficiency, however, at least from the standpoint of Jewish philosophy, is that they were unable to demonstrate an intelligible relation between the universal and the particular, reason and revelation. Such a demonstration, based on the premise of the harmony of Judaism and secular society, would have to wait for a more philosophically robust thinker, Hermann Cohen.

CHAPTER FOURTEEN

HERMANN COHEN AND THE JEWISH NEO-KANTIANS

1. Introduction

As we saw in the preceding chapter, Moses Mendelssohn's interpretation of Noahide law was revolutionary in the history of Judaism, as he constituted Noahide law as philosophically prior to the more historically contingent Mosaic law. The medieval rationalists, on the other hand, always considered Noahide law to be a prelude to the fully revealed Mosaic law, the latter being clearly superior to the former. Aside from the question of whether or not this traditional doctrine can be reinterpreted as Mendelssohn did and still not contradict its sources, his reinterpretation presented two philosophical problems: (1) By reducing Judaism to a particularistic phenomenon, at best a transitional entity standing between unenlightened parochialism behind it and wholly enlightened humanity ahead of it, does this not make a *philosophy of Judaism* impossible? Mendelssohn would have had to answer affirmatively inasmuch as Judaism for him is devoid of what would be for him philosophically relevant content. (2) If this is the case, then, as philosophy (and culture in general) advances along universal lines, does not particularistic Judaism necessarily recede into obscurity, or as the Talmud characterized a similar approach, "the Torah is placed folded in a corner and whoever is interested will come and study it"?[1] By situating philosophy and Judaism in absolute separation, Mendelssohn made the development of Judaism, at least in a rationally self-conscious way, almost impossible. By making it philosophically peripheral, he offered little to make an integration of the universal and particular possible within Judaism.[2] As such he laid the groundwork, however much he did not intend to so, for an inevitable choice between particularistic *old* Judaism, or the *new* universalistic European secular civilization. Mendelssohn's reinterpretation of the Noahide laws established the idea, accepted by many later Jewish intellectuals, that integration between universal philosophy and Jewish tradition was an impossibility.

These problems were inherited by the most systematic philosopher of modern Judaism, Hermann Cohen (1842–1918). He was faced with three alternatives: one, return to the medieval position that regarded revelation as the inner core of Judaism; (2) continue the nineteenth-century tradition of considering Judaism largely obsolete, needing only a proper burial; and (3) try to correlate philosophy and Judaism in such a way that each required the other for its fulfillment. Cohen, committed to the historical development of Judaism, settled on the third option. With the combination of his familiarity with classical Jewish sources and his profound philosophical ability, he was able to develop a philosophy of Judaism unequalled in modern times in terms of its systematic comprehension. I want to show how Noahide law lies at the very heart of his correlation of Judaism and philosophy.

2. Cohen's Theory of Noahide Law

Like Mendelssohn, Cohen developed a theory of Noahide law in response to changed historical circumstances. Whereas Mendelssohn developed his theory of Judaism's affirmation of universal law in order to facilitate the *entry* of committed Jews into the mainstream of European civilization, Cohen developed his theory in order to counteract the charges made in the late nineteenth century that committed Jews could not possibly *remain* within that mainstream because Judaism was antithetical to it. As early as 1880, Cohen confronted Heinrich von Treitschke, the German historian, regarding the supposed incompatibility of Judaism and the universalism of modern Germany.[3] Cohen's article, however, was almost entirely apologetic, containing no analysis of Jewish universalism within. Nevertheless, despite the limitations of this article, it was regarded later by Cohen as his reaffirmation of Judaism.[4] Early in his career, he did not consider himself a Jewish thinker, but rather an explicator of Kant's ideas. Historical events caused him to enlist his philosophical gifts in the service of rethinking Judaism for his time.

In 1888 Cohen participated in an important trial. A teacher in Marburg, where Cohen had achieved fame as a professor, was sued by the Jewish community for slandering Judaism. The teacher charged that Talmudic law permitted the robbery and defrauding of gentiles. These charges were part of a surge in intellectual anti-Judaism, sparked in large measure by the work of the Catholic cleric August Rohling, whose *Talmudjude* had been published in 1871.[5] Cohen was summoned to offer expert testimony. In the course of his testimony he offered the broad outlines of his theory of Noahide law. He wished to demonstrate that Judaism indeed had a doctrine of universal law, one concerned with the rights of gentiles as well as Jews. However, like any systematic representation, Cohen's treatment of Noahide law involved the input of his own views on ethics. As a Kantian, Cohen would have been the first to admit that no datum simply presents itself. He writes: "the literary sources . . . remain mute and blind if I do not approach them with a concept which I myself lay out as a foundation in order to be instructed by them and not simply guided by their authority."[6]

In representing the Noahide laws, Cohen, following the Talmud, emphasizes their restriction to the *seven* precepts mentioned in the Tosefta.[7] From this limitation he draws the following conclusion:

Nothing more is demanded. The belief in the Jewish God is not demanded . . . The Noahide is not a believer but a citizen (*Staatsbürger*). Therefore, this institution constitutes a unique factor in the history of religious politics . . . The positive connection with the faith community (*Glaubensgemeinschaft*) is not constituted as necessary for the civil community . . . The Noahide was not recognized as a believer but as a moral (*sittlicher*) human being.[8]

Cohen was arguing here that Judaism, even ancient Judaism, recognized that citizenship should not have any prerequisites outside of a commitment to obey civil law. This is presented to show that Judaism is not parochial, opposed to the secular state. Even the prohibition of idolatry is interpreted as a repudiation of the immoral practices associated with ancient idolatry.[9]

Furthermore, Cohen was impressed that the first Noahide law (at least in the Babylonian Talmud's version of the Tosefta) was the law of adjudication. For Cohen it is not just a specific provision for rectification of illegalities, but rather the essential characterization of the civil nature of Noahide law. He writes:

the precept of the "judicial institutes," to which the Noachide must submit, deserve particular attention . . . The concept of the Noachide is the foundation for natural law not only as an expression of the objective law but also as a determination of the subject . . . the Noachide is the *forerunner of natural law* for the state and for freedom of conscience.[10]

Cohen's insistence on the centrality of the Noahide laws for a philosophical constitution of Jewish ethical teaching emerges strongly in his review of Moritz Lazarus' *The Ethics of Judaism*. Lazarus, a social psychologist of the *Volkgeist* school, presented a systematic treatment of Jewish ethics. He judges Noahide law as a "decidedly particularistic doctrine . . . it is characteristic that in these supposed Noachian laws no mention is made of altruistic virtues, of charity and love, which are considered of the essence of the Jewish code."[11] Cohen criticizes Lazarus for misidentifying the essence of Jewish ethics:

objective lawfulness. Lazarus is guilty of sentimental subjectivism. The Noahide law, for Cohen, is "the idea of right and adjudication is the classical
expression of universal justice."[12]

As a Jew, Cohen was proud that two seventeenth-century Christian
students of jurisprudence, John Selden (d. 1654) and Hugo Grotius (d. 1645),
recognized this fact in their respective designations of Noahide law as the
Jewish version of the doctrine of the "law of nations" (*ius gentium*).[13] Grotius,
especially, was anxious to find any precedents he could for the constitution of a
system of international law transcending any religious foundations.[14] Cohen's
primary interest, unlike that of Grotius, was not jurisprudence per se. Rather,
as a philosopher and, later, as a philosopher of Judaism, Cohen was interested
in constituting an ethical foundation for Judaism. Since, for him, ethics is
universal by nature, non-Jewish recognition of this universal ethical-legal
element within Judaism was a welcome confirmation of his own views, a
confirmation that helped demonstrate that these views were not merely a subjective distortion of the Jewish sources.

However, the full thrust of Cohen's argument is far more than apology. It
follows, instead, from his philosophical attempt to show that ethics can be
constituted independently of religion and that this is authentic Jewish teaching as well. He argues:

Jewish moral teaching (*Sittenlehre*) constitutes the inner source, strictly the substantial principle of Jewish religious teaching (*Glaubenlehre*). Jewish ethics (*Ethik*) is
the principle of the Jewish religion. It is the principle and not the consequence.[15]

Jewish ethics in its most universal form is the Noahide law. Much later Cohen
speaks of the Noahide law as "an original (*ursprungliche*) Torah of their own,
which is the foundation for law and state."[16] All of this reflects Cohen's interpretation of Judaism along Kantian lines. For Cohen insisted that both for
Judaism and for Kant ethics is of primary importance. Religion itself must be
justified on purely ethical grounds.

3. Kant's Autonomous Ethics

As a disciple of Kant, Cohen's theory of ethics was based on moral autonomy.[17]
To paraphrase the Talmud: in order to understand the disciple one must first
understand the master.[18] We must, then, appreciate Kant's idea of moral
autonomy and, then, how Cohen shaped it and thereby showed the necessity
of Judaism for both its history and its horizon.

Kant's insistence on the autonomous nature of morality was revolutionary.
He characterized ethics as *rationally autonomous*, that is, ethical precepts are

both essentially intelligible and man-made.[19] This can best be understood by contrasting it with three other alternative views of ethics, explicitly or implicitly rejected by Kant, namely, (1) ethical precepts are neither man-made nor intelligible; (2) they are man-made but not intelligible; and (3) they are intelligible but not man-made. All three of these alternatives were discussed in the classical Jewish sources. What Cohen attempted to do was to show that moral autonomy was distinctive of the best in traditional Jewish ethical teaching and, moreover, that this idea alone made Judaism ethically respectable in the world after Kant. By seeing these alternatives in Jewish tradition, we can see how a critical treatment of that tradition parallels Kant's critical treatment of the history of ethics.

The first alternative was advocated by those Jewish thinkers who stressed the absolute transcendence of God. Its classical expression is: "The Holy One blessed be He said, 'I have made a statute, I have decreed a decree and you are not permitted to transgress My decree!'"[20] The problem with this approach is that, first of all, certain commandments, especially those pertaining to inter-human relationships (*bein adam le-havero*), were considered to be rationally evident.[21] Secondly, there were persistent attempts to uncover the reason for even the most obscure ritual commandments (*shimiyot*). Finally, this position implies that God is a capricious tyrant issuing irrational orders.[22] The chief weakness of this view is that it presents God as morally appalling. Therefore, it was the tendency of many traditional Jewish theologians to accept this assumption only tentatively.[23] This tendency can perhaps be seen as early as the Tannaitic period when Elijah, the messianic herald, is presented as one who will solve heretofore insoluble problems in the Law.[24] One can find little if any support in the normative Jewish tradition for the view that total absurdity reflects the unique will of God.

The second alternative was judged by tradition as the rationalization of immorality. This approach allowed humans to legislate for themselves without restraint. The recognition of the primacy of human-made law means no external restraints, that is, a divine lawgiver. The recognition of the unintelligibility of human-made law means that there are no internal restraints, that is, reason. Such an approach was considered to be the elevation of human caprice: "there is no law (*layt din*) and no Judge (*layt dayyan*)."[25] The Bible deems the denial of God to be a moral rather than a theoretical error: "the despicable one says in his heart, 'God is not there . . . ' The Lord scrutinizes the sons of man from heaven to see if there is anyone discerning (*maskil*), seeking (*doresh*) God" (Ps. 14:1–2).

The third alternative is the position of classical natural law theory. It is based on the assumption that ethics has a metaphysical foundation, that our understanding of the intelligibility of the external world is the basis for our discovering what ought to be done. In Jewish tradition the greatest proponent of this position was Maimonides.[26] For him, human obligation is rooted in the way God has created the universe and involved himself in its continuing operation. The primary project of his whole theological enterprise was to provide a coherent and sufficient metaphysical foundation for Jewish law and ethics. Cohen's attempts to use Maimonides as a precedent for his own distinctly Kantian ethical approach, an approach based on the rejection of classical natural law theory and the metaphysical assumptions underlying it, were distortions of Maimonides' position, as Julius Guttmann argued.[27]

Although the third alternative was more attractive than the other options, it was rejected by Kant. His rejection was based both on his own view of metaphysics and the phenomenology of ethics.

Kant's rejection of classical theistic metaphysics followed from his assumption that concepts are only valid if required by our understanding of sense experience. Since the concept of God as the foundation of all being is not required for this understanding, such a concept is epistemologically unsound. This rejection was expressed by Kant in his attempt to show that the classical proofs for God's existence are all based on the irrational assumption of the identity of thought and experience.[28] Just because we can conceive of a supreme being does not by extension assure the truth of this conception. Furthermore, Kant also claimed that the very intelligibility of the external world was actually our comprehension of how we order our experience of that world so that it will be intelligible to *us*, that is, phenomenal. Theocentric and cosmocentric views of reality are rejected, and we are left with a decidedly anthropocentric view.[29]

Even a secular natural law theory could not survive this new Kantian design. Moreover, a theistic natural law, one that inferred the existence of God from the intelligible structure of the universe, was doubly unacceptable. Cohen was aware of the revolutionary implications of Kant's philosophy. Yet he was convinced that its inner logic could actually provided a new and compelling philosophical foundation for Judaism—a Judaism ethical in character only—far superior to what Jewish philosophers had offered in the past.

Kant's philosophical revolution, at first glance, appears to be a return to Protagoras—that "man is the measure of all things."[30] However, whereas Protagoras argued that human ethical standards are of singularly human creation, Kant insisted that these standards are human creations shaped by the *inner* laws of human consciousness. Just as our discovery of the inner laws of consciousness, qua knowledge, grounded the intelligibility of sense experience, so our discovery of the inner laws of our consciousness, qua will, now grounds the intelligibility of the world ethically presented. Furthermore, one could view the world as a realm of our own making in a way one could not possibly view the external world experienced by the senses.[31] This accounts for the greater importance of ethics than anything else in the hierarchy of values. In short, ethics could be rationally constituted without recourse either to God or nature. Such a constitution could only be autonomous, that is, self-legislated, because Kant's metaphysical assumptions denied intelligibility to God and nature, the two non-human realms, because neither was now considered necessary for human understanding. An unintelligible "otherness" (*heteronomy*) cannot very well be authoritative for any rational person. Thus we legislate for ourselves based on our own self-understanding.

Kant's rejection of heteronomy in ethics was not only the result of his rejection of the metaphysical foundation of the classical natural law theory. He also rejected heteronomy based on the phenomenology of moral life. In a heteronomous ethic the ground of ethics is itself non-ethical. In natural law theory, therefore, at least as Kant understood it, one acts for the sake of some sort of perfection that is a state of human bliss. Moral acts, then, are means to a higher, non-moral end.[32] However, morality is unique precisely because it operates on its own *immediate* awareness of duty, according to Kant, not on some *projected* sense of well-being.[33] Only this distinction saves morality from becoming simply a form of prudence (*Klugheit*). Only this distinction enables morality to generate categorical imperatives, based on the general idea of humanity rather than being limited to conditional, hypothetical options, based on the particular circumstances of the situation of various people.[34] This emphasis on virtue for its own sake was not lost on Cohen, who found significant parallels in classical Jewish sources that condemned anyone performing a commandment for the sake of reward.[35]

Kant's doctrine, in and of itself, appears to ignore history and deny religion. For if humanity can legislate for itself based upon individual self-understanding, then human nature is a constant that transcends the changing shape of human history. How *humankind* comes to this self-understanding, why it is present at some times and places more than at others, does not seem to be of much interest to Kant.[36] As for religion, its insistence on affirming a divine lawgiver contradicts Kant's stress on autonomy.

Nevertheless, Kant did not choose to either ignore or deny the centrality of religious life. He was determined to find a place for it in his ethical design. He did this by making belief in the existence of God a postulate of pure practical reason:

> . . . there is not the slightest ground in the moral law for a necessary connection between morality and proportionate happiness of a being which belongs to the

world as one of its parts and is dependent on it. Not being nature's cause, his will cannot by its own strength bring nature, as it touches on his happiness, into complete harmony with his practical principles. Nevertheless . . . such a connection is postulated as necessary . . . Therefore also the existence is postulated of a cause of the whole of nature, itself distinct from nature, which contains the ground of the exact coincidence of happiness with morality.[37]

Ethics requires a belief in God so that our moral will is regarded as *really efficacious* and not just internal intention, which would make it impractical.[38] God enters at this point. God functions at best as a postulated subsequent efficient cause needed only to put some finishing touches to the ethical system. No doubt Kant was sincere in his reconstruction of theology, even having written *Religion within the Limits of Reason Alone* to further this point. In this book, he generally follows Spinoza's low view of Judaism's spirituality and philosophical relevance.[39]

Such a secondary role for God and Judaism could not satisfy someone like Cohen, who was so seriously committed to both. Moreover, the almost complete neglect of history in reflection on human ethics disappointed Cohen, as he followed instead Hegel's emphasis on history.[40] As a philosopher and a Jew, therefore, Cohen attempted to show that Kantian autonomous ethics could be considerably deepened if seen from the point of view of both the faith and the tradition of Judaism.

4. Cohen's Ethical Monotheism

Although, for Cohen, the concept of ethical autonomy is independent of history and its contingencies, the history of ethics is important inasmuch as ethics is the foundation of human culture, and it is only in the context of human culture that ethics can be efficacious. Cohen insists on "historical considerations":[41]

It is, however, an unhistorical view that the story (*Geschichte*) of ethics was independent of religion. The science of ethics must be independent of religion. This independence is conditioned by its method and its problematic, which are entirely separate from religion . . . But ethics borrows its material, just as much so, from religion . . . And so ethics gives thanks to the great fundamental proposition concerning love of neighbor in the so-called Mosaic teaching.[42]

Cohen was quite correct that the concept of the *ger toshav*, the gentile having civil rights in a Jewish polity, long proceeded the concept of Noahide law, that Noahide law was the rabbinic attempt to constitute the status objectively.[43] For Cohen, the discovery of the *humanity* of the non-Jew, a humanity ethically con stituted, was the earliest discovery of the idea of *human qua human*, the subject required for autonomous ethics. He notes that the form of "love your neighbor as yourself" (*kamokha*—Lev. 19:18) is the same as that of "the *ger* who dwells among you, you shall love him as yourself (*kamokha*), because you were *gerim* in the land of Egypt . . . " (Lev. 19:34).[44] He considers the discovery of this concept momentous in human history.[45] Although there were those in the rabbinic tradition who insisted that one's "neighbor" (*re'a*) was his fellow Jew,[46] there were also those who saw Hillel's dictum, "what is hateful to you, do not do it to your fellowman (*haverakh*)," as being a paraphrase of the commandment to love one's neighbor as himself.[47] Hillel's dictum was clearly universal inasmuch as it was addressed to a non-Jew inquiring about Judaism.[48] (It is easy to see why it was so often quoted by nineteenth-century Germany teachers and preachers.)[49]

If this were the total extent of Judaism's contribution to the history of ethics, it would certainly deserve the perpetual gratitude of the philosophy of ethics. Nevertheless, this gratitude would be a backward glance. It would in no way indicate that Judaism is of any present or future importance for ethics. Furthermore, in Cohen's idealistic view of history, history is essentially a continuum of ongoing progress into the future.[50] This project into the future determines the meaning of the past. This is what distinguishes history from obscurantism.

Cohen was aware of this. His philosophical idealism, reflecting Hegel's influence, saw *humanity* suggested by the Jewish concept of "fellowman" as an ideal to be realized in the future. Cohen introduced the messianic idea, or "messianic age," as Judaism's unique contribution to the horizon of ethics. Cohen sees the messianic age as the very essence of history and a decidedly Jewish contribution to civilization:

The ideality of the Messiah, his significance as an idea, is shown in the overcoming of the person of the Messiah and in the dissolution of the personal image in the pure notion of time, in the concept of the age. Time becomes future and only future . . . man's existence (*Dasein*) is preserved and elevated (*hebt sich auf*) in this being of the future. Thus, the thought of *history* comes into being for human life and for the life of the peoples.[51]

In its concept of the messianic age, Judaism has presented the horizon for the future of humankind, a culture ethically constituted. Since that future idealization is still not a reality in history, the Jewish people and Judaism are ethically justified in maintaining their separate identity. To merge with a humanity not yet messianically fulfilled could only be pseudo-messianic. It would deprive humanity of the necessary benefit of Judaism's continuing contribution. The mission of Judaism is to teach ethical monotheism until the world is ready to accept it. The preservation of the true vision of ethical monotheism requires the separate preservation of Jews.[52]

This too can be seen in Cohen's concept of the Noahide. The recognition of the humanity of the Noahide non-Jew as an ethical personality is the historical emergence of the ideal of a united humankind. Nevertheless, one must recognize that the idea is *not yet* realized in human history. Thus Cohen's philosophical idealism, which enabled him to correlate the concept of the Noahide as the background of ethical humankind with the concept of the messianic age as the horizon of ethical humankind, this philosophical idealism enabled him to compellingly argue against the Jewish assimiliationists of his time.[53] Even his deep German patriotism did not lead him to equate the Germany of his day with the fully realized kingdom of God on earth.[54] Thus the Noahide and the Jew, as ideal types, are correlated as the universal and the particular. Clearly, the universal is the goal of the particular and, therefore, is more important than it. However, the universal, which is the full brotherhood of man seen in the concept of the Noahide, is still unrealized, as the ideal and the real have not yet merged. Cohen refuses to allow Judaism to prematurely submerge itself into humanity, because *humankind is not yet humanity*.

In his later thought Cohen connected the idea of the messianic age with the idea of one God, with monotheism. The idea of God's singular oneness qua Being is correlated with humankind's becoming through the process of messianic realization.[55] God's singular oneness, then, is humankind's ideal.[56] In this correlation Cohen sees the Jewish God idea as presenting ethics with the true horizon of its fulfillment. Thus, unlike Kant, Cohen conceives of the idea of God as much more than a postulate guaranteeing the ultimate efficacy of personal virtue. The idea of God, for Cohen, is even more than the guarantee of the historical fulfillment of all humankind. Rather, God as the idea of Being (but not as a personal commanding will)[57] is seen as the ground of the messianic ideal, the final goal of all of humankind's ethical striving. Kant's "Kingdom of Ends" is transformed by Cohen into the "Kingdom of God."[58] This would have been impossible without Cohen's conscious involvement with his Jewish background and aspirations.

4. Cohen's Influence

As the founder of the Marburg school of neo-Kantianism, Cohen had a wide influence on a younger generation of philosophers. Perhaps his best known disciple was Ernst Cassirer (d. 1945). Cohen also inspired liberal Jewish theologians, although his best disciples, Rosenzweig[59] and Leo Baeck,[60] broke

with their master's Kantianism. However, they did not depart from his interpretation of Noahide law, and consequently an analysis of their own ideas is
out of place here.

Cohen's theory of Noahide law was used, however, by his disciples Felix
Perles and Julius Guttmann. They did not add substantially to Cohen's view of
the Noahide, but their use of Talmudic sources inspired a criticism that,
although directed against them, in effect showed that Cohen's theory was
inconsistent with Talmudic traditions. Of course, one can take a traditional
teaching and use it to illuminate a new context. However, if that illumination
contradicts the clear meaning of that traditional teaching, then it cannot
be accepted as a development of it. The rabbis stated: "the clear meaning
(*peshuto*) cannot be overridden."[61]

Perles, in a *Festschrift* for Cohen's seventieth birthday,[62] argued that the rabbinic dictum, "greater is he who is commanded and practices than he who is
not commanded and practices,"[63] implies a recognition of autonomous ethics
in Judaism. This is explicitly based on the work of the Jewish neo-Hegelian
Samuel Hirsch (d. 1889),[64] but one can see how it fits into Cohen's approach.
He himself had said almost the same thing. Perles, like Cohen, interprets
"commanded" as "ethically necessary" as opposed to merely optional.[65] God as
the one who commands now becomes the support for the rational ethical
commandment itself.

In an indirect criticism of Perles' interpretation, Isaak Heinemann made
the following points:[66] (1) the Talmud only recognizes autonomous acts as
possible; (2) if there are autonomous acts, then they are those which are commanded; (3) for rabbinic Judaism, autonomous ethics is only a possibility for
gentiles. For Jews there are only revealed ethics in the normative sense. In his
critique, Heinemann identifies the Noahide law with this autonomous possibility. What emerges from Heinemann's critique is a reaffirmation of the rab-
binic-medieval assumption, namely, even if there is a moral law rationally
apprehended, that law is at best an inferior prelude to the divinely revealed
Torah. Israel, the recipient of the Torah, then, clearly stands above the rest of
humankind. Heinemann's argument is not with the philosophical assumptions of Cohen and his disciples, but rather with their historical assumption
that rabbinic texts lend themselves to these neo-Kantian interpretations.

Even a scholar as philosophically sophisticated as Guttmann attempted the
same type of exegesis. In an early essay (1908), he wrote:

They also thought that there are commandments—according to the striking
Talmudic statement (B. *Yoma* 67b)—that even were it not written it ought to have
been written . . . The basic idea in Kant's moral teaching, that the good law which we
legislate for ourselves and which we must realize . . . This foundation of Kant's is

indeed typical of the ethics of Judaism . . . in complete semblance of Kant's method.[67]

In opposition to this type of use of the rabbinic sources, E.E. Urbach notes that for the rabbis the authority of the law is due to its being revealed and written. He sees the rabbinic speculations noted by Cohen, Perles and Guttmann as being simple reflections of what might have been had there been no revelation. Such speculations, however, do not imply that there is in effect a non-revealed law that Judaism recognizes.[68]

The historical importance of this type of criticism is twofold. First, it indicates how the classical Jewish sources, especially the rabbinic sources, do not lend themselves to interpretation based on a philosophical system essentially antithetical to them. Secondly, this type of criticism indicates how persuasive Cohen was in convincing subsequent scholars, even those who did not follow his Kantian approach, that natural law theory and Kantian autonomous ethics are one and the same. Therefore, scholars such as Urbach assume that by showing that autonomy plays a very minor role in rabbinic thought that there is no basis for a Jewish natural law theory in the rabbinic sources. However, as we have seen, classical natural law theory posited a heteronomous rational norm. As such, revelation can be seen as both direct and indirect. Natural law, then, is indirect revelation. Direct revelation is from God and constitutes the unique relationship between God and Israel. Indirect revelation is inferred from humankind's relationship with their fellow humans. Direct revelation is divine in its source; indirect revelation is divine in its intent. The latter is the prelude to the former. One of the main reasons, it seems to me, that there has been a reluctance to see a tradition of Jewish natural law type theory, beginning in the rabbinic sources, is because of the unconscious acceptance of Cohen's assumptions, even by those who opposed his conclusions. What Jewish natural law theorizing after Cohen must do, then, is to reinterpret this tradition in such a way so as to avoid the metaphysical assumptions of the medievals, assumptions that, since Cohen and Kant before him, cannot be accepted as the sufficient theoretical basis of this doctrine. However, to move beyond Cohen in this area, one must appreciate the profundity of his effects and at the same time understand the insufficiencies of the pre-Kantians.

CHAPTER FIFTEEN

CONCLUSION

This study has been an attempt to show how philosophy arose and developed in Judaism, that it was not a foreign element grafted onto it but was, instead, an inner need, a desire to constitute a Jewish anthropology. Humanity in general and the Noahide became synonyms.

In the past, there were attempts to limit or eliminate philosophical reflection from Jewish thought. In 1305, the rabbinate of Barcelona endeavored to ban the study of philosophy, led by Solomon ibn Adret (Rashba). Rashba argued that one devoted "to the books of the Greeks makes them the root (ikkar) and uproots (oker) the Torah of the Lord!"[1] Such a charge, heard less today but not absent, must be answered.

If Jewish philosophy is to be a permissible Jewish activity, it must find its justification in the most evident structure of Judaism—halakhah. This was done best by Maimonides, I believe. The Talmud records the following dictum:

Rav Safra said in the name of R. Joshua b. Hananyah . . . that one should divide his years of study into a third of the time for Scripture, a third for Mishnah, a third for Talmud.[2]

In codifying this prescription, Maimonides writes:

One ought to divide his study time into three parts: one third for the Written Torah, one third for the Oral tradition, and one third for understanding and comprehending a subject from beginning to end and inferring one thing from another and comparing one thing with another and understanding the principles by which the Torah is interpreted so that he knows the essence of these principles . . . This is what is called Gemara.[3]

For Maimonides, Talmud or Gemara is primarily a method of inquiry, and all method is ultimately a philosophy of its subject matter. If Talmud is method, then it can be extended beyond its previous explication in a particular body of literature, for method is necessarily less explicit than data. This understanding of Talmud as method in the deepest sense is the greatest Jewish justification of philosophical reflection I know.[4] As a method of inquiry, rather than a competing source of wisdom, it at all times respects the independent integrity of the object of its concern.[5]

Inquiries can be of two types: either they proceed out from the core towards the periphery, or they begin at the periphery and proceed inward to the core. Aristotle distinguishes between discourse from first principles and discourse towards first principles. In what we would later term the "cultural disciplines," he advises the second method of inquiry because these disciplines do not deal with objects "known in themselves,"[6] that is, immediately intelligible at the core (*ratio per se*). The method of inquiry is not only determined by the historical situation of the subject, but, even more so, by the very structure of the object itself. For only an object that is constituted as a deductive model admits of a method of inquiry where one proceeds from first principles to conclusions. As for Judaism, such a process of understanding would only be possible if Judaism were constituted dogmatically, that is, if at its core we found certain elementary propositions from which everything subsequent is then systematically deduced. Leaving the much-debated question of the role of dogma in Judaism aside, no one could successfully maintain that the core of Judaism is dogmatic.[7]

One evident example ought to suffice to prove this point. The *Mishneh Torah* is the most systematic exposition of Judaism ever written. It is designed to systematize halakhah, the most evident structure of Judaism. Nevertheless, its system is not deductive. Even though it begins with such dogmas as the existence of God and the revelation of the Torah, it does not deductively proceed from these central dogmas to more specific questions. These dogmas are taken as general assumptions, but the various laws of the *Mishneh Torah* are not presented as further specifications of these general principles in any deductive way.[8]

Therefore, Judaism itself requires a process of understanding that penetrates inward rather than deducing outward if its intelligibility is to be grasped. This process of beginning at the periphery, then, is not just a technique for marginal Jews who are alienated from Judaism. It is, rather, the way that any Jew, no matter how immersed one is in Judaism, must proceed in a philosophical reflection on Judaism.

The success of Jewish philosophy ultimately depends on the ability of the particular Jewish philosopher. Some attempts have been brilliant successes, others dismal failures. However, I believe that Judaism itself admits of philosophical reflection as a legitimate method of inquiry. Philosophy is possible for Judaism. As such Judaism is an authentic challenge for any committed Jew who is stirred by philosophical *eros* to discover the essential structures of the object of his primary interest. As Plato taught, philosophical *eros* is first aroused by paradox.[9] The paradox here is that I am conscious of being both human and Jewish. Ordinary classification indicates that the species "Jew" is a subset of the genus "humanity." Jewish tradition, on the other hand, suggests that the Jew is *sui generis*, someone apart from humanity at large.[10] This paradox, then, manifests itself in the fundamental feeling of ambivalence. Philosophical *eros* is the philosopher's desire to resolve his ambivalence. I do not think that Judaism precludes this desire by making its resolution impossible.

The question now arises: does halakhah admit of philosophical reflection?

The surprising fact is that most philosophical reflections on Judaism have not only avoided Noahide law as a starting point, but have avoided halakhah in general. This is because of a basic misunderstanding in Jewish philosophy. If it can be cleared away, we can better understand the method at work here.

This misunderstanding is based on the assumption that the systematic structure admitting philosophical analysis is evidently deductive. Since halakhah is not a process where first principles are set down and thereafter specified, it seems to elude philosophical analysis. It seems unstructured in comparison with the impressive dogmatic edifices of some other religions. Halakhah can scarcely be conceived by means of a mathematical model.[11] For this reason much of Jewish philosophy has begun elsewhere because of the basically non-architectonic character of halakhah. Nevertheless, this approach is based on a misunderstanding of philosophical method, namely, it does not appreciate philosophy as a process of discovery. In a process of discovery one begins with seemingly disjointed data and only *subsequently* glimpses the essential structures.[12] Therefore, philosophy can begin *wherever* the boundaries of the particular philosopher's primary interests are experientially located, as Socrates demonstrated. Indeed a dogmatic structure actually hampers the critical function of philosophy, as the history of European philosophy, beginning with Socrates, has shown repeatedly.

At this level the relation between Judaism and the external world, which the concept of the Noahide constitutes the border of Judaism, functions in two ways: one as a criterion of the possibility of divine revelation to humanity; the other as a criterion of human potentiality for knowledge of God. In both of these ways the philosophical problem of natural law permanently enters into the discussion. In both of these ways we have before us a true *beginning* that philosophical reflection requires.

Noahide law functions as a criterion of the possibility of revelation as follows. It asserts that the people of Israel did not come to Sinai as a moral *tabula rasa*. It asserts, in a way that can be clarified by the Kantian notion of the *a priori* conditions of experience, that the Torah specified and ultimately

particularized what humankind already had in general. However, this specification and particularization are not subsumed within the general categories
that the people of Israel as humans, that is, as Noahides, already have. Both
the experience and content of revelation *came into* this world, but were not
produced by it. Just as the *a priori* categories that enable experience to be possible, for Kant, do not themselves produce that experience,[13] so the moral categories expressed in the Noahide laws do not produce revelation. Revelation
only *presupposes* these categories as conditions, not as grounds. This is why
throughout this study I have several times made the philosophical distinction
between a *conditio sine qua non* and a *conditio per quam*. The former provides
the necessary background for revelation; the latter would provide its sufficient
ground. Therefore, my central argument with a philosopher like Hermann
Cohen is that, because his theology is built upon Kant's ethical construction-
ism rather than on Kant's much more empirically sensitive epistemology, he
makes Noahide law and all that it signifies for him *conditio per quam* rather
than the *conditio sine qua non* of Judaism. In other words, by overemphasizing
its importance, he misses its true significance for Jewish philosophy. The
notion of preconditions saves Judaism from this type of extinction at the
hands of philosophy.

Recognizing that Judaism has intelligible preconditions also saves Jewish
philosophy from the historical and philosophical pitfalls of what we call fundamentalism. Fundamentalism insists on regarding Judaism as something
absolutely unique at all levels and rejects any suggestion that it has analogues
in the world at large. This approach is anti-historical, suggesting at times that
those who do find these analogues in the world are motivated by anti-Jewish
bias. The recognition of the intelligible preconditions enables one to see the
very generality that makes analogy possible as the background of Judaism.
Judaism's uniqueness, then, is not at the *prima facie* level, but rather it is discovered within, something often unseen and unsaid. The philosophical snare
of fundamentalism is its attempt to particularize language, to see the forms of
Jewish expression as absolutely unique. However, this approach is belied by
the fact that Jewish theologians throughout history freely appropriated the
language and concepts of various philosophies in their fruitful attempts to
understand Judaism. Recognizing the preconditions of revelation enables one
to maintain the crucial distinction between the uniqueness of experience and
the generality of descriptive language.

Finally, in more theological language, this approach sees creation as the
background for revelation. Creation has a permanent order, a *nature* that God
placed in it and declares "very good." In our case our nature is social. Although
revelation is not a natural development from creation, it does, nevertheless,

enter into the created order. Thus the Bible compares revelation with natural human sociality as well as with the rest of nature: "Can two walk together without agreement? Does the lion roar if he has no prey? . . . when the Lord God speaks, who will not prophesy?" (Amos 3:3, 8). And: "Surely the stork in the heavens knows her appointed seasons; and the turtledove and the swallow and the crane observe the time of their coming; but My people do not know the just law (*mishpat*) of the Lord" (Jer. 8:7).

These comparisons presuppose something essential in common between the two orders, that of creation and that of revelation. What they share in common is normativity: both created nature and revelation manifest their own law. Because created nature, including human sociality, precedes revelation, the law of revelation presupposes creation's law. Thus it is said about Abraham that he was to command his progeny "to keep the way of the Lord to do righteousness and just law . . . " (Gen. 18:19). However, this "way of the Lord," this divine law, cannot contradict natural justice per se as indicated by Abraham's challenge to God, "Will the Judge of the whole earth not do justly?" (Gen. 18:25). Moreover, the justice of this revealed law is to be evident to the nations of the world that are bereft of Sinaitic revelation: ". . . for it is your wisdom and understanding in the view of the nations, who will hear these statutes and will say . . . [they are] statutes and just laws, according to this whole Torah which I place before you today" (Deut. 4:6, 8). And, finally, it is "My just laws" of Lev. 18:5 that the rabbis considered to be rational.[14]

Noahide law functions, also, as a criterion of human potentiality in relation to revelation. Jewish tradition has emphasized again and again that the Torah was revealed because humanity needed it. As such, the Torah came in response to human nature at its deepest level. Need precedes response in human experience. The philosophical understanding of the Torah by those who walk in its paths is greatly enriched and stimulated by reflection on what human needs are being addressed by the specific commandments of the Torah and, indeed, the Torah *in toto*. The experience of need is what makes humanity aware of the gap between what we are and what we are to be. Awareness of need allows us to translate our present lack into the active thrust of desire. However, all of this would be futile and meaningless without previous knowledge of the correlation between need and response. Our discovery of our nature, at least in part, is the result of understanding that our desires intend real objects. The view that Noahide law is a Jewish formulation of natural law means that the Torah can be accepted as the complete response to our needs in the world, precisely because its precepts have a general affinity with those humanly discoverable laws that have *already* responded to recognizable human needs. If the Torah did not have anything in common with what we already know about our nature and the law that this knowledge discovers, then acceptance of the Torah would be nothing more than an irrational leap of faith. The Torah itself would always be unintelligible because no intelligible preconditions would apply to it.

Finally, the relation between Noahide law as natural law and the revealed law of the Torah indicates that humans' desire to draw near to God is the culmination of their desire to draw near to their fellow humans in community. Indeed, God reveals himself to the *people of Israel*, and, therefore, to every member of it as a social creature. God's revelation presupposes the elect people of Israel, and the whole life of this elect people intends God's revelation. The people of Israel say, "If Thy presence does not go with us, do bring us up out of this place" (Ex. 33:15). Additionally: "In Thy presence, Lord, is my whole desire . . ." (Ps. 38:10). The concept of Noahide law suggests that Israel acknowledges that they experienced this desire for ultimate communion even before its ultimate object revealed himself to them. Before God appeared other humans appeared. The life of this earlier communion and the laws that govern it were with the people of Israel when they stood at Sinai, when the desire that intended communion in general heard its ultimate object. The life of this earlier communion and the laws that govern it are now with the people of Israel as they travel from Sinai to "Jerusalem rebuilt," from revelation to redemption.

AFTERWORD

MATTHEW LAGRONE

THIS AFTERWORD is designed to fill out some of the larger concerns of *The Image of the Non-Jew in Judaism*. David Novak's book is a thick historical delineation of the concept on the Noahide from rabbinic times to the twentieth century. This section touches on some of his concerns subsequent to the original publication of the book. In particular, it considers the philosophical underpinnings of natural law and their relationship to Noahide law; the use of natural law thinking in Jewish history, especially since Emancipation; and Novak's analysis of Marvin Fox's and Devora Steinmetz's attitudes towards natural law.

2. The Relationship of Noahide and Natural Law

Noahide law is related to natural law as a particular manifestation of the universal idea of a rational moral law that all are bound to without the specific obligations of a revealed law. Natural law, properly defined, is the universally applicable—at all times, everywhere and for everyone—and rationally evident standard of human action in the world. It provides an objective basis for a small but essential part of human morality, a basis that is outside any human particularities, ontologically prior to any law-making person or body. Natural law is known through our rational capacity, which all people share. The concern for natural law theorists, at least those writing out of a religious tradition, does not center around matters of ritual and liturgy, which are indubitably particular; rather, they focus on the foundations of inter-human relations and the elementary moral standards that make interaction possible and desirable. Noahide law is, as noted above, the translation of this conception of natural law into a specifically Jewish conceptual vocabulary. It is natural law anchored in a historical tradition. All religions contain some conception, whether fully formulated or not, of laws that include all of humanity. That is, there are moral expectations of other people, not merely one's own community. Concern for the moral life of one's community alone is tribalism, and Noahide law acts as an internal philosophical structure to avoid such an ethically disastrous outcome; it is a danger for all religious groups. These moral expectations have shaped Judaism's approach to other cultures, establishing criteria, a sort of bright-line test, to determine whether Jews can live and thrive in a particular non-Jewish environment. And these expectations frame attitudes toward the public square where people with prior, and perhaps conflicting, commitments can come together, it is hoped, for political flourishing. Natural law, then, allows a way out of a crude social contract theory where   people must conceal their existing convictions to participate in the public square. Possessors of older traditions may meet in a secular space without bracketing primary commitments, or fearing that secular space will become secularized (and as a result risk becoming the primary community for everyone), lacking any recognition of a truth that transcends any particular human political arrangement. The way that Jews have contributed to public life and the moral discourse that surrounds it is through Noahide law, even if many Jews have not named it as such.

The foregoing leads to a central question for natural law theory: Is natural law—and by logical extension, Noahide law—theological or philosophical? It can best be found at the intersection of the two, making both stronger. The main interest of theology is revelation, and revelation is decidedly unique, given to one historical community and consequently not universal because it is not repeatable. Natural law cannot be fully identified with theology (although many outstanding natural law theorists are theologians), because that would reduce natural law to apologetics, the confirmation of a tradition's particularities. The benefit of a properly constituted natural law theory for theology is that the former can demonstrate that the latter is not irrational. That is to say, natural law shows the rationality of law, and that accepting a law, even if its source is ultimately divine, does not by extension entail blind faith. The role of natural law within philosophy, on the other hand, is quite different. Philosophy is about our fundamental conception of the world, at least as it pertains to the universal world of ideas. Natural law allows the generalizations of philosophy to be part of intercultural contact, translating the abstract sphere of ideas into the reality of human relations.

Within a religion of revelation like Judaism the use of natural law presents the possibility of demanding too much or too little from the religion. Unlike a thinker such as Aristotle who consistently stressed the superiority of the general, Judaism, because of its status as a revealed religion, emphasizes the particular. If natural law claimed to be more than universal principles of human conduct, then it would encroach upon the distinctive covenantal character of Judaism. That is, it would threaten to overwhelm Judaism with a claim of being equal to or greater than its specific revelation, and Judaism would become but a division of natural religion. Natural law, at best, operates as a system of principles instead of a body of normative law, wide-ranging categories instead of explicit prescriptions. This does not mean that natural law has no real-world application, only that it is not positive law. Ideally, natural law would place itself above the temporizing political bargains necessary for human society but below direct divine revelation, as it cannot claim to be part of any unique revelation. Natural law emerges from the one thing humans have in common, and that is reason, and reason is greater than practical politics yet inferior to a covenanted community. On the other hand, if Judaism denies natural law, asserts that everything is revelation and reason is merely practical and outside the ambit of truth, then Jewish and gentile relations would be reduced to nothing but power politics where the strong subsume the weak at best and crush them at worst—such a relationship would be similar to that of the hammer and the nail. In this situation, concern for a common moral truth would be shelved. The rabbis' discovery of Noahide law, then, is a recognition that there is a moral category separate from revelation.

Noahide law, then, may be defined as: (1) the Jewish understanding of natural law, (2) the engagement of Judaism with philosophy, (3) the particular construal of universal truths and (4) a border concept, mediating between the Jewish world and the gentile world, a moral space between the interstices of traditions that also overlaps with them.

3. Noahide Law in History

Noahide law was never part of a functioning Jewish legal system. It surfaced in the rabbinic attempt to discover within the classical resources of the tradition a thread of thought that spoke to universal, inter-human concerns. Jews resided among gentiles and, more often than not, lived under their political authority, so surely the tradition must have something to say about these relations and this could only be done by locating common moral features. Consequently, the theoretical Noahide was constructed (although construction does not mean invention). The biblical model that the rabbis could point to was the ger toshav, the non-Jew who lived under Israelite rule in the biblical era and was afforded rights. Of course, the Noahide had no historical connection to the institution of the ger toshav, and Noahide law thus was never applied in history. In any case, the ger toshav was never a full member of Israelite society, unlike the Noahide, who was imagined (usually) as the morally equal other.

The absence of a historical Noahide was an advantage. The Noahide covenant, unlike its Mosaic parallel, does not celebrate any historical event, and is not anchored in the memory of any community. As it was a philosophical-theological construct, the rabbis were not bound by the particular contexts of history; therefore, they could swim in the depths of philosophical reflection rather than wade in the shallows of historical limitation. In the rabbinic imagination, this law appeared before the revelation at Sinai and is binding on gentiles eternally. Before Sinai, of course, all humanity was non-Jewish and by extension Jews were Noahides until the superior and explicit revelation to Moses and the people of Israel. The rabbis interpreted Noahide law through aggadah, moral and theological speculation, not halakhah, the normative rabbinic explication of divine law. When they discussed the Noahide, the rabbis were considering human beings per se, and this was the strength of aggadah. Rabbinic conclusions about the nature of the Noahide were not normative in aggadic contemplation but rather were deliberations on the rational and moral grounds of inter-human relationships at both the individual and communal level. The rabbinic construction of the Noahide allowed Jews to justify the moral constitution of gentile society. If these societies among whom they lived adhered to the seven principles of Noahide law (or what more or less approximates it), then they were morally respectable. It is a recognition of a common moral ground that permitted a covenanted people to live under the rule of those outside of the Sinaitic covenant, and, ideally, Noahide law should act as proof for those who question whether Judaism contains a universal standard of justice and fairness. Thus the Noahide represents the contemporary non-Jew, the one with whom Jews attempt to discover some significant moral commonality without at the same dismissing particularism, which has been the error of much of liberal Jewish thought from Mendelssohn forward.

Natural law thinking through the concept of the Noahide had been a conscious part of Judaism since rabbinic times, but the modern era presented three distinct challenges to natural law theorists in the Jewish tradition. With greater personal and communal contact with the non-Jewish world, natural law/Noahide law provided a language of inter-human discourse for Jews to engage the gentile world in dialogue. When the historical context has allowed for greater Jewish interaction, the utility of the rabbinic conception of the Noahide has correspondingly increased. The need for a very public and self-aware natural law from the sources of Jewish tradition emerged from the debates about Jewish emancipation in the eighteenth and nineteenth centuries, the destruction of most of European Jewry in the Holocaust, and the establishment of the State of Israel. These events transformed Jewish life to a degree not witnessed since the ruin of independent religious and national life in the land of Israel following the first Roman–Jewish war (66–73 CE).

Emancipation involved the Jewish pursuit of equal civil, social and religious rights in Europe. Jews would end their alienation from gentile society and enjoy the benefits of citizenship, and to justify this significant transformation philosophically oriented thinkers such as Moses Mendelssohn employed natural law to bolster Jewish claims to equality. Conversion to Christianity, contra Heine, was not to be the passport to secular society, but instead a language of universal rights independent of any particular tradition. Noahide law, the specifically Jewish form of natural law, gave Jews an idiom to both justify their participation in the wider political and cultural life and to endorse the normativity of gentile morality. Emancipation, in theory if not always in practice, was intended to offer a space for a meeting of moral and political equals. In practice, for many Jews emancipation meant entering modernity as "a man on the street" rather than as a Jew, relinquishing particularism for universalism (the irony, of course, was that the springtime promise of universalism turned into a different kind of particularism). For Jews to enter this space with integrity—that is, without diminishing their commitment to Jewish practice—it follows that the justification for this entrance must emerge from the sources of the tradition.

The second major event in the development of a Jewish understanding of natural law appears after the Holocaust. While the majority of victims of the National Socialists were Jews, this tragedy had universal implications, and many, though not all, Jews treated it as a universal tragedy. The disproportionate number of Jews engaged in humanitarian work today reveals the universal significance of the phrase, "Never again." For other Jews, the distinctiveness of the Holocaust—that it is foremost a Jewish catastrophe—cannot be diminished. This latter group tends to avoid natural law assessments of the Holocaust's implications. But for those who affirm a universal background to a particular event, natural law considerations are indispensable. Jewish suffering in the Holocaust is the peak example of the violation of human beings per se. Again, Noahide law supplies a specifically Jewish vocabulary of human rights. Rights-talk works best when it comes from a tradition that precedes and transcends the secular public square where we discuss rights.

The creation of the State of Israel represents the third key event in instigating the conscious use of natural law. In this historically novel situation—a people deprived of its ancestral land regains that land—the Jewish people now for the first time in at least 2000 years are a majority in one independent location, governing non-Jewish minorities. Israeli law is a crazy quilt of legal systems, including halakhah in matters of personal status (for Jews alone), but it is not a theocracy in the classical sense—that is, rule by divine law—or in the more contemporary sense of rule by clerics. Rather, it is a secular state that must negotiate morally and politically with its citizens and neighbors. Natural law thinking in this case provides a point of moral commonality between the Jewish majority and the non-Jewish minority. While Jewish sovereignty has been restored for the first time in two thousand years, the same conditions do not apply. When Jews had self-government in the biblical period, a non-Israelite who was part of the polity was a *ger toshav* (resident alien) who had rights but not did not enjoy the privileges of Israelites. In the modern State of Israel, the category of the *ger toshav* is inoperable. Citizens, Jewish or gentile, are afforded equal protection under the law. Historically, Noahide law has been employed to justify Jews living under non-Jewish sovereignty. The laws determine whether a particular gentile society broadly follows Noahide law; if so, Jews may reside in that society and even use its courts. The situation in contemporary Israel, of course, reverses the power dynamic. Jews now have political authority over gentiles, but this fact does not unmake the need to utilize Noahide/natural law-type thinking. It continues to be indispensable to ensure that Jewish authorities treat their gentile minority as moral and legal equals.[1]

4. Debate with Marvin Fox

The late American Jewish philosopher, Marvin Fox, was one of the most prominent and articulate critics of the natural law position in Judaism. In his *Interpreting Maimonides,* Fox argued that Judaism did not have, and indeed could not have had, a natural law, contending that the tradition knows only the positive law of biblical commandment and rabbinic halakha.[2] In the Hebrew Bible, right and wrong are known only by way of divine fiat; reason cannot discover moral absolutes on its own. Reason is constrained by local circumstance, accidents of geography and era, its vision limited to our temporary life. Reason understands moral law, but it does not discover it. The great majority of the commandments are ritual in nature and addressed to Jews alone, leaving only a handful of divine laws with universal application. The Bible does not have a word for nature, and does not speak to human beings through reason. Human reason may, after the fact, detail *ta'amei ha-mitzvot* (reasons for the commandments), but they are limited by necessarily imperfect human knowledge.

Fox denies that those passages in the Talmud that appear to support a natural law position do in fact support such a supposition. For instance, he points to a famous extract from tractate Eruvin (100b), where several laws referring to inter-human relations correspond to the animal world. In this passage, the rabbis suggest that, in the absence of direct divine revelation, humans could have learned proper social behaviors from certain animals: a cat's modesty, a dove's chastity, et al. Some philosophically-naïve supporters of a natural law in Judaism have designated this sentiment as articulating an explicit natural law-type of thinking among the rabbis. Fox counters, however, proposing that the passage is far more limited in its intentions: this non-normative statement offers several models of socially advantageous action, action that would be worth mimicking in want of revelation. But Fox contends that these are not the only models available to us in nature, as humans could have plumped for less worthy options such as the unrestrained sexual habits of the rabbit. Reason presents no absolute, formal criteria for choosing right and wrong, but revelation and its authoritative interpretation does contain that criteria.

As for medieval thinkers such as Saadiah Gaon, Maimonides and Joseph Albo, Fox also denies any place of importance for natural law in their respective philosophies. Regarding Saadiah's insistence that the commandments are accessible to reason, Fox insists that such rationalism does not equal an enthusiasm for natural law. Instead, Saadiah's descriptions of *taamei ha-mitzvot* are indeed based on the rationality of divine law, but this does not as a consequence signify that divine law could be accessed by independent reasoning. The commandments suggest themselves to our experience and we can formulate a sound basis for them, yet all of this occurs only *ex post facto*. We can appreciate the functionalism of the commandments as they pertain to inter-human relations, but we have no method to determine whether they are decisively true exclusive of revelation.

Regarding Maimonides' difficult statement in *Hilkhot Melakhim* (8:11) about the world-to-come (*olam haba*) and the Noahide, Fox opts to diminish the natural law interpretation of this passage. Maimonides, according to Fox, held that non-Jews achieve salvation through conscious acceptance of the Noahide commandments as *divine* laws; that is to say, they acknowledge revelation. Salvation is not gained, however, by means of rational speculation about universal moral law, as the Noahide commandments are *communicated* and not *discovered*. And while all the *mitzvot* have reasons—they aim to perfect the political body and the individual soul—that fact does not by extension mean that they are rationally evident. Maimonides, despite his reputation for rationalism, limits rationally accessible commandments to the first two of the Ten Commandments: the existence of God and the prohibition of idolatry. The remainder of the *mitzvot* cannot be retrieved through reason. Fox summarizes his view of natural law in Maimonides' thought thusly: divine law agrees with human nature, but is not itself natural.

While Novak notes that the work of Saadiah, Maimonides, Albo and others actually contain a comprehensive appreciation for natural law, his disagreement with Fox emerges more at the philosophical level than that of intellectual history. Novak argues, contra Fox, that the Noahide laws were constructed by the rabbis as a universal moral law for all because these laws were part of ordinary human life, and thus were universalizable.[3] Our knowledge that murder is always wrong, for instance, precedes any legal transmission of this moral and political truth, because murder, the unwarranted destruction of human life, cuts away at the foundation of society and we experience society as something both good and necessary. If people had to wait for divine instruction in preventing antisocial behavior as extreme as murder, society would not have been possible, and consequently this means that we have an understanding of the prohibition of murder that is prior to, though not greater than, its formal proscription at Sinai. Although natural law is prior in time to revelation, it does not have ontological preference. The commandments that address inter-human relations, then, impart no new moral data unknown to human experience. The experience of natural law prepared Jews for the greater and more specific Sinaitic revelation, as they came to the Sinai encounter with a familiarity of living under a law. Jews were Noahides before revelation, and the moral norms of Noahide law under which they lived made it possible for them to accept the specifications of the Torah.

Fox's denial of the rationality of the commandments per se—he does agree that we can discover good reasons for them after the fact—is also disputed. The rationality of inter-personal commandments, such as the prohibition of murder, is inferred at the primary level of meaning, that is, these commandments are descriptive of human nature as such. Reasons for non-rational commandments, such as *shaatnez* (the forbidden mixture of wool and linen), can only be inferred at the secondary level because they are outside of immediate human experience; that is, they can be understood after the fact. These commandments also contain a meaning remote from mundane human understanding, a meaning unavailable to the limits of reason. This meaning is covenantal. The non-rational, often ritual, commandments are an intimate part of the covenant, what Jonathan Sacks terms "the mutual commitment between God and the people Israel."[4] Fox appears to collapse rational and non-rational commandments, whereas the rabbis very clearly distinguished between them. The rational inter-human commandments—that is, the laws ordering moral responsibility—do not introduce something new into human experience, that is to say, they do not reshape human nature as if it were merely soft wax.

The austere halakhic positivism of Fox suggests two questions: why did God give commandments to Israel, and why did the Israelites accept? The answer to the first question remains outside of human purview—"My thoughts are not your thoughts, nor your ways My ways, says the Lord" (Is. 55:8). The reply to the second question cannot be adequately answered by Fox's positivism, assuming as it does a God who acts without intentions accessible to human reason. Novak argues that the Israelites were not coerced to accept the Torah at Sinai. Instead, they accepted because of their experience with God's goodness in the exodus from Egypt. The Israelites responded confidently and consented freely to the commandments because they believed that God cared for them, as he demonstrated by liberating them from servitude. This liberation gave the Israelites a template for discerning the difference between good and evil. Novak's view of the rationality of Israel's free covenantal acceptance parallels a famous passage from *Mekhilta de-Rabbi Ishmael*:

"I the Lord am your God" (Exod. 20:2). Why were the 10 Commandments not proclaimed at the beginning of the Torah? A parable: what is this like? Like a human king who entered a province and said to the people: Shall I reign over you? They replied: Have you conferred upon us any benefit that you should reign over us? What did he do then? He built a city wall for them, he brought in the water supply . . . Similarly, God said to Israel: "I the Lord am your God who brought you out of the land of Egypt. You shall have no other gods." He thus said to them: "Am I He whose reign you have accepted in Egypt?" They replied: "Yes." So He went on: "Now, just as you have accepted My reign, accept My decrees."[5]

The Israelites in this aggadic passage demand reasons for assenting to God's sovereignty. God first had to prove that his rule was not arbitrary, and the Israelites desired evidence of God's providential concern. They ultimately chose to live within the parameters of the covenant because they knew that the divine decrees they had just accepted were not isolated from general human experience.

It is worth briefly noting a recent, and important, piece of scholarship that also deals with the role and relevance of natural law (and much else besides) in Judaism, Devora Steinmetz's *Punishment and Freedom*.[6] Steinmetz's work, which centers around how the rabbis made law, considers the differences between natural and Noahide law, and natural and positive law. In an otherwise excellent study, it is confused about the rabbinic understanding of the nature and intent of law.

Steinmetz maintains that the rabbis rejected natural law, arguing that they deny that humans are capable of deriving the moral *ought* from the factual *is*. For her, the "nature" in natural law refers to *nature out there*—the blank, amoral material world—rather than to *human nature*. According to Steinmetz, classical natural law focuses on the *is*, because its moral cues are taken from the natural world. Novak asks: can such an approach refer to any actual law? Law concerns itself with the *ought*, which cannot be found in nature out there but only in human nature. Linking the *ought* of law with human nature makes possible the conditions for humans to be freely acting moral agents, otherwise our behavior would be merely instinctual. For the rabbis, because of their creation-centered theology, law occurs within human sociality not in the natural world. The Greek sense of nature, on the other hand, is at a far remove from the rabbinic sense of the same. The distance between God and creation in the Greek philosophical imagination is telescoped, both bound by the same eternal nature. God does not surpass nature in this system. For the rabbis, of course, while God is intimately concerned with creation and creature, the gap between God and created nature, human or otherwise, cannot be measured on a scale of difference by degree as in Greek thought but rather as a difference of kind. Instead, the rabbis developed their own version of natural law, a law that today we refer to as Noahide law.[7]

Despite some contemporary attempts to transform the rabbinic construction of the Noahide into a practical reality, Novak argues that the *sheva mitzvot bnei Noah* were never a Jewish legal instrument, and that it is not the obligation of Jews to adjudicate Noahide law for gentiles, if indeed the latter even wished for such a situation. Jews and gentiles share the same moral insight, accessible through reason. Ultimately, Noahide law allows for a positive valuation of pluralism, a recognition that particularistic beliefs will not converge but that there is sufficient shared morality that can be arrived at without the benefit of direct divine revelation.

ABBREVIATIONS

Talmud

B	Babylonian Talmud
P	Palestinian Talmud
Arakh.	*Arakhin*
AZ	*Avodah Zarah*
BB	*Bava Batra*
Betz.	*Betzah*
Bek.	*Bekorot*
Ber.	*Berakhot*
Bik.	*Bikkurim*
BK	*Bava Kamma*
BM	*Bava Metzia*
Dem.	*Demai*
Edu.	*Eduyot*
Eruv.	*Eruvin*
Git.	*Gittin*
Hag.	*Hagigah*
Hor.	*Horayot*
Hul.	*Hullin*
Ker.	*Keritot*
Ket.	*Ketubot*
Kid.	*Kiddushin*
KL	*Kl'ayim*
MS	*Ma'aser Sheni*
Mak.	*Makkot*
Meg.	*Megillah*
Me'il.	*Me'ilah*
Men.	*Menahot*
MK	*Moed Katan*
Naz.	*Nazir*
Ned.	*Nedarim*
Neg.	*Nega'im*
Nid.	*Niddah*

Ohol.	*Oholot*
Pes.	*Pesahim*
San.	*Sanhedrin*
Shab.	*Shabbat*
Shevu.	*Shevu'ot*
Shevi.	*Sheviit*
Sot.	*Sotah*
Suk.	*Sukkah*
Ta'an.	*Ta'anit*
Tam.	*Tamid*
Tem.	*Temurah*
Ter.	*Terumot*
Yad.	*Yadayim*
Yev.	*Yevamot*
Zab.	*Zabim*
Zev.	*Zevahim*

Rabbinic Sources

BaR	*Bamidbar Rabbah*
BR	*Bereshit Rabbah*
CR	*Canticles Rabbah*
DR	*Devarim Rabbah*
EH	*Even ha'Ezer*
GA	*Hilkhot Gezelah v'Avedah*
HM	*Hoshen Mishpat*
IB	*Hilkhot Issurai Bi'ah*
KM	*Kesef Mishneh*
LT	*Lekah Tov*
M	*Mishnah*
Mekh.	*Mekhilta de-Rabbi Ishmael*
Mel.	*Hilkhot Melakhim*
MiT	*Midrash Tannaim*
MM	*Magid Mishneh*

MN	Moreh Nevukim		Tan.	Tanhuma
MRE	Mishnat R. Eliezer		Tesh.	Teshuvah
MT	Midrash Tehillim		Tos.	Tosafot
OH	Orah Hayyim		VR	Vayikra Rabbah
PM	Penai Mosheh		YD	Yoreh Deah
PR	Pesikta Rabbati		YS	Yalkut Shimoni
PRE	Pirkei Rabbi Eliezer		YT	Hilkhot Yesodai ha-Torah
PRK	Pesikta de-Rav Kahana			
KE	Korban ha'Edah		**Other Sources**	
KR	Kohelet Rabbati		Ant.	Josephus, Antiquities
RSN	Hilkhot Rotzeah u'Shmirat ha-Nefesh		EJ	Encyclopedia Judaica
			ET	Encyclopedia Talmudit
SA	Shulhan Arukh		HUCA	Hebrew Union College Annual
SER	Seder Eliyahu Rabba		JBL	Journal of Biblical Literature
SEZ	Seder Eliyahu Zuta		JE	Jewish Encyclopedia
SH	Sefer Hasidim		JQR	Jewish Quarterly Review
SM	Sefer ha-Mitzvot		LTJ	Law and Theology in Judaism
SR	Shemot Rabbah		MGWJ	Monatsschrift für die Geschichte
T	Tosefta			und Wissenschaft des Judenthums

NOTES

CHAPTER 1. The Origins of the Noahide Laws

1 See B. *Hul.* 141a–b; *Igeret Rab Shereira Gaon* 1.5, ed. A. Hyman (Jerusalem, 1967), 37–38; Maimonides, *Hakdamah le-Mishnah*, 62–63. Cf. I.H. Weiss, *Dor Dor Ve-Dorshav* (Jerusalem, n.d.), 1:194 ff.

2 T. *AZ* 8.4 following MS Vienna, ed. Zuckermandel, 47.

3 *Seder Olam*, ch. 5; B. *San.* 56a–b.

4 See I Kgs 21:13, Job 2:9 and R. Gordis, "Studies in Hebrew Roots of Contrasted Meanings," *JQR* (July 1936), 27.1:33 ff. Cf. B. *San.* 45b–46a and P. *Naz.* 7.1 (55d) re Deut. 21:23.

5 *BR* 16.6; *CR* 1.16; *PRK*, Ba-Hodesh, 202–203. Cf. *BR* 34.8 for another sequence. For the whole question what was commanded to Adam and what was commanded to Noah, see *Tan.*, Yitro, ed. Buber, no. 2: 35a and esp. n. 7 thereon. The order presented by Maimonides in *Mel.* 9.1 is not based on a textual precedent, but seems to be based on apodictic sequence.

6 B. *San.* 56b.

7 This is Rashi's interpretation of this verse in his comment to Hosea thereto as well as in his comment to B. *San.* thereto. Cf. Ibn Ezra in his comment to the verse in Hosea who connects the use of the word *tzav* here with its use in Is. 28: 10, 13.

8 In *Targum Onkelos* the word *elohim* is translated by *dayana*. For the difference between the secular (*kol*) and sacred (*kodesh*) meaning of *Elohim*, see B. *San.* 66a.

9 See Deut. 24:1; M. *Git.* 9.10; B. *Git.* 90a.

10 On the notion of stealing from God, see T. *Ber.* 4.1 re Ps. 24:1 and S. Lieberman, *Tosefta Kifshuta: Zeraim* (New York, 1955), 55–56; B. *Ber.* 35a; P. *Ber.* 6.1 (9d) and P. *Kid.* 1.6 (61a).

11 *BR* loc. cit.

12 *CR* loc. cit.

13 See B. *San.* 59b re Gen. 9:3.

14 See e.g. B. *BK* 2a, *Rashi* and *Tos.*, s.v. *ha-shor*; P. *BK* 1.1 (2a); Maimonides, *Hakdamah le-Mishnah*, 50–51.

15 T. *AZ* 8.6–8; B. *San.* 56b, bot. See P. *KL* 2.7 (27a).

16 Ibid.

17 *Yad Ramah* to B. *San.* 56b. For the use of the verb *ylf* as a term denoting strict legal derivation, see B. *Hag.* 10b and parallels. For the attempt to specify Gen. 2:16, arguing that the core of the Noahide laws do not need revelation, see Saadiah Gaon, *Emunot ve-De'ot*, 9.2.

18 Cf. e.g. B. *Yev.* 54a.

19 See e.g. D. Hoffmann, *Die Wichtigsten Instanzen gegen die Graf-Wellhausen Hypothese* (Berlin, 1904).

20 See B. *San.* 59a re Deut. 33:4 and B. *AZ* 3a, *Tos.*, s.v. *she-afilu*.

21 See e.g. Hermann Cohen, "Ein Bekenntnis in der Judenfrage," in *Jüdische Schriften* (Berlin, 1924), 2:73 ff.; D. Hoffmann, *Die Schulchan Aruch und die Rabbinen über das Verhältnis der Juden zu Andersgläubigen* (Berlin, 1885).

22 See S.R. Hirsch, *Judaism Eternal*, ed. and trans. I. Grunfeld (London, 1956), 1:203 ff.

23 "Das religiose Element ist damit erkennbare Grundlage der Rechtserwicklung ueber-haupt," *Nachalat Z'vi* (1937), 7:230. Biberfeld largely depended on B.W. List, *Graeco-italische Rechtsgeschichte* (Jena, 1884), 550 ff. Also, see Biberfeld's "Judaism and International Law," in *Israel of Tomorrow*, ed. L. Jung (New York, 1946), 174 ff.

24 Trans. I. Levy, *Genesis*, 2nd edn. (New York, 1971), 1:61. Nevertheless, see his comments to Gen. 3:24 (94) and Gen. 9:27 (192–193), which seem to indicate that *derekh eretz* is presupposed by the Torah. In his comment to Lev. 18:4 (2.2:478–479) Hirsch acknowledges a conception of right which preceded what revelation teaches. However, without revelation such a conception of right, for him, can only be utilitarian. See N.H. Rosenbloom, *Tradition in an Age of Reform: The Religious Philosophy of Samson Raphael Hirsch* (Philadelphia, 1976), 315–318. For a critique of Hirsch's fideism, see Isaak Heinemann, *Ta'amei ha-Mitzvot be-Sifrut Yisrael* (Jerusalem, 1957), 2:94–95.

25 "Dieses 'Urgesetz' ist, was in einzelnen nachzuweis sein wird, nichts anderes als das noachidische Rechtssystem," *Nachalat Z'vi* (1936), 6:311. For the ancient theory that Jewish law is the prototype of later law, see Philo, *De Specialibus Legibus*, 4.61; Josephus, *Contra Apionem*, 1.165 ff., 2.15 and 279–281; Tertullian, *Apologia*, 45.4.

26 *Universal Jewish History* (New York, 1948), 1:121–122. A similar approach is found in Aharon Lichtenstein, *The Seven Laws of Noah* (New York, 1981).

27 See esp. Julius Wellhausen, *Prologomena to the History of Ancient Israel*, trans. A. Menzies (New York, 1956), 365 ff.

28 *Torah Shlemah* (New York, 1956), 17:222.

29 Even a non-fundamentalist such as Solomon Schechter held the same view. See "Higher Criticism—Higher Anti-Semitism," in *Seminary Addresses and Other Papers* (Cincinnati, 1915), 36–39. Cf., however, *Studies in Judaism* (New York, 1896), 1:xii ff.

30 *YS*, Beshalah, 257.67.

31 B. *San.* 56b re Ex. 15:25.

32 *Toldot ha-Halakhah* (New York, 1934), 1:335–336.

33 See B. *BK* 38a re Hab. 3:6.

34 See e.g. Gen. 6:12, 13:13, 18:23, 20:11, 34:7 (cf. 29:26); Ex. 1:7; Amos 1:3–2:4. None of these passages, however, refers to a specific code for non-Jews.

35 *Kuzari* 3.73, trans. H. Hirschfeld (New York, 1964), 193–194. See the notes of Moscato, *Kol Yehudah*; Halevi, *Otzar Nehmad*; *Das Buch Kuzari*, trans. D. Cassel (Leipzig, 1853), 302. See also Rabbenu Bahya and Malbim to Gen 2:16; R. Yehiel M. Epstein, *Arukh ha-Shulhan he'Atid: Melakhim* (Jerusalem, 1973), 78.2:89.

36 See e.g. B. *Hag.* 4a; Maimonides, *Hakdama le-Mishnah*, 33–34; *ET* 2, s.v. *asmakhta* (I); also Tchernowitz, *Toldot ha-Halakhah*, 1:62–66.

37 See P. *Pes.* 6.1 (33a); B. *Pes.* 66a and *Rashi*, s.v. *vekhi*; *ET* 5, s.v. *gezerah shavah*. Cf. Maimonides, *Ishut*, 1.2; *Mamrim*, 1.1–2; *SM*, *shoresh* 2 and Nahmanides' comment thereto.

38 Finkelstein, "Some Examples of Maccabean Halakha," in *Pharisaism in the Making* (New York, 1972), 226 (originally in *JBL* 49:20–42). See also his *The Pharisees* (Philadelphia, 1938), 2:597 and 709, n. 22.

39 Trans. from the Ethiopic by R.H. Charles, *Apocrypha and Pseudepigrapha of the Old Testament* (Oxford, 1913), 2:24. Earlier scholars who interpret Jubilees 7:20 similarly are: K. Kohler in *JE*, 7:302, and *Jewish Theology* (New York, 1918), 48 ff.; E. Schürer, *Geschichte des jüdischen Volkes im Zeitalter Jesu Christi* (Leipzig, 1909), 3.4:170; Ginzberg, *Legends*, 5:193, n. 67; M. Guttman, *Das Judentum und seine Umwelt* (Berlin, 1927), 99. Note also K. Hruby, "La Révélation dans la théologie rabbinique," *L'Orient Syrien* (1966), 11.1:26–27, n. 17.

40 "Die sogenanten sieben noachidischen Gesetze koennen selbverstaendlich fuer unser Verfasser gar nicht in Frage kommen, da nach ihm die Gerechten noch vor der Offenbarung am Sinai die Vorschriften der Thora pflichtmaessig beobachten, und unter ihnen warnen auch Noach und seine Sohne." *Das Buch Jubilaen und die Halacha* (Berlin, 1930), 34. See also pp. 4 and 59, n. 231; Tchernowitz, *Toldot ha-Halakhah*, 1:334. (Later in this work, however, Tchernowitz seems to agree with Finkelstein's theory of a specifically Noahide law in Jubilees. See 4:351–352.) Re Noah's observance of the whole Torah, see Jub. 6:3, 7:38–39; M. Zucker, *Rab Saadiah Gaon's Translation of the Torah* (Heb.) (New York, 1959), 448–451.

41 e.g. M. *Kid.*, end; B. *Yoma* 28b; P. *Ber.* 2.3 (4c); *Tan.*, Lekh-Lekha, ed. Buber, 29b. Cf. *CR* 1.6. See Ginzberg, *Legends*, 5:259, n. 275.

42 For the subsequent Christian use of LXX on Deut. 25:26 to argue for the impossibility of compliance with the Law, see Gal. 3:10–12. For Jewish replies, see *Men.* 43b re Num. 15:40; P. *Ned.* 3.9 (38b) and Nahmanides to Deut. 25:26. Cf. P. *MS* 5.5 (56c) re Deut. 26:14.

43 *Bek.* 20b. Cf. B. *Shab.* 31a.

44 See B. *Eruv.* 21a re Job 11:9.

45 B. *Yev.* 47b. For the difference between major (*hamurah*) and minor (*qalah mitzvoth*), see Maimonides, *Commentary on the Mishnah*, 2.1.

46 See B. *BK* 15a and parallels.

47 Review of *Pharisaism in the Making* in *Conservative Judaism* (Spring 1974), 28.3:64–65.

48 *Ant.*, 13.257.

49 Ibid., 13.296 and B. *Ber.* 29a.

50 *Ant.*, 13.297–298; *Bellum Judaicum*, 2.119 ff.; B. *Hor.* 4a and parallels.

51 Cf., also, Jub. 15:26–27 and LXX on Est. 8:17—"Many of the peoples were circumcised and became Jews (*Ioudaizon*) because of the fear of the Jews." As a reaction we might see the later rabbinic rejection of the converts from the time of Mordecai and Esther (B. *Yev.* 24b; *Gerim* 1.7). Cf. Josephus, *Vita*, 112–113.

52 Surely Heinrich Graetz was engaging in some nineteenth-century apologetics when he wrote: "Zum ersten Male zeigt hier das Judenthum in seinem Fuersten Johann Hyrkanos Undulsamkeit gegen andere Culte und liegte Religionszwant auf": *Geschichte der Juden* (Leipzig, 1888), 3.1:72. Cf. Weiss, *Dor Dor ve-Dorshav*, 1.117.

53 *Ant.*, 13.401–402; B. *Kid.* 66a and B. *Ber.* 48a.

54 B. *San.* 57a.

55 *Jewish and Roman Law* (New York, 1966), 1:26–27. I myself tended to follow my teacher's view (*LTJ* 1:114) before examining the concept of *ius gentium* more closely in historical perspective.

56 *Digest* I, 2, 2, 28. See D. Daube, "The Peregrine Praetor," *The Journal of Roman Studies*

(1951), 41.1–2:66–70. For further discussion of the concept and history of *ius gentium*, see R. Sohm, *The Institutes: A Text-Book of the History and System of Roman Private Law*, 2nd edn., trans. J.C. Leslie (Oxford, 1901), 69 ff.; A.H.J. Greenridge, *Roman Public Life* (New York, 1970), 207; E. Levy, "Natural Law in Roman Thought," *Gesammelte Schriften* (Cologne, 1963), 1:4 ff.

57 B. *AZ* 64b. See P. *Yev.* 8.1 (8d); also S. Lieberman, *Greek in Jewish Palestine* (New York, 1942), 81–82.

58 "Ohne das Noachidenprinzip ist diese Gesetzbestimmt unbegreiflich." Guttmann, *Das Judenthum und seine Umwelt*, 110. Cf. I.H. Herzog, *The Main Institutions of Jewish Law* (London, 1965), 1:xxiii.

59 *AZ* 10.6 and *Mel.* 8.7. Re majority rule, see B. *Ber.* 9a and *Hul.* 11a re Ex. 23:2.

60 *Arakh.* 29a. See Maimonides, *Shemitah ve-Yovel*, 10.8–9.

61 *Sifra*, Behar, 107a; P. *Shevi.* 10.2 (39c); *Arakh.* 32b re Lev. 25:10. See Maimonides, *Shemitah ve-Yovel*, 10.3, 5; but cf. *Arakh.* 21b–32a, *Tos.*, s.v. *hitkin*.

62 Thus Maimonides saw Jewish sovereignty and Jewish suzerainty over gentiles in its domain as the *conditio sine qua non* for both the *ger toshav* and the full enforcement of the Noahide laws. See *AZ* 10.5–6 with notes of *Rabad* and *KM*; *IB* 14.8 with note of *Rabad*, who emphasizes that without the Jubilee and the economic sovereignty it entails, the *ger toshav* would be an intolerable economic burden on the Jewish community. For Maimonides' view of the quasi-*ger toshav* today, see *Milah*, 1.6; *Shab.* 20.14.

63 See also Ex. 20:10; Lev. 16:29, 17:8–13, 18:26; Num. 9:14, 15:15–29, 19:10; Deut. 5:14.

64 See also Gen. 15:13, 23:4; Ex. 2:22, 18:3, 22:20; Lev. 19:34, 25:35, 47; Deut. 10:19, 16:11, 14, 23:8.

65 See B. *Yev.* 46a; P. *Kid.* 4.1 (65b); B. *Shab.* 135a and B. Bamberger, *Proselytism in the Talmudic Period* (New York, 1968), 38 ff. Cf. B. *AZ* 64b.

66 *Sifra*, Behar, 110a. See Targumim to Lev. 25:47; B. *Kid.* 20a–b and *Arakh.* 30b; also, B. Epstein, *Torah Temimah* (New York, 1962), n. 76 to Lev. 25:13, for an explanation of the etymology used here.

67 Meek, "The Translation of *Ger* in the Hexateuch," *Journal of Biblical Literature* (1930), 49:177.

68 See Num. 18:1–24.

69 Lev. 25:13–18. See T. *Neg.* 6.2. There is an opinion in P. *Dem.* 5.8 (24d) and P. *Git.* 4.9 (46b) re Lev. 25:23 which permits permanent gentile ownership of real estate in the Land of Israel. However, this is not the plain meaning of the text, nor is it accepted as law. See B. *Git.* 47a and *Ter.* 1.10. See P. *Kid.* 1.5 (60c) for the earlier importance of maintaining one's ancestral estate.

70 *Sifre: Bamidbar*, no. 78. For an attempt to see the descendants of Jethro as a special class of *gerim* having limited landed status in the Land of Israel, see *Sifre: Devarim*, 823–825. Thus the full investigation of the *ger toshav* into the Land of Israel could only be part of a future messianic agenda. See Ez. 47:22–23.

71 See I.L. Seligmann in *Encyclopedia Mikra'it*, 2:546.

72 *Ancient Israel* (New York, 1965), 1:74.

73 *Israel: Its Life and Culture* (Copenhagen, 1926), 1:40–41. Pedersen's proof texts are: Josh. 16:10, 17:13; Jud. 1:28, 30, 33, 35. For rabbinic qualification of the severity of the

proscription of tolerance of the Canaanites in Deut. 20:16, see *Sifre: Devarim*, no. 200; P. *Shevi.* 6.1 (36c); B. *Git.* 46a, *Tos.*, s.v. *kayvan*.

74 M. *Yad.* 4.4 re Deut. 23:4 and Is. 10:13; B. *Ber.* 28a and parallels; *PRK*, Nahamu, re Ruth 2:11, 263.

75 See A. Bertholet, *Die Stellung der Israeliten und der Juden zu Fremden* (Freiburg, 1896), 27–36; Schürer, *Geschichte*, 3.4:175; G.F. Moore, *Judaism* (Cambridge, MA, 1927), 1:328; R. Vinogradoff, *Outlines of Historical Jurisprudence* (Oxford, 1932), 1:95–96; A.R.W. Harrison, *The Law of Athens* (Oxford, 1968), 1:189, 195.

76 See M. Rostovtzeff, *The Social and Economic History of the Hellenistic World* (Oxford, 1941), 1:334, 509; 2:1103–1104.

77 See A. Berger, *Encyclopedic Dictionary of Roman Law* (Philadelphia, 1953), 391.

78 See ibid., 626, 647; W.W. Burkland and P. Stein, *A Text-Book of Roman Law from Augustus to Justinian* (Cambridge, 1963), 96–97; N.D. Fustel de Coulanges, *The Ancient City*, trans. W. Small (Garden City, NY, n.d.), 196.

79 See Meek, "The Translation of *Ger*," 179; Thucydides, *The Peloponnesian War*, 1.9 and Moore, *Judaism*, 3:107, note thereon.

80 Philo, *Fragments* II, ed. Mangey, 677—quoted in Moore, *Judaism*. At times, however, Philo does use *proselytos* and *epelytos* as synonyms. See *De Specialibus Legibus*, 1.51–52; also, Lieberman, *Greek in Jewish Palestine*, 80.

81 B. *Yev.* 24b. See *BaR* 8.4 and *IB* 13.15. For the notion of the essentially political character of the Messiah, see B. *Ber.* 3b re Deut. 15:11 and *Mel.* 11.1ff. Cf. P. *San.* 6.7 (23d).

82 *Toldot ha-Halakhah*, 1.296. The early Christian historian Eusebius refers to *gerim* as being of "mixed descent" (*tous epimiktous*). See *Ecclesiastical History*, 1.7.13. Women, on the other hand, seem to have become part of the people of Israel by marriage. See Deut. 21:10–13; Ruth 2:10–12. For the later rejection of this type of informal conversion, see Ezra 9:1–2; Neh. 13:23–27. B. *Kid.* 21b–22a.

83 See B. *Yev.* 46a–57b.

84 *Toldot ha-Emunah ha-Yisraelit* (Jerusalem, 1953), 5:459, n. 5; see 3:636. Cf. E. Bickerman, *From Ezra to the Last of the Maccabees* (New York, 1962), 82–83.

85 See Tchernowitz, *Toldot ha-Halakhah*, 1:296–298.

86 *MRE*, sect. 20 (end), 374. See P. *Yev.* 8.1 (8d). However, for a later dating of this work, locating it as being from the school of Saadiah Gaon (*c.*1000), see Moshe Zucker, "Towards a Solution of the Problem of the 32 Exegetical Principles, etc.," *Proceedings of the American Academy of Jewish Research* (1954—Hebrew section), 23:1ff. Cf. B. *AZ* 20a, *Tos.*, s.v. *lehaqdim* and *Ker.* 9a. B. *Yev.* 48b makes this an option for a slave.

87 B. *AZ* 65a. Only *Meiri*, 256, codifies this opinion. Re a "confirmed idolater," see *Hul.* 13b, top.

88 See Josephus, *Ant.*, 14.110 (*sebomenon ton theon*). However, Josephus does not consider them Jews in a formal sense.

89 See *Hul.* 4a.

90 *Contra Apionem*, 2.123, trans. H. St. John Thackeray (Cambridge, MA, 1926), 340–341.

91 Ibid., 2.210, pp. 376–379. See 2.279–283. Josephus (*Bellum Judaicum* 2.463) refers to non-Jewish "Judaizers" in Syria as "ambiguous" (*amphibolos*).

92 *Satires*, 14.96, trans. G.C. Ramsey (Cambridge, MA, 1940), 271–273. Cf. Tacitus, *History*, 5.5.

93 This might very well be the background for the Talmud's exemption of gentiles from the obligation to die if forced to participate in public idolatry (B. *San.* 74b–75a and P. *San.* 3.6 [21b] re II Kgs 5:18–19; P. *Shevi.* 4.2 [35a] re Lev. 22:32). See Salo Baron, *A Social and Religious History of the Jews*, rev. edn. (New York, 1952), 1:179; J. Juster, *Les Juifs dans L'Empire Romain* (Paris, 1914); also Lieberman, *Greek in Jewish Palestine*, 85–86. For the view that religious innovation is a civic crime, see Plato, *Euthyphro*, 3b; *Apology*, 24c. For Jewish exemption from public idolatry, see P. *AZ* 5.4 (44d).

94 Klausner, *From Jesus to Paul*, trans. W.F. Stinespring (Boston, 1961), 43.

95 See e.g. *BR* 28.5; *DR* 2.15; P. *Meg.* 1.11 (72b).

96 *Mekh.*, Mishpatim, 312. In the variant in *Avot de-Rabbi Natan*, A, ch. 36, p. 54 the mention of *yirai shamayim* is absent. See T. *Hor.*, end, re Ps. 135; 19 ff.:447. (Cf. version in B., Vilna edn. and Samuel Avigdor b. Abraham, *Minhat Bikkurim* thereto.) See *MRE* 303. Re gentile quasi-Judaism, see P. *Meg.* 3.2 (74a) and parallels.

97 B. *Shab.* 31a. See *Avot de-Rabbi Natan*, A, ch. 26, p. 27a; *LTJ* 1:173, n. 29; also, *Didache*, 1.1. For historical background, see Guttmann, *Das Judenthum und seine Umwelt*, 48, n. 1; Heinemann, *Ta'amei ha-Mitzvot*, 1:46. Re gentile morality making for an affinity with Judaism, see Philo, *De Vita Mosis*, 2.17.

98 Agus, *The Evolution of Jewish Thought* (New York, 1959), 68. See his *Jewish Identity in an Age of Ideologies* (New York, 1978), 8.

99 *Das Judenthum und seine Umwelt*, 110. Guttmann argued that the absence of a specific doctrine of *seven* Noahide laws in Hellenistic Jewish literature was the result of a philosophically influenced rationalization of the Palestinian doctrine found in Jub. 7:20. Nevertheless, Jub. 7:20 does not present such a doctrine, as Albeck proved. Secondly, Guttmann's theory is based on no other source.

100 Philo, 2:373–374. Samuel Belkin attempted to locate a reference to the legal institution of the *ger toshav* in Philo, *Fragments*, 2:677. See *Philo and the Oral Law* (Cambridge, MA, 1940), 47–48. However, earlier, G.F. Moore discounted this inference, arguing that Philo was speculating, not describing a juridical fact. See *Judaism*, 1:328, n. 1.

101 Wolfson, *Philo* (Cambridge, MA, 1947), 2:183–187.

102 See note 40.

103 See Wolfson, *Philo*, 2:192 ff.

104 *De Specialibus Legibus*, 1.3, trans. F.H. Colson (Cambridge, MA, 1935), 4–7.

105 See *Republic*, 507b.

106 *Legum Allegoria*, 2.86.

107 I. Heinemann, "Die Lehre vom ungeschriebenem Gesetz in jüdischen Schriften," *HUCA* (1928), 4:150 ff.

108 See esp. *SR* 30.6 and *CR* 2.16.

109 P. *AZ* 2.1 (40c). See *BR* 98.9 and *MT* 2.5:89a and notes thereon; B. *Ber.* 57b re Zeph. 3:9.

110 *Hul.* 92a–b. Menahem Azariah di Fano (d. 1620) attempted to combine the traditions of *seven* Noahide laws and *thirty* Noahide laws by making the seven laws seven categories having a total of thirty precepts. See *Asarah Ma'amarot* 3.21, Frankfurt am Main edn., 103 ff.; also, A. Greenbaum, "Thirty Commandments according to R. Samuel b. Hofni" (Heb.), *Sinai* (1973), 72.4–5:205 ff.

111 See esp. B. *San.* 58b, bot., 74b, bot.; also, P. *Ber.* end, re Ps. 12:1 and *Peirush me-Ba'al Sefer Haredim.* Most probably, the choice of the number seven was because of its symbolic value. See Guttmann, *Das Judenthum und seine Umwelt*, 102.

112 See Schürer, *Geschichte*, 3.4:179–180. Cf. Bertholet, *Die Stellung*, 328 ff.

113 Krauss, "Les Préceptes des Noachides," *Revue des Études Juives* (1903), 47:33. Cf. Krauss, "The Jews in the Works of the Church Fathers," *JQR* (old series—1894), 4:258–295. The text under discussion is *Sibylline Oracles* 5.86–89.

114 See Acts 10:2, 13:16, 18:4. Cf. Klausner, *From Jesus to Paul*, 42.

115 Davies, *Paul and Rabbinic Judaism*, 2nd edn. (London, 1955).

116 This point is debated by Davies (App. A, 325–328) in a polemic with Karl Barth. Arguably, I think Barth insists that Paul's theology precludes any "natural theology" or natural law morality. Paul's one reference to a "natural" precept *(he physis aute didaskei)* is in I Cor. 11:14. See *Theological Dictionary of the New Testament*, ed. G. Friedrich, trans. G.W. Bromiley (Grand Rapids, MI, 1974), 9:272–273. However, this passage refers to the customary accepted length of the hair of a woman as opposed to that of a man. This is simply a recognition of customary human behavior *(minhag ha-olam)*. One finds similar observations by the rabbis. See e.g. the use of *derekh* on B. *Yoma* 11b and *Men.* 34a re Deut. 6:9. One can say that Jewish thinkers cannot affirm a concept of natural law similar to that developed in Greek philosophy based on the idea of *physis.* However, that does not preclude a Jewish concept of natural law based on different ontological premises. See Leo Strauss, *Natural Right and History* (Chicago, 1953), 81–82.

117 For the sexual connotation of this term, see Tobit 8:7. For its connotation with idolatry, see e.g. Wisdom of Solomon 14:12, 22–27.

118 See e.g. Clement of Alexandria, *Exhortation to the Greeks*, ch. 2 ff.

119 See note 114.

120 See Bamberger, *Proselytism*, 135–138; Baron, *History*, 1:375, n. 15. The question of the exact criteria for *gerut* was thus the subject of much debate in the Tannaitic period. See B. *Yev.* 46a–47b; *Kid.* 3.14 (64d); Bamberger, 38 ff. Perhaps the connection of the Noahide laws with the institution of the *ger toshav* was to emphasize the primacy of normativity in all *gerut*. The New Testament indicates (Acts 15:1 ff.) that the *halakhah* of *gerut* was *the* issue that led to the normative split with Judaism.

121 B. *San.* 58b, bot. Samuel Atlas argued that restraint is the heart of natural law teaching. See *Netivim be-Mishpat ha-Ivri* (New York, 1978), 39.

122 This conclusion surely rejects the view of Heinrich Graetz that the Noahide laws were formulated during the time of Rabban Gamliel II (*c.*80 CE) as a recognition of the "ja halb und halb Judaer" status of non-idolatrous gentiles. See *Geschichte der Juden*, 3.1:350. Cf. *Meiri* to B. *Yev.* 48b, 192. This notion of the continued quasi-Jewish status of non-idolatrous gentiles is followed by a number of modern scholars who interpret the statement of R. Johanan b. Nappaha, "whoever renounces idolatry is called a Jew" (B. *Meg.* 13a re Est. 2:5 and Dan. 3:12). See Bamberger, *Proselytism*, 36, n. 5; H. Loewe in *A Rabbinic Anthology*, ed. C.G. Montefiore and H. Loewe (New York, 1963), 252–253; R. Loewe, "Potentialities and Limitations of Universalism in the Halakhah," in *Studies in Rationalism, Judaism and Universalism: In Memory of Leon Roth*, ed. R. Loewe (London, 1966), 137. Nevertheless, the statement is an aggadic statement about Mordecai *the Jew* (see *Maharsha* to B. *Meg.* 13a; also B. *San.* 61b re Ex. 20:5). One should also remember

R. Johanan's opposition to gentile study of the Torah (B. *San.* 59a, top). Finally, this statement seems to be of the genre of statements such as "whoever repudiates idolatry is like one who has accepted the whole Torah" (B. *Kid.* 40a re Jer. 6:19 and Ezek. 14:15; both texts refer to Jews). See also B. *San.* 19b re I Chron. 1:18 and *Rashi* thereto.

123 *Sifra*, Emor, 98a. See *Men.* 73a–b; P. *Dem.* 3.1 (23b); *Ter.* 4.15.

124 See M. *Men.* 9.8.

125 B. *San.* 58b–59a. See *SR* 25.15; *DR* 1.18; B. *Hag.* 13a re Ps. 147:20. Cf. *Mekh.*, Ki Tissa, 343; B. *Ned.* 31a. The statement of R. Johanan might well be referring to Christian plagiarism of Jewish teachings. See S. Lieberman, *Hellenism in Jewish Palestine*, 2nd edn. (New York, 1962), 18–19 and n. 111. See *Ker.* 9a. For modern halakhic treatments of this question, see J. David Bleich, "Teaching Torah to Non-Jews" *Tradition* 18.2 (Summer 1980), 192–211.

126 See B. *AZ* 3a and *Tos.*, s.v. *she-afilu*.

127 See *ET* 2:37–39.

128 See e.g. M. *Hor.* 3.8; also Finkelstein, *The Pharisees*, 1:82–83.

129 See e.g. Ignatius, *To the Magnesians*, ch. 10.

130 *Mel.* 10.9. See M. *Ter.* and *Rambam* thereto. Cf. *Responsa Pe'er ha-Dor*, Amsterdam edn. (1750), no. 50. See *supra*. Maimonides interprets the Talmud's use of the verse, "Day and night they shall not cease" (*l'o yishbotu*—Gen. 8:22) as referring to the gentile observance of the Sabbath on the seventh day or any other day. Rashi, on the other hand, interprets it as a prohibition of complete gentile rest (*menuhah b'alma*—cf. *Radbaz* to Maimonides, loc. cit.) However, Rashi is here interpreting the query of Rabina, a fifth-century Babylonian Amora. An Amora of this period would not be as directly anti-Christian as an earlier Palestinian Amora such as Resh Lakish. For Rashi's awareness of Sunday as a peculiarly Christian holy day, see B. *Ta'an.* 27b, Rashi, s.v. *mipnei ha-Notzrim*.

131 See *Ma'aseh Korbanot*, 3.2–3; also *Zev.* 116a.

132 See *infra*.

133 B. *San.* 74a; P. *San.* 3.6 (21b); also, *Sifra*, Aharai-Mot, 86a re Lev. 18:5. Cf. P. *San.* 10.3 (29c); *SR* 15.8. Sometimes in order to emphasize the severity of other sins the rabbis compared them to these three sins. See e.g. T. *BM* 6.17; P. *BM* 5.8 (10d); also, P. *San.* 6.7 (23d).

134 See Baron, *History*, 2:102 ff.

135 B. *Kid.* 40b. See B. *BK* and B. *AZ* 18a.

136 *Sifre: Devarim*, no. 41, pp. 85–86 and notes thereon; B. *Ber.* 61b. See L. Finkelstein, *Akiva* (Philadelphia, 1936), 258 ff.

137 *Nimukai Joseph* to *Alfasi*, B. *San.* 74a–b (Vilna edn., 17b). See *YT* 5.7.

138 B. *San.* 74a–b; *Mel.* 10.2

139 See B. *Pes.* 25a–b.

140 B. *San.* 74a.

141 T. *BK* 9.31, p. 366; also, B. *Shab.* 105b. Cf. *MN* 2.33; E.E. Urbach, *Hazal: Emunot ve-De'ot* (Jerusalem, 1971), 417–418. For the notion that Abraham rejected idolatry by ratiocination, see *BR* 38.13; Ginzberg, *Legends*, 1:189 ff., 5:210, n. 10.

142 *Sifra*, Aharei-Mot, 86a; also, B. *Yoma* 67b. For the connection of the point of this *baraita* with the seven Noahide laws, see *LT* to Gen 2:16; 10b.

143 For important variant readings, see R. Rabinovicz, *Dikdukai Sofrim* to B. *Yoma* 67b.
     Max Kadushin, in an apparent polemic against any natural law type interpretation of
     this passage, writes, "Obviously the contrast is between the laws which the nations of
     the world and Israel possess in common and those that Israel alone possesses. The
     former, then, are universal laws . . . 'It stands to reason' simply refers to the fact that
     those things are universal . . . so universal as to be found among various animals."
     Worship and Ethics (Evanston, IL, 1964), 45. Here Kadushin is referring to the
     statement of R. Johanan that "even if the Torah had not been given, we would have
     learned (*hayyinu lemaydeen*) modesty from the cat, etc." (B. *Eruv.* 100b). However,
     despite the fact that the rabbis did not use the categories of Stoic philosophy or Roman
     jurisprudence, the texts of B. *Yoma* 67b and B. *Eruv.* 100b both imply the *inherent
     reasonableness* of these laws, and this makes the analogues from the non-Jewish world,
     even the non-human world, relevant. Otherwise, what made *certain* universal practices
     morally praiseworthy, and *certain* other universal practices morally blameworthy?
     Clearly, the definition of right is logically prior, for the rabbis, to the *selection* of
     pertinent examples from life. By eliminating this necessary rational precondition,
     which is clearly expressed by the term *ba-din hu* (see e.g. B. *San.* 2b), Kadushin's
     interpretation begs the question. These texts affirm more than a mere *consensus
     gentium.*

144 Re Ishmael, see T. *Sot.* 6.6 and Lieberman, *Tosefta Kifshuta: Nashim* (New York, 1973),
     670–671. Re Esau, see *PR* 47b. Cf. *Sifre: Devarim*, no. 31, p. 50 and note thereon; also B.
     BB 16b and *Tos.*, s.v. *b'a.*

145 See Ginzberg, *Legends*, 5:278, n. 51 and 223, n. 82.

146 B. *San.* 57a, top.

147 See ibid., 45b–46a re Deut. 21:23; 109a; P. *San.* 6.6 (23c), 7.9 (25b); *Ker.* 7b.

148 See M. *Neg.* 7.1; *Sifra*, Metzor'a, 74a; B. *Naz.* 54a; B. *Hor.* 10a; also, B. *Shab.* 135a–b.

149 See B. *San.* 56b–57a; *Mel.* 9.1.

150 10b–11a. For rabbinic use of this type of induction, see P. *Ber.* 2.3 (4c).

151 See B. *BB* 118a. Thus Guttmann refers to *dinim* as "die aber kein singulars, sondern ein
     summarisches Gebot darstellt und das Verhueten von Unrecht zur Aufgabe hat." *Das
     Judenthum und seine Umwelt*, 105.

152 See M. *Ber.* 5.3; B. *Ber.* 33b.

153 See *BR* 23.6–7 re Gen. 4:26, p. 227 and notes thereon.

154 See *infra*, 66–71.

155 *BR* 38.8 and B. *San.* 109a interpret this as *avodah zarah*. Another opinion in this
     gemara and *LT* op. cit. interpret it as blasphemy. Both acts are, however, direct denials
     of God.

156 See B. *San.* 94a–b and *Hul.* 89a. Cf. *Ibn Ezra* to Ex. 8:15.

157 See *infra*, 55–56.

158 See M. *San.* 5.5.

159 See Abravanel's comment thereto, *contra* B. *Sot.* 11b re Ex. 1:15.

160 Cf. B. *San.* 58b for a more restricted interpretation. Cf., however, *Meiri*, 288 thereto.

161 See *BR* 80.6.

162 See ibid., 26.5.

163 See B. *San.* 57a and *Tos.*, s.v. *dikhteeb.*

164 See *infra*, 104–105.

165 See *Sifra*, Aharei-Mot, 86b; B. *Shab.* 33a.

166 See note 10.

167 See *Ibn Ezra* thereto; cf. Targumim of *Onkelos* and *Pseudo-Jonathan* and *BR* 67.4 thereto.

168 See Gen. 13:7; *BR* 40.5. Cf. *YS*, Shemot, no. 187 re Ps. 111:6 and *Rashi* to Gen. 1:1, beg.

169 See Ex. 21:6; Deut. 24:7; *Mekh.*, Yitro, 232–233; M. *San.* 11.1; *LTJ* 2:88–89, 200.

170 See B. *San.* 91a and Ginzberg, *Legends*, 5:436–437, n. 233.

171 Cf., however, Atlas, *Netivim*, 25–26.

CHAPTER 2. The Law of Adjudication

1 B. *San.* 56b; also, T. *AZ* 8.4.

2 *Mel.* 9.14. See Epstein, *Torah Temimah* to Num. 25:5; also B. *San.* 35a, top.

3 Ibid., 8.10 note 10.11: "The Jewish court is obligated to appoint judges for these resident aliens to adjudicate for them on the basis of these laws in order that society not be destroyed. If the court deems it proper (*ra'u*) that they appoint their own judges, let them appoint them. And if they deem it proper to appoint Jewish judges, let them do so." See the comment of R. Abraham ibn Zimra (*Radbaz*) thereto. Radbaz emphasizes that Jewish judges are only appointed if qualified non-Jewish judges are unavailable.

4 See B. *Meg.* 9a for the attempt to soften Jacob's curse in Gen. 49:5–7. Cf. LXX and *Targum Onkelos* thereto.

5 Nahmanides interprets B. *San.* 58b, viz., "the death penalty is their warning" as only applying to an act when restraint (*meni'ah*) should have been exercised. In his comment to Gen. 26:5 Nahmanides disputed with Rashi, who held that Abraham observed the full Sinaitic law before it was publicly revealed. (For the rabbinic sources of Rashi's view, see *supra*, 245, n. 41.) Nahmanides held that Abraham is praised for observing Noahide law plus a few other details. See *Mel.* 9.1.

6 *Malmad ha-Talmidim*, Noah, ed. Mekitsei Nirdamim, 12b. See Mishpatim, 72a, and Kasher, *Torah Shlemah*, 17: 218.

7 For Maimonides' essentially political concept of the Messiah, see *Mel.*, chs. 11–12; also B. *Ber.* 34b.

8 Comment to Deut. 6:20. See *Hinukh*, nos. 49, 58; R. Meir Simhah of Dvinsk, *Meshekh Hokmah*, ed. A. Abraham (Jerusalem, 1972), Mishpatim (re Ex. 24:3), 133; Epstein, *Arukh ha-Shulhan he-Atid*: *Mel.* 79.15:93.

9 Comment to Gen. 6:2. See his comment to Gen. 6:11; also, José Faur, *Iyunim be-Mishneh Torah le-ha-Rambam* (Jerusalem, 1978), 143.

10 B. *San.* 56b.

11 *Responsa Ha-Ramo*, ed. A. Siev (Jerusalem, 1970), no. 10: 45–46. See *ET* 3:355.

12 Ibid. See *BR* 34.7 re Deut. 18:12; also, Finkelstein, "Some Examples of Maccabean Halakhah," in *Pharisaism* 223–224, n. 4. There is the notion in the Talmud (*Bek.* 13a, bot.) that *be-dinayhem* refer to "their laws" stipulated for *them* by the Torah (*she-paskah lahem*).

13 No. 2.

14 *Mekh.*, Yitro, 188. See n. 1 thereon for the parallels.

15 See B. *Ber.* 21b and parallels; also, Abravanel's comment to Num. 16:1.

16 See B. *Pes.* 6a–b and parallels and Sforno's comment to Num. 9:1. For the rabbinic transfer of biblical verses from one context to another, see e.g. B. *Kid.* 43a. For an analysis of the theology underlying these exegetical principles, see Heschel, *Torah min ha-Shamayim* (London, 1962), 1:199 ff.

17 *Zev.* 116a. Note *AZ* 24b, *Tos.*, s.v. *Yitro*, which attempts to resolve this dispute by stating that Jethro arrived before the giving of the Torah, but did not give his juridical advice until after the giving of the Torah. Chavel notes in his edition of Nahmanides' Torah commentary (Jerusalem, 1959, 1:374–375) that this is the basis of Nahmanides' view. However, nowhere does Nahmanides state this explicitly. In fact he explicitly accepts the view of R. Joshua. Also, see *Rashbam* to Ex. 18:1, who argues on purely literary grounds that Jethro came after the giving of the Torah.

18 See *YS*, Yitro, no. 273; Abravanel to Ex. 18:1 ff., q. 5.

19 See B. *San.* 15b, Rashi, s.v. *mah*; *Tos.*, s.v. *shor*. Cf., however, *PRK*, Ba-Hodesh, 211; *LTJ* 2:24–27. See the view of Rava on B. *San.* 27a and Atlas, *Netivim*, 31, n. 2.

20 T. *Sot.* 8.6, ed. Lieberman, 205 following MS Erfuhn. See *MT* 2.5.

21 P. *Sot.* 7.5 (21d). See *BaR* 14.35 for the notion that the Noahides had prophets who taught them their own law.

22 B. *Sot.* 35b. For the use of this principle for a pre-Sinaitic situation when it could not have been referring to Jewish law, see B. *BK* 92a and B. *Mak.* 9b.

23 See *Letter of Aristeas*, sect. 65; Philo, *De Vita Mosis*, 2.7, 37–39; B. *Meg.* 9a and *Soferim* 1.8.

24 *KR* 2.11; *VR* 1.10.

25 Lieberman, *Hellenism in Jewish Palestine*, 200–202.

26 B. *BK* 113a–b. Note: "a *ger toshav* . . . is always judged by their law." *Mel.* 10.12. See *Sifre: Devarim*, no. 16.

27 See Rabinovicz, *Dikdukai Sofrim* thereto. Note the conceptual justification for such a latter emendation given by Meiri thereto, 330. Over and above its precise denotation as a proper noun, "Canaan" in the Bible also connoted an untrustworthy person. See Hos. 12:8 and *Radak* thereto. Its connotative sense of untrustworthiness in later texts of the Talmud has definite precedence.

28 See *Sifre: Devarim*, no. 202; P. *Shevi.* 6.1 (36c); B. *Sot.* 35b–36a and *Tos.*, s.v. *lerabbot*; B. *AZ* 26b and *Tos.*, s.v. *ve'lo*.

29 See *SM*, pos. no. 187.

30 Note how Maimonides carefully terms a gentile accepting Noahide law as *ke-ger toshav* (*Milah*, 1.6).

31 M. *BK* 4.3. Cf. M. *San.* 9.2.

32 In T. *BK* 4.3 this is presented as the view of R. Meir. Another view is presented which states that the Jewish law of *tam* and *mu'ad* applies to both the goring ox of a Jew and that of a gentile. However, neither Talmud quotes the opinion.

33 B. *BK* 38a. For another example of a ruling power examining the laws of a vassal state, see P. *BM* 2.5 (8c). For another example of the legal effects of a lack of reciprocal trust, see *Bek.* 13b. Cf. B. *BM* 49a.

34 Cohen, *Jewish and Roman Law*, 1:25.

35 B. *BK* 38a. Cf. B. *AZ* 2a, bot., where the verb *hiteer* is used to describe gentile release from observing the seven laws as direct divine commandments. See *infra*, 146–148

36 For the attempt to determine moral culpability on an individual basis, see B. *Ber.* 7a re Ex. 34:7 and Deut. 24:16. It need hardly be pointed out that the notion of inherited guilt was used against Jews throughout history. *The High Holiday Prayerbook*, ed. B. Bokser (New York, 1959), 430 ff. (*eleh ezkarah*).

37 P. *BK* 4.3 (4b), also T. *BK* 4.2.

38 *Nizkei Mammon*, 8.5. See De Boten, *Lehem Mishneh* thereto. See also ibid., 10.1, also B. *BK* 41a; P. *BK* 4.2 (4b). Cf. M. *BK* 4.6 and P. *BK* 4.5 (4b). B. Jackson argues that the rule that an ox pays full damages reflects Roman law and that Maimonides' point that it does not pay any damages reflects Islamic law. See his "Maimonides' Definitions of *Tam* and *Mu'ad*," *The Jewish Law Annual* (1978), 1:171.

39 Cf. *BR* 41.7; *SER*, ch. 28.

40 T. *AZ* 3.3; B. *AZ* 26a. However, see P. *AZ* 2.1 (40c) and *Meiri*, 58.

41 B. *BK* 113b. "Graetz, *MGWJ* (p. 495), shows clearly that the whole controversy whether robbery of a heathen was permissible was directed against the iniquitous *Fiscus Judaicum* imposed by Vespasian and enacted with much rigor by Domitian." *Students' Edition of the Babylonian Talmud: Bava Kamma*, trans., with notes, E.W. Kirzner (London, 1956), 664, n. 6. For another example of where strict justice had to be sacrificed for political survival in Jewish law, see M. *Git.* 5.6; T. *Git.* 3.10 and Lieberman, *Tosefta Kifshuta: Nashim*, 841–842; P. *Git.* 5.7 (47b). For the legal difference between gentiles who persecute Jews and those who do not, see *Semag*, neg. no. 152.

42 See T. *BK* 10.15. For Jewish arguments against charges of misanthropy, see Josephus, *Ant.*, 16:30, 42–43.

43 *Sifre: Devarim*, no. 344. For further discussion of these points, see *infra*, 127–128.

44 Page 122. No doubt Meiri's reasoning as brought by Ashkenazim *Sheetah Mekubetzet* (*BK* 38a) influenced the subsequent printed reading of "Canaanite." Cf. *SER*, chs. 15 and 28.

45 *Meiri: Ket.* (15b), 67–68.

46 *Arakh.* 32b re Lev. 25:10.

47 B. *Kid.* 15b–16a.

48 Ibid., s.v. *lekhidetanya*.

49 See Maimonides, *Hametz u-Matzah*, 4.2 and *MM* thereto.

50 B. *Kid.* 16a, s.v. *b'akum*. Cf. *Bek.* 13b, *Tos.*, s.v. *ke-m'an d'amar*. For the argument that such acts are evil *per se*, see Luria, *Yam shel Shlomo: BK* 10.20. Cf. *Avot de-Rabbi Natan*, A, ch. 2.5a; B. *BB* 16b, *Tos.*, s.v. *b'a*; B. *San.* 57b, *Tos.*, s.v. *le-na 'arah*.

51 See *LTJ* 2:25–27.

52 M. *San.* 4.2. See T. *San.* 7.2.

53 P. *San.* 4.7 (22b). See *PM* thereto. Cf. M. *San.* 7.3 and B. *San.* 52b.

54 For the question of whether the patriarchs and their children observed Jewish or non-Jewish law before Sinai, see *supra*, 245, n. 41.

55 M. *BM*, end.

56 B. *BM* 119a. Re Shapur I, see J. Neusner, *A History of the Jews in Babylonia: The Early Sassanian Period* (Leiden, 1966), 2:68–69.

57 Note to B. *BM* 119a, also B. *Hag.* 13a re Ps. 147:19–20. For the permission to study Noahide law with non-Jews, see B. *AZ* 3a, top.

58 Ibid., s.v. *shbor malka*. Cf. B. *BB* 64a, *Rashbam*, s.v. *bi-zeman*. Also, *sbor malka* was sometimes used as a euphemism for Jewish civil authority. See B. *BB* 115b.

59 For the sake of clarity I have combined the readings of ed. Horovitz-Rabin, 246, and ed. Lauterbach, 3:2. See *Tan.*, Shoftim, ed. Buber, 14b; *YS*, Shemot, no. 273.

60 M. *Git.* 9.8.

61 See B. *Git.* 88b and *Tos.*, s.v. *u-ba'akum*; B. *San.*, end.

62 M. *Git.* 1.5. Cf. B. *BK* 113b–114a and *Meiri*, 332. *LTJ* 1:128–129.

63 *Mordecai: Git.* no. 324. *Responsa Rashba*, 4, no. 126 and 7, no. 148; *SA: HM* 66.6–7.

64 See B. *Git.* 9b, s.v. *al'al-pi*.

65 See *SA: HM* 26.1–4; 68.1. For permission to use the *arka'ot* of the gentiles for specific Jewish self-interest, see T. *AZ* 1.8 and B. *AZ* 13a.

66 B. *BB* 54a, s.v. *dina*. (The Gemara presents this view on B. *Git.* 10b. See *GA* 5.13, 18; *Teshuvot ha-Ramban*, no. 47:75–76, and *MM* thereto.) See *Digest*, 1.4.1.

67 See Atlas, *Netivim*, 6, n. 2.

68 B. *Git.* 9b, s.v. *hutz*.

69 For the ethical inadequacies of social contract theory, see Strauss, *Natural Right and History*, 119.

70 Prov. 1:13–14. Halevi, *Kuzari*, 2.48; also Plato, *Republic*, 351D; also, ibn Daud, *Ha-Emunah ha-Ramah*, ed. S. Weil, 75.

71 See B. *Yev.* 89b; B. *Kid.* 19b.

72 B. *BB* 54b.

73 *Zekhiyyah u-Mattanah*, 1.14–15. See also B. *Ned.* 28a with *Tos.*, *Asheri*, and *Ran*, s.v. *be-mokes*.

74 See R. Zvi Hirsch Chajes (d. 1855), *Torat Neviim*, ch. 7 in *Kol Kitvei Maharetz Chajes* (Jerusalem, 1958), 1:46–47; Hobbes, *Leviathan*, chs. 14–24.

75 For the most insightful critiques of social contract theory, see Max Scheler, *Formalism in Ethics*, trans. M.S. Frings and R.L. Funk (Evanston, IL, 1973), 528–531; Reinhold Niebuhr, *The Self and the Dramas of History* (New York, 1955), 165. Earlier in the nineteenth century, German social philosopher Ferdinand Tönnies developed the thesis that contractual society (*Gesellschaft*) was subsequent to traditional society (*Gemeinschaft*). See his *Fundamental Concepts of Sociology*, trans. C.P. Loomis (East Lansing, MI, 1957), esp., 65 ff. Also, C.J. Friedrich, *The Philosophy of Law in Historical Perspective*, 2nd rev. edn. (Chicago, 1963), 138 ff.

76 *Responsa Rashba*, 6, no. 254. See Karo, *Bet Yosef* to *Tur: HM* 26, end; Isserles to *SA: HM* 369, end; Rashba attempted to limit this principle to royal prerogatives only. He rules that Jewish recognition of *royal* law does not extend to the ordinary courts (*arkaot*), in order that Jewish civil authority not be totally eclipsed. See *Responsa*, 3, no. 109; also, S. Shilo, *Dina de-Malkhuta Dina* (Jerusalem, 1974), 66–68. Rashba sees *dina de-malkhuta dina* as analogous to the specific privileges accorded a Jewish king (see I Sam. 8:9 ff.; B. *San.* 20b). This distinguishes *dina de-malkhuta*. See *Responsa*, 2, no. 134. Along the lines of Rashba's concern that Jewish law be eclipsed, see Rosh, *Responsa Rabbenu Asher*, no. 55, who argues against *hokhmat ha-teva* (= *ratio naturalis*)

as a halakhic criterion and R. Isaac Lampronti, *Pahad Yitzhak*, s.v. *pesulin min ha-Torah*, who rejects *dat ha-teva* (= *ius naturale*) as a halakhic criterion. See also L. Land-man, "Law and Conscience," *Judaism* (Winter 1969), 18.1: 27–28. Cf. J. Lauterbach, *Rabbinic Essays* (Cincinnati, 1951), 130–134.

77 See Cohen, *Religion der Vernunft aus den Quellen des Judenthums* (Darmstadt, 1966), 38; *Jüdische Schriften* (Berlin, 1924), 3:86.

78 *Malki ba-Kodesh*, 2, no. 2, pt. 2 quoted in Shilo, *Dina*, 83, n. 103. Also, see I.Z. Meltzer, *Even ha-Ezer Nizkei Mammon*, 8.5; Rashi (*Men.* 38b, s.v. *aryokh*) sees *dina de-malkhuta dina* as the basis for the Talmud's acceptance of Samuel's authority in *all* civil matters (*be-dinai, Bek.* 49b).

79 The noun *din* comes from the verb *doon*, which has both a logical and a legal denotation (cf. *krinein* in Greek). See e.g. B. *San.* 2b. For the relation of law and logic, see Cohen, *Religion der Vernunft*, 12, 32.

80 M. *Kid.* 1.5.

81 B. *BB* 45a.

82 *Rashbam* thereto following the emendation of *Bach*. See *Tos.*, s.v. *dina*, quoting Rashba, who indicates that gentile law might be different than Jewish law in this case, hence the need for extra effort at retrieval.

83 Maimonides, *Mekhirah*, 19.3–4; Rabbenu Jonah to *Alfasi*, Vilna edn., 24b; also, B. *BK* 9a.

84 *Hiddushai ha-Rashba* thereto.

85 *KM* to Maimonides, *Mekhirah*, 19.3–4.

86 *Hiddushai ha-Ritba*, ed. M.Y. Blau (New York, 1954), 84b and n. 746 thereto.

87 Cf. B. *Git.* 28b, bot.

88 *Alfasi*, op. cit.; Maimonides, *Mekhirah*, 19.3–4; Rabbenu Jonah and the insertion in *Rashbam*, s.v. *afilu* base it on the fact that Amemar was a later authority (*batraah*) than Rava or R. Pappa, who ruled otherwise above. For this principle of legal decision, see e.g. *Alfasi, Eruv.*, end, and B. *Ber.* 13b, *Tos.*, s.v. *amar Rava*.

89 Cf. *LTJ* 1:122–123; 2:202, n. 13.

90 Maimonides, *Mekhirah*, 19.3–4.

91 *Tur: HM* 225, beg., and *Bet Yosef* thereto; *SA: HM* 225, beg.

92 *Meiri*, 194.

93 *Bach* to *Tur: HM* 225. Cf. *SA: EH* 24.1 for a similar type interpretation.

94 For the problems with Maimonides' seeming rejection of the principle of *dina de-malkhuta dina* here, see *KM* to Maimonides, *Mekhirah*, 19.3–4.

95 *Avot* 3.2. See B. *AZ* 4a and, esp., B. *Ber.* 58a re I Chron. 29:11; also, *Zev.* 102a and *Men.* 98a re Ex. 11:6.

96 B. *San.* 39b.

97 See *LTJ* 2:22–27.

98 For attempts to morally discourage usury with gentiles, see B. *San.* 25b; B. *Mak.* 24a; *Meiri*, 116 thereto; B. *BM* 70b–71a, *Tos.*, s.v. *tashikh* and *Maharasha* thereto. Albo (*Ikkarim*, 3.25) limits the right to take interest only to idolaters without "religion" (*dat*), but prohibits taking interest from Noahides, who are like *gerai toshav*. R. Isaac Abravanel in his comment to Deut. 23:20 attempts to answer Christian charges that

the permission to Jews to take interest from gentiles indicates the moral inferiority of Judaism. Along these lines, see B. Nelson, *The Idea of Usury*, 2nd edn. (Chicago, 1969). Maimonides, on the other hand, rules that taking interest from a gentile is at least biblically mandatory. See *Malveh ve-Loveh*, 5.1–2 and *Rabad* and Rozanis, *Mishneh le-Melekh* thereto. Cf. *Edu.* 12.5.

99   B. *BM* 62a–b.

100   See M. *BM* 5.10.

101   See B. *Kid.* 13b, *Tos.*, s.v. *malveh*; B. *San.* 10a, *Tos.*, s.v. *meshum*, end; *Bek.* 48a, *Tos.*, s.v. *malveh*.

102   B. *San.* 59a. Cf. " . . . quod civile, non idem continuo gentium; quod autem gentium, idem civile esse debet." Cicero, *De Officiis*, 3.69. See B. *Yev.* 22a; Maimonides, *Mekirah*, 13.7.

103   Thus the rabbis were even willing to "apply many of the limitations set by the gentiles on animals to be offered in addition to their own restrictions." Lieberman, *Hellenism in Jewish Palestine*, 129. See B. *Git.* 56a; B. *AZ* 51a.

CHAPTER 3. The Law of Blasphemy

1   Finkelstein, *Pharisaism in the Making*, 226.

2   For the designation of God's name as the "four lettered name," see B. *Kid.* 71a and Philo, *De Vita Mosis*, 2.115.

3   B. *San.* 56a.

4   M. *San.* 7.5. See *Sifra*, Emor, 104b.

5   *AZ* 2.7.

6   B. *San.* 46a. See *Mel.* 9.3.

7   Ibid.

8   Ibid., 66a. See 46b, bot.

9   On B. *San.* 71b and P. *Kid.* 1.1 (58c) we find the law that a Noahide who blasphemed and then converted to Judaism is exempt from punishment, because blasphemy is more severely punished by Jewish law than by Noahide law. See B. *San.*, *Tos.*, s.v. *ben noah*; also, Radbaz to *Mel.* 10.4, who emphasizes the religious change brought about by conversion, hence the change in judgment of a crime against God.

10   See Plato, *Phaedo*, 98c.

11   B. *Naz.* 23b (see Rashi and *Tos.*, s.v. *Tamar*); B. *Hor.* 10b; also, B. *Ber.* 63a re Prov. 3:6.

12   See *YT*, beg.

13   M. *San.* 10.1.

14   B. *San.* 101b, also T. *San.* 12.9:433. See M. *Sot.* 7.6; B. *Sot.* 38a; *Sifre: Nas'o*, no. 43; *BR* 11.10.

15   Cf. Abulafia, *Yad Ramah*, 87b. For the use of the Tetragrammaton in the priestly blessing, see B. *Sot.* 38a re Num. 6:27.

16   T. *Sot.* 13.8, ed. Lieberman, 234; B. *Yoma* 39b. Cf. B. *Pes.* 50a.

17   B. *Sot.* 38a, *Tos.*, s.v. *harai*; Maimonides, *Tefillah*, 14.10 re B. *Kid.* 71a.

18   For anti-Gnostic measures, see M. *Ber.* 5.3; M. *Meg.* 4.9; P. *Ber.* 1.5 (3c); B. *Ber.* 12a.

19   B. *Kid.* 71a.

20 *MN* 1.62. See B. *AZ* 17b–18a and *Tos.*, s.v. *hogeh*; *LTJ* 2:160–163.

21 P. *San.* 10.1 (28b).

22 See *Otzar ha-Geonim: Sanhedrin*, ed. H.Z. Taubes (Jerusalem, 1966), 526.

23 *Hul.* 6a.

24 I Sam. 17:10. See Num. 31:2–3 and Rashi thereon; P. *Meg.* 1.4 (70c).

25 II Macc. 10:4. Note P. *Suk.* 5.1 (55b), where Jews are contrasted with "barbarians."

26 See Liddell and Scott, *A Greek–English Lexicon*, s.v. *barbaros*; also, H.D.F. Kitto, *The Greeks*, rev. edn. (Baltimore, 1957), 7–9.

27 For the notion that gentile abandonment of idolatry will give them "pure speech," see B. *Ber.* 57b re Zeph. 3:9. Blasphemy as a specifically religious crime, as opposed to mere sedition, seems to have been a uniquely Jewish idea in antiquity. See W.F. Cobb, "Blasphemy," in *Encyclopedia of Religion and Ethics* (Hastings), 2:670a. See B. *San.* 45b–46a re Deut. 21:23; P. *San.* 6.6 (23c), 7.9 (25b); *Ker.* 7b.

28 B. *San.* 60a. Cf., however, ibid., re Jud. 3:20 as an exception to usual gentile irreverence.

29 Ibid., P. *San.* 7.8 (25a–b); P. *MK* 3.7 (83b). For Rabshakeh's blasphemy, see I Kgs 18:32. For Hezekiah as a paragon of virtue, see B. *Pes.* 46a and B. *BK* 17a.

30 For similar legal logic, see M. *Sot.* 9.9 ff.

31 See *AZ* 2.10; Rosh, *Sanhedrin*, ch. 7, no. 2; *Tur: YD* 340.

32 See *supra*, 41–45.

33 B. *Ber.* 21b; P. *Ber.* 7.3 (11c). Rabbenu Jonah Gerondi (d. 1263) indicated that even when we speak of *Hillul Ha-Shem* in private we mean acts essentially public (comment to *Avot* 4.4).

34 B. *San.* 74a–b. Cf. B. *Ber.* 61b.

35 Ibid., 74a.

36 Ibid., 74b re II Kgs 5:18–19; *Mel.*, 10.2. See *supra*, 248, n. 93.

37 P. *BM* 2.5 (8c).

38 By Hellenistic times, the term *barbaros* had a clearly pejorative meaning in a moral sense.

39 See the version in *DR* 3.5, where the Arab is reported to have said, "blessed is the Lord, God of Simon b. Shetah." The midrashic version is presented in the context of an exegesis of the verse, "And you shall know that the Lord your God is *the* God, the faithful God" (Deut. 7:9). See P. *BB* 2.11 (13c).

40 *PM* to P. *BM* 2.5 (8c).

41 *GA* 11.3, also B. *BK* 113b and M. *Git.* 5.9 and T. *Git.* 3.13–14.

42 *KM* thereto. See *SH*, no. 358. Cf., however, B. *San.* 76b re Deut. 29:18 and Rashi thereto. B. *Ket.* 15b and Rashi thereto.

43 See B. *Git.* 46a.

44 B. *Shab.* 31a.

45 B. *BK* 99b–100a; B. *BM* 24b. Cf. M. *BM* 4.2.

46 For the relation between blasphemy and *Hillul Ha-Shem*, see P. *San.* 6.7 (23c).

47 See P. *Dem.* 4.3 (24a); P. *Git.* 5.9 (47c) and P. *AZ* 1.3 (39c). Cf. B. *AZ* 8a re Ex. 34:15.

48 B. *Ber.* 7a re Is. 56:7.

49 See *Sifre: Devarim*, no. 26; A. Marmorstein, *The Old Rabbinic Doctrine of God: The Names and Attributes of God* (New York, 1968), 1:43 ff.

50 In B. *BK* 99b–100a and B. *BM* 30b the concept of *gemilut Hasidim* is connected with *lifnim mi-shurat ha-din* based on the exegesis of Ex. 18:20 (see also *Mekh.*, Yitro 198). For *gemilut Hasidim* as *imitatio Dei*, see *Targum Pseudo-Jonathan* to Deut. 34:6 and B. *Sot.* 14a.

51 *Sifra*, Emor, 104b. For a similar exegesis, where the designation of locale is interpreted as the issue of a quarrel, see *BR* 22.8 re Gen. 4:8, 213–214 and notes thereon.

52 See V. Aptowitzer, "Zekher le-Zekhut ha'Em bi-Sifrut Yisrael," *Ha-Mishpat ha-Ivri* (1927), 2:9–23.

53 See *VR* 32.4.

54 B. *Yev.* 45b; B. *Kid.* 68b. See M. *Yev.* 7.5 with Maimonides' comments; B. *Yev.* 44b–45a; *Alfasi; Yev.* 15a, Vilna edn.; B. *Yev.* 16b, *Tos.*, s.v. *ke-sabar*; P. *Kid.* 3.12 (64d); *IB* 15.4; Aptowitzer, "Zekher," 13, n. 12; J.D. Bleich, "Survey of Recent Halakhic Literature," *Tradition* (Fall 1977), 16.5:85–88.

55 See T. *Kid.* 4.16; P. *Yev.* 1.6 93a), 7.6 (8b), 7.7 (8c); P. *Kid.* 3.12 (64d) re Num. 1.18; *BR* 19.3; B. *Kid.* 75b, *Tos.*, s.v. *ve-R. Ishamel* and *hashata*; *Piskai Tosafot*, no. 142; B. *Bek.* 47a and *Tos.*, s.v. *ve-l'o*; B. *Yev.* 78b; Nahmanides to Lev. 25:9; A. Geiger, *Urschrift und Übersetzungen der Bibel* (Breslau, 1857), 54.

56 See *supra*, 22–23; also, B. *BB* 109b re Num. 1:20 for the rule that family pedigree follows the father.

57 *Sifre, Ki Tetz'e*, no. 24k; M. *Kid.* 3.12.

58 *Tan.*, Korah, ed. Buber, 46b.

59 *VR* 32.5 (Cf. M. *Ket.* 7.6). The emphasis there is on the word *vayetz'e* as a term connoting promiscuity. Cf. *BR* 80.1 re Gen. 43:1; *SR* 1.1 re Gen. 21:11.

60 *VR* 32.4.

61 Ibid., 32.7. See *DR* 9.4; *KR* 4.3; T. *Kid.* 5.4; B. *Kid.* 72b; P. *Kid.* 3.13 (65a) re Ezek. 36:25.

62 Cf. Is. 56:3–5.

63 See Job 21:19–21.

64 B. *Ber.* 7a; B. *San.* 27b. For attempts to justify inherited guilt as a punishment for sinful parents and as a general social precaution, however, see B. *Yev.* 22b re Ecc. 1:15; B. *Sot.* 37b re Deut. 27:15; B. *Yev.* 27b re Lev. 19:29; T. *Kid.* 1.4; *Sifra*, Kedoshim, 90b; B. *Shevu.* 39a–b; T. *Sot.* 7.2; B. *Kid.* 71b re Jer. 31:1; Shadal to Ex. 20:5.

65 *BR* 19.20; *MT* 18.3, 68b; *MRE*, ch. 5, pp. 95, 97; *PRK*, Selihot, 2:382, *SEZ*, ch. 6.

66 M. *Hor.* 3.8.

67 B. *MK* 12b–13a and *Tos.*, s.v. *netybah*; *SA: HM* 108.2; A. Gulak, *Yesodai ha-Mishpatim ha-Ivri* (Berlin, 1927), 2.7, p. 16.

68 M. *Kid.* 3.13. For the question of the Jewish status of the slave, see *LTJ* 2:93–96.

69 B. *Kid.* 69a. See *Alfasi, Kid.* 30a, Vilna edn. and *Ran* thereto. The solution, however, does not apply to female *mamzerot* since the status of this type follows the female line. See *Tur: EH* 4 and, esp., Karo, *Bet Joseph* thereto.

70 B. *Kid.* 70b–71a re Mal. 3:3; *Mel.* 12.3.

71 B. *Kid.* 71a, top, Rashi, s.v. *kesef*. Cf. B. *Pes.* 62b and Maharasha thereto.

72 B. *Kid.* 68a; also, B. *Ket.* 29a, Rashi, s.v. *bo'u*. Cf. M. *Yev.* 4.13 and B. *Yev.* 49a–b. For general rabbinic reluctance in this area, see B. *Git.* 33a, *Tos.*, s.v. *v'afka'inu; LTJ* 2:61–63.

73 See e.g. B. *Mak.* 2a re Deut. 19:19 and *Tos.*, s.v. *me'idin*.

74 See B. *Kid.* 73a; *IB* 15.21.

75 See *LTJ* 1:1–14; 2:xiii–xvi.

76 See Agus, *Jewish Identity in an Age of Ideologies*, 391.

77 See B. *Shevu.* 35a; *Targum Onkelos* to Gen. 3:5; *MN* 1.2; Marmorstein, *The Old Rabbinic Doctrine of God*, 1:43 ff.

78 See B. *San.* 38b; P. *Ber.* 9.1 (12d).

79 See e.g. Ex. 8:15 and Rashi and Ibn Ezra thereto.

80 See *Mekh.*, Mishpatim, 317; B. *San.* 66a.

81 See, e.g., I Kgs. 18:27; Ps. 115:4–8; I Chron. 16:26.

82 *Ant.*, 4.207, trans. H. St. John Thackeray (Cambridge, MA, 1930), 574–575.

83 See E.R. Goodenough, *The Jurisprudence of the Jewish Courts in Egypt* (Amsterdam, 1968), 206–212.

84 *Contra Apionem*, 2.144. See *DR* 6.4 re: Ps. 50:20.

85 See *infra*, 373–374; 386–387.

86 *De Vita Mosis*, 2.205–206, trans. F.H. Colson (Cambridge, MA, 1935), 550–551.

87 *De Spec. Leg.*, 1.51, 53, pp. 126–129. For Philo's insistence of Judaism's tolerance of the popular manifestations of polytheism, see *De Spec. Leg.*, 2.164–167. See Justin Martyr, *Dialogue with Trypho*, chaps. 8 and 55 re: Deut. 4:19.

88 See Wolfson, *Philo*, 2:123.

89 "Keter Malkhut," trans. Israel Zangwill in *Selected Religious Poetry of Solomon ibn Gabirol*, ed. I. Davidson (Philadelphia, 1923), 86–87. For a Talmudic basis on this idea, see *Men.* 110a re: Mal. 1:11.

CHAPTER 4. The Law of Idolatry

1   T. *AZ* 8.4, p. 473.

2   B. *San.* 56a.

3   Ibid., 56b.

4   On the same page the view of the Tanna, R. Judah, is reported that Adam was only prohibited re idolatry. Cf. T. *Shevu.* 4.6.

5   *BR* 16.16; *CR* 1.16; *PRK*, Ba-Hodesh, 202.

6   *Supra*, 39–40.

7   *Mel.* 9.1.

8   See B. *Mak.* 24a; *SM*, pos. no. 1 and neg. no. 1; *MN* 2.33. T. *Shevu.* 3.6.

9   *Supra*, 19–23.

10 B. *AZ* 64b. See note 4; also, B. *San.* 38b re Gen. 3:9, Hos. 7:7, Jer. 22:9.

11 Deut. 14:21; *Sifre: Devarim*, no. 104; P. *Yev.* 8.1 (8d). See *Mekh.*, Mishpatim, 321 and *Rashi* to Ex. 22:30; also, B. *AZ* and *Tos.*, s.v. *lehakdeem*.

12 See *Zev.* 116b re Lev. 17:2; Maimonides, *Ma'aseh Korbanot*, 19.16.

13 See Ex. 12:38.

14 See *SR* 42.6; 43.8.

15 See Gen. 26:34–35; Num. 25:1–3; *Bek.* 5b; *BaR* 20.23.

16 See M. *San.* 2.4; B. *Kid.* 68b re Deut. 7:4; Philo, *De Specialibus Legibus*, 3.29; Josephus, *Ant.*, 8.191–193; *IB* 12.7. Cf. B. *Yev.* 76a–b; P. *San.* 2.6 (20c).

17 See T. *AZ* 4.6; B. *AZ* 8a, 36b. For the less explicit ban on intermarriage with gentile monotheists, see *IB* 12.5. Thus the early Reform theologian Samuel Holdheim attempted to show that there is no ban at all on such marriages. See his *Gemischte Ehen zwischen Juden und Christen* (Berlin, 1850). For an earlier form of Holdheim's argument, see the view refuted by R. Moses de Leon, *Sefer Shekel ha-Kodesh* (London, 1911), 63–66; I. Tishby, *Mishnat ha-Zohar* (Jerusalem, 1961), 2:626; Yitzhak Baer, *Toldot ha-Yehudim be-Sefarad ha-Notzrit* (Tel Aviv, 1959), 141–155; *LTJ* 2:177–178. Because of the waning hold of idolatry per se, beginning in the Hellenistic period, idolatry was seen by some sources as being a cover for sexual license. See Wisdom 14:12, 22–27; *Avot de-Rabbi Natan*, A, ch. 3; T. *BK* 9.31; B. *Shab.* 104b; B. *San.* 63b, 106a and Ginzberg, *Legends*, 6:134–134, n. 785. See also B. *Yoma* 69b; *KR* 7.13.

18 See commentary of A.S. Hartom thereto (Tel Aviv, 1972), 14. Cf. *Rashi* thereto.

19 See M. *AZ* 4.7; T. *AZ* 6.7; B. *AZ* 54b; *Mekh.*, Yitro, 226.

20 See *Rashi* to Jer. 10:11.

21 See Hab. 2:18–20; *AZ*, beg.

22 *Sifre: Devarim*, no. 174; B. *Yev.* 90b re Deut. 18:15; P. *Ta'an.* 2.8 (65d) and *KE* thereto re Gen. 35:11; P. *Meg.* 1.11 (72c).

23 *YT* 9.3. See *Hakdamah le-Mishneh*, 25.

24 T. *AZ* 4.5. See B. *Ket.* 110b; B. *AZ* 8a; *Ramban* to Gen. 28:21 and Lev. 18:25 re II Kgs 17:26.

25 See Ex. 18:11; Josh. 2:11; *Mekh.*, Yitro, 194–195.

26 See B. *Git.* 45a, *Rashi*, s.v. *el adonav*. Note how it is emphasized that Jethro, the convert, had to become a virtual recluse because of his monotheism. See *SR* 1.35. Furthermore, the Talmud (B. *San.* 74b–75a; P. *San.* 3.6 [21b]) cites II Kgs 5:18–19 as proof that a gentile need not die for *kiddush ha-shem*, viz., being forced to participate in public idolatry.

27 See Is. 13:11, 16:6, 24:1–5; Ezek. 25. When the Talmud assumes that idolatry is prohibited to gentiles after the Sinaitic revelation (B. *San.* 59a), *Rashi* (s.v. *la-zeh*) brings as proof Deut. 18:12: " . . . and because of these abominations the Lord your God disinherits them before you" (see T. *AZ* 8.7; ibid., 56a re Deut. 18:12). However, this is not so much a moral indictment as an indication of the covenantless status of these gentiles. Unlike Israel, they simply do not know any better. See *Rashbam* to Deut. 18:12, also *YS*, Bo, no. 187 re Is. 11:16 and *Rashi* to Gen. 1:1. Nahmanides (Lev. 18:25) and Bahya (Deut. 31:16) both interpret the divine punishment of the Samaritans with lions (II Kgs 17:25 ff.) as being for their idolatry in the land of Israel. However, the text only states "they did not fear the Lord." They themselves believed this was their sin for they regarded YHWH as "the god of the land" and continued "serving their gods." Their polytheistic syncretism was only regarded by the scriptural author as invalid for Jews.

28 Cf. Ps. 36:2.

29 See *Sifre: Devarim*, no. 354 re Deut. 33:19.

30 Re the mighty acts of God towards Israel impressing gentiles, see e.g. Ex. 7:5, 14:4 and 18; I Kgs 8:41–43; Is. 24:14–15, 25:1–8, 45:3–8 and 18–24, 55:4–5, 60:1 ff.; Ezek. 29:6

and 9, 30:8 and 25–26; Ps. 47:2–5 and 10, 98:2–3, 105:1 ff., 117:1–2. Sometimes the universally evident power of God is emphasized. See e.g. Ps. 49: 2–3, 66:1–5, 67:2–7; Job 40:6 ff. Where acknowledgment of God involves rejection of idolatry, as in Ps. 97:7, the intent is messianic. See P. *AZ* 4.7 (44a). See also Jer. 16:19–20 and *Radak* thereto. Moreover, the terror of the mighty acts of God can cause gentiles to return to their idols with renewed fervor. See Is. 41:1–7 and *Radak* to v. 5.

31   Kaufmann, *The Religion of Israel*, trans. M. Greenberg (Chicago, 1960), 163–164. This view was also put forth, in more traditional form to be sure, by R. Solomon ibn Adret in the thirteenth century (*Responsa Rashba*, 4, no. 334) and later by Rabbenu Bahya. The latter writes: "Therefore, we do not find in the entire Torah in any place that Scripture considers the nations guilty of idolatry, but only Israel who are specified as His portion" (comment to Deut. 31:15 re Deut. 4:19–20, p. 452). He continues, re II Kgs 17:26, that gentile idolatry is only considered prohibited when practiced in Eretz Israel, even when the Jews are not there. See also Lev. 18:27–28; *SR* 15.23 re Lev. 26:1. See *Rashbam* to Deut. 4:19. Furthermore, it is worth noting that the condemnation of the Jewish survivors of the Temple's destruction by Ezekiel (33:24–25), a condemnation that lists idolatry among *their* sins, was interpreted on T. *Sot.* 6:9 to refer to gentiles for their violation of all the Noahide laws.

32   Kaufmann, 127. Cf. Wellhausen, "Israel," in *Encyclopedia Britannica*, reprinted in Eng. trans. of *Prolegomena to the History of Ancient Israel*, trans. A. Menzies, 437: "The expression 'YHWH is the God of Israel' . . . certainly did not mean that the almighty Creator of heaven and earth was conceived of as having first made a covenant with this one people that by them He might be truly known and worshipped. It was not as if YHWH had originally been regarded as the God of the universe who subsequently became the God of Israel; on the contrary, He was primarily Israel's God, and only afterwards (very long afterwards) did He come to be regarded as the God of the universe."

33   Kaufmann, 128. See W. Eichrodt, *Theology of the Old Testament*, trans. J.A. Baker (Philadelphia, 1967), 2:182–183.

34   See Is. 14:26, 18:3, 34:1; Jer. 1:14, 10:10, 25:17, and 31, 27:2–11, 28:8; Amos 9:7.

35   For the rabbinic developments of this idea, see *SR* 34.1; B. *San.* 7a re Ex. 25:22.

36   Kaufmann, 164.

37   See Ex. 18:11–12; Josh. 2:9–11; *Zev.* 116a.

38   Kaufmann, 165.

39   See Is. 2:3, 56:3 and 6–8; Micah 4:1–4; Zech. 8:20–23.

40   See Josephus, *Ant.*, 13.62–68; O. Kaiser, *Isaiah 13–39: A Commentary*, trans. R.A. Wilson (Philadelphia, 1974), 106–109; *Men.* 109b–110a. Rashi, quoting *Seder Olam* (ch. 23), sees the builders of this altar as Egyptian troops of King Hezekiah, whom the king permitted to return to Egypt. These troops are seen as *yirai ha-Shem*, viz., they accepted the one God but not the yoke of the commandments. See *Radak* thereto and *Men.* 109b, *Tos.*, s.v. *ve-he'aleh; LTJ* 2:154–155.

41   Kaufmann, 391 and 392, n. 6. See A.J. Heschel, *The Prophets* (Philadelphia, 1962), 169–170.

42   The term *ha-Shem elohai yisrael* does not mean that God is the automatic guarantor of Israelite claims. See Eichrodt, *Theology of the Old Testament* (Philadelphia, 1961),

1:192–193. It does mean, however, that God's universal power is not inconsistent with his special presence to Israel. For rabbinic discussion of whether this term is sacred, see P. *Meg.* 1.9 (71d); cf. B. *Shevu.* 35b.

43 Trans. R. Gordis, *The Book of God and Man* (Chicago, 1965), 285. See *LT* 10b re Gen. 2.16 that uses this as a proof of the Noahide ban on idolatry.

44 B. *BB* 15a–b.

45 See e.g. Gen. 14:18–20.

46 T. *Ber.* 6.2, ed. Lieberman, 33.

47 *Tosefta Kifshuta: Zera'im* (New York, 1955), 103–104.

48 B. *Ber.* 57b. See, esp., the note of Zevi Hirsch Chajes thereto.

49 The point is debated on B. *AZ* 24a. On P. *AZ* 2.1 (40c) one Amora interpreted Zeph. 3:9 to mean full conversion.

50 *Ber.* 10.9.

51 *KM* thereto in answer to *Tur: OH* 224.

52 The source in the Mishnah (M. *Hul.* 2.7) indicates that the original context of this statement concerned the appropriateness of slaughtering animals of gentiles to be sacrificed on the altar of the Temple (see *Hul.* 28b–39a; M. *Zev.* 4.6 and *Zev.* 47a). Later the principle was applied in other contexts. See B. *Git.* 45a and *Hul.* 13a. Cf. P. *AZ* 2.3 (41b) and 2.7 (41c). For R. Eliezer's anti-gentile views, see T. *San.* 13.2; B. *San.* 105a re Ps. 9:18.

53 B. *Git.* 45b and parallels. Cf. B. *Shab.* 116a and *YT* 6.7.

54 B. *Kid.* 40a re T. *Peah* 1.4. See *Hinukh*, no. 31. Thoughts per se are not the subject of halakhic norms. See B. *Kid.* 49b; Maimonides to M. *Kid.* 2.3; *Meiri* to B. *Kid.* 40a, ed. Sofer, 202.

55 P. *Peah* 1.1 (16b) re Obad. 1:10; also, B. *Kid.* 40a, *Tos.*, s.v. *mahshabah*.

56 See *Hul.* 39b.

57 B. *AZ* 64b; P. *Yev.* 8.1 (8d).

58 B. *San.* 60b. See B. *Git.* 52b–53a; P. *Git.* 5.5 (47a).

59 See *LTJ* 2:176–178.

60 See *Responsa Ramo*, no. 124.

61 B. *San.* 56b.

62 Ibid., 57a.

63 See ibid., 10a, *Rashi*, s.v. *malkot*.

64 T. *AZ* 5.3, p. 408. See M. *AZ* 4.4; P. *AZ* 4.4 (43d). B. *AZ* 53a. Cf. *Mekh.*, Yitro, 226; M. *AZ* 4.7.

65 See B. *BK* 69a.

66 M. *Dem.* 6.10; B. *Kid.* 17b. See T. *Dem.* 6.12–13; Maimonides, *Ma'akholot Asurot*, 13.22. Only during the time of the Amoraim was it assumed that a *ger* would also desire to uproot idolatry from his *gentile* father's house. See P. *Dem.* 6.10 (25b).

67 M. *AZ* 2.3; B. *AZ* 29b.

68 B. *Pes.* 6b.

69 This is analogous to the concepts in Roman law of *ius ad rem* and *ius in personam*. Ultimately, the former presupposes the latter, viz., property relations are based on personal relationships. See Hans Kelsen, *The Pure Theory of Law*, trans. M. Knight (Berkeley, CA, 1970), 130–132.

70 M. *Pes.* 2.2.

71 M. *AZ* 4.4; B. *AZ* 52a re Deut. 27:15.

72 See M. *Zev.* 12.4.

73 B. *AZ* 52a.

74 P. *Yev.* 8.1 (8d).

75 See B. *AZ* 64b.

76 For the use of the term *bitul* to denote legislative repeal of an earlier law, see M. *Edu.* 1.5. (Cf. *lex posterior derogate priori.*)

77 The Greek *latria* comes from the verb *latrein* and is the same as the Hebrew *avodah* from the verb *avd*. Cf. *Avot* 1.2 and Romans 9:4. Also, in *avodah zarah*, that which is "strange" can be both the *object* of worship or the *method* of worship. For *zarah* denoting even unacceptable Jewish worship, see *Sifra*, Shemini, 45b re Lev. 10:1. Cf. *Mekh.*, Yitro, 223: B. *BB* 110b.

78 M. *AZ* 4.4.

79 P. *AZ* 4.4 (43d), viz., he rejects it as involving the logical fallacy of *post hoc ergo propter hoc*.

80 See T. *AZ* 5.3–4.

81 P. *AZ* 4.4 (44a).

82 For the actual procedure of desecration, see M. *AZ* 4.5.

83 See *Mekh.*, Bo, 47, and note thereon.

84 *AZ* 8.9.

85 See Maimonides, *Milah*, 1.6; *Shab.* 20.14. In *Tur: YD* 146, the non-idolatrous gentile is termed *ger toshav*. Karo, *Bet Yosef* thereto, indicates that Muslims are an example of such non-idolatrous gentiles.

86 *Arakh.* 29a. See *IB* 14.8; Maimonides, *Shemitah ve-Yovel*, 10.9.

87 M. *Shevu.* 3.6; B. *Hag.* 10a re Ps. 119:106 and *Tos.*, s.v. *legayyem*; *Tem.* 3b re Ps. 119:106 and Deut. 10:20; *Shevu.* 5.16 and *Radbaz* thereto; *SM*, pos. no. 7 (end).

88 See his comment to Gen. 37:2; *contra* B. *Ber.* 28b.

89 B. *Meg.* 9a–b. Cf. *Letter of Aristeas*, sect. 65; Philo, *De Vita Mosis*, 2.7, 37–39. See also T. *Meg.*, end; B. *Kid.* 49a; *Avot de-Rabbi Natan*, A, 13b; Maimonides to *Avot* 1.11.

90 See *Rabbenu Bahya* to Gen. 1:18; also, Kittel, *Biblia Hebraica* (Stuttgart, 1951), 268, note to Deut. 4:19, who suggests emending *otam* to *otot*. Such an emendation suggested on B. *Meg.* 9b. Cf. Jer. 10:2 as interpreted on B. *Shab.* 156a.

91 Septuagint, 6th edn. (Stuttgart, n.d.), 1:293. All of the other Greek versions cited in Origen's *Hexapla* (ed. F. Field, Oxford, 1875, p. 280) translate the verse similarly to LXX. However, note the Vulgate thereto (ed. G. Nolli, Rome, 1955, 523): " . . . *quae creavit Dominus Deus tuus in ministerium cunctis gentibus quae sub caelo sunt.*"

92 The present LXX text corroborates the emendations of Gen. 2:2, 5:1.

93 Josephus, *Contra Apionem*, 2.237–238; *Ant.*, 4.207; Philo, *De Vita Mosis*, 2.205 re LXX to Ex. 22:27.

94 B. *Meg.* 9b, s.v. *leha'ir*. See *Rashi* to Deut. 4:19; *AZ* 2.1; *MN* 2.5.

95 B. *AZ* 55a. See ibid., 4b re Deut. 6:6; Ps. 36:3 and *Targum Pseudo-Jonathan* to Deut. 4:19.

96 See *Men.* 29b re Prov. 3:34.

97 See M. *AZ* 4.7; T. *AZ* 6.7; B. *AZ* 54b; *Mekh.*, Yitro, 226. For Jews, concern with the heavenly bodies was considered necessary, specifically because of the calculation of the calendar, generally to acknowledge its creation by God. This was clearly to dissociate it from idolatrous connotations. See B. *Shab.* 75a re Is. 5:12 and Deut. 6:6; also, B. *RH* 24a and B. *AZ* 43a re Ex. 20:20.

98 B. *Meg.* 9b, s.v. *asher.* Cf. T. *Meg.* 3.41.

99 P. *Meg.* 1.9 (71c).

100 *Hiddushei Aggadot* to B. *Meg.* 9b.

101 M. *Hul.* 1.1.

102 T. *Hul.* 1.1. See *Hul.* 13a. Cf. Acts 15:20, 29; 21:25; Tertullian, *Apologia*, 9.13; Strack and Billerbeck, *Kommentar zum Neuen Testament aus Talmud und Midrasch* (Munich, 1924), 2:729–739.

103 *Hul.* 13b.

104 Ibid. "The phrase is the exact equivalent to *mos maiorum* that was so dear to Cicero and the Roman jurists, which they deemed as such an important source for their law." Cohen, *Jewish and Roman Law*, 2:386. The Koran, on the other hand, sees the argument from ancestral custom as an unacceptable reason for idolatrous practices. See Sura 43:20–30.

105 See Maimonides, *Shehitah*, 4.12, and *KM* thereto.

106 This is the law in the absence of certainty. See B. *BK* 46a. As Rashi notes on *Hul.* 13b, top, if only a minority are idolaters, the majority are not tainted. Cf. B. *Kid.* 80a.

107 B. *Shab.* 116a. Cf. B. *AZ* 27b; also, *Sifre: Devarim*, no. 87 re Deut. 13:8.

108 This can even be the case with a Jewish practice. See P. *Sot.* 7.6 (22a); B. *Betz.* 4b, bot.; *LTJ* 2:182.

109 Faur, *Iyunim*, 227–229. Cf. *Hul.* 13b, *Tos.*, s.v. *akum.*

110 It should be noted that the full exegesis of Gen. 2:16 as the pre-Sinaitic basis for the Noahide laws is recorded in the name of R. Johanan (B. *San.* 56b).

111 This is why the standards for non-Jewish cultus were much more lenient than those for Jewish cultus. See *Zev.* 115b–116a; P. *Meg.* 1.11 (72b).

112 B. *AZ* 41b; *Me'il.* 14b and *Tos.*, s.v. *u-mutteret.*

113 See B. *Git.* 14a.

114 See Bamberger, *Proselytism.*

115 B. *Shab.* 156a. For attempts to reconcile this doctrine with the numerous rabbinic statements that take *mazal* seriously, see *Responsa Rashba*, 1, no. 148; *Responsa Rashba* (attributed to Nahmanides), no. 285 and *Rabbenu Bahya* to Deut. 8:18. For even R. Johanan's recognition of heavenly powers, see B. *San.* 67b. See also *Nid.* 16b re Deut. 10:12, *Tos.*, s.v. *ha-kol* à la B. *Ber.* 10a. Cf. *Tosafot ha-Rosh* thereto.

116 Cf. B. *Suk.* 29a. See B. *Yoma* 54a and *Rabbenu Bahya* to Ex. 25:18; *Malbim* to Deut. 4:19.

117 See *supra*, 63–65.

118 See *MN* 2.5.

119 *Men.* 110a. See LXX to Deut. 9:26; *Radak* to Mal. 1:11; Urbach, *Hazal*, 118–119.

120 See *SR* 15.18 and B. *AZ* 41b re I Sam. 5:4–5, where the representative character of idolatry is recognized. Note: "However, the truth is that to the Rabbis symbols are the same as idols, as mere fetishes. Although the Rabbis were not so naïve as to think their

heathen contemporaries to be mere fetishists, this distinction did not in their eyes lessen the idolatrous character of this worship." Lieberman, *Hellenism in Jewish Palestine*, 126. See also B. *Ket.* 33b and *Tos.*, s.v. *ilmalai*.

121 *Encounters between Judaism and Modern Philosophy* (New York, 1973), 188–189. On the other hand, Kaufmann consistently maintained that pagans recognized the limitations of the gods and, thereby, acknowledged an infinite "metadivine" realm. See *The Religion of Israel*, 21 ff. Nevertheless, this theory has little empirical data behind it. For an excellent critique of Kaufmann, see Faur, *Iyunim*, 195–210.

122 See Eliade, *The Sacred and the Profane* (New York, 1961), 11.

123 *SM*, pos. no. 7.

124 See *infra*, 93–94.

125 See Plato, *Republic*, 511B, 532Bff.

126 *Truth and Symbol*, trans. J.T. Wilde, W. Kluback and W. Kimmel (New York, 1959), 39. See also P. Ricoeur, *The Symbolism of Evil*, trans. E. Buchanan (New York, 1967), 15.

127 Ibid., 159–160. Cf. P. Tillich, *Dynamics of Faith* (New York, 1957), 43; Jacques Ellul, *The Meaning of the City*, trans. D. Pardee (Grand Rapids, MI, 1970), 18, n. 3.

128 B. *San.* 63b.

129 *Rashi* thereto, s.v. *l'o yigrom*.

130 See Abulafia. *Yad Ramah* thereto, 60b; *Meiri* thereto, 239.

131 *Mekh.*, Mishpatim, 332. Because of the Jews' refusal to take non-Jewish oaths, the institution of *More Judaico* arose in the Middle Ages. See *JE*, 9:367 ff.

132 Cf. T. *AZ* 4.6.

133 Re Jacob's covenant with his idolatrous father-in-law, Laban (Gen. 31:30), see *SH* following MS Parma, no. 1395.

134 See *Shevu.* 12.1 for an oath as an act of worship (*me-darkhei avodah hi*).

135 See e.g. M. *BK* 6.4 and B. *BK* 60a; B. *BB* and *Tos.*, s.v. *z'ot*; also, B. *Kid.* 43a re II Sam. 12:9.

136 See e.g. M. *San.* 63b.

137 B. *San.* 63b.

138 Ibid., *Tos.*, s.v. *asur*. Cf., however, *Responsa Rashi*, ed. Elfenbein, no. 180; also, *SER*, ch. 7 (end). *Rosh* presents and elaborates on Rabbenu Tam's innovative ruling by citing B. *Meg.* 28a (see *Tos.*, s.v. *titi*) that he believes that the ruling of the father of Samuel was not generally followed even in Amoraic times, but was, rather, considered a standard of unusual piety. Note how a Christian scholar expresses this point: ". . . l'interdiction de la idolatrie n'implique pas ipso facto pour les Noachides, l'acceptation positive du monothéisme . . . on ne peut demander aux Noachides que la foi en Dieu, créateur du ciel et de la terre, sans que cette exclue des intermédiares." Hruby, "La Révélation dans la theologie rabbinique," 28, n. 17.

139 B. *AZ* 2a, *Tos.*, s.v. *asur*; 57b, s.v. *l'afookai*. In an important *responsum* on this subject, R. Ephraim ha-Kohen of Vilna notes that this type of association of God and a sacred personality is in essence the same as the association of God and Moses in Ex. 14:31. See *Responsa Sha'ar Ephraim*: *OH*, no. 24. As background, see *Men.* 73b, top.

140 *Bek.* 2b, *Tos.*, s.v. *shem'a* ala B. *AZ* 6b. See T. *MK* 1.12; *Responsa Ribash*, no. 119.

141 "Soblanut Datit be-Shitato shel Rabbi Menahem ha-Meiri," *Zion* (1953), 18:18–19. See his *Exclusiveness and Tolerance* (Oxford, 1961), 34–35; Faur, *Iyunim*, 230.

142 M. *Neg.* 12.5; B. *RH* 29a and parallels; *Bek.* 40a; *Hul.* 56a; P. *San.* 4.1 (22a). Cf. M. *Yad.* 4.3. See also E.E. Urbach, *Ba'alei ha-Tosafot* (Jerusalem, 1955), 57.

143 B. *Ber.* 19b and parallels. See *Men.* 49b, *Rashi*, s.v. *hasa* and *amar layh* and *Tos.*, s.v. *Rav.*

144 B. *San.* 63a; also, B. *Suk.* 45b.

145 See *Aykhah Rabbati*, intro., 10 re Jud. 10:6. For the various views of the specifics of this permission, see *ET* 2:350.

146 B. *San.* 63a re Ex. 32:4. See *SR* 42.3.

147 See e.g. *SR* 43.8.

148 See *Shevu.* 11.2.

149 Abulafia, *Yad Ramah* to B. *San.* 63a, p. 60b. Cf. *Rabbenu Jonah* thereto, Leghorn edn., 46a.

150 See M. *Eruv.* 6.5 and *Rashi* thereto (on B. *Eruv.* 71a) and B. *Eruv.* 71b.

151 Faur, *Iynunim*, 231, n. 10 referring to E.J. Martin, *A History of the Iconoclastic Controversy* (London, 1931), 121 ff. Cf. *Responsa Rashba*, 7, no. 502 (see also no. 320).

152 Katz, *Exclusiveness and Tolerance*, 163–164.

153 See esp. *Ramo* to *SA*: *OH* 156.1; *YD* 140.3 and 151.10.

154 See e.g. *Ramo* to *SA*: *YD* 123.1, 124.19 and *Shakh* thereto. Cf. B. *AZ* 57b, *Tos.*, s.v. *l'afookai* (end).

155 See Katz, op. cit.

156 See *infra*, 195–199.

157 See commentary to M. *AZ* 1.4 and *AZ* 9.4; *Ma'akhalot Asurot*, 11.7; *Teshuvot ha-Rambam*, ed. J. Blau (Jerusalem, 1957), no. 448, 2:726; Faur, *Iyunim*, 230 ff.

158 *Teshuvot ha-Rambam*, no. 149; 1:284–285.

159 *Mel.* 11, end (uncensored, ed. M. Rabinowitz, Jerusalem, 1962), 416–417.

160 See B. *Ned.* 11b.

161 *Sifre: Devarim*, no. 170. See *Men.* 64a and *Tos.*, s.v. *ba'alei*; *AZ* 3.2. Cf. Plato, *Republic*, 409B.

162 See e.g. Is. 44:6–20; Ps. 115:2–8. Kaufmann's thesis that monotheism had so permeated Israel that the biblical authors had no understanding of the ideology behind idolatry (*The Religion of Israel*, 77 ff.) has found little scholarly acceptance. See Faur, *Iyunim*, 197–199.

163 Cf. H.A. Wolfson, *The Philosophy of the Church Fathers*, 3rd rev. edn. (Cambridge, MA, 1970), 305 ff.

164 *Arakh.* 4.13. See T. *San.* 8.7; B. *San.* 28a; P. *San.* 1.1 (18a) re Is. 44:6 and B. *Yev.* 101a.

165 See M. *Ber.* 5.3; M. *Ber.* 33b; *LTJ* 2:127–128; Jonas, *The Gnostic Religion* (Boston, 1958), 42–43, 236–237.

166 *Nid.* See P. *Ber.* 9.1 (12d) re Gen. 1:26. For other examples of where a *direct* relationship with God makes one his *shuttaf*, see B. *Ber.* 63a re Job 22:25; B. *Shab.* 119b re Gen. 2:1; *MRE* 321.

167 See Deut. 18:10–12; B. *San.* 65b.

168 Quoted in Taubes, *Otzar ha-Geonim: Sanhedrin*, 389. See *Ibn Ezra* to Ex. 20:20; also *Targum* to Cant. 1:7.

169 Quoted in *Franz Rosenzweig: His Life and Thought*, 2nd rev. edn., trans. N. Glatzer (New York, 1961), 346–347. See also *Judaism despite Christianity*, trans. D. Emmet and E. Rosenstock-Huessey (New York, 1971), 113.

170 Ibid., 341. See *Zohar*, ed. Pinchas, 237b re Ex. 35:1, 5.

171 B. *Yoma* 52a. For the notion that Israel does not need angelic intermediaries, see *SR* 23.7; also B. *Sot.* 33a and *Rashi*, s.v. *yahid* re Job 36:5.

172 See comment to M. *AZ* 1.1, 2.4, 4.7; *MN* 2.33, 3.29, 37, 45.

173 See *LTJ* 1:136 ff., 2:7 ff., 28 ff., 40 ff., 163.

174 Maimonides, in his introduction to *Moreh Nevukim*, indicates that he is writing this treatise as the "science of the Law in its true sense" (trans. S. Pines, Chicago, 1963, 5). Written for the "religious man" who has "studied the sciences of the philosophers and come to know what they signify." Clearly, then, philosophy causes religious persons to reason philosophically about the Torah. Methodologically, such a person is a philosopher (see e.g. 3.10). However, if philosophy determines its object to be only what is immediately and universally accessible to reason and the senses, precluding biblical prophecy (see 2.32), then such a religious person is not a philosopher. The philosophical meaning of Maimonides' theological analyses is not to be rejected just because he himself did not claim to be a philosopher in the more specific sense of that name in his day (others did—see Gersonides, *Milhamot ha-Shem*, 3.1), any more than Amos' utterances are not prophecy just because he claimed not to be a prophet in the sense that name was used in his own day (see Amos 7:14). See also L. Strauss, *Persecution and the Art of Writing* (Glencoe, IL, 1952), 42–43.

175 See *MN* 1.51 (beg.).

176 For the notion that Maimonides' philosophical speculation is a thing apart from his work as a halakhist and a theologian, see I. Husik, "The Philosophy of Maimonides," in *Maimonides Octocentennial Series* (New York, 1935), 4:4 ff.; Strauss, *Persecution*, 38 ff.; Gershom Scholem, *Major Trends in Jewish Mysticism* (New York, 1941), 28–29. For a critique of this whole line of interpretation, see D. Hartman, *Maimonides: Torah and Philosophic Quest* (Philadelphia, 1976), 20 ff. For a critique of Strauss, see J. Guttmann, *Philosophies of Judaism*, trans. D.S. Silverman (New York, 1964), 434, n. 125.

177 *SM*, pos. no. 7:37.

178 *Hellenism in Jewish Palestine*, 214.

179 See *SM*, intro., p. 3.

180 *Shevu.* 11.2.

181 *Hellenism*, 214–215.

182 B. *Shevu.* 35a–b. See *Shevu.* 12.3 and, esp., *Radbaz* thereto.

183 For another example of where Maimonides, although having to accept popular superstition that had been endorsed by earlier halakhah, nevertheless qualified it with a new definition, see *AZ* 11.11–12 re B. *San.* 101a and *Alfasi: San.*, ch. 11, end. Cf. *Tur: YD* 179 and, esp., Karo, *Bet Yosef* thereto.

184 Re inconsistent oaths, see B. *Hag.* 10a and *Rashi* thereto; B. *Ned.* 28a; *Shevu.* 6.1; B. *Eruv.* 64b, *Tos.*, s.v. *potehin*.

185 *Shevu.* 11.1.

186 See *AZ* 2.1. The Talmud faced the same problem re the veneration of the Temple. It used the same logic as Maimonides later used re oaths. See B. *Yev.* 6a–b and *Tos.*, s.v. *yakhol*; *Sifra*, Kedoshim, 90b; *SM*, pos. no. 21; *Bet ha-Behirah*, 7.1; *MN* 3.45.

187 *Teshuvot ha-Rambam*, 2, no. 148:726. For his negative view of contemporary Muslims, see *Igeret Teman*, ed. M. Rabinowitz (Jerusalem, 1960), chs. 1 and 4.

188 Ibid., no. 293:548–550 ala P. *Bik.* 1.4 (64a). See *Bik.* 4.3 and Rozanis, *Mishneh le-Melekh* thereto; *LTJ* 1:72 ff.

189 B. *Yev.* 22a and parallels.

199 M. *BM* 4,10; B. *San.* 94a.

191 *Teshuvot ha-Rambam*, 2:550.

192 For *beriyot* as denoting humanity in this context, see *Avot* 1.12.

193 *MN* 3.29, p. 515. Maimonides also understood the commandment of *Kiddush ha-Shem* to be the Jewish mission to proclaim monotheism. See *SM*, pos. no. 9.

194 See *Men.* 110a and *Rashi*, s.v. *v'et* ala the emendation of *Bach*, no. 2.

195 *Mel.* 9.1.

196 See Aristotle, *Metaphysics*, 1049b5 ff.; *MN* 1.55. See also Rambam *Millot ha-Higayon*, ed. L. Roth (Jerusalem, 1965), sect. 11, pp. 74 ff. See further *LTJ* 2:190, n. 14.

197 *Mel.* 8, end.

198 *AZ* beg.

199 Ibid., 1.2. For the prohibition of having images of the sun, moon and stars, see B. *AZ* 43a–b.

200 Over and above the arguments from heavenly motion that Maimonides derived from Aristotle, he also argued that the contingency of existence required an Absolute Being as its ultimate explanation. See *MN* 1.57 following Bahya ibn Pakudah, *Hovot ha-Levavot*, 1.5.

201 *AZ* 1.3.

202 *MN* 1.4–5. See Aristotle, *Metaphysics*, 1072a20 ff.

203 Ibid., 1.49 and 2.6 and 3.45. See *YT* 2.3.

204 Along these lines, see *MN* 2.6 and Aristotle, *Metaphysics*, 1074b1–15. Also, see Epstein, *Torah Temimah* to Deut. 4:6, also B. *Shab.* 75a.

205 Even in ancient times Abraham was portrayed as a philosopher. See Josephus, *Ant.*, 1.155–156; *BR* 64.4; *BaR* 14.7; Ginzberg, *Legends*, 5:210, n. 16. Cf. Hebrews 3:2.

206 See Guttman, *Philosophies of Judaism*, 157 ff.

207 *SM*, pos. no. 7.

208 See *YT* 1.7–9; *MN* 1.59.

209 *MN* 1.52. See *LTJ* 2:33 ff.

210 *MN* 1.58.

211 See F. Bamberger, *Das System des Maimonides* (Berlin, 1935), 34.

212 See *MN* 3.32.

213 See *Tesh.* 3.7. Cf. note of Rabad thereto. See *MN* 1.35.

214 See *AZ* 11.16. For Maimonides' view of the essential universality of truth, see e.g. *Kiddush ha-Hodesh*, 17.24.

215 *SM*, pos. no. 7.

216 *MN* 1.58, p. 131. See *Millot ha-Higayon*, sect. 13. Note the critique of Aquinas, *Summa Theologiae*, 1, q. 13, a. 5 and *LTJ* 2:36–37.

217 See Loewe, "Potentialities and Limitations of Universalism in the Halakhah," 140.

218 For Maimonides' official approval of Ibn Tibbon's translation of *MN*, see the latter's introduction thereto.

219 See *MN* 3.27. Cf. e.g. *The Metaphysics of Avicenna: A Critical Translation-Commentary*, ed. P. Morewidge (New York, 1973), 151–152.

220 Comment to M. *AZ* 4.7.

221 Ibid., ed. J. Kappah (Jerusalem, 1965), 239.

222 *AZ* 1.3. See *MN* 2.39, 3.29.

223 Comment to M. *AZ* 4.7.

224 *YT* 5.1. See *MN* 2.33.

CHAPTER 5. The Law of Homicide

1 See the commentary of *Shadal* thereto, 25. *Targum Yerushalmi* renders *al ha-adam* as *yat adom*; LXX renders it *tō Adam*. The Targum of *Onkelos* and *Pseudo-Jonathan* translate it as *al adam*, although this might be reflecting the rabbinic exegesis of these words. See *LTJ* 2:115, 204, n. 82. (On 115 there I indicated erroneously that all the Targumim render the phrase *yat Adam*.)

2 B. *San.* 56b. Note the translation of Buber and Rosenzweig: "Er, Gott, begot *über den Menschen* ..." (*Die fünf Bücher der Weisung*, Cologne, 1954, 13).

3 For the whole problem of determining whether a scriptural commandment is historically limited (*le-she'ah*) or not (*le-dorot*), see *SM, shoresh* 3.

4 *De Decalogo*, 170, trans. F.H. Colson (Cambridge, MA, 1937), 90–91. The designation of a social institution as both "necessary" and "useful" seems to follow Aristotle, *Politics*, 1254a20. Cf. *Avot* 3.2.

5 Ibid., 132, pp. 72–73. Cf. Aristotle, *Politics*, 1253a1.

6 *RSN* 4.9. For discussion of which is worse, murder or idolatry, see P. *San.* 8.8 and 9 (26c).

7 *De Decalogo*, 133–134, pp. 72–73.

8 *Republic*, 501B. See Wolfson, *Philo*, 1:112–113 and D. Novak, *Suicide and Morality* (New York, 1975), 28 ff.

9 *Laws*, 871D.

10 *BR* 34.14, p. 326. See *Mekh.*, Yitro, 233 and D. Novak, "Judaism and Contemporary Bioethics," *Journal of Medicine and Philosophy* (Dec. 1979), 4.4:361 ff. Cf. B. *Yev.* 61a re Ezek. 34:31 and *Tos.*, s.v. *kivray* and *ayn*.

11 *Avot* 3.14.

12 For the social emphasis, see e.g. P. *Ber.* 1.5 (3c) re Deut. 11:17; Saadiah, *Emunot ve De'ot*, 3.2; Halevi, *Kuzari*, 3.11; *Hinukh*, no. 34. For the theological emphasis, see *Zohar*, Yitro, 90a.

13 B. *BK* 15a.

14 According to T. *BK* 4.2 *tam* and *mu'ad* law is only for Jews.

15 See M. *Neg.* 12.5; also, R. Moses di Trani, *Bet Elohim* (Venice, 1576), *sha-ar ha-yesodot*, ch. 27.

16 See Amos 3:2; B. *Yev.* 22a.

17 See M. *BM* 7.1; M. *Ket.* 6.4; B. *Yev.* 89b, bot.; B. *Ber.* 19b, bot.

18 See B. *San.* 8a, bot.; B. *BK* 84b; *San.* 5.8–9.

19 B. *San.* 57a; *BR* 18.5 re Gen. 2:24, p. 167, Venice edn. (1545).

20 See B. *San.* 10a, bot., and *Rashi*, s.v. *malkot*; also, T. *Shevu.* 4.6.

21 Note: "... even when the Rabbis altered a law they never abrogated it. They retained *the integrity of the law*. By integrity I mean partial applicability ... that was necessary not to impugn the *Lawgiver* with a lack of moral sensitivity which may undermine not only this law, but laws in general." D. Weiss Halivni, "Can a Religious Law be Immoral?", in *Perspectives on Jews and Judaism: Essays in Honor of Wolfe Kelman* (New York, 1978), 166–167.

22 R. Gordis, "A Dynamic Halakhah: Principles and Procedures of Jewish Law," *Judaism* (Summer 1979), 28.3:273. Cf. B. *San.* 71a.

23 There are two views of when exactly the Romans removed this power from Jewish courts. The first, and most accepted, view is that this power was removed 40 years prior to the destruction of the Second Temple. See P. *San.* 1.1 (18a), 7.2 (24b); B. *San.* 41a; B. *AZ* 8b. For the apparent corroboration of this, see John 18:31 and R. Brown, *The Anchor Bible: The Gospel According to John xiii–xxi* (Garden City, NY, 1970), 849–850; also, A.N. Sherwin-White, *Roman Society and Roman Law in the New Testament* (Oxford, 1963), 36–37. The second view is that this power was only removed when the Temple was destroyed. See T. *San.* 9.11; B. *San.* 52b; B. *Ket.* 30a–b. For the attempt to reconcile these two views, see B. *AZ* 8b, Tos., s.v. *ela*; B. *Ket.* 30a, Tos., s.v. *me-yom*. However, the crucial point of all this speculation about capital punishment is that it was a theoretical exercise at the time it was being engaged in. The one eyewitness account of capital punishment in the Talmud, that of R. Eleazar b. Zadok (T. *San.* 9.11; P. *San.* 7.2 [24b]; B. *San.* 52b) was rejected because (1) testimony from a child's experience is not considered accurate, and (2) what he saw was considered to be a Sadducee practice. For substitutes for capital punishment after the power had been removed, see B. *San.* 27a, bot. and *SA: HM* 425, beg., and note of Isserles thereto; *Responsa Ribash*, no. 251. See also Haim H. Cohen, *The Trial and Death of Jesus* (New York, 1977), 31–32, 346–350, n. 43.

24 M. *Mak.* 1.10. Cf. B. *San.* 35a re Is. 1:21 and *Rashi* thereto; B. *San.* 42b and Rashi, s.v. *ki*. For other examples of R. Akiva's abhorrence of capital punishment, see *Sifra*, Kedoshim, 90a and B. *San.* 63a re Lev. 19:26.

25 B. *Mak.* 7a. For another example of R. Akiva's making a biblical law inoperable, see M. *Zab.* 2.2.

26 See B. *San.* 78a.

27 See B. *Mak.* 7a and Tos., s.v. *ke-makhol*; *RSN* 2.8 and *KM* thereto. For the use of probability in determining the cause of death, see e.g. M. *Git.* 7.3; T. *Git.* 5.2; P. *Git.* 7.4 (48d); B. *Git.* 73a and Tos., s.v. *m'ay*.

28 *Ant.*, 13.294, trans. R. Marcus (Cambridge, MA, 1943), 374–375. See 20.199 and Finkelstein, *The Pharisees*, 2.286 ff.

29 B. *BM* 83b. For the whole question of turning over guilty Jews to the Roman authorities, see T. *Ter.* 7.20; P. *Ter.* 8.4 (46b); *BR* 94, end; also, D. Daube, *Collaboration with Tyranny in Rabbinic Law* (Oxford, 1965) and E.J. Schochet, *A Responsum of Surrender* (Los Angeles, 1973).

30 *Meiri*, 332. See Maimonides, *Hovel u-Mazik*, 8.9. This was no doubt why the rabbis refused to locate a biblical prohibition for murdering a gentile. See T. *San.* 8.5; B. *San.* 57a; P. *AZ* 2.2 (40d).

31 See T. *Yev.* 14.7; B. *Yev.* 25b (cf. T. *Yev.* 4.5; P. *Yev.* 2.11 [4b]) and B. *Git.* 28b. Cf. B. *BK* 114a.

32 See T. *San.* 12.3 and 14.3; B. *BK* 90b re Ex. 21:18; B. *San.* 51b re Lev. 21:9. Re R. Akiva's consistency irrespective of the practical results, see e.g. M. *Naz.* 7.4; B. *Kid.* 68a; *Men.* 89a and parallels. Re R. Akiva's exegetical approach, see *BR* 1.14 and 22.2 re Deut. 32:47; Finkelstein, *Akiva*, 171 ff. For the general question of consistency in halakhic approach, see T. *Suk.* 2.3 and parallels; B. *Eruv.* 7a and parallels.

33 See M. *Ket.* 9.2. Cf. T. *San.* 7.5.

34 See e.g. M. *Sot.* 8.5 re Deut. 20:8; T. *Sot.* 7.22; B. *Sot.* 44a; *Mel.* 7.15; D. Halivni, *Mekorot u-Mesorot: Nashim* (Tel Aviv, 1968), 473.

35 B. *Mak.* 5b.

36 For the close relation between lashes and the death penalty, see B. *San.* 10a, bot., *Rashi*, s.v. *malkot*.

37 T. *San.* 11.1.

38 See B. *Betz.* 19a and *Hul.* 13b.

39 B. *San.* 72b re Ex. 22:1. See *LTJ* 1:132–135.

40 P. *San.* 5.1 (22c). See *ET* 11, s.v. *hatra'ah*.

41 See e.g. B. *Pes.* 112a, bot.

42 See Weiss, *Dor Dor ve-Dorshav*, 1:142–143 and 2:23; Finkelstein, *The Pharisees*, 1:286 ff. Cf. B. *RH* 21b re Deut. 17:6; B. *Git.* 17b and *Tos.*, s.v. *zenut*.

43 See P. *San.* 6.3 (23b, bot.).

44 See *Mekh.*, Mishpatim, 327 and note thereon; B. *San.* 37a; P. *San.* 4.9 (22b); P. *Sot.* 3.4 (19a, top). Also, see *Avot* 1.9; T. *San.* 6.6; Tchernowitz, *Toldot ha-Halakhah*, 4:173–174; Finkelstein, *The Pharisees*, 2:67, n. 76.

45 B. *San.* 54b and parallels. Cf. B. *Yev.* 3b, bot.

46 Punishments are not inferred from the text of Scripture but must be explicitly prescribed. See B. *San.* 54a and parallels.

47 *Tam.* 1.4. See Lipschuetz, *Tiferet Yisrael* thereto.

48 For the notion of witnesses as surrogates for the whole people, see S. Atlas, *Netivim*, 246–247, and D. Novak, "Annulment in Lieu of Divorce in Jewish Law," *The Jewish Law Annual* (1981), 4:190. For this reason, perhaps, in most cases when a Jew was condemned to death all lesser charges against him were dropped (M. *Ket.* 3.2; B. *BK* 22b), viz., the attention of the whole people was to be directed to ridding their society of the murdered as an act of public atonement (*kapparah*—see Deut. 21:8; also, M. *San.* 11.4 re Deut. 17:3). Since the execution of a Noahide criminal was a matter of justice, devoid of these sacral connotations, this rule was not considered to pertain to him. See B. *Eruv.* 62a., *Tos.*, s.v. *ben Noah* ala B. *BK* 114a. Cf. Sherwin-White, *Roman Society and Roman Law in the New Testament*, 35.

49 For the preclusion of *hatra'ah* for gentiles, see B. *San.* 57b re Gen. 9:5; *BR* 52.5 re Gen. 20:3 and 52.10 re Gen. 20:7.

50 M. *Mak.* 2.3.

51 B. *Mak.* 9a.

52 This seems to be the point of Issi b. Akiva, that after the giving of the Torah the law of homicide became more lenient for Jews (*tahat she-huhmaru hekalu*). *Mekh.*, Mishpatim, 263. Here the verse being interpreted is Ex. 21:14 that prescribes death for

premeditated murder, which the preceding text in *Mekh.* interprets as a limitation (*lehotz'i et shogeg*).

53 B. *Mak.* 9a–b.

54 M. *BK* 2.6.

55 *RSN* 5.4.

56 *Mel.* 10.1.

57 *Lehem Mishnah* thereto.

58 B. *Mak.* 9a, *Rashi*, s.v. *lefikhakh* re B. *San.* 57a (for this type of analogy, see *Hul.* 17a). See B. *Yev.* 47b and *Rashi*, s.v. *u'modi'een*; also, *Meiri* to B. *San.* 56b, 224.

59 Ibid., s.v. *d'omer.*

60 T. *Sot.* 8.6, ed. Lieberman, 205. See *supra*, 40–41.

61 B. *Sot.* 35b.

62 B. *BK* 92a. See B. *Sot.* 10a re Gen. 38:14 and *BR* 85.14. For the notion of prophets being provided for the gentiles to teach them morality, see *BaR* 14.34.

63 B. *Hor.* 4b.

64 See B. *San.* 33b. For the notion that the Written Torah is available to all, see B. *Ber.* 8a, bot.

65 See M. *Hor.* 1.3 and Maimonides, *Shegagot*, 14.2.

66 B. *San.* 8b, bot. See T. *Mak.* 2.10; B. *Kid.* 55b–56a; B. *San.* 40b and *Tos.*, s.v. *minayyin*; *BR* 19.1 and Zundel, *Etz Yosef* thereto ala *Avot* 4.13: *KR* 1.39; Urbach, *Hazal*, 525.

67 Ibid., s.v. *ela.*

68 *San.* 12.2. See *IB* 1.3 and *MM* thereto. Cf. B. *Hor.* 3b.

69 Ibid., *MM* thereto.

70 See *infra*, 203–205.

71 *Israël et l'humanité* (Paris, 1914), 688: " . . . cette excuse n'est point admise pour le Noahide dont la loi éminément exclusivement rationelle s'impose d'elle-même à la conscience humaine." See Atlas, *Netivim*, 2.

72 B. *San.* 57b. See P. *Kid.* 1.1 (58c); *Tan.*, Shoftim, beg., ed. Buber, 14b and Ki Tetz'e, 10, 20a–b; *PRK*, Zakhor, 45. In this latter text self-incrimination is also mentioned as sufficient for executing a Noahide. *Mel.* 9.14 does not codify this view, but it is brought in *Hinukh*, nos. 26 and 192. See A. Kirschenbaum, *Self-Incrimination in Jewish Law* (New York, 1970), 62 ff., 96–99. Cf. *Meiri* to B. *San.* 56b, p. 224 and n. 8 thereon. For the differences in Persian law, see B. *BK* 113b–114a and *Meiri* thereto, 332. For other consequences of the more lenient gentile law of testimony, see e.g. B. *BK* 114a and *GA* 6.3.

73 A. Schmiedl, "Comparisons between Roman and Talmudic Law" (Heb.), *Ha-Schachar* (1880), 10:52 ff. On p. 53 Schmiedl notes that required *hatra'ah* corresponds to the Roman rule, "constitutiones principium nec ignorare nec dissimulare permittimus." See also T. Mommsen, *Römisches Strafrecht* (Berlin, 1955), 401 ff.

74 *BR* 34.14, p. 325.

75 B. *Kid.* 43a. See M. Greenberg, "Rabbinic Reflections on Defying Illegal Orders: Amasa, Abner and Joab," *Judaism* (Winter 1970), 19.1:30–37.

76 B. *Kid.*, 42b. See B. *BK* 60a; B. *BM* 10b and *Tos.*, s.v. *ishah*; B. *San.* 29a, bot.

77 M. *Ber.* 5.5.

78 See *Dor Dor ve-Dorshav*, 1:142; Finkelstein, *The Pharisees*, 2:685, n. 6.

79 B. *San.* 19a–b. See S.B. Hoenig, *The Great Sanhedrin* (Philadelphia, 1953), 186; Atlas, *Netivim*, 156 ff.

80 M. *San.* 2.2. For the reported courage of Simon b. Shetah in the face of Hasmonean power, see B. *Kid.* 66a, bot.

81 *Bellum Judaicum*, 1.209–211, trans. H. St. John Thackeray (Cambridge, MA, 1927), 96–99.

82 *Ant.*, 14.167, pp. 540–543. For Sammaias' refusal to fear Herod, see ibid., 15.2–4, 307. See also Abravanel's comment to II Sam. 12.

83 *Jewish and Roman Law*, 2:599. See also Aristotle, *Nicomachean Ethics*, 1136b30.

84 Note e.g. H.H. Cohn and L.I. Rabinowitz in *EJ*, 5:147a, "the whole tendency of the rabbis was toward the complete abolition of the death penalty."

85 M. *Mak.* 1.10. See Saadiah, *Emunot ve-De'ot*, 4.2 and *Hinukh*, no. 77.

86 B. *Mak.* 7a.

87 B. *San.* 53a re Num. 35:21.

88 P. *Sot.* 9.6 (23d).

89 M. *Sot.* 9.9.

90 P. *Sot.* 9.9 (24a); B. *Sot.* 47b. Actually the plain meaning of this verse is that the man is innocent of causing his wife's punishment if she is guilty of infidelity (*Rashi, Rashbam*), or of even causing her humiliation if she is innocent (*Sforno*).

91 See *LTJ* 1:158, n. 8.

92 See comment to Num. 5:31, ed. Chavel, 3:26.

93 M. *San.* 6.4; P. *San.* 6.6 (23c, bot.).

94 B. *San.* 46a (and B. *Yev.* 90b ala *Avot* 1.1) according to *Rashi* and Abulafia, *Yad Ramah* thereto. Maimonides (*RSN* 2.4–5) and *Meiri*, 197, consider the power of the court to be parallel to royal power to execute those who violate his decrees. The examples of the use of this extraordinary power by the court are for violations of rabbinic laws. Re royal prerogatives in capital punishment, see B. *Kid.* 43a re II Sam. 11:11 and *Rashi* and *Tos.*, s.v. *mored*; B. *San.* 49a re Josh. 1:18; B. *Meg.* 15a, top. Re the notion that violation of rabbinic laws deserves death, see P. *Ber.* 1.3 (3b) re Ecc. 10:8; B. *Ber.* 4b, top, and L. Ginzberg, *Peirushim ve-Hiddushim be-Yerushalmi: Ber.* 1:150.

95 Capital punishment is a general power of society to be applied or not applied as the authorities see fit. See Hugo Grotius, *De Jure Belli ac Pacis*, 2.5. Note: "c'est là un maximum dont la société dispose pour se défendre dans les cas ou elle le jugerait nécessaire, mais il n'y faut pas voir le châtiment applicable indistinctement dans toutes les circonstances . . . " Benamozegh, *Israël et l'humanité*, 702. See B. *San.* 58b re Ex. 2:12; *Mel.* 10.6 and *KM* thereto, and, especially, *Meiri*, 228; also, Atlas, *Netivim*, 32–33. S. Federbush, *Mishpat ha-Melukhah be-Yisrael*, 2nd rev. edn. (Jerusalem, 1973), 44 ff.

96 M. *San.* 9.5.

97 B. *San.* 81b. See B. *Yoma* 66b; *Mel.* 3.10; *MN* 3.40. For the elimination of *hatra'ah* in the case of mass idolatry, see M. *San.* 10.4. Cf. *AZ* 4.6, however, for quasi-*hatra'ah*.

98 *RSN* 4.9.

99 *San.* 20.4. See M. *San.* 4, end. Re greater latitude for the execution of murderers, as opposed to those guilty of other capital crimes, see B. *San.* 45b re Num. 35:17 and *San.* 13.7.

100 See *KR* 7.33 and *Ramban* to Deut. 19:13.

101 *Bet Yosef* to *Tur. HM* 2. See *Responsa Rashba*, 3, no. 393.4, no. 311 and *Responsa Rashba Attributed to Ramban* (Warsaw, 1883), no. 279. The notion that judicial authority had to respond to the situation of a particular place and time is pre-Toraitic was invoked by R. Moses Schreiber to justify contemporary judicial authority independent of specific statute. See *Responsa Hatam Sofer, OH*, no. 208 (last page).

102 *Git.* 4:2.

103 B. *BM* 30b. For the question of using an *aggadah* as a halakhic precedent, see *LTJ* 2:71–72.

104 See B. *BK* 99b–100a; B. *BM* 24b; also, B. *Ber.* 7a re Is. 56:7.

105 Ibn Adret also permits Jewish judges, appointed by gentile kings, to exercise capital punishment to Jews under their jurisdiction in case of "great need and with deliberation." He bases this on the legal power of kingship, a power recognized by Jewish law even when some of the king's Jewish subjects are adversely affected. See *Responsa Rashba*, 2, no. 290; 5, nos. 338, 343, 345.

106 B. *San.* 57b. "Another view is that this extension of the Noachidic laws was intended, on the contrary, as a protest against the widespread Roman practice of abortion and infanticide." I. Jakobovits, *Jewish Medical Ethics* (New York, 1959), 181. This is based on Weiss, *Dor Dor ve-Dorshav*, 2:22. The plain meaning of the verse is, "whosoever sheds human blood, *by* humans shall his blood be shed." See *Targum Onkelos* and *Rabbenu Bahya* thereto. Cf. LXX to Ex. 21:22 and Josephus, *Contra Apionem*, 2.202.

107 *Mel.* 9.4. See *SM, shoresh* 3.

108 M. *Ohol.* 7.6; *Mekh.*, Mishpatim, 276; B. *Ket.* 36b; B. *BK* 43a re Ex. 21:22; Josephus, *Ant.*, 4.278, 290.

109 B. *San.* 59a.

110 Ibid., *Tos.*, s.v. *leyka*. Cf. *Hul.* 33a, *Tos.*, s.v. *ehad* and P. *Shab.* 14.4 (14d); P. *AZ* 2.2 (40d).

111 *YT* 5.7. re M. *Ohol.* 7.6.

112 B. *San.* 80b and *Tos.*, s.v. *ubar*.

113 B. *BK* 91a and *SM*, neg. no. 57.

114 *Responsa Havot Yair* (Lemberg, 1896), no. 31. Cf., however, R. Jacob Emden, *Responsa Yabetz* (Lemberg, 1884), 1, no. 43.

115 *Responsa Noda bi-Yehuda* (Vilna, 1904), *HM* 2, no. 59. Cf. R. Yom Tov Lipmann Heller, *Tosafot Yom Tov* to M. *Nid.* 5.3. For further discussion of abortion, see D.M. Feldman, *Birth Control and Jewish Law* (New York, 1968), 284–294; J.D. Bleich, *Contemporary Halakhic Problems* (New York, 1977), 325 ff.; *LTJ* 1:114 ff.; Novak, "Judaism and Contemporary Bioethics," 355–357.

CHAPTER 6. The Law of Sexual Relations

1 B. *San.* 56b. Re sexual misconduct as the grounds for divorce, see Deut. 24:1; M. *Git.* 9.10; *LTJ* 2:6 ff.

2 *De Spec. Leg.* 3.14–15: 482–483. See Plato, *Laws* 838B–C; also, S.D. Luzzatto, *Yesodai ha-Torah*, no. 43, ed. A.Z. Eshkoli (Jerusalem, 1947), p. 53.

3 *De Spec. Leg.* 3.25–26, pp. 488–489. Cf. Augustine, *De Civitate Dei* 15.16; Freud, *Collected Papers*, trans. J. Strachey (London, 1950–52), 4:205–206.

4   *De Spec. Leg.* 3.29.

5   See Plato, *Timaeus* 29E and *Republic* 532B–533D; A.J. Lovejoy, *The Great Chain of Being* (New York, 1960), 24–66; Novak, *Suicide and Morality*, 33–34

6   T. *AZ* 8.4, p. 473; B. *San.* 57b. See *Tos.*, s.v. *ve-hakhamin*. Cf. B. *San.* 59a.

7   B. *San.* 58b; P. *Kid.* 1.1 (58b–c).

8   See M. *Ket.* 1.5; T. *Ket.* 1.4; B. *Ket.* 12a. Cf. P. *Ket.* 1.5 (25c).

9   *Sifra*, Aharai-Mot, p. 85b; B. *San.* 57b.

10 B. *San.* 58a.

11 *Mel.* 9.6.

12 The Canon Law, also, makes a similar recognition; e.g. "lex huius modi naturalis modificata est per ordinem discreti et honesti moris . . . " *Die Summa Decretorum des Magister Rufinus*, ed. H. Singer (Paderborn, 1902), 7.

13 B. *Yev.* 22a. See *SH*, no. 691. For the earlier Tannaitic view of conversion as rebirth, see P. *Bik.* 1.4 (64a) re Gen. 17:5; *LTJ* 1:72 ff.

14 P. *Yev.* 11.2 (12a). See B. *Yev.* 97b–98a. For the similar Roman law, see Cohen, *Jewish and Roman Law*, 1:281.

15 *BR* 18.5

16 P. *Yev.* 11.1 (11d). Cf. P. *San.* 5.1 (22c) and *PM* thereto. For *re'iyah* as possession rather than mere right, see e.g. B. *Pes.* 5b re Ex. 13:7.

17 See *Rashbam* to Lev. 20:17.

18 B. *San.* 58b. See *Tos.*, s.v. *mipnei*; also, *Teshuvot ha-Rambam*, no. 111 and *Shakh* to *SA*: *YD* 269.1.

19 *BR* 22.1. See note of Albeck on 205.

20 For a certain tolerance of quasi-incest, see B. *Yev.* 62b–63a; B. *San.* 76b re Is. 58.7; Maimonides, *IB* 2.4 and *MM* thereto; B. *Git.* 17a.

21 B. *Hor.* 10b re Hos. 14:10. See B. *Naz.* 23b re Pr. 18:1.

22 B. *Yev.* 22a.

23 *IB* 14.12.

24 B. *San.* 103b. See B. *BB* 115b re Gen. 36:24.

25 B. *Yoma* 69b; B. *San.* 64a. Cf. B. *Sot.* 47a and B. *Kid.* 81b. See Feldman, *Birth Control in Jewish Law*, 88.

26 See Sophocles, *Oedipus Rex*, 1270–1274.

27 M. *Git.* 4.5 and M. *Edu.* 1.13. See B. *Git.* 43b and P. *Git.* 4.5 (46a).

28 B. *Git.* 42a, top.

29 *Jewish and Roman Law*, 1:28, n. 97.

30 M. *Yev.* 6.6.

31 B. *Yev.* 61b–62a.

32 Ibid., 62a.

33 See B. *BK* 15a, top, and Halivni, *Mekorot u-Mesorot: Nashim*, 70.

34 See Maimonides, *Avadim* 14.17, 19.

35 P. *Yev.* 2.6 (4a)

36 Along the lines of the refusal to totally deny gentile familial lines, see B. *San.* 52b re Lev. 20:10 and *Rashi*, s.v. *ahereim* and *Tos.*, s.v. *perat*; B. *Sot.* 26b and *Tos.*, s.v. *yatza*; B. *Kid.* 21b, *Tos.*, s.v. *eshet*; B. *AZ* 36b; Maimonides, *IB* 12.1–4 and *Mel.* 8.3.

37 *IB* 15.6. See *MM* thereto; Rosh (*Yev.*, ch. 6, no. 8 and Weil, *Korban Nathaniel* thereto);
    Meiri, 228—all follow Maimonides. *Contra* Maimonides, see *Bek.* 47a; B. *Yev.* 62a,
    Rashi, s.v. *bnai Noah* and *Tos.*, s.vv. *R. Johanan, bnei*; B. *Hag.* 2b, *Tos.*, s.v. *l'o*; *SA: EH* 1.7
    and Ashkenazi, *Be'er Haytev* thereto.

38 B. *San.* 59b. See *Tos.*, s.v. *ve-ha.*

39 See *Alfasi* to B. *Yev.* 62a, Vilna edn., 19b.

40 See *supra*, 36–38.

41 *Ishut* 1.1. See *MN* 3.49.

42 *Ishut* 1.4.

43 See note to ibid. and note to Maimonides, *Na'arah Betulah* 2.17 (and *KM* thereto); also,
    Responsa Rashba 3, no. 371. Cf. *Mel.* 4.

44 P. *Kid.* 1.1 (58c). See *BR* 18.5, p. 166 and Albeck's note thereon. Cf. P. *BB* 8.1 (16a, top).

45 See *KE* thereto, s.v. *she-lo.* For the Christian rejection of divorce, see Mark 10:11–12;
    Matt. 5:31–32 and 19:9; I Cor. 7:11 ff. Cf. *LTJ* 1:6 ff.

46 See *LTJ* 1:31 ff.

47 For theoretical halakha as opposed to practical, see *ET* 9:339–340.

48 *Seridai Esh: EH* (Jerusalem, 1966), no. 22, 46–47.

49 *Mel.* 9.8.

50 See *infra*, 209–211.

51 For the subsequent Orthodox hostility to Mendelssohn, see e.g. R. Moses Schreiber,
    Responsa Hatam Sofer: YD, no. 338.

52 *LTJ* 1:159, no. 26.

53 See *Teshuvot ha-Rambam*, no. 105:158–159 and *KM* to Maimonides, *Ishut*, 1.4; R. David
    Hoffmann, *Responsa Melamed le-Ho'il* (Frankfurt am Main, 1926), 3, no. 8. The
    question of whether two Jews married according to Noahide law was discussed by R.
    Isaac bar Sheshet Parfat, who ruled that this Noahide status only applies to non-Jews
    (*Responsa Ribash*, no.6). He cites, among others, Rabad on concubinage. Nevertheless,
    Ribash dealt with Jews married in a Christian ceremony. Following extensive analysis
    one could apply his conclusion to civil marriage as well, but he himself obviously was
    unaware of such a peculiarly modern possibility.

54 See Novak, "Annulment in Lieu of Divorce in Jewish Law," 189.

55 *Book of Beliefs and Opinions* 3.2, trans. S. Rosenblatt (New Haven, 1948), 141. See
    Nahmanides to Gen. 2:24.

56 See Maimonides, *Na'arah Betulah* 2.17 and *MN* 3.49; *LTJ* 2:198, nn. 154 ff.

57 B. *San.* 57b–58a.

58 B. *Kid.* 31a; P. *PE* 1.1 (15c). See Yellin, *Yefeh Aynayim* to B. *Kid.* 31a, for further parallels.

59 See e.g. *Tan.*, Kedoshim, no. 15; Ginzberg, *Legends*, 5:278, n. 51.

60 See B. *Shab.* 146a and parallels.

61 See *supra*, 1.

62 B. *Eruv.* 18a. See B. *Ber.* 61b re Ps. 139:5; B. *Meg.* 9a; B. *Ket.* 8a; B. *San.* 38b, top, Rashi.

63 *MT* 139.5:265a. See *BR* 8.1; 18.2; 22.2; P. *Ber.* 9.1 (12a); B. *Shab.* 95a; *PRE*, ch. 22;
    Ginzberg, *Legends*, 5:90, n. 48.

64 See K.L. Moore, *The Developing Human*, 2nd edn. (Philadelphia, 1977), 288 ff.

65 *Symposium* 191D–192B.

66 Cf. the use of term *sitra ahra* in the kabbalistic literature for the feminine aspect of being. See Gershom Scholem, *Kabbalah and its Symbolism*, trans. R. Manheim (New York, 1965), 157. My use of the term "other side" does not connote the demonic aspects of the kabbalistic use.

67 B. *San.* 58a, Rashi, s.v. *ve-devak*.

68 Even between heterosexual partners it was often considered degrading. See e.g. *BR* 80.5 re Gen. 34:2.

69 See *Hinukh*, no. 29.

70 *BR* 50.5; *Tan.*, Va-yera, no. 12.

71 See T. *San.* 13.8.

72 M. *AZ* 2.1.

73 T. *AZ* 3.2, p. 463.

74 B. *Ned.* 51a.

75 *Torah Temimah* to Lev. 18:22.

76 M. *Kid.* 4.14; B. *Kid.* 82a; P. *Kid.* 4.11 (66c).

77 *SA: EH* 24.1; *Bach* to *Tur: EH* 24. Cf. B. *Kid.* 80a where the Amora, R. Judah, indicates that the dispensations of the sages only apply to *kesherim*. Re Christian sexual mores affecting those of Jews, see *SH*, no. 1101.

78 B. *Yev.* 76a.

79 Ibid., s.v. *ha-mesollelot*. See also B. *Shab.* 65a, Rashi, s.v. *gane'an*; Karo, *Bet Yosef* to *Tur: EH* 20.

80 *IB* 21.8. See *Rambam* to M. *San.* 7.4

81 Aharai-Mot, 86a. See B. *San.* 54b re I Kgs 14:24.

82 *VR* 23.9.

83 See Kohut, *Arukh Completum*, 2:311; also, *BR* 26.5.

84 *Hul.* 92a–b.

85 *Lives of the Caesars* 4.28.

86 See C. Albeck, *Mav'o le-Talmudim* (Tel Aviv, 1969), 302–304.

87 B. *San.* 58a.

88 B. *San.* 105b re I Kgs 1:2. The whole motif of seeing Balaam's sins as sexual (e.g. *VR* 1.13 re Deut. 23:11) comes from the fact that the Torah (Num. 31:16) mentions Balaam as the instigator of the seduction of the Israelite men by the Midianite women at Ba'al Peor (Num. 25:1 ff.). Re Balaam, see B. *San.* 106a–b; P. *San.* 10.2 (28d).

89 B. *Yev.* 63a.

90 See *BR* 18.4; *LTJ* 2:13–14.

CHAPTER 7. The Law of Robbery

1 *Supra*, 34. For another exegetical attempt to derive the prohibition of *gezel* from a specific verse, see B. *San.* 57a re Gen. 9:3.

2 *Emunot ve-De'ot*, 3.2, pp. 141–142. Much the same argument was put forth by Kant, *The Fundamental Principle of the Metaphysics of Morals*, 2.4, trans. T.K. Abbot (New York, 1948), 40.

3 *Supra*, 41–45.

4 T. *AZ* 8.5, p. 473; B. *San.* 57a.

5 B. *San.* 86a re Lev. 19:11; B. 111a re Lev. 19:13.

6 *Supra*, 254, n. 41.

7 *Supra*, 43–44.

8 *Supra*, 195–199.

9 B. *San.* 57a; *Mel.* 9.9.

10 See *supra*, 271, n. 20.

11 B. *San.* 59a.

12 See e.g. M. *Kid.* 1.1 and B. *Kid.* 3a–b, 11a–b.

13 B. *San.* 57a.

14 See *Hul.* 33a.

15 Deut. 21:10 ff. For the qualifications and justifications of this privilege, see *Sifre*, Devarim, nos. 211 ff.; B. *Kid.* 21b–22a.

16 See *supra*, 98–100.

17 *Supra*, 78–80., and *infra*, 195–199.

18 P. *BM* 4.2 (9c).

19 *BR* 31.5, pp. 279–280.

20 B. *San.* 57a.

21 M. *San.* 11.1.

22 B. *San.* 85b. See *GA* 9.2 and *LTJ* 2:87 ff.

23 *Etz Yosef* to *BR* 31.5.

24 *De Decalogo*, 137, trans. F.H. Colson (Cambridge, MA, 1937), 74–75.

25 B. *Yev.* 79a. See P. *Kid.* 4.1 (65c).

26 *Tesh.* 2.10 ala *Avot* 5.11. See M. *BK* 8.7 re Gen. 20:7, 17; *Hinukh*, no. 130.

27 B. *San.* 59a, s.v. *mishum* ala B. *Yoma* 87b. Note how the same mercenary image was projected on Jews by medieval Christians. *Shylock*: "I hate him for he is a Christian; but more for that in low simplicity he lends out money gratis, and brings down the rate of usance here with us in Venice." *The Merchant of Venice*, 1.2. in Shakespeare, *Complete Works*, ed. W.J. Craig (London, 1945), 195. See *supra*, 256, n. 98.

28 B. *Yev.* 47a.

29 Ibid., 47b.

30 Ibid., s.v. *u-modee'in*. See B. *San.* 57a, *Rashi*, s.v. *tza'ara* re Lev. 19:13 and 5:23; also, *ET* 5:487 ff.

31 Ibid., s.v. *ve-lo* ala B. *San.* 57a. In the commentary, *Tosafot Yeshenim* (roughly contemporaneous with Rashi), the reason given for so informing the would-be convert is that because of his love of money he might return to his old gentile ways and not fulfill his new Jewish charity obligations (cf. B. *Kid.* 17a, bot.). Similarly, see *Meiri*, 189.

32 B. *San.* 57a, s.v. *yisrael*. Although there is no direct rabbinic precedent for this, to my knowledge, Rashi's emphasis that *re'a* means "fellow Jew" has precedence. See e.g. M. *BK* 4.3 re Ex. 21:35 (cf. M. *BK* 1.2); M. *San.* 9.1–2; *infra*, 301, n. 46.

33 B. *Yev.* 47b, s.v. *u-modee'in*. There *Tosafot Yeshenim* writes: " . . . *as they do in their* law."

34 *Netivim*, 33.

35 *Mel.* 9.1. For the notion that *she'urin* are specifically determined by Jewish tradition, see B. *Yoma* 80a.

36   See *infra*, 227–228.

37   *Netivim*, 33–34.

38   Ibid., 35–37.

39   Ibid., 37. This should be compared with the rabbinic view that Noahides can only offer whole burnt offerings (*olot*), but not peace offerings (*shelamim*), i.e., those offerings eaten in fellowship. See *Zev.* 116a and *Sifra*, Vayikra, 13a re Lev. 3:1. For the notion that a breakdown of covenantal mutuality caused the rabbis to reinstitute harsher Noahide standards, see R. Samson Raphael Hirsch, *Commentary to the Pentateuch*: Lev. 25:14 (3.2:747) re B. *BM* 47b and *Bek.* 13b.

40   See *Netivim*, 1–2.

41   See B. *BM* 21a–b.

42   B. *BM* 22b. See *GA* 15.16.

43   Ibid., s.v. *yatmay*.

44   See B. *Ned.* 43a, bot., and *ET* 10:53 ff.; *LTJ* 1:170, n. 18.

45   T. *BM* 2.15, p. 374. Instead of *salmah* the Samaritan text reads *simlah*. See Kittel, *Biblia Hebraica*, thereto.

46   M. *BM* 2.5. For this exegetical principle, see *Sifra*, intro., no. 2, 1a.

47   B. *BM* 27a. See *Tos.*, s.v. *mah* ala B. *BK* 66a and P. *BM* 2.1 (8b).

CHAPTER 8. The Law of the Torn Limb

1   B. *San.* 59a ala T. *AZ* 8.6. See *Rashi*, s.v. *ve-rabbanan*, and *Shadal* to Gen. 9:4.

2   B. *San.* 56a.

3   Ibid., 59b.

4   Ibid., 56b, s.v. *akhol*.

5   Ibid., 59b.

6   Ibid., 56a–57a.

7   M. *AZ* 2.3. See T. *AZ* 4.7.

8   B. *AZ* 32a–b; P. *AZ* 2.3 (41b).

9   *Supra*, 78–80.

10   See *Hellenism in Jewish Palestine*, 129 and *supra*, 257, n. 103.

11   *Hul.* 121b.

12   Ibid., 33a.

13   Ibid., cf. B. *San.* 58b re Gen. 9:6.

14   Ibid., 121b. See M. *Hul.* 1.1 and 9.1 and *Hul.* 121a.

15   Ibid., 33a. See 102a, Rashi, s.v. *be-ma'y* and *Tos.*, s.v. *ela*.

16   B. *San.* 63a.

17   No. 6.

18   *Hul.* 33a, s.v. *ehad*.

19   *Shehitah*, 1.2.

20   *Mel.* 9.10, 13.

21   *Infra*, 156–157.

22   Rashba, *Torat ha-Bayit he'Arokh*, 30b; *Tur. YD* 27 (beg.); *SA: YD* 27.1 (see *Shakh* and *Taz* thereto).

23 *KM* to *Shehitah*, 10.2. This law is absent from *SM* (because of the principle of either *shoresh* 2 or 4).

24 *Meiri* to *Hul.* 33a; 60a.

25 *Supra*, 30–35.

26 See *Mekh.*, Mishpatim, 321 ala MS Oxford.

27 B. *Pes.* 22b (and *Tos.*, s.v. *ever*) and B. *AZ* 6a–b.

28 T. *AZ* 8.6:473. See M. *Hul.* 9.7 and M. *Ker.* 3.8.

29 *Hul.* 33a and B. *San.* 59a.

30 Note: "The propositions of logic describe the scaffolding of the world, or they represent it. They have no 'subject-matter'." Wittgenstein, *Tractatus Logico-Philosophicus*, 6.124:128–129.

31 *Supra*, 37, and *infra*, 167–172, 176–180, 209–211, 214–216.

32 *Before Philosophy: The Intellectual Adventure of Ancient Man* (Harmondsworth, 1949), 12, 35. For the difference between the pre-philosophic and philosophic concepts of nature, see Strauss, *Natural Right and History*, 81 ff.

33 T. *AZ* 8.6 and 8; B. *San.* 56b ff.

34 See B. *San.* 59a, Rashi, s.v. *ki ha-dam*.

35 Ibid., 57a, top.

36 Ibid., See *Rashi*, s.v. *me-ha'of* and *v'eedakh*.

37 Ibid., 60a. See *She'ilot de-Rav Ahay Gaon*, no. 99.

38 Ibid., s.v. *et hukkotai*. See *Tos.*, ibid.

39 *Yad Ramah* thereto: 57a. See, esp., B. *BK* 55a re Gen. 1:25 and *Tos.*, s.v. *le-meenayhu* and *Hul.* 60a–b re Ps. 104:31 and *Tos.*, s.v. *nirkeeb*.

40 P. *KL* 1.7 (27b). See *PM* thereto.

41 *De Spec. Leg.*, 4.204:136–137. See Wolfson, *Philo*, 1:187, n. 139; 2:342 ff.

42 Ibid., 4.210:138–139. "This word is very inadequate as a translation for *kosmos* ... It is something higher than mere *taxis*, and thus can be used to signify good behavior and adornment and the perfection of the cosmic system." Note on ibid. by F.H. Colson.

43 *Ramban* to Lev. The rabbinic reference is to *Sifra*, Aharai-Mot, 86a and B. *Yoma* 67b. See *Rabbenu Bahya* to Ex. 22:17 and C. Henoch, *Ha-Ramban ke-Hoker u-Mekubbal* (Jerusalem, 1978), 385 ff. Cf., *MN* 3.26.

44 *Ramban* to Gen. 26.5.

45 B. *San.* 67b and parallels. See M. *San.* 7.11 and *Rambam* thereto. For the prohibition of witchcraft, see ibid. and 59b–60a re Ex. 22:17–18.

46 "What does reverence for life say about the relations between men and the animal world? Whenever I injure life of any sort, I must be quite clear whether it is necessary. Beyond the unavoidable I must never go, not even with what seems insignificant." *The Philosophy of Civilization: Civilization and Ethics*, 2nd edn., trans. C.T. Campion (London, 1929), 2:256.

47 *MN* 3.48:598–599. See *infra*, 172.

48 See note 8.

49 See *supra*, 89–96; also, *infra*, 167–172.

50 599. See *Responsa Ribash*, 4, no. 253.

51 *MN* 3.27. See 3.49 (beg.); also *DR* 6.1.

52   *Supra*, 165–167.

53   *MN* 3.49 ala B. *AZ* 20b; Aristotle, *Nicomachean Ethics*, 1118b2 ff.; *Rhetoric*, 1370a18 ff.
     Cf. *MN* 2.36; 3.8.

54   B. *BK* 85a.

55   Ibid., s.v. *she-neetnah*. See B. *Ber.* 60a; *Hul.* 55b; Siracides 38:1–3; *Tur: YD* 336. Cf.
     Maimonides, *Hovel u-Mazeek*, 6.4. B. *Mak.* 7a for *bi-yedai shamayim* as a synonym for
     nature.

56   *Ramban* to Lev. 26:11.

57   *Rambam* to M. *Ned.* 4.4 ala B. *BK* 81b and B. *San.* 73a; *Ned.* 6.8. See Josephus, *Ant.*,
     8.45–46; Ginzberg, *Legends*, 6:291, n. 48; M. Hengel, *Judaism and Hellenism*, trans.
     J. Bowden, 2 vols. (London, 1974), 1:241; Jakobovits, *Jewish Medical Ethics*, 1 ff.

58   M. *Pes.* 4.9 (B. *Pes.* 56a). See B. *Ber.* 10b; P. *Pes.* 9.1 (36c) and *KE* and *PM* thereto;
     MN 3.37.

CHAPTER 9. Aggadic Speculation

1   *Sifre: Devarim*, no. 343, pp. 396–397; *PR* 99a–b; *MiT*, 210; *PRE*, ch. 41. See
     Tchernowitz, *Toldot ha-Halakha*, 1:311. For a possible historical context for this idea, see
     Urbach, *Hazal*, 472–473; also, J. Heinemann, *Aggadot te-Toldotaihem* (Jerusalem,
     1974), 156 ff.

2   See *supra*, 66–71.

3   See Ex. 24:7 and B. *Shab.* 88a, bot.

4   See *VR* 13.2.

5   *Mekh.*, Yitro, 221–222. See B. *Yev.* 48b, bot.

6   See Ginzberg, *Legends*, 6:31, n. 181.

7   B. *AZ* 2b–3a; B. *BK* 38a. The *derasha* is found in *Mekh.*, loc. cit. The use of the verse
     from Hab. 3:6 was undoubtedly because the message of this biblical section opens
     with the words, "God comes from Teman, the Holy One from the mountain of Paran
     . . ." (3:3), which is the direct parallel to Deut. 33:2, the verse used in the earlier
     Tannaitic *derashah* (see *Rashi* on these two verses). See also *Aykhah Rabbati* 1.29, 37
     and esp. P. *Kid.* 1.7 (61b) and *KE* thereto ala B. *Kid.* 39b.

8   *Supra*, 19–23.

9   P. *Shevi.* 6.1 (36c). See *VR* 17.6; *DR* 5.13; also, B. *Git.* 46a, *Tos.*, s.v. *kayvan*; *Tan.*, Shoftim
     (end).

10   See B. *Ber.* 5b. Cf. *Avot* 3.1.

11   None of the Noahide laws in any way involves the recognition of a historical event.
     Furthermore, whereas Israel's acceptance of the covenant is an indispensable element
     in its effectiveness, the acceptance of Noahide law by gentiles is not explicitly
     mentioned in scripture. Thus e.g. Cain's complaint, "Am I my brother's keeper?"
     (Gen. 4:9) implies that moral responsibility is contingent on personal acceptance of
     that responsibility. In scriptural law one cannot become a *shomer* without his explicit
     prior consent. See Ex. 22:6 and *Mekh.*, Mishpatim, 298. Hence God's refusal to accept
     Cain's excuse means that moral responsibility does not presuppose an act of personal
     commitment, i.e., a covenant. On the other hand, for Jewish acceptance of the Sinaitic
     covenant as an essential part of the effectiveness, see B. *Shab.* 88a re Est. 9:27; Novak,
     "Judaism and Contemporary Bioethics," 360–361.

12　B. *Kid.* 31a and parallels.

13　Ibid., *Tos.*, s.v. *gadol*.

14　Ibid., *Tos.*, s.v. *de-l'a*. See *Hiddushei Ritva* thereto.

15　See *SA: OH* 38.3; *LTJ* 1:15 ff., 2:145–146.

16　M. *Kid.* 1.7.

17　See B. *San.* 90a, bot.

18　See e.g. Maimonides, *Shofar*, 2.4 and *MM* thereto; *LTJ* 1:174, n. 10.

19　See *SR* 15:23 and *Tan.*, Ekev, 3 (end).

20　See Heinemann, *Taamei ha-Mitzvot* 1:23–24; also S. Israeli, "Exemptions from Noahide Law" (Heb.), *Ha-Torah ve-ha-Medinah* (1954–57), 7–8:337–338. For the notion that the gentiles only have *hokhmah* not *Torah*, see *Aykhah Rabbati* 2.17 re Obad. 1:8; also, *Tur: OH* 244 and Bach thereto re the *berakhah* for seeing a gentile sage.

21　See Heinemann, *Aggadot ve-Toldotaihem*, 160–161, who emphasizes the increasing separatist tendency in the Amoraic development of the legend of the offering of the Torah to the gentiles and their rejection of it.

22　T. *San.* 13.2: 434; B. *San.* 105a. See T. *Ned.* 2.4 re Jud. 14:3; *PR*, addendum, 192a.

23　See M. *Hul.* 2.7; *Hul.* 13a and B. *Git.* 45a; *supra*, 115.

24　See B. *San.* 105a, *Rashi*, s.v. *matneeteen* and *m'ay*; *YS*, Kedoshim, no. 626 re Lev. 20:26 and Isaiah, no. 429 re Ps. 132:9; also, *Tesh.* 3.5 and *Mel.* 8, end. Cf. M. *San.* 10.1.

25　See *supra*, 28–30.

26　See *supra*, 30–35.

27　See *Meiri* to B. *San.* 59a, p. 229.

28　*SR* 30.6 re Ps. 147. The term *golem* means an undefined mass without fine details. See e.g. B. *San.* 22b.

29　*Etz Yosef* thereto. See B. *BK* 5b and *Tos.*, s.v. *le-hilkhotaihen*; P. *BK* 1.1 (2b) and *PM* thereto ala *Avot* 6, end; Nahmanides' note to *SM*, *shoresh* 14, end; *Hinukh*, no. 416.

30　B. *BM* 115b and parallels. See B. *Kid.* 34a; *SM*, *shoresh* 4.

31　See *supra*, 101–105.

32　B. *San.* 59a and *Rashi*, s.v. *v'aliba*; P. *MK* 3.5 (82c); Maimonides, *Abel*, 1.1; *Hinukh*, no. 264; also, B. *Shab.* 135a–b and B. *BK* 64b.

33　See esp., *VR* 9.3 re Gen. 3:24 and Zundel, *Etz Yosef* thereto; *Avot* 3.17; *Hinukh*, 331; Guttmann, *Das Judenthum und seine Umwelt*, 333.

34　B. *AZ* 2b–3a; B. *BK* 38a; also, P. *BK* 4.3 (4b).

35　B. *BK* 38a, *Tos.*, s.v. *ela* ala B. *Yev.* 61a (see *Tos.*, s.v. *kivrai* and *ein*; also 62a re Gen. 22:5) and B. *BM* 114b. B. *Meg.* 9a re Gen. 49:7 and *Rashi* thereto; B. *BB* 58a, *Tos.*, s.v. *metzayen*. Note, however, *Hul.* 5a re Lev. 1:2 where the distinction between *adam* and *behemah* is that between the righteous and the wicked (see M. *Sot.* 2.1). Maimonides, on the other hand, makes the question a purely halakhic one, devoid of the theological foundation of making ontological distinctions between Jews and non-Jews. See *Tum'at Met*, 1.13.

36　For further anti-gentile attitudes of R. Simon, see B. *Yev.* 103a–b and parallels. For a Karaite critique of R. Simon's view, see H.H. Ben-Sasson, "*De'ot*, etc.," in *Salo W. Baron Jubilee Volume* (Jerusalem, 1974), 3:74–76.

37　See e.g. T. *Eruv.* 5.19; *Sifra*, Metzor'a, 74b re Lev. 14:47; T. *Neg.* 7.10; Maimonides, *Tum'at Tzara'at*, 16.7; M. *Naz.* 9.1 and B. *Naz.* 61a–61b.

38　See e.g. M. *MK* 1.2 and B. *MK* 5a.

39　*Das Judenthum und seine Umwelt*, 182–183. For an earlier apologetic attempt to play down the implications of R. Simon's opinion, see M. Lazarus, *The Ethics of Judaism*, trans. H. Szold (Philadelphia, 1900), 1:264.

40　Perhaps the most famous result of this theological assumption is found in the emendation of M. *San.* 4.5, viz., "whoever destroys a life (*nefesh ahat*) it is as if he destroyed an entire world." The version in the printed edn. of B. reads: ". . . a Jewish life (*nefesh ahat be-yisrael*) . . ." See Rabinovicz, *Dikdukai Sofrim* thereto and *San.* 12.3. Cf. M. *Ter.* 8.12 and T. *Ter.* 7.20. From the context of this mishnah it is clear that the whole text is concerned with humanity in general. See *Shadal* to Gen. 9:6. See also T. *San.* 9.7; B. *San.* 46b re Deut. 21:23 and Rashi's Torah commentary thereto.

41　Along these lines, gentile refusal to accept the Torah was used aggadically to justify gentile slavery.

42　B. *Shab.* 33b. See B. *AZ* 2b.

43　B. *Yev.* 103a–b; B. *Naz.* 23b; B. *Hor.* 10b. See Wisdom 2:24; also, B. *Shab.* 145b–146a; B. *AZ* 22b.

44　See Scholem, *Major Trends in Jewish Mysticism*, 156 ff.

45　*Zohar*, Balak, 192a–b. Cf. Bereshit, 25a, top; Shemot, 3a, top; Emor, 91b, top. Already in certain Amoraic accounts, the *reasons* for gentile rejection are not mentioned. See e.g. *Aykhah Rabbati*, intro., 24 and 3.3; *MT* 149.2.

46　*Gevurot ha-Shem*, ch. 72. See Katz, *Exclusivism and Tolerance*, 141–142.

47　*Avodat ha-Kodesh*, 1.23. This is based on *PR* 67b. Cf. B. *AZ* 4b re Deut. 4:6; 55b re Deut. 4:19.

48　See *Zohar*, Va-year, 108b; Va-yehi, 220a; Shemot, 17a; Yitro, 86; Be'ha'alotekha, 152b; Ha'azinu, 286; also, see *Zohar Hadash*, Midrash ha-Ne'elam, 18b–19b and Tishby, *Mishnat ha-Zohar*, 44–45.

49　See esp. *Zohar*, Noah, 71b, and R. Moses Cordovero (*Ramak*) *Shiur ha-Komah* (Jerusalem, 1965), 41:45–46. The Hasidic masters R. Menahem Mendel of Rimanov and R. Menahem Mendel of Kotzk both were willing to see Noahide law as pre-Sinaitic rational law. However, revealed law made such rational law superfluous. See *Torat Menahem*, Naso (end), and *Ohel Torah*, Likkutim—quoted in I. Werfel, *Sefer ha-Hasidut* (Tel Aviv, 1947), 44a and 77b.

50　See *BR* 63.7 and 10.

51　*Avodat ha-Kodesh*, 3.21 a la *Zohar Hadash*, 29b. See Ginzberg, *Legends*, 5:187, n. 51. Cf. *KR* 3.14. For the notion of Abraham's observance of the whole Torah prior to Sinaitic revelation, see *supra*, 245, n. 41.

CHAPTER 10. Maimonides' Theory of Noahide Law

1　*Mel.* 9.1.

2　For other examples of Maimonides' use of *netiyat ha-da'at* to denote moral reasoning, see *YT* 5.7; *GA* 4.16.

3　*Mel.* 8, end.

4　See *supra*, 20.

5　See *Mamrim*, beg.; comment to M. *San.* 1.6 ala B. *San.* 17a re Num. 11:16. Cf. *Mishneh Torah*, intro. for a more literal interpretation of Mosaic tradition.

6 Maimonides notes, basing himself on the text from *Mel.* 8, end, that a gentile is only rewarded by God *if* they accept a commandment because of their belief in Mosaic prophecy. (See *Teshuvot ha-Rambam*, I, no. 148. Cf. *Mel.* 10.10 and Radbaz thereto re B. *Kid.* 31a; also, *Talmud Torah*, 1.3; comments to M. *Ter.* 3.9 and M. *Mak.*, end). None of this, however, implies that an act in compliance with Noahide or Mosaic law, not performed from these theological motives, is itself legally invalid. See B. Wein, *Hikrai Halakha* (Jerusalem, 1976), 14–15, n. 12; 16–17.

7 See B. *Pes.* 114b. For the debate on this general question, see B. *RH* 28a–29a; Maimonides, *Shofar*, 2.4 and *MM* thereto; *LTJ* 1:136 ff., 174, n. 10. On the other hand, Jacob Emden concluded, in a response to Mendelssohn, that Maimonides held that the *mitzvot* qua commandments require *kavanah*. Therefore, only Noahides who observe the Noahide laws because of their belief that they are revealed merit eternal bliss. See *infra* 206–209. However, even this only implies that *kavanah* only affects the other-worldly consequences of the commandments. It does not suggest that without *kavanah* the acts themselves are without value. See S. Schwarzschild, "Moral Radicalism and 'Middlingness' in the Ethics of Maimonides," *Studies in Medieval Culture* (1977), 11:87, n. 64.

8 See *Tesh.* 3.5. Maimonides' rabbinic sources seem to be T. *San.* 13.2 and B. *San.* 105a. (See *supra*, 147–148). His use of *hasidim* rather than *tzaddikim* (the original term in both T. and B.) is based on the following text from *MRE*, ch. 6:121: ". . . but the saints of the nations of the world (*hasidai ummot ha'olam*), when they perform the seven commandments commanded to the sons of Noah . . . by virtue of Noah our father commanding us from revelation (*mi-pi ha-gevurah*) . . . but if they perform the seven commandments and say, 'from so-and-so we heard,' or from their own opinion (*ha-da'at mekhara'at*) . . . they only receive reward in this world." (For Maimonides' citation of this work as his source, see *Teshuvot ha-Rambam*, ed. A. Freimann, no. 124:117. For another recognition by Maimonides of the importance of this work, see *SM*, pos. no. 5.) Zvi Hirsch Chajes, who was unfamiliar with this textual evidence, nevertheless concluded that even without rabbinic sources Maimonides' ruling was consistent with his system. See *Torat ha-Neviim*, ch. 11, in *Kol Kitvei Maharetz Chajes*, 1:66. It is likely that Maimonides preferred *hasid* to *tzaddik* because the former denoted a greater spirituality than the latter. See e.g. B. *AZ* 20b re Ps. 89:20; *Shemonah Perakim*, ch. 6, beg.; *MN* 3.51. A *tzaddik* is only a person who is legally innocent. See e.g. Deut. 25:1 and *Sifre: Devarim*, no. 286.

9 *Hekhr'e ha-da'at* is a rabbinic term designating an inductive argument. See e.g. P. *San.* 1.1 (18b); T. *Hul.* 8.1 (Cf. *Hul.* 90b). It should be contrasted with *hekhr'e ha-katuv*, viz., an argument based on the Torah. See e.g. *Sifra*, intro., 1a. The difference in these two types of proof is akin to the rabbinic distinction between *ker'a* and *sevar'a*. See e.g. B. *Ber.* 4b; B. *Kid.* 13b; B. *AZ* 34b. See also M. Guttmann, "Maimonide sur l'universalité de la morale religieuse," *Revue des Études Juives* (1935), 99:41. Maimonides' understanding of *hekhr'e ha-da'at* can be equated with his understanding of what in Arabic is called *qiyas*, viz., inductive-type estimation. See *MN* 2.23 (beg.).

10 A number of modern scholars (Katz, *Exclusiveness and Tolerance*, 175, n. 5; Guttmann, "Maimonide") have argued that the text from *MRE* makes this stipulation not Maimonides' own original opinion as R. Joseph Karo (*KM* to *Mel.* 8, end) assumed.

11 Saadiah regarded all the pre-Sinaitic commandments to be *sikhliyot*, exclusive of

Passover. He refused to endorse any of the various rabbinic opinions concerning the exact number and content of the Noahide laws. He simply stipulated that he would only accept as pre-Sinaitic commandments those explicitly mentioned in the Torah. See M. Zucker, *Hasagot al Rav Saadiah Gaon me'et Rav Mubashshir, etc.* (New York, 1955), 78, n. 50. In *Emunot ve-De'ot*, 92, Saadiah judges the core of Noahide law as rational.

12 *Shemonah Perakim*, ch. 6, ed. and trans. J. Kifih (Jerusalem, 1965), 258, re B. *Yoma* 67b. See comment to M. *Peah*, beg.

13 *MN* 1.71 ff.

14 See note 11 and *LTJ* 2:6–7; also, I. Efros, *Studies in Medieval Jewish Philosophy* (New York, 1974), 123–124.

15 See *Shemonah Perakim*, intro., ch. 5, beg.; *MN* 3.51.

16 See Strauss, *Persecution and the Art of Writing*, 40–41.

17 B. *Pes.* 50b and parallels. See *Hakadamah le-Perek Helek*, 114–117.

18 *Mel.* 9.1. Note: "R. Jannai said that to the earlier ones You gave them a smell (*reyah*) of the commandments . . . but when we came to Sinai it was like a man who pours out from the spout of a barrel. You poured out for us all the commandments." *Tan.*, Yitro, ed. Buber, no. 2, p. 35 re Cant. 1:3.

19 See *SM*, *shoresh* 2, viz., commandments not specifically stated in the Written Torah are not included among the 613. In *Mel.* 9.1 Maimonides notes that the Noahide laws are *generally* included in the Torah.

20 For Maimonides' acknowledgment of his debt to Aristotle, see A. Marx, "Texts by and about Maimonides," *JQR* (April 1935), 25.4:379–380. See *supra*, 265, n. 198; *LTJ* 1:119.

21 *MN* 3.45.

22 *MN* 2.36, p. 369.

23 *MN* 1.2.

24 *MN* 2.36.

25 *MN* 1.51, p. 112.

26 See Aristotle, *Physics*, 194b16 ff., and *MN* 2.1.

27 See *Tesh.* 5.5 for the assertion that free choice is prior to religious doctrine.

28 Ibid., 5.4. See *Shemonah Perakim*, ch. 8.

29 See *MN* 3.32.

30 See *MN* 2.29.

31 Maimonides emphasizes in *MN* 1.1 intellect, not will, as the point in common between humanity and God. See *YT* 4.8. This idea has many Jewish and non-Jewish expressions. See e.g. Plato, *Phaedrus*, 248A; *Theaetetus*, 176A–B; *Laws*, 899D; Philo, *De Opificio Mundi*, 69 (beg.); Epictetus, *Discourses*, 1.9; Clement of Alexandria, *Exhortation to the Greeks*, 10. For a critique of this idea, see Novak, "Judaism and Contemporary Bioethics," 361 ff.; *LTJ* 2:108 ff.

32 3.17, p. 469.

33 Note: "Choice (*proairesis*) is manifestly a voluntary act (*hekousion*). But the two terms are not synonyms, the latter being the wider. Children and the lower animals as well as men are capable of voluntary action, but not of choice." Aristotle, *Nicomachean Ethics*, 1111b5, ed. and trans. H. Rackham (Cambridge, MA, 1926), 128–129.

34 *Shemonah Perakim*, ch. 1 (end).

35 See *MN* 1.2.

36 *MN* 1.69.

37 *MN* 2, intro., no. 18; 2.36; Aristotle, *De Anima*, 430a15, 431a1–5; *Metaphysics* 1049b25 ff. See A.J. Reines, *Maimonides and Abravanel on Prophecy* (Cincinnati, 1970), xxxi ff.

38 Maimonides' Neoplatonism came via Avicenna. For the relation between emanation and the four Aristotelian causes, see Morewidge, *The Metaphysics of Avicenna*, 264 ff. Cf. Aquinas, *Summa Theologiae*, 1, q. 79, aa. 3–4; q. 84, a. 4. For a view of the Aristotelian Active Intellect that deems it mentally immanent, however, see W.D. Ross, *Aristotle* (New York, 1959), 146 ff.

39 *MN* 2.12.

40 Ibid.

41 *MN* 1.69, p. 170.

42 *MN* 1.65. See H.A. Wolfson, *Repercussions of the Kalam in Jewish Philosophy* (Cambridge, MA, 1979), 111–112.

43 *MN* 2.19.

44 See *SM*, neg. no. 365; *MN* 2.25, 3.25–26 and 31.

45 Although Maimonides asserts that "there is a reason for every commandment" (*MN* 3.26), "there is more that we do not understand than we do understand" (*MN* 3.49). In terms of essence/function (*hokmah*) we understand much; in terms of existence/entity (*ratzon*) we understand little. Maimonides is dealing with two types of teleology: functional teleology that answers "how"; existential teleology that answers "why." See Z. Diesendruck, "Die Teleologie bei Maimonides," *HUCA* (1928), 4:499 ff. Cf. Plato, *Republic*, 427B–C; *Laws*, 738B–C; Novak, *Suicide and Morality*, 51–54.

46 Re the combination of wisdom and will in divine creativity as an artistic act ala Plato, *Philebus*, 26E–28D, see Efros, *Studies in Medieval Jewish Philosophy*, 164–165. For the suggestion that Maimonides' teleology, being more comprehensive than Aristotle's, has important affinities to the later thought of Plato, see Diesendruck, "Die Teleologie," and his "Ha-Takhlit ve-ha-Te'arim be-Torat ha-Rambam," *Tarbiz* (Jan. 1930), 1.3:106 ff.

47 *MN* 2.40, pp. 381–382.

48 For the influence of Avicenna on this point, see Pines' intro. to *MN*, xcix.

49 See comment to M. *AZ* 4.6 and *supra*, 94–95, where idolatry is the mystical device used by political leaders to unify a community.

50 *MN* 2.40, p. 384. See *BaR* 22.6 re Jer. 9:22 and Ecc. 9:11; also, E.I.J. Rosenthal, "Torah and Nomos in Jewish Philosophy," in *Studies in Rationalism, Judaism and Universalism*, ed. R. Loewe (London, 1966), 218 ff.

51 See *De'ot*, 3.3 ala *Avot* 2.2; *MN* 2.32, 36; 3.8, 51.

52 *MN* 3.34, p. 534. Both Plato (*Statesman*, 294A–C) and Aristotle (*Politics*, 1286a7 ff.) recognize that generality is the strength of the law, as does Maimonides. However, whereas for Maimonides this generality is the law's advantage, viz., it brings political unity out of individual diversity, for Plato and Aristotle, it suggests that *who* the political leader is is more important that *what* the laws are, because such a leader can better deal with individual cases and their respective peculiarities. (See also *Nicomachean Ethics*, 1132a20). For Maimonides, the Torah as a created entity (*MN* 1.65)

is natural, therefore, unchanging and unchangeable. For Plato and Aristotle, on the other hand, a specific law code is a human invention. Because of the specificity of the Torah, Maimonides' natural law doctrine is more specific. For the importance of generality in Talmudic jurisprudence, see e.g. M. *Ber.* 1.3 and *Sifre: Devarim*, no. 34 re Deut. 6:7; B. *Eruv.* 63b (bot.); B. *Ber.* 12a; B. *Kid.* 80a; B. *BM* 39b; *Hul.* 9a, 11a. Cf. Philo, *De Spec. Leg.*, 1.3.

53   Re the immutability of the Torah, see *MN* 3.41.

54   See *MN* 3.18, 51.

55   For the synthesis of intellection and imagination in the prophet, see *MN* 2.37.

56   See *MN* 3.54.

57   *MN* 2.40, p. 382.

58   *Mel.* 8.11. For MSS that confirm the reading of the *editio princeps*, see Faur, *Iyunim*, 151, n. 43.

59   Mendelssohn stressed, in a letter to the Christian theologian Lavatar (see *Schriften*, jub. edn., 7:11, note c; also note 114 in this chapter), that this was the correct reading. Kook argued for this reading as part of his emphasis on universal sanctity (see *Igrot Rayah*, Jerusalem, 1961, 1:99). See also *The Code of Maimonides—Book XIV: The Book of Judges*, trans. A.M. Hershman (New Haven, 1949), 230 and 308; B.Z. Bokser, "Morality and Religion in the Theology of Maimonides," in *Essays on Jewish Life and Thought: Presented to Salo Wittmayer Baron* (New York, 1959), 155, n. 6; S. Schwarzschild, "Do Noachites Have to Believe in Revelation?," *JQR* (April 1962), 52.4:302; *A Maimonides Reader*, ed. I. Twersky (New York, 1972), 221. For a similar textual problem, see Ginzberg, *Legends*, 6:115–116, n. 658.

60   The form *ein . . . ela* is extremely common in Tannaitic texts. See e.g. B. *Ber.* 5a re Job 5:7.

61   *YT* 7.1. Cf. *Tesh.* 102. For Maimonides, himself a physician, sages were frequently physicians. Indeed *al hakim* in Arabic often means a physician. Today we call such people *applied* rather than *pure* scientists. See *Hakdamah le-Mishnah*, 68–69; Faur, *Iyunim*, 189, n. 69. S. Munk translates the *hakam* (*rajal illumai*) of *MN* 1.2 as "un homme de science"—*Le Guide des égarés* (Paris, 1856), 37.

62   *De'ot*, 1.4. Cf. B. *Meg.* 16a re Est. 6:13.

63   *MN* 3.54, p. 633. See Pines' n. 10 thereto.

64   Certain Jewish neo-Kantians seized upon this and attempted to show that Maimonides placed morality above metaphysics like Kant. (See *infra*, 216–220). Nevertheless, one cannot argue for the superiority of ethics over metaphysics in Maimonides' system inasmuch as true ethics presupposes metaphysics. Just as for Maimonides God operates as both final (wisdom) and efficient (will) cause, so metaphysics, the "divine science," functions as both the origin and the goal of ethics. For the classical presentation of this view, see Hermann Cohen, "Charakteristik der Ethik Maimunis," *Jüdische Schriften*, 3:238–259; *Religion der Vernunft*, 6:94–95; Diesendruck, "Die Teleologie bei Maimonides," end; Atlas, *Netivim*, 10–15; Schwarzschild, "Moral Radicalism and 'Middlingness' in the Ethics of Maimonides," end. Concerning this whole approach, all influenced by Cohen, note: "Cohen saw a corrective to his doctrine of God . . . especially in Maimonides' doctrine of attributes, to whose metaphysical presuppositions Cohen failed to do justice." Guttmann, *Philosophies of Judaism*, 357.

65 See *MN* 2.32 re B. *Shab.* 92a and B. *Ned.* 38a.

66 *MN* 2.40, p. 382.

67 *MN* 2.10, p. 272. See Pines' n. 11 thereon.

68 *MN* 1.72.

69 *MN* 3.43, p. 571. Thus the commentator Moses Narboni explains Maimonides' remark, "the Law, although it is not natural enters into what is natural" (*MN* 2.40), as referring to the fact that "the languages are not natural." In other words, language as intelligent expression is not a manifestation of physical nature per se. Cf. Aristotle, *Politics*, 1253a10.

70 *MN* 1.72. See Joseph ibn Tzaddik, *Olam Katan*, an influential philosophical work almost exclusively devoted to this theme.

71 See *MN* 2.23.

72 *MN* 1.72, p. 190. See *Ma'amar Tehiyyat ha-Metim*, ed. M. Rabinowitz (Jerusalem, 1960), 374, where Maimonides attempts to bring biblical and rabbinic precedents for his theory of nature. See also R. Bahya ibn Pakudah, *Hovot ha-Levavot*, 3.4.

73 Thus Maimonides states that any pagan practice that "required speculation concerning nature is permitted" (*MN* 3.37, p. 543). In other words, the law of the Torah does not contradict nature as does idolatry, which prescribes "things not required by reasons concerning nature." See comment to M. *Pes.* 4, end; *Shab.* 19.12 ala B. *Shab.* 67a. Cf. *MN* 3.20. 46.

74 *MN* 3.49, p. 609. Cf. *Me'il.* 17a.

75 See *MN* 3.43.

76 This double use of "nature" has philosophical precedent in Aristotle: " . . . nature then, *qua* genesis proclaims itself as the path (*hodos*) to nature *qua* goal (*eis physis*) . . . Towards what, then, does it grow? Not towards its original state at birth, but towards its final state or goal (*eis ho*). It is, then, the form (*morphē*) that is nature; . . . 'form' and 'nature' are ambiguous terms (*dichōs legetai*) . . . " (*Physics*, 193b12–13, trans. F.M. Cornford, Cambridge, MA, 1929, 114–117). See 199a30; *Metaphysics*, 1015a15; also, Plato, *Republic*, 423D and 429A.

77 See *MN* 1.34; 3.51.

78 *MN*, intro.

79 For Maimonides' insistence on the congruity of Torah and reason, precisely because both follow a "natural order," see *Ma'amar Tehiyyat ha-Metim*, ch. 6. Cf. Philo, *De Vita Mosis*, 2.48.

80 The translation of Judah al-Harizi reads, "it is included (*ha-nikhlelet bi-khlal*) among the laws of nature (*hukkai ha-tev'a*)." In other words, by entering the natural/physical order the Torah has natural/physical significance. See *LTJ* 1:144.

81 Thus it is incorrect to assume that Maimonides means here that the *end* of the Torah is natural (i.e., social), but *its* source is divine, as does Faur in "Mekor Hiyyuvan shel ha-Mitzvot le-Da'at ha-Rambam," *Tarbiz* (1968), 38.51. He repeats this same interpretation in his "Understanding the Covenant," *Tradition* (Spring 1968), 9.4:47, and his *Iyunim*, 168. For Maimonides the end of the Torah is not determined by humanity's *social* nature, but by its *rational* nature. Only the initial intelligibility of the Torah is social. This is what Maimonides means by stating, "the Torah has an introduction (*mav'o*) in the natural." He is not referring to its source at all in this passage. I cannot

agree with Faur's understanding of "nature" in Maimonides, or with his assumption that reason and revelation are mutually exclusive concepts. (See Wolfson, *Philo*, 2:310–311). For Faur's sustained polemic against natural law theory in Maimonides in particular and Judaism in general, see his "The Origin of the Distinction between Rational and Divine Commandments in Medieval Jewish Philosophy," *Augustianum* (1969), 9:299–304; "Understanding the Covenant," 40 ff.; *Iyunim*, 63 ff., 145 ff., 174 ff.

82 *MN* 3.27. Maimonides sees the political end of the Torah exemplified in the virtue of "awe of God" (*yirat ha-Shem*). See *MN* 3.24, 52 (end). Just as the political end chronologically precedes the intellectual end, so does *yirat ha-Shem* chronologically precede "love of God" (*ahavat ha-Shem*), the virtue that exemplified the intellectual end of the Torah. See *Tesh.* 10.1–2; *Igeret Teman*, ch. 1, pp. 123–124; *MN* 3.24 (end).

83 Whereas Faur reads the text to *MN* 2.40 too literally, Reines does not seem to read it literally enough. He writes: "The Law is not natural in that it is the artificial creation of men; it enters into the natural by realizing the natural providential purpose" ("Maimonides' Concept of Mosaic Prophecy," *HUCA* [1969–1970], 40–41:359, n. 127). Maimonides does not ascribe the Torah to human invention, but rather to Moses' unambiguous *normative* prophecy (see *MN* 2.35, 39). The Torah's "entering into what is natural" refers to its relevance for humanity's physical/social nature. Its end, by contrast, is referred to as "divine" (see *MN* 1.34; 2.40).

84 *MN* 3.27, p. 510. Pines, in his introduction to *MN*, makes the point that for Aristotle "the perfect philosopher, who has outgrown . . . the need for intellectual companionship, belongs to the city only insofar as he has to provide for his physical necessities. Qua philosopher, he is self-sufficient" (lxxxviii). Along these lines, one should compare *Republic*, 516 ff. and *Nicomachean Ethics*, 1177b1. Also, see Novak, *Suicide and Morality*, 22 ff. It is clear, then, that Maimonides' political philosophy is more Platonic (via Alfarabi, whose influence he acknowledged. See Marx, "Texts by and about Maimonides," 379); Schwarzschild, "Moral Radicalism," 76.

85 *Mel.* 9.1.

86 *Supra*, 89–96.

87 *MN* 2.33, p. 364.

88 B. *Mak.* 24a. See *IB* 14.2.

89 *Supra*, 89–96.

90 Indeed in his earliest work, *Millot ha-Higayon* (sect. 8, pp. 44–45), Maimonides classified the concepts of *mefursamot* and *mekubbalot* as something clearly evident, not requiring proof for their existence. Those *mefursamot* most universally followed are, for Maimonides, the most true. In *MN* 1.51 he did not include them in this category. It would seem that as Maimonides' thought developed he realized that even the more universally prevalent *mefursamot* were only true in a relative sense. In his more mature thought he seems to have followed Aristotle more closely in seeing intelligible nature as a truer foundation for morality than *consensus gentium*. See Aristotle, *Rhetoric*, 1373b5; *Nicomachean Ethics*, 1134b20. It would seem that, following Aristotle, *Topica*, 100a25–30 and *Prior Analytics*, 24a24–24b10, the *muskalot* are known via the "demonstrative syllogism" (*ex endoxōn*). For Aristotle the *endoxa* are not unintelligible. See *Nicomachean Ethics*, 1094b25; Philo, *De Ebrietate*, 34, 84; Wolfson, *Philo*, 1:150, n. 32. See also Efros, *Studies in Medieval Jewish Philosophy*, 13, 73–77; R.L. Weiss,

"Introduction," in *The Ethical Writings of Maimonides* (New York, 1975), 22–23. It would seem that the great project of Maimonides' philosophy of law was to ground the *mefursamot* of the Torah in the realm of the *muskalot*, thus giving them greater intelligibility.

91 See *MN* 3.31.

92 *YT*, beg.

93 See *AZ* 11.16.

94 See *MN* 1.59.

95 *Mel.* 9.3.

96 *Supra*, 58.

97 *Tesh.* 3.7.

98 *RSN* 4.9.

99 *MN* 3.26, p. 507. See 3.28.

100 In the *Mishneh Torah* Maimonides refers to *arayot* as being a matter between humanity and God. Earlier in *Shemonah Perakim* (ch. 6:259) he classified *arayot* among the "traditional" (*shimiyot*) commandments. However, he may well be referring to certain prohibited incestuous relations whose particular rationale is not evident, rather than the general concept of incest whose rationale is evident. See *supra*, 113–117.

101 *Ishut*, 1.1, 4.

102 *MN* 3.49, pp. 601–602. Re the importance of maintaining family lines of descent, thus requiring the prohibition of random sexual relations, see *Na'arah Betulah*, 2.17. Cf. Saadiah Gaon, *Emunot ve-De'ot*, 3.2.

103 *MN* 3.27.

104 See *Nicomachean Ethics*, 1103a15.

105 *MN* 3.33, p. 532. See 3.11.

106 This complete synthesis must be the result of the most direct possible prophetic apprehension. Any mediation would lessen its simple unity and force. This is why Maimonides emphasized points about Mosaic prophecy in contrast to other types of prophecy, viz., (1) it is immediately apprehended (*YT* 7.6; *MN* 2.45); (2) it is immediately normative (*MN* 2.39). Here we see a logical connection between the descriptive and prescriptive aspects of Mosaic prophecy, which corresponds to the political and intellectual aims of the Mosaic Torah. Prophecy which is mediated, on the other hand, can only result in much more tentative prescriptions. Thus the Mosaic Torah is not rooted in imagination (*contra* Reines, "Maimonides' Concept of Mosaic Prophecy," 353 ff.).

107 *MN* 3.35, p. 536.

108 *MN* 3.40, p. 556. See *GA* 1.11; *SM*, neg. no. 266.

109 See *supra*, 37–38.

110 See B. *San.* 59b.

111 *MN* 3.48, pp. 598–599. See B. *Ned.* 65a and Maimonides' comment to M. *AZ* 2.3.

112 *MN* 3.48, p. 599.

113 Jacobs, *Principles of the Jewish Faith* (New York, 1964), 316.

114 See Mendelssohn, *Schriften*, jub. edn., 16: 178–180. See *infra*, 206–209. The same point was expressed earlier by Moses Chefetz in *Melekh'et Shlemah* (Venice, 1710), quoted in Guttmann, *Das Judenthum und seine Umwelt*, 300, n. 1.

115   *Tractatus Theologico-Politicus*, ch. 5 (end) in *Opera*, ed. C. Gebhart (Heidelberg, 1925), 3:79–80. Spinoza emphasizes the view of Joseph ibn Shem Tov, who in *Kevod Elohim* (ed. Ferrara, 1556, 29a) stated that Maimonides limited the category of *hasidai ummot ha'olam* to literal believers in Mosaic revelation. (Nevertheless, Shem Tov presents the text in *Mel.* 8.11 a reading *aval me-hakhmaihem*). See also Isaac Abravanel's comment to Ex. 19:1; 21:1; R. Moses de Trani, *Beit Elohim*; *Sha'ar ha-Yesodot*, chs. 42, 47. This view was also expressed by Spinoza's Amsterdam teacher, Manasseh b. Israel, in his *The Conciliator*, trans. E.H. Lindo (New York, 1972), I, q. 172, p. 277. See Guttmann, "Maimonide sur la universalité de la morale religieuse," 43. For a recent halakhic endorsement of this interpretation, see M. Feinstein, *Igrot Moshe* (New York, 1964), *OH*, no. 25, 2:196–197.

116   Hermann Cohen accused Spinoza of using an incorrect reading that stated *ve-l'o* instead of the correct *ela*. He based this on M. Joel's monograph, "Spinozas Theologische-Politische Traktät," in *Beiträge zur Geschichte der Philosophie* (Breslau, 1876), 2:55–57. See *Jüdische Schriften*, 3:347 ff.; also, *Religion der Vernunft*, 386. Cohen characterizes Maimonides' dissatisfaction with "freien Vernunft . . . von relative Geltung" in favor of morality as "einer politischen Verpflichtung" (350). (See also Atlas, *Netivim*, 6, 9). Nevertheless, Leo Strauss was correct when he pointed out that the reading that Spinoza was using is the one used in all printed editions of the *Mishneh Torah*, a reading that did not shock Jewish traditionalists. See *Spinoza's Critique of Religion* (New York, 1965), 23–24. For Cohen's concept of Noahide law, see *infra*, 214–216. Cohen's dislike for Spinoza actually stemmed more from his rejection of Spinoza's pantheism than from Spinoza's interpretation of Maimonides. See *Jüdische Schriften*, 1:292–293; also, *Ethik des reinen Willens*, 3rd edn. (Berlin, 1921), 470.

117   *Tractatus Theologico-Politicus*, ch. 5, trans. R.H.M. Elwes (New York, 1951), 60. See S. Schwarzschild, "Do Noachites Have to Believe in Revelation?" (pt. 2), *JQR* (July 1962), 53.1:46 ff.

118   "Maimonides and Aquinas on Natural Law," *Dine Israel* (1972), 3:xiv, xxvii. See Fox's prolegomenon to A. Cohen, *The Teaching of Maimonides* (New York, 1968), xli–xlii. Also, Bokser, "Morality and Religion in the Theology of Maimonides," 139; A. Kirschenbaum, "Ha-Berit im Bnei Noah," *Dine Israel* (1975), 6:47. As a precedent for this anti-natural law interpretation of Maimonides, see Abravanel's comment to Ex. 19:1 ff. Note, however: "Maimonides, counter to what Fox ascribes to him, does not claim that *nomos* (as distinct from Torah) lacks a legitimate ground for moral obligation. Maimonides only distinguishes between a law that aims solely at political well-being, and a law that leads humanity to spiritual perfection. If Fox is correct that Maimonides believed a moral system lacking the sanction of divine authority does not bind a rational man, it is difficult to understand how a '*nomos* society' could realize its goal. Maimonides only claims that law exclusively concerned with social and political well-being is limited; he does not say it fails as a moral system." Hartman, *Maimonides: Torah and Philosophic Quest*, 260, n. 38. Also see Lichtenstein, "Does Jewish Tradition Recognize an Ethic Independent of Halakha?" in *Modern Jewish Ethics*, ed. M. Fox (Columbus, OH, 1975), 63.

119   See *MN* 2.35. Cf. Halevi, *Kuzari*, 1.95, 103; 2.14.

120   See *MN* 3.29.

121   *Shemitah ve-Yovel*, end. See Atlas, *Netivim*, 13–14.

122 *Kobetz Teshuvot ha-Rambam v'Igrotav*, ed. A. Lichtenberg (Leipzig, 1859), 2:23b–24a. See *Hakdamah le-Perek Helek*, 124 (top). All of this is a far removed from Maimonides' statement in the *Mishneh Torah* that "the world-to-come is only reserved (*tzafun*) for *tzaddikim* and they are Israel" (*IB* 14.4). In the printed text of the Talmud (B. *Yev.* 47a, bot.) and *Alfasi* (Vilna edn., 16a) it does not exactly state that *tzaddikim* are only Israel. Nevertheless, the context of the passage seems to indicate that only full conversion to Judaism makes a person one of the righteous. This Jewish version of *extra ecclesiam nulla salus* seems to be according to R. Eliezer b. Hyrkanus' views (see *supra*, 146–147). In *Mel.* 8.11 Maimonides codifies R. Joshua's view, viz., the righteous gentiles also merit the bliss of the world-to-come. The contradiction between *IB* 14.4 and *Mel.* 8.11 is not created by Maimonides' theology as much as by the disparity between two respective *halakhot*, which he as a *posek* was required to codify.

123 See *MN* 3.54.

124 *Supra*, 37–38.

CHAPTER 11. Albo's Theory of Noahide Law

1 *Ikkarim*, 1.7. In general, I have followed the translation of I. Husik (Philadelphia, 1929), with my own variations when deemed necessary. See E. Schweid's *Sefer ha-Ikkarim le-Rabbi Yosef Albo* (Jerusalem, 1967), 7 ff., for the best introduction to Albo's work.

2 *Ikkarim*, 1.5.

3 *Politics*, 1253a2.

4 Lerner, "Natural Law in Albo's *Book of Roots*," in *Ancients and Moderns*, ed. J. Cropsey (New York, 1964), 132, 142. Husik attempted to see Aquinas' division of law (i.e, *lex aeterna, lex naturalis positiva, lex divina*—*Summa Theologiae*, 1–2, q. 93, a. 1) as an influence on Albo's division. See also J. Guttman, "An Investigation of the Sources of *Sefer ha-Ikkarim*" (Heb.), in *Sefer ha-Ikkarim*, 2 vols. (Jerusalem, n.d.), 2:935. If there is any influence at all it is more terminological than conceptual. Aquinas' view of *lex naturalis* is far more comprehensive than Albo's *daat tiv'it*. For *daat tiv'it*, see J. Klatzkin, *Thesaurus Philosophicus*, 5 vols. (Berlin, 1928), 1:149.

5 For the influence of Avicenna on both Maimonides and Albo on this point, see Guttman, "An Investigation," 932; Pines' introduction to the *Guide*, xcix.

6 *Ikkarim*, 3.7.

7 Such a man would be either superhuman or subhuman. See Aristotle, *Nicomachean Ethics*, 1177b1 ff.

8 B. *Eruv.* 110b.

9 *Ikkarim*, 3.1.

10 Ibid., 4.4.

11 Ibid., 1.5.

12 Ibid., 1.7. Note H.L.A. Hart, who, although arguing against natural law theories (e.g. Aquinas) based on a universal teleology, nevertheless accepts a minimal natural law theory similar to Albo's: "Reflections on some very obvious generalizations—indeed truisms—concerning human nature and the world in which men live, show that as long as these hold good, there are certain rules of conduct which any social

organization must contain if it is to be viable . . . Such universally recognized principles of conduct which have a basis in elementary truths concerning human beings, their natural environment, and aims, may be considered the *minimum content* of Natural Law, in contrast with the more grandiose and more challengeable constructions which have been proffered under that name." *The Concept of Law* (Oxford, 1961), 188–189.

13 Note: "the State is but an agency entitled to use power and coercion . . . an instrument in the service of man. Putting man at the service of that instrument is political perversion." Jacques Maritain, *Man and the State* (Chicago, 1951), 13.

14 *Ikkarim*, 1.5.

15 Ibid.

16 See Hegel, *Logic*, trans. A.V. Miller (London, 1969), 107.

17 *Ikkarim*, 1.9.

18 See B. *San.* 56b; *Tesh.* 5.4–5.

19 *Ikkarim*, 3.7. For the difference between a legal system based on "rights" as opposed to one based on "goods," see John Rawls, *A Theory of Justice* (Cambridge, MA, 1971), 446, and R. Dworkin, *Taking Rights Seriously* (Cambridge, MA, 1978), 171–172.

20 *Ikkarim*, 1.3.

21 The same sort of developmental logic is found in Talmudic jurisprudence. The biblical presentation of human adjudication of divine law (Deut. 17:11) is interpreted in the Talmud as being equally the basis of positive rabbinic innovations such as kindling the Hanukkah lights. See B. *Shab.* 23a. In other words, human-made law is not only regulative of divine law, it is also itself a legitimate supplement to it. For the rabbinic effort to qualify the biblical prohibition of adding to divine law (Deut. 4:2, 13:1) by making the prohibition apply only to specifics of individual laws rather than to the law as a whole, see e.g. *Sifre: Devarim*, no. 82; B. *San.* 88b.

22 *Ikkarim*, 1.7.

23 Cf. *MN* 3.51.

24 Cf. Aristotle, *Nicomachean Ethics*, 1134b18.

25 *Ikkarim*, 1.6.

26 Ibid. See *LTJ* 2:4–6.

27 Aristotle, *Politics*, 1254a18 ff.

28 *Ikkarim*, 1.5.

29 Ibid., 1.8.

30 Ibid., 1.6. See *Nicomachean Ethics*, 1094a15.

31 Ibid., 1.7.

32 See Plato, *Republic*, 491C, and M.J. Adler, *The Time of Our Lives* (New York, 1970), 84 ff.

33 See *Republic*, 449C ff.

34 *Ikkarim*, 1.7.

35 *Politics*, 1261a5 ff.

36 Cf. Saadiah, *Emunah ve-De'ot*, intro., 6.

37 *Ikkarim*, 1.8.

38 *MN* 2.40.

39 "Nu rein geoffenbartes goettliches Gesetz bildet eine Religion und daher die staedige Bezeichung für Religion 'Dath Elohith.' 'Goettliches Gesetz' ist . . . die Anerkennung

goettlicher Gebote als unserer Pflichten." A. Taenzer, *Die Religionsphilosophie Josef Albos* (Frankfurt am Main, 1896), 7–8.

40 *Ikkarim*, 1.17. See Halevi, *Kuzari*, 1.25.

41 Cf. *Ramban* to *SM*, pos. no. 1; *LTJ* 1:145–149.

42 *Ikkarim*, 1.19. See Wolfson, *The Philosophy of the Church Fathers*, 112 ff.

43 See Klatzkin, *Thesaurus Philosophicus*, 2:248–249.

44 *Ikkarim*, 1.10. See comment of Abravanel to Ex. 21:1 ff.

45 Ibid., 1.8. Cf. Aquinas, *Summa Theologiae*, 2-2, q. 99, a. 2.

46 See *Euthyphro*, 6D.

47 See e.g. *Republic*, 472D ff.

48 See *Nicomachean Ethics*, 1106a10.

49 *Kuzari*, 1, intro., p. 35.

50 See e.g. ibid., 1.88–89.

51 *Ikkarim*, 1.8. For the notion that punishment be equal to the crime (*middah ke-neged middah*) even in divine retribution, see B. *San.* 90a, bot.

52 *Ikkarim*, 4.36.

53 See Lerner, "Natural Law in Albo's *Book of Roots*," 145, n. 10.

54 B. *BK* 83b–84a; B. *Ket.* 38a. See the view of Saadiah Gaon quoted in *Ibn Ezra* to Ex. 21:24.

55 See *Ikkarim*, 1.8, re punishment for visible crime only in conventional law.

56 Ibid., 1.18.

57 Ibid., 1.17.

58 Ibid., 2.5 (end).

59 Ibid., 2.1 (end).

60 Ibid., 2.4 (end)

61 Ibid., 2.1. In 2.11 he sees the Torah as arguing against Epicureanism, using the term *lehorot*.

62 Ibid., 2.5 (end). See *MN* 2.1, no. 4. For references, see Husik, 2:7–8, n. 1.

63 Ibid., 2, intro.

64 Ibid., 2.1.

65 Ibid., 1.7.

66 Ibid., 3.7.

67 Ibid., 3.26.

68 Ibid., 3.6.

69 See *Mel.* 9.1.

70 B. *San.* 56b.

71 *MN*, intro. See *Ikkarim*, 2, intro.

72 *Ikkarim*, 3.28.

73 Ibid., 1.5. See 3.6.

74 Ibid., 1.6.

75 Ibid., 1.7.

76 *AZ* beg.

77 *Ikkarim*, 3.7.

78 *Ikkarim*, 1.25. See 1.23.

79 The problem with this line of reasoning is that its logical conclusion should be that an oracle is more "divine" than a fixed permanent revelation which must be expressed in universals, however circumscribed their sets may be. See *LTJ* 1:81–82.

80 *Ikkarim*, 1.17.

81 See *supra*, 13–17.

82 For the difference between an allusion (*zekher*) and a proof (*ray'ah*), see e.g. B. *Ber.* 2b re Neh. 4:14 and *Tos.*, s.v. *al-pi*. The terms *zekher*, *remez*, and *asmakhta* are virtually the same in meaning.

83 *Ikkarim*, 3.19.

84 Ibid., 1.18.

85 See ibid., 1.7. Cf. *MN* 2.39.

86 "These are the rational laws, being the basis and preamble of the divine law, proceeding it in character and time . . . For the divine laws cannot become compete until the social and rational laws are perfected." Halevi, *Kuzari*, 1.48:111.

87 See Husik, intro., pp. xxi ff.

CHAPTER 12. Late Medieval Developments

1 *Meiri* to B. *San.* 57a, p. 226.

2 *Meiri* to B. *AZ* 20a, p. 46. He refers to pre-Christian and pre-Muslim gentiles as being from "earlier faiths" (*ha'emunot ha-kedumot*). See *Meiri* to B. *Kid.* 17b, p. 108.

3 See Katz, *Exclusiveness and Tolerance*, 120–121.

4 See Kohut, *Aruch Completum*, 3:169.

5 *Meiri: Avot*, intro., 16. See *MN* 2:40. For a similar approach, see R. Zvi Hirsch Chajes, "Torat Nevi'im," in *Kol Sifrei Mahoratz Chajes* I, 8–9, 70, 205.

6 *Meiri* to B. *BK* 38a, p. 122.

7 See *supra*, 44–45.

8 *Meiri* to B. *San.* 59a, p. 229.

9 *Meiri* to B. *Yev.* 48b, p. 192.

10 Thus we find in the twelfth-century *Decretum* of Gratian, the oldest part of the collected Canon Law: "Moralia mandata ad naturale ius spectant, atque ideo nullam mutabilitatem recepisse monstrantur . . . naturale ergo ius ab exordio rationalis creaturae incipiens, ut supra dictum est, manet immobile." Quoted in I. Husik, "The Law of Nature, Hugo Grotius, and the Bible," *HUCA* (1925), 1:387–388. Also, see Aquinas, *Summa Theologiae*, 2-2, q. 98, a. 5.

11 *Arakh.* 29a. See also Chajes, *Ateret Zevi—Tiferet Yisrael* in *Kol Kitvei Maharatz Chajes*, 1:490.

12 See *supra*, 285, n. 8.

13 *Shab.* 20.14. See *Milah*, 1.6.

14 See *supra*, 85–86.

15 See *supra*, 83–86.

16 See *supra*, 144–145.

17 *Meiri* to B. *Kid.* 21a: 181. See *Tos.*, s.v. *de-la*.

18 B. *San.* 58b–59a. For a thorough discussion of later halakhic treatments of this theme, see David Hoffman, *Responsa Melamed le-Ho'il*, 2, no. 77, pp. 82–83.

19 See *Mel.* 10.9.

20 *Meiri* to B. *San.* 59a: 229.

21 See *Men.* 73b and parallels; P. *Dem.* 3.1 (23b); *Ter.* 4.15.

22 See *supra*, 28–30.

23 *Mel.* 10.10.

24 Thus *Radbaz* to *Mel.* 10.10 prohibits non-Jewish use of objects such as *tefillin*.

25 See *EJ*, 13:1260–1261.

26 See *supra*, 28.

27 See *LTJ* 2:127–128.

28 See *Encyclopedia of Religion and Ethics* (Hastings), 8:407 ff.

29 *Bi'ur Halakha* to *SA*: *OH* 304.3. See Abraham Gumbiner, *Magen Avraham* thereto. Also, note Akiva Eiger to *SA*: *YD* 241, end.

30 B. *AZ* 64b.

31 See *EJ*, 2:159 and 8:1134 ff.

32 *Hul.* 4a.

33 See *Mel.* 10.8 and Abraham Eisenstadt, *Pithai Teshuvah* to *SA*: *YD* 264.1, n. 5; also *LTJ* 2:221–222.

34 B. *San.* 59b re Deut. 33:4.

35 *Tan.*, Vayera, ed. Buber, 44b. See *SR* 47.1; P. *Peah* 2.4 (10a); *PR* 14b; also, B. *Git.* 60b and *Tos.*, s.v. *atmohei* and *Tem.* 14b.

36 See *supra*, 253, n. 23. For the Christian claim of "true Israel," see Epistle of Barnabas, 4.6.

37 *Responsa Pe'er Ha-Dor*, no. 50.

38 See *supra*, 86–87, 91–92.

39 *Lehem Shamayim* (New York, 1950) to *Avot* 4.11.

40 See *EJ*, 10:762 ff.

41 See e.g. B. *Ber.* 5a re Ex. 24:12.

42 *Mekharai ha-Yahadut* (Warsaw, 1931), 2:24 ff. See Heinemann, *Ta'amei Ha-Mitzvot*, 2:69.

43 For Luzzatto's anti-Reform position, see his comment to Lev. 7:18, pp. 402–403.

44 Comment to Ex. 20:2, pp. 320–321. See his *Yesodei ha-Torah*, nos. 34–36:47 ff.; T. *San.* 8.4 and B. *San.* 38a.

45 See N.H. Rosenbloom, *Luzzatto's Ethico-Psychological Interpretation of Judaism* (New York, 1965), 59 ff.

46 See *supra*, 144–145.

47 Comment to Ex. 22:20, p. 346. Cf. David Hume, *An Inquiry Concerning the Principles of Morals*, ed. C.W. Hendel (New York, 1957), App. I, 104 ff.

48 Comment to Lev. 18:5, p. 417.

49 Comment to Deut. 6:5, pp. 516 ff. See R. Israel Lipschuetz, *Tiferet Yisrael* to *Avot* 3.17; also, to *Avot* 2.14 and M. *BK* 4.3.

50 *Israël et l'humanité*, 496, 614.

51 Ibid., 461–462. See also 508.

52 Ibid., 468. See *Be-Shbilai ha-Mussar*, trans. S. Marcus (Jerusalem, 1966), 118 ff.

53 Ibid., 566.

54 See e.g. *BR* 36.8.

55 *Israël et l'humanité*, 630–631.

56 Aimé Pallière, *The Unknown Sanctuary*, trans. L.W. Wise (New York, 1928), 157–158.

57 See *supra*, 11–13.

58 See *JE*, 2:684.

59 "Israel and the Oikoumenē," in *Studies in Rationalism, Judaism and Universalism*, 56–67.

CHAPTER 13. Moses Mendelssohn and his School

1 See Guttmann, *Philosophies of Judaism*, 291 ff.

2 See *supra*, 84–86, 195–199.

3 See *supra*, 173–175.

4 The letter is dated Oct. 26, 1773, *Schriften*, jub. edn. 16:178–180.

5 The reply is dated Nov. 1773 (ibid.).

6 See *Shofar*, 2.4 ala B. *RH* 28b–29a; *LTJ* 1:140.

7 See *Schriften*, 16:166 ff. This was concerning Mendelssohn's unorthodox views regarding delayed burial. See A. Altmann, *Moses Mendelssohn: A Biography* (Tuscaloosa, AL, 1973), 288 ff.; *LTJ* 2:106–107.

8 *Jerusalem*, trans. M. Samuels (London, 1838), 2:96–97.

9 See *supra*, 156–160.

10 *Schriften*, jub. edn., 7:11, note c.

11 *MN* 3.29.

12 Note: "With these ideas Mendelssohn affirms the fundamental spirit of the western European civilization of his day. Medieval rationalists did not fully comprehend the universal consequences of the rational concepts of religious truth; in the reality of the medieval world, the religious communities remained isolated in their exclusiveness." Guttman, op. cit., 298.

13 See *supra*, 189–194, 203–205.

14 See e.g. Gal. 3:10–14.

15 See Altmann, *Moses Mendelssohn*, 36 ff.

16 Schiller, *Werke*, ed. J. Mueller (Berlin, 1967), 1:64. See M. Meyer, *The Origins of the Modern Jew* (Detroit, 1967), 13 ff.

17 *Jerusalem and Other Jewish Writings*, trans. A. Jospe (New York, 1969), 66. *Schriften*, ed. M. Brasch (Leipzig, 1880), 2:424.

18 See *supra*, 285–286, n. 11.

19 *Emunot ve-De'ot*, 3.6.

20 Ibid., 1.6.

21 *Jerusalem*, ed. Jospe, 65.

22 Ibid., 61–62.

23 "Historical truths, or accounts of the occurrence of the primitive world . . . and as

historical truths, they cannot according to their nature be received otherwise than *on trust*; authority alone gives them the necessary evidence." *Jerusalem*, 2:151–152.

24 See *Morgenstuden*, ch. 17 in *Schriften*, 1:434 ff.; Altmann, op. cit., 123 ff.

25 *Jerusalem*, ed. Jospe, 62; *Schriften*, 2:419. Note: "The Supreme Bring revealed them to all rational beings . . . and inscribed them in their soul in a character legible and intelligible *at all times* and *in all places*." *Jerusalem*, 2:150.

26 For a traditional critique of Mendelssohn's overemphasis on the centrality of Noahide law, see Benamozegh, *Israël et l'humanité*, 506 ff.

27 *Moses Mendelssohn*, 295.

28 *Jewish Philosophy in Modern Times*, 15. See Agus, *Jewish Identity in An Age of Ideologies*, 12 ff.

29 Warsaw, 1886.

30 Note: "Thank the God of your forefathers, thank God who is all love and mercy, that the error appears to be gradually vanishing. The nations are now tolerating and bearing with one another, while to you also they are showing kindness and forbearance, which . . . may grow to true brotherly love." *Jerusalem*, 1:116. (The quote is from the full text of Mendelssohn's introduction, which is included in Samuels' translation of *Jerusalem* as a supplement.)

31 *Divrei Shalom v'Emet*, 3. Note Mendelssohn: "Revealed *religion* is one thing, revealed *legislation* is another . . . All this is the *universal religion of mankind*, and not Judaism." (*Jerusalem*, 2:10).

32 Ibid., 5–6.

33 See *VR* 9.3.

34 *Divrei Shalom v'Emet*, 7.

35 Ibid., 9.

36 Ibid., 222–223.

37 For a critique of this portrayal, see Simon Rawidowicz, *Studies in Jewish Thought* (Philadelphia, 1974), 345–346. Cf. Y. Kaufmann, *Golah ve-Nekhar* (Tel Aviv, 1930), 22 ff.

CHAPTER 14. Hermann Cohen and the Jewish Neo-Kantians

1 B. *Kid.* 66a.

2 For Cohen's critique of Mendelssohn on this point, invoking the example of Noahide law among others, see "Deutschtum und Judenthum" (I), *Jüdische Schriften*, 2:257–259.

3 The article was entitled "Ein Bekenntnis in der Judenfrage," *Jüdische Schriften*, 2:73 ff. See 3:73.

4 See S.H. Bergman, *Faith and Reason: An Introduction to Modern Jewish Thought*, trans. A. Jospe (Washington, DC, 1961), 28–31.

5 Rohling's work brought forth a whole series of responses, the most complete being *Israel und die Völker* (Leipzig, 1922) by the Austrian rabbi and statesman Josef Bloch. In this work Bloch presents a wide selection of rabbinic sources to disprove Rohling's point. His work does not, however, deal with the sources systematically either on the conceptual or historical level.

6   *Religion of Reason*, trans. Kaplan, intro., 4. Cf. *Critique of Pure Reason*, B93.

7   See *supra*, 11–13.

8   "Die Nachstenliebe im Talmud," *Jüdische Schriften*, 1:159–160.

9   Ibid., 163.

10 *Religion of Reason*, 8.16:122–123. See "Liebe und Gerechtigkeit in den Begriffen Gott und Mensch," *Jüdische Schriften*, 3:86. Cohen's use of the term "natural" must be understood not as nature qua external world, but nature in Kant's sense, viz., an ideal construct of pure practical reason. See *Critique of Practical Reason*, trans. L.W. Beck (Indianapolis, 1956), 1.1.2:72; Novak, *Suicide and Morality*, 87–88.

11 *The Ethics of Judaism*, 1:221–222.

12 "Das Problem der jüdischen Sittenlehre: Eine Kritik von Lazarus' *Ethik des Judenthums*," *Jüdische Schriften*, 3:30.

13 See *Jüdische Schriften*, 1:160–161; *Religion of Reason*, 8.17:124.

14 See *De Jure Belli ac Pacis*, prol., sect. 8 and 1.16, 2.5. For the radical character of Grotius' theory, see E. Bloch, *Natürrecht und menschliche Würde* (Frankfurt, 1961), 63–64.

15 "Das Problem der jüdischen Sittenlehre," *Jüdische Schriften*, 3:5. For Cohen, "Sittenlehre" is the material content of Jewish tradition; "Ethik" is Judaism's religious philosophy (10–11).

16 *Religion of Reason*, 8.17:124.

17 Most expressive of Cohen's conviction of the inner identity of Kant's philosophy and Judaism is the following from his 1880 answer to Treitschke: "Die Kantische Ethik trifft zwar inhaltlich in ihrem Imperativ voellig zusammen mit dem Rigorismus der israelitischen Sittenlehre," *Jüdische Schriften*, 2:76. At the beginning of this essay Cohen speaks of Germany as "Nation Kants" (73). Nevertheless, this inner identity is philosophically constituted; one cannot naïvely assert their historical identity. See *Jüdische Schriften*, 3:12–13.

18 *Nid.* 14b.

19 "The *autonomy* of the will is the sole principle of all moral laws and of the duties conforming to them; *heteronomy* of choice, on the other hand, not only does not establish any obligation but is opposed to the principle of duty and to morality of the will." *Critique of Practical Reason*, 1.1.1, theorem 8:33.

20 *BaR* 19.1. See *LTJ* 2:38–40.

21 See *supra*, 31–35.

22 See e.g. B. *Shab.* 88a and B. *AZ* 2b–3a.

23 See Heinemann, *Ta'amei ha-Mitzvot*, 1:11 ff.

24 See e.g. M. *BM* 1.8; *Avot de-Rabbi Natan*, A, ch. 34:51a.

25 *VR* 28.1 and parallels.

26 See *supra*, 154–156.

27 *Philosophies of Judaism*, 357. See *supra*.

28 See *Critique of Pure Reason*, B612 ff.

29 See Novak, *Suicide and Morality*, 91–97.

30 *Theaetetus*, 152A, 166D.

31 See *Critique of Pure Reason*, B575 ff.

32 See *Critique of Practical Reason*, 1.1.2:59 ff.

33 See *Fundamentals Principles of the Metaphysic of Morals*, 12 ff.

34 Ibid., 33 ff.

35 See e.g. *Religion of Reason*, 15.36:325–326 ala *Avot* 1.3.

36 Cf. Y. Yovel, "The Highest Good and History in Kant's Thought," *Archiv für Geschichte der Philosophie* (1972), 54:238–283.

37 *Critique of Practical Reason*, 1.2.2.5:129.

38 See *Jüdische Schriften*, 3:18.

39 Ibid., 3:2.

40 For the influence of Hegel on Cohen, see *Ethik des reinen Willens*, 254 ff.

41 *Religion of Reason*, 8.12:120. See intro., 15:33.

42 "Zum Prioritaetsstreit über das Gebot der Nächstenliebe," *Jüdische Schriften*, 1:175–176. For Cohen such a *Grundsatz* is surely a *Vernunftsatz*, *contra* Mendelssohn (*supra*, 209–211.).

43 See *supra*, 19–23.

44 *Jüdische Schriften*, 1:148–149. See 194.

45 "Die Fremdenliebe ist somit ein schoepferisches Moment in der Entstehung des Begriffs vom Menschen als dem Nächsten," *Jüdische Schriften*, 1:150. See *Religion of Reason*, 17:391.

46 See P. *Ned.* 9.4 (41c) and *KE* thereto; *SM*, pos. no. 206 and *De'ot*, 6.3 (cf. *Abel*, 14.1); *Hinukh*, no. 243. See also Ernst Simon, "The Neighbor (*Re'a*) Whom We Shall Love," in *Modern Jewish Ethics*, ed. M. Fox, 29 ff.

47 See *Sifra*, Kedoshim, 89a; *Targum Pseudo-Jonathan* to Lev. 19:18 ala B. *Shab.* 31a; Bahya ibn Pakudah, *Hovot Ha-Levavot*, 8.3.33; *Semag*, pos. no. 9; Hasdai Crescas, *Or ha-Shem*, 2.6.1.

48 See Heinemann, *Ta'amei ha-Mitzvot*, 1:46.

49 Thus in his rejection of this whole tendency, Franz Rosenzweig wrote to Martin Buber in 1923: "wir hoeren aus dem überdruss zitierten Geschichte von Hillel und dem Proselyten . . . und halten uns an sein letztes, nicht an sein erstes Wort: geh und lerne." "Die Bauleute," *Kleinere Schriften*, 109. Afterwards (109–110), he praises Buber for liberating Judaism from a reduction to Kantianism.

50 See Rotenstreich, *Jewish Philosophy in Modern Times*, 52–54.

51 *Religion of Reason*, 13.20:249. Cohen's use of Hegel's key term *Aufhebung* (in verbal form) is highly significant. *Aufhebung* is the process where something is elevated and transformed onto a higher level. See Hegel, *Logic*, 107 and W. Kaufmann, *Hegel: A Reinterpretation* (Garden City, NY, 1965), 180–181; also, W.S. Dietrich, "The Function of the Idea of Messianic Mankind in Hermann Cohen's Later Thought," *Journal of the American Academy of Religion* (June 1980), 48.2:245–258.

52 See *Religion of Reason*, 13.44:255 ff. Cf. 17:389–390. Such a view was by no means a uniquely liberal German-Jewish one. See e.g. R. Samson Raphael Hirsch, *Commentary on the Pentateuch*: Lev. 20:26 (3.2:584–585).

53 See "Deutschtum und Judenthum" (II), *Jüdische Schriften*, 2:310–311.

54 "Das Deutschtum muss zum Mittelpunkte eines Staatsbundes werden, der den Frieden der Welt begrunden und in ihm die wahrhafte Begründung einer Kulturwelt stiffen wird," *Jüdische Schriften*, 2:287.

55 See *Religion of Reason*, 6.596; also, *Ethik des reinen Willens*, 454.

56 See "Religion und Sittichkeit," *Jüdische Schriften*, 3:134–135, also 289; *Religion of Reason*, 6.2:95; *Ethik des reinen Willens*, 457 ff.

57 See Guttmann, *Philosophies of Judaism*, 366; Rotenstreich, *Jewish Philosophy in Modern Times*, 56–57. Cf., however, Franz Rosenzweig, "Hermann Cohens jüdische Schriften," *Kleinere Schriften*, 332.

58 See *Religion of Reason*, 16:345; "Das Gottesreich," *Jüdische Schriften*, 3:169 ff. For Kant's notion of Kingdom of Ends, see *Fundamental Principles of the Metaphysics of Morals*, 50–51.

59 See *Der Stern der Erlösung* (Frankfurt, 1921), intro.

60 See Baeck's last work, *Diese Volk: Jüdische Existenz* (Frankfurt, 1955), 1:114, 178; (Frankfurt, 1957), 2:324. For his earlier Kantianism, however, see "Romantic Religion" in *Judaism and Christianity*, ed. and trans. W. Kaufmann (Philadelphia, 1958), 254–255.

61 B. *Yev.* 24a.

62 "Die Autonomie der Sittlichkeit im jüdischen Schriftum" in *Judaica Festschrift zu Hermann Cohens siebzigtum Geburtstage* (Berlin, 1912), 107–108.

63 B. *Kid.* 31a.

64 Quoting Hirsch's *Religionsphilosophie der Juden* (Leipzig, 1842), 33.

65 *Religion of Reason*, 15.39:324.

66 "Die Lehre vom umgeschreibenem Gesetz in jüdischen Schriftum," 160–161.

67 *Dat u-Mada*, trans. S. Asch (Jerusalem, 1955), 226–227.

68 *Hazal*, 283 ff.

CHAPTER 15. Conclusion

1 *Responsa Rashba*, no. 414, 1:150. For the historical background of this ban, see F.I. Baer, *A History of the Jews in Christian Spain*, trans. L. Schoffman (Philadelphia, 1978), 1:236 ff., 289 ff. Centuries later, S.D. Luzzatto distinguished between philosophy beginning from premises antithetical to Judaism (especially "Greek" metaphysics) and "true" philosophy which is in harmony with Judaism. He claims that this latter philosophy has not yet been written. See his comment to Deut. 6:5. Cf. B. Lonergan, *Method in Theology* (New York, 1972), 24–25; A. Nygren, *Meaning and Method*, trans. P.S. Watson (Philadelphia, 1972), 359–360.

2 B. *Kid.* 30a.

3 *Talmud Torah*, 1.11–12. See also B. *Shab.* 31a (bot.) and Rashi, s.v. *hebanta*. For an analysis of the antecedents and consequents of this text, see I. Twersky, "Some Non-Halakhic Aspects of the *Mishneh Torah*," in *Jewish Medieval and Renaissance Studies*, ed. A. Altmann (Cambridge, MA, 1967), 106 ff. On the other hand, Faur, in his *Iyunim be-Mishneh Torah le-ha-Rambam* (53), insists that Maimonides only means "legal thought" similar to the use of Gemara on B. *BM* 33a. However, he neglects to quote the crucial inclusion of *pardes*, i.e., physics and metaphysics, in *ha-gemara*. For other Maimonidean sources dealing with the order of studies, see *Hakdamah le-Mishneh*, 79 ff.; comment to *Hag.* 2.1; *MN*, intro., 3.51.

4 For those who are not philosophically inclined, however, Talmud/Gemara is ultimately the particular body of literature that subsequently came to bear this name. See B. *Kid.* 30a, *Tos.*, s.v. *lo* based on B. *San.* 24a.

5 Note: "Die erste und grundlegende Aufgabe der mittelalterlichen Philosophie ist die gesetzliche Begründung der Philosophie, d.i., vor allem der Nachweiss, dass die zum philosophieren verpflichtet und also ermachtigt sind." Leo Strauss, *Philosophie und Gesetz* (Berlin, 1935), 48. See his *Persecution and the Art of Writing*, 88–89.

6 *Nicomachean Ethics*, 1095a30–1095b10. Cf. 1094b10.25 and Plato, *Republic*, 510B; Wilhelm Dilthey, *Gesammelte Schriften* (Leipzig, 1914), 7.79–80. For the importance of philosophical reflection as *Philosophie von unten*, see Husserl, "Philosophy as Rigorous Science," in *Phenomenology and the Crisis of Philosophy*, trans. Q. Lauer (New York, 1965), 121–122 and n. 60 thereon. Franz Rosenzweig argued for the Jewishness of this method. Note: "Und wir tragen das Leben von der Peripherie her, wo wir es fanden . . . ins Zentrum . . . dass dies Zentrum nu rein jüdisches Zentrum sein kann." "Neues Lernen," *Kleinere Schriften* (Berlin, 1937), 98.

7 See *LTJ* 1:155, n. 2.

8 See *Mishneh Torah*, intro. ala B. *Ber.* 5a.

9 See *Symposium*, 202E, where philosophical *eros* is experienced as the "ambivalence" (*metaxu*) of the immortal and the mortal; *Republic*, 523C, where the "paradoxical" (*to enantion*) "calls" (*parakalounta*) the mind to "reflection" (*episkepsasthai*); *Theaetetus*, 155C–D, where "wonder" (*to thaumazein*), the beginning of philosophy, results from the experience of "contradiction" (*paradexometha*). Note, also, Hegel's critique of the formalism of Kant's moral philosophy in *Phaenomenologie des Geistes*, 6.c.b., ed. Hoffmeister (Hamburg, 1952), 434 ff., and Sartre's critique of the lack of motivation in Husserl's phenomenology in the *The Transcendence of the Ego*, trans. F. Williams and R. Kirkpatrick (New York, 1957), 102–103.

10 Cf. Aristotle, *Topics*, 109, and B. *Yev.* 61a and Tos., s.v. *v'ein*. Note: "This, however, contains an ambiguity, insofar as the Israelite is a son of Adam and a son of Abraham." Hermann Cohen, *Religion of Reason*, 8.5:115.

11 Cf. Joseph Soloveitchik, "Ish ha-Halakha," *Talpiot* (1944), 1.3–4:665.

12 See Franz Rosenzweig, "Apologetische Denken," *Kleinere Schriften*, 41–42. Cf. D. Neumark, *Toldot ha-Philosofia be-Yisrael* (New York, 1921), 5–6.

13 See *Critique of Pure Reason*, B165.

14 *Sifra*: Aharei-Mot, 6a; B. *Yoma* 67b.

Afterword

1 For a fuller sense of the philosophical underpinnings of these three events, see D. Novak, *Natural Law in Judaism* (Cambridge, 1998), 1–12.

2 M. Fox, *Interpreting Maimonides: Studies in Methodology, Metaphysics and Moral Philosophy* (Chicago, 1990).

3 D. Novak, *Jewish Social Ethics* (Oxford, 1992), 25–29.

4 J. Sacks, *Crisis and Covenant: Jewish Thought after the Holocaust* (Manchester, 1992), 1.

5 Quoted in M. Walzer, M. Lorberbaum and N. Zohar (eds.), *The Jewish Political Tradition*, vol. 1: *Authority* (New Haven, 2000), 27–28.

6 D. Steinmetz, *Punishment and Freedom: The Rabbinic Construction of Criminal Law* (Philadelphia, 2008).

7 D. Novak, Review of "Freedom and Punishment." *Journal of Religion* 90.1 (Jan. 2010), 93–94.

BIBLIOGRAPHY

Bible and Commentaries

ABRAVANEL, ISAAC. *Commentary on the Pentateuch*. Amsterdam, 1768.

——*Commentary on the Former Prophets*. Jerusalem, 1955.

BAHYA B. ASHER. *Commentary on the Pentateuch*, ed. C.B. Chavel, 3 vols. Jerusalem, 1971.

Biblia Hebraica, ed. R. Kittel. Stuttgart, 1951.

EPSTEIN, BARUCH HA-LEVI. *Torah Temimah*, 5 vols. New York, 1962.

Die fünf Bücher des Weisung, trans. M. Buber and F. Rosenzweig. Cologne, 1954.

GORDIS, ROBERT. *The Book of God and Man*. Chicago, 1965.

HARTOM, A.S. *Commentary on Isaiah*. Tel Aviv, 1972.

HIRSCH, SAMSON RAPHAEL. *Commentary on the Pentateuch*, trans. I. Hunfeld, 6 vols. New York, 1961.

The Holy Scriptures. Philadelphia, 1917.

IBN EZRA, ABRAHAM. *Commentary on the Pentateuch*. In *Mikra'ot Gedolot*. New York, 1951.

KAISER, O. *Isaiah 13–39: A Commentary*, trans. R.A. Wilson. Philadelphia, 1974.

KASHER, M.M. *Torah Shlemah*. New York, 1956.

KIMHI, DAVID. *Commentary on Prophets and Writings*. In *Mikra'ot Gedolot*. New York, 1951.

LUZZATTO, SAMUEL DAVID. *Commentary on the Pentateuch*, ed. P. Schlesinger. Tel Aviv, 1965.

MALBIM, MEIR LEIBUSH. *Commentary on the Pentateuch*, 2 vols. Jerusalem, 1957.

MEIR, SAMUEL B., *see* Rashbam

MEIR SIMHAH OF DVINSK. *Meshekh Hokhmah*, ed. A. Abraham. Jerusalem, 1972.

NAHMANIDES, *see* Ramban

RAMBAN (NAHMANIDES). *Commentary on the Pentateuch*, ed. Chavel, 2 vols. Jerusalem, 1963.

RASHBAM (SAMUEL B. MEIR). *Commentary on the Pentateuch*, ed. Bromberg. Jerusalem, 1959.

RASHI. *Commentary on the Pentateuch*. In *Mikra'ot Gedolot*. New York, 1951.

——*Commentary on the Pentateuch*, ed. M. Rosenbaum and A.M. Silberman, 2 vols. London, 1946.

——*Commentary on the Prophets and Writings*. In *Mikra'ot Gedolot*. New York, 1951.

SFORNO, OBADIAH. *Commentary on the Pentateuch*. In *Mikra'ot Gedolot*. New York, 1951.

Septuagint, 6th edn., ed. A. Rahlfs, 2 vols. Stuttgart, n.d.

The Torah. Philadelphia, 1962.

Vulgate, ed. G. Nolli, 3 vols. Rome, 1955.

Hellenistic Jewish Sources

Apocrypha and Pseudepigrapha of the Old Testament, ed. R.H. Charles, 2 vols. Oxford, 1913.

JOSEPHUS. *Contra Apionem*, ed. and trans. H. St. John Thackeray. Cambridge, MA, 1926.

——*Antiquities of the Jews*, ed. and trans. H. St. John Thackeray et al., 6 vols. Cambridge, MA, 1930–65.

——*Bellum Judaicum*, ed. and trans. H. St. John Thackeray, 2 vols. Cambridge, MA, 1927.

——*Vita*, ed. and trans. H. St. John Thackeray. Cambridge, MA, 1926.

Letter of Aristeas, ed. and trans. M. Hadas. New York, 1951.

ORIGEN. *Hexaplar*, ed. F. Field. Oxford, 1875.

PHILO. *De Decalogo*, ed. and trans. F.H. Colson. Cambridge, MA, 1937.

——*De Ebrietate*, ed. and trans. F.H. Colson. Cambridge, MA, 1930.

——*Fragments*, ed. T. Mangey, vol. 2 of *Opera*. Erlangen, 1785.

——*Legum Allegoria*, ed. and trans. G.H. Whitaker. Cambridge, MA, 1929.

——*De Specialibus Legibus*, ed. and trans. F.H. Colson. Cambridge, MA, 1937.

——*De Vita Mosis*, ed. and trans. F.H. Colson. Cambridge, MA, 1935.

Rabbinic Sources

Avot de-Rabbi Natan, ed. Solomon Schechter. New York, 1967.

Babylonian Talmud. Vilna edn., 1898.

Bamidbar Rabbah. New York, 1957.

Bereshit Rabbah, ed. Theodor–Albeck, 3 vols. Jerusalem, 1965.

Canticles Rabbah. New York, 1957.

Devarim Rabbah. New York, 1957.

Dikdukai Sofrim, ed. R. Rabinovicz, 2 vols. New York, 1976.

Eichah Rabbati. New York, 1957.

Esther Rabbati. New York, 1957.

Igeret Rab Shereira Gaon 1.5, ed. A. Hyman. Jerusalem, 1967.

Igeret Teman, ed. M. Rabinowitz. Jerusalem, 1960.

Kohelet Rabbati. New York, 1957.

Lekha Tov, ed. S. Buber. Vilna, 1884.

Mekhilta der Rabbi Ishmael, ed. Horovitz–Rabin. Jerusalem, 1960.

Mekhilta der Rabbi Ishmael, ed. J. Lauterbach, 3 vols. Philadelphia, 1949.

Midrash Tannaim, ed. D. Hoffman, 2 vols. Berlin, 1909.

Midrash Tehillim, ed. S. Buber. Vilna, 1891.

Mishnah, ed. H. Albeck, 6 vols. Tel Aviv, 1957.

Mishnah. Vilna edn., 1892.

Mishnat Rabbi Eliezer, ed. H. Enelow, 2 vols. New York, 1934.

Otzar ha-Geonim, ed. B.M. Lewin, 13 vols. Jerusalem, 1928–43.

Otzar ha-Geonim: Sanhedrin, ed. H.Z. Taubes. Jerusalem, 1966.

Pesikta Rabbati, ed. M. Friedmann. Vienna, 1880.

Pesikta de-Rav Kahana, ed. B. Mandelbaum, 2 vols. New York, 1962.

Pirkei Rabbi Eliezer. Antwerp, n.d.

Seder Eliyahu Rabba, ed. M. Friedmann. Vienna, 1904.

Seder Eliyahu Zuta, ed. M. Friedmann. Vienna, 1904.

Seder Olam, ed. B. Ratner. New York, 1946.

She'iltot de-Rav Ahai Gaon, ed. E.M. Kenig. Jerusalem, 1940.

Sifre: Bamidbar, ed. M. Friedmann. Vienna, 1864.

Sifre de-Bay Rav, ed. H. Weiss. Vienna, 1862.

Sifre: Devarim, ed. L. Finkelstein. Berlin, 1939.

Students' Edition of the Babylonian Talmud, trans. E.W. Kirzner. London, 1956.

Tanhuma, ed. S. Buber. Vilna, 1885.

Tanhuma, printed edn. Jerusalem, 1962.

Targum Onkelos. In *Mikra'ot Gedolot*. New York, 1951.

Targum Pseudo-Jonathan. In *Mikra'ot Gedolot*. New York, 1951

Targum Yerushalmi. In *Mikra'ot Gedolot*. New York, 1951.

Tosefta, ed. M.S. Zuckermandel. New York, 1963.

Tosefta, ed. S. Lieberman, 4 vols. (*Zera'im–Nashim*). New York, 1955–73.

Vayikra Rabbah, ed. R. Margaliot, 4 vols. Jerusalem, 1953.

Yalkut Shimoni, 2 vols. New York, 1944.

Commentaries on Rabbinic Sources

ABRAHAM B. DAVID OF POSQUIÈRES, *see* Rabad

ABULAFIA, MEIR. *Yad Ramah*. Salonika, 1798.

ADRET, SOLOMON IBN, *see* Rashba

ANATOLI, JACOB. *Malmad ha-Talmidim*. Lyck, 1866.

ASHKENAZI, BEZALEL. *Sheitah Mekubetzet*. In Babylonian Talmud. Vilna edn., 1898.

ASHKENAZI, JUDAH. *Be'er Haytev*. In *Shulhan Arukh*. Lemberg edn., 1873.

BACH (JOEL SIRKES). *Bayit Hadash*. In *Tur*. Jerusalem, 1969.

CHAJES, ZVI HIRSCH. Notes on Babylonian Talmud. Vilna edn., 1898.

DE BOTEN, ABRAHAM. *Lehem Mishneh*. In *Mishneh Torah*. Vilna edn., 1900.

EDELS, SAMUEL, *see* Maharsha

EIGER, AKIVA. Notes on *Shulhan Arukh*. Lemberg edn., 1873.

EISENSTADT, ABRAHAM. *Pithai Teshuvah*. In *Shulhan Arukh*. Lemberg edn., 1873.

EMDEN, JACOB. *Lehem Shamayim*. New York, 1950.

Encyclopedia Talmudit, 16 vols. Jerusalem, 1955–80.

GERONDI, JONAH. *Rabbenu Yonah* on *Alfasi*. In Babylonian Talmud. Vilna edn., 1898.

GINZBERG, LOUIS. *Peirushim ve-Hiddushim be-Yerushalmi: Berakhot*, 4 vols. New York, 1941–63.

HA-KOHEN, SHABBATAI, *see* Shakh

HA-LEVI, DAVID, *see* Taz

HELLER, YOM TOV LIPMANN. *Tosafot Yom Tov*. In Mishnah. New York, 1963.

IBN HABIB, JOSEPH. *Nimuqai Yosef*. In Babylonian Talmud. Vilna edn., 1898.

ISHBILI, YOM TOV B. ABRAHAM, *see* Ritba

ISSERLES, MOSES, *see* Ramo

KARO, JOSEPH. *Bet Yosef*. In *Tur*. Jerusalem, 1969.

——*Kesef Mishnah*. In *Mishneh Torah*. Vilna edn., 1900.

KOHUT, ALEXANDER. *Arukh Completum*, 8 vols. Vienna, 1926.

LIEBERMAN, SAUL. *Tosefta Kifshuta*, 9 vols. New York, 1955–73.

LIPSCHUETZ, ISRAEL. *Tiferet Yisrael*. In Mishnah. New York, 1963.

LURIA, SOLOMON. *Yam shel Shlomo*, 2 vols. New York, 1953.

MAHARSHA (SAMUEL EDELS). *Hiddushai Halakhot-Hiddushai Aggadot*. In Babylonian Talmud. Vilna edn., 1898.

MAIMONIDES, *see* Rambam

MEIR, SAMUEL B., *see* Rashbam

MEIRI, MENACHEM. *Bet ha-Behirah: Avodah Zarah*, ed. Sofe. Jerusalem, 1964.

——*Bet ha-Behirah: Avot*, ed. A. Sofer. Jerusalem, 1964.

——*Bet ha-Behirah: Bava Batra*, ed. Menat. Jerusalem, 1971.

——*Bet ha-Behirah: Bava Kamma*, ed. K. Schlesinger. Jerusalem, 1967.

——*Bet ha-Behirah: Hullin*, Parma edn. New York, 1945.

——*Bet ha-Behirah: Ketubot*, ed. A. Sofer. Jerusalem, 1968.

——*Bet ha-Behirah: Kiddushin*, ed. A. Sofer. Jerusalem, 1963.

——*Bet ha-Behirah: Makkot*, ed. S. Strelitz. Jerusalem, 1966.

——*Bet ha-Behirah: Sanhedrin*, ed. A. Sofer. Jerusalem, 1965.

——*Bet ha-Behirah: Yevamot*, ed. S. Dickman. Jerusalem, 1968.

MORDECAI B. HILLEL. *Mordecai*. In Babylonian Talmud. Vilna edn., 1898.

NAHMANIDES, *see* Ramban

RAMBAM (MAIMONIDES). *Commentary on the Mishnah*, ed. and trans. J. Kappah, 3 vols. Jerusalem, 1964–67.

——*Hakdamah le-Perush ha-Mishnah*, ed. M. Rabinowitz. Jerusalem, 1961.

RAMBAN (NAHMANIDES). *Hiddushai Ramban*, 2 vols. Bnai Barak, 1959.

——Notes on Maimonides' *Sefer ha-Mitzvot*. Jerusalem, 1962.

——*Peirush mi-Ba'al Sefer Haredim*. In *Palestinian Talmud*. Vilna edn., 1922.

RABAD (ABRAHAM B. DAVID OF POSQUIÈRES). Notes on Maimonides' *Mishneh Torah*. Vilna edn., 1900.

——Notes on *Sifra*, ed. H. Weiss. Vienna, 1862.

RAMO (MOSES ISSERLES). Notes on *Shulhan Arukh*. Lemberg edn., 1873.

RASHBA (SOLOMON IBN ADRET). *Hiddushai Rashba,* 3 vols. Jerusalem, 1963.

RASHBAM (SAMUEL B. MEIR). Notes on *Bava Batra.* In Babylonian Talmud. Vilna edn., 1898.

RASHI. Notes on *Babylonian Talmud.* Vilna edn., 1898.

RITBA (YOM TOV B. ABRAHAM ISHBILI). *Hiddushai Ritba,* 3 vols. New York, 1970.

——Notes on *Bava Batra,* ed. M.Y. Blau. New York, 1954.

ROZANIS, JUDAH. *Mishneh le-Melekh.* In *Mishneh Torah.* Vilna edn., 1900.

SAMUEL AVIGDOR B. ABRAHAM. *Minhat Bikkurim.* In Babylonian Talmud. Vilna edn., 1898.

SHAKH (SHABBATAI HA-KOHEN). *Siftai Kohen.* In *Shulhan Arukh.* Lemberg edn., 1873.

SIRKES, JOEL, *see* Bach

TAZ (DAVID HA-LEVI). *Turai Zahav.* In *Shulhan Arukh.* Lemberg edn., 1873.

Tosafot. In Babylonian Talmud. Vilna edn., 1898.

Tosefta Yeshenim. In Babylonian Talmud. Vilna edn., 1898.

VIDAL OF TOLOSA. *Maggid Mishneh.* In *Mishneh Torah.* Vilna edn., 1900.

YELLIN, ARYEH LEIB. *Yefeh Aynayim.* In Babylonian Talmud. Vilna edn., 1898.

ZUNDEL, HANOKH. *Etz Yosef.* In *Midrash Rabbah.* New York, 1957.

Codes and Responsa

ADRET, SOLOMON IBN, *see* Rashba

ALFASI, ISAAC. *Codification of Babylonian Talmud.* Vilna edn., 1898.

ASHER B. YEHIEL, *see* Rosh

BACHRACH, HAYIM YAIR. *Responsa Havot Yair.* Lemberg, 1896.

EMDEN, JACOB. *Responsa Yabetz.* Lemberg, 1884.

EPHRAIM HA-KOHEN. *Responsa Sha'ar Ephraim: Orah Hayyim.* New York, 1958.

EPSTEIN, YEHIEL MICHAL. *Arukh ha-Shulhan he-Atid: Melakhim.* Jerusalem, 1973.

FEINSTEIN, MOSHE. *Igrot Moshe,* vol. 2. New York, 1964.

HA-LEVI, AARON. *Sefer ha-Hinukh.* Jerusalem, n.d.

HATAM SOFER (MOSES SCHREIBER). *Responsa Hatam Sofer: Orah Hayyim, Yoreh Deah.* New York, 1958.

HIRSCHENSOHN, HAYYIM. *Malki ba-Kodesh,* 3 vols. St. Louis, 1919–23.

ISSERLES, MOSES, *see* Ramo

JACOB B. ASHER. *Tur,* 6 vols. Jerusalem, 1969.

KARO, JOSEPH. *Shulhan Arukh,* 7 vols. Lemberg edn., 1873.

LAMPRONTI, ISAAC. *Pahad Yitzhak,* 6 vols. Lyck, 1846.

LANDAU, EZEKIEL. *Noda bi-Yehuda,* 2 vols. Vilna, 1904.

MAIMONIDES, *see* Rambam

MELTZER, I.Z. *Even ha'Ezel,* 3 vols. Tel Aviv, 1962.

MOSES OF COUCY. *Sefer ha-Mitzvot ha-Gedolot,* 2 vols. Jerusalem, 1959.

NAHMANIDES, *see* Ramban

Piskai Tosafot. In Babylonian Talmud. Vilna edn., 1898.

RADBAZ (DAVID IBN ABI ZIMRA). *Responsa ha-Radbaz,* 2 vols. Warsaw, 1852.

RAMBAM (MAIMONIDES). *The Code of Maimonides—Book XIV: The Book of Judges,* trans. A.M. Hershman. New Haven, 1949

—— *Hilkhot Melakhim,* ed. M. Rabinowitz. Jerusalem, 1962.

—— *Kobetz Teshuvot ha-Rambam v'Igrotav,* ed. A. Lichtenberg. Leipzig, 1859.

—— *Mishneh Torah,* 5 vols. Vilna, 1900.

—— *Responsa Pe'er ha-Dor.* Amsterdam, 1750.

—— *Sefer ha-Mitzvot,* ed. Heller. New York, 1946.

—— *Teshuvot ha-Rambam,* ed. J. Blau, 3 vols. Jerusalem, 1957.

—— *Teshuvot ha-Rambam,* ed. A. Freimann. Jerusalem, 1934.

RAMBAN (NAHMANIDES). *Teshuvot ha-Ramban,* ed. C. Chavel. Jerusalem, 1975.

RAMO (MOSES ISSERLES). *Responsa Ha-Ramo,* ed. Ziv. Jerusalem, 1970.

RASHBA (SOLOMON IBN ADRET). *Responsa Rashba,* 6 vols. Bnai Barak and Tel Aviv, 1958–73.

—— *Responsa Rashba Attributed to Nahmanides.* Warsaw, 1883.

—— *Torat ha-Bayit he'Arokh.* New York, 1952.

RASHI. *Responsa Rashi,* ed. I. Elfenbein. New York, 1943.

RIBASH (ISAAC B. SHESHET). *Responsa Ribash.* Constantinople, 1547.

ROSH (ASHER B. YEHIEL). *Codification of the Babylonian Talmud.* Vilna edn., 1898.

—— *Responsa Rabbenu Asher.* Vilna, 1881.

—— *Tosafot ha-Rosh.* Vilna edn., 1898.

SCHREIBER, MOSES, *see* Hatam Sofer

SHESHET, ISAAC B., *see* Ribash

WEINBERG, YEHIEL J. *Seridai Esh: Even ha'Ezer,* vols. 3 and 4. Jerusalem, 1966.

ZIMRA, DAVID IBN ABI, *see* Radbaz

Medieval Jewish Theological Works

ALBO, JOSEPH. *Sefer ha-Ikkarim,* ed. and trans. I. Husik, 5 vols. Philadelphia, 1929.

BAHYA IBN PAKUDAH. *Hovot ha-Levavot,* ed. and trans. H. Hyamson. Jerusalem, 1962.

CHEFETZ, MOSES. *Melekh'et Shlemah.* Venice, 1710.

CORDOVERO, MOSES. *Shiur ha-Komah.* Jerusalem, 1965.

CRESCAS, HASDAI. *Or ha-Shem.* Ferrara, 1555.

DI FANO, MENACHEM AZARIAH. *Asarah Ma'amarot.* Frankfurt, 1698.

GERSONIDES, *see* Ralbag

HALEVI, JUDAH. *Das Buch Kuzari,* trans. and comm. D. Cassel. Leipzig, 1853.

—— *Kuzari.* Vilna, 1905.

—— *Kuzari,* trans. H. Hirschenfeld. New York, 1964.

IBN DAOUD, ABRAHAM. *Ha'Emanah ha-Ramah*, ed. Weil. Frankfurt, 1852.

IBN GABBAI, MEIR. *Avodat ha-Kodesh*. Jerusalem, 1954.

IBN GABIROL, SOLOMON. *Selected Religious Poetry*, ed. and trans. I. Davidson. Philadelphia, 1923.

IBN SHEM TOV. *Kevod Elohim*. Ferrara, 1556.

IBN TZADDIK, JOSEPH. *Olam Katan*, ed. Horowitz. Breslau, 1903.

LOEWE, JUDAH, *see* Maharal

MAHARAL (JUDAH LOEWE). *Gevurot ha-Shem*. Tel Aviv, n.d.

MAIMONIDES, *see* Rambam

MANASSEH B. ISRAEL. *The Conciliator*, trans. E.H. Lindo. New York, 1972.

MOSES DE LEON. *Sefer Shekel ha-Kodesh*. London, 1911.

MOSES DI TRANI. *Bet Elohim*. Venice, 1576.

NAHMANIDES, *see* Ramban

RALBAG (GERSONIDES). *Milhamot ha-Shem*. Riva di Trenta, 1560.

RAMBAM (MAIMONIDES). *Dalalat al-Ha'min*, ed. S. Munk. Paris, 1856.

—— *Le Guide des égarés*, trans. S. Munk, 3 vols. Paris, 1856.

—— *Guide of the Perplexed*, trans. S. Pines. Chicago, 1963.

—— *Igeret Teman, Ma'amar Tehiyyat ha-Metim*, trans. Samuel ibn Tibbon. Jerusalem, 1960.

—— *A Maimonides Reader*, ed. and trans. I. Twersky. New York, 1972.

—— *Millot ha-Higayon*, ed. L. Roth. Jerusalem, 1965.

—— *Moreh Nevukim*, trans. Judah al-Harizi, 2 vols. Warsaw, 1904.

—— *Moreh Nevukim*, trans. Samuel ibn Tibbon, with Narboni and Shem Tov commentaries. Warsaw, 1872.

—— *Moreh Nevukim*, trans. and comm. J. Kappah. Jerusalem, 1972.

RAMBAN (NAHMANIDES). *Kitvei Ramban*, ed. C. Chavel, 2 vols. Jerusalem, 1963.

SAADIAH GAON. *Emunot ve-De'ot*, trans. Judah ibn Tibbon. Jerusalem, 1948.

Sefer Hasidim. Jerusalem edn., 1966.

Zohar, ed. R. Margaliot, 3 vols. Jerusalem, 1970.

Zohar Hadash, ed. R. Margaliot. Jerusalem, 1953.

Christian and Muslim Sources

BARNABAS. *Epistle of Barnabas*, ed. and trans. K. Lake. Cambridge, MA, 1912.

CLEMENT OF ALEXANDRIA. *Exhortation to the Greeks*, ed. and trans. B.W. Butterworth. Cambridge, MA, 1919.

Didache, ed. and trans. K. Lake. Cambridge, MA, 1912.

EUSEBIUS. *Ecclesiastical History*, ed. and trans. K. Lake and J.E.L. Oulton, 2 vols. Cambridge, MA, 1932.

IGNATIUS. *To the Magnesians*, ed. and trans. K. Lake. Cambridge, MA, 1912.

JUSTIN MARTYR. *Saint Justin Martyr: Dialogue with Trypho*, trans. T.B. Falls. Washington, DC, 1948.

The Koran, trans. N.J. Dawood. Harmondsworth, 1956.

Novum Testamentum Graece, ed. E. Nestle. Stuttgart, 1960.

TERTULLIAN. *Apologia*, ed. and trans. T.R. Glover. Cambridge, MA, 1931.

Theological Dictionary of the New Testament, ed. G. Friedrich, trans. B.W. Bromiley. Grand Rapids, MI, 1974.

Prayerbooks

The High Holiday Prayerbook, ed. B. Bokser. New York, 1959.

High Holy Day Prayerbook, ed. and trans. B. Adeser. New York, 1959.

Secondary Sources

Books

AQUINAS, THOMAS. *De Veritate*, trans. R.W. Schmidt, 3 vols. Chicago, 1954.

—— *Summa Theologiae*, ed. P. Caramello, 3 vols. Rome, 1962.

ADLER, MORTIMER J. *The Time of Our Lives*. New York, 1970.

AGUS, JACOB. *The Evolution of Jewish Thought*. New York, 1959.

—— *Jewish Identity in an Age of Ideologies*. New York, 1978.

ALBECK, CHANOCH. *Das Buch Jubilaen und die Halacha*. Berlin, 1930.

—— *Mav'o le-Talmudim*. Tel Aviv, 1969.

ALTMANN, ALEXANDER. *Moses Mendelssohn: A Biographical Study*. Tuscaloosa, AL, 1973.

ARISTOTLE. *De Anima*, ed. and trans. W.S. Hett. Cambridge, MA, 1936.

—— *Categories*, ed. and trans. H.P. Poole. Cambridge, MA, 1938.

—— *Metaphysics*, ed. and trans. H. Trendennick. Cambridge, MA, 1933.

—— *Nicomachean Ethics*, ed. and trans. H. Rackham. Cambridge, MA, 1926.

—— *Physics*, ed. and trans. F.M. Cornford. Cambridge, MA, 1929.

—— *Politics*, ed. and trans. H. Rackham. Cambridge, MA, 1927.

—— *Prior Analytics*, ed. and trans. H. Trendennick. Cambridge, MA, 1938.

—— *Rhetoric*, ed. and trans. S.H. Freese. Cambridge, MA, 1926.

—— *Topics*, ed. and trans. E.S. Forster. Cambridge, MA, 1960.

ATLAS, SAMUEL. *Netivim be-Mishpat ha-Ivri*. New York, 1978.

AVICENNA. *The Metaphysics of Avicenna: A Critical Translation-Commentary*, ed. P. Morewidge. New York, 1973.

AUGUSTINE. *De Civitate Dei*, trans. G.G. Walsh et al. Garden City, NY, 1958.

BAECK, LEO. *Dieses Volk: Jüdische Existenz*, 2 vols. Frankfurt, 1955 and 1957.

BAER, YITZHAK. *A History of the Jews of Christian Spain*, trans. L. Schoffman, vol. 1. Philadelphia, 1978.

—— *Toldot ha-Yehudim be-Sefarad ha-Notzrit*. Tel Aviv, 1959.

BAMBERGER, BERNARD. *Proselytism in the Talmudic Period*. New York, 1968.

BAMBERGER, FRITZ. *Das System des Maimonides*. Berlin, 1935.

BARON, SALO. *A Social and Religious History of the Jews*, vols. 1 and 2. New York, 1952.

BELKIN, SAMUEL. *Philo and the Oral Law.* Cambridge, MA, 1940.

BENAMOZEGH, ELIJAH. *Be-Shbilai ha-Mussar.* Jerusalem, 1966.

—— *Israël et l'humanité.* Paris, 1914.

BERGER, ADOLF. *Encyclopedic Dictionary of Roman Law.* Philadelphia, 1953.

BERGMAN, SHMUEL. *Faith and Reason: An Introduction to Modern Jewish Thought,* trans. A. Jospe. Washington, DC, 1961.

BERTHOLET, A. *Die Stellung der Israeliten und der Juden zu Fremden.* Freiburg, 1896.

BIBERFELD, PHILIP. *Universal Jewish History,* vol. I. New York, 1948.

BICKERMAN, ELIAS. *From Ezra to the Last of the Maccabees.* New York, 1962.

BLEICH, J. DAVID. *Contemporary Halakhic Problems.* New York, 1977.

BLOCH, ERNST. *Naturrecht und menschliche Würde.* Frankfurt, 1961.

BLOCH, JOSEF. *Israel und die Völker.* Leipzig, 1922.

BROWN, R. *The Anchor Bible: The Gospel According to John xiii–xxi.* Garden City, NY, 1970.

BURKLAND, W.W., and P. STEIN. *A Text-Book of Roman Law from Augustus to Justinian.* Cambridge, MA, 1963.

CHAJES, ZVI HIRSCH. *Kol Kitvei Maharetz Chajes,* 2 vols. Jerusalem, 1958.

CICERO. *De Officiis,* ed. and trans. W. Miller. Cambridge, MA, 1928.

COHEN, BOAZ. *Jewish and Roman Law,* 2 vols. New York, 1966.

COHEN, HERMANN. *Ethik des reinen Willens,* 3rd edn. Berlin, 1921.

—— *Jüdische Schriften,* ed. B. Strauss, 3 vols. Berlin, 1924.

—— *Religion of Reason out of the Sources of Judaism,* trans. S. Kaplan. New York, 1972.

—— *Religion der Vernunft aus den Quellen des Judenthums,* 3rd edn. Darmstadt, 1966.

COHEN, HAIM H. *The Trial and Death of Jesus.* New York, 1977.

DAUBE, DAVID. *Collaboration with Tyranny in Rabbinic Law.* Oxford, 1965.

DAVIES, W.D. *Paul and Rabbinic Judaism,* 2nd edn. London, 1955.

DEVAUX, ROLAND. *Ancient Israel,* 2 vols. New York, 1965.

Digest (Corpus Juris Civilis), trans. C.H. Munro. Cambridge, MA, 1891.

DILTHEY, WILHELM. *Gesammelte Schriften,* vol. 3. Leipzig, 1914.

DWORKIN, RONALD. *Taking Rights Seriously.* Cambridge, MA, 1978.

EFROS, ISRAEL. *Studies in Medieval Jewish Philosophy.* New York, 1974.

EICHRODT, W. *Theology of the Old Testament,* trans. J.A. Baker, 2 vols. Philadelphia, 1961–67.

ELIADE, MIRCEA. *The Sacred and the Profane.* New York, 1961.

ELLUL, JACQUES. *The Meaning of the City,* trans. D. Pardee. Grand Rapids, MI, 1970.

Encyclopedia Judaica, 10 vols. Jerusalem, 1970.

EPICTETUS. *Discourses,* trans. P.E. Matheson. New York, 1940.

FACKENHEIM, EMIL. *Encounters Between Judaism and Modern Philosophy.* New York, 1973.

FAUR, JOSÉ. *Iyunim be-Mishneh Torah le-ha-Rambam.* Jerusalem, 1978.

FEDERBUSH, SIMON. *Mishpat ha-Melukhah be-Yisrael*, 2nd rev. edn. Jerusalem, 1973.

FELDMAN, D.M. *Birth Control and Jewish Law*. New York, 1968.

FINKELSTEIN, LOUIS. *Akiva*. Philadelphia, 1936.

—— *Pharisaism in the Making*. New York, 1972.

—— *The Pharisees*, 2 vols. Philadelphia, 1938.

FOX, MARVIN. *Interpreting Maimonides: Studies in Methodology, Metaphysics and Moral Philosophy*. Chicago, 1990.

FRANKFORT, HENRI, ET AL. *Before Philosophy: The Intellectual Adventure of Ancient Man*. Harmondsworth, 1949.

FREUD, SIGMUND. *Collected Papers*, trans. J. Strachey. London, 1950–52.

FRIEDRICH, CARL. *The Philosophy of Law in Historical Perspective*. 2nd rev. edn. Chicago, 1963.

FUSTEL DE COULANGES, N.D. *The Ancient City*, trans. W. Small. Garden City, NY, n.d.

GEIGER, ABRAHAM. *Urschrift und Übersetzungen der Bibel*. Breslau, 1857.

GINZBERG, LOUIS. *The Legends of the Jews*, 6 vols. Philadelphia, 1909–28.

GOODENOUGH, ERWIN R. *The Jurisprudence of the Jewish Courts in Egypt*. Amsterdam, 1968.

GRAETZ, HEINRICH. *Geschichte der Juden*. Leipzig, 1888.

GREENRIDGE, A.H.J. *Roman Public Life*. New York, 1970.

GROTIUS, HUGO. *De Jure Bellis ac Pacis*, 2 vols. Oxford, 1925.

GULAK, ASHER. *Yesodai ha-Mishpatim ha'Ivri*, 2 vols. Berlin, 1927.

GUTTMANN, JULIUS. *Dat u-Mada*, trans. S. Asch. Jerusalem, 1955.

—— *Philosophies of Judaism*, trans. D.S. Silverman. New York, 1964.

GUTTMANN, MICHAEL. *Das Judenthum und seine Umwelt*. Berlin, 1927

HALIVNI, DAVID WEISS. *Mekorot u-Mesorot: Nashim*. Tel Aviv, 1968.

HARRISON, A.R.W. *The Law of Athens*. Oxford, 1968.

HART, H.L.A. *The Concept of Law*. Oxford, 1961.

HARTMAN, DAVID. *Maimonides: Torah and Philosophic Quest*. Philadelphia, 1976.

HEGEL, G.W.F. *Logic*, trans. A.V. Miller. London, 1969.

—— *Phaenomenologie des Geistes*, ed. J. Hoffmeister. Hamburg, 1952.

HEIDEGGER, MARTIN. *Sein und Zeit*, 8th edn. Tübingen, 1957.

HEINEMANN, ISAAK. *Ta'amei ha-Mitzvot be-Sifrut Yisrael*, 2 vols. Jerusalem, 1957.

HEINEMANN, JOSEPH. *Aggadot ve-Toldotaihem*. Jerusalem, 1974.

HENGEL, MARTIN. *Judaism and Hellenism*, trans. J. Bowden, 2 vols. London, 1974.

HENOCH, CHAIM. *Ha-Ramban ke-Hoker u-Mekubbal*. Jerusalem, 1978.

HERZOG, ISAAC H. *The Main Institutions of Jewish Law*, 2 vols. London, 1965.

HESCHEL, ABRAHAM JOSHUA. *God in Search of Man*. New York, 1955.

—— *The Prophets*, Philadelphia, 1962.

—— *Torah min ha-Shamayim*, 2 vols. London, 1962.

HIRSCH, SAMSON RAPHAEL. *Judaism Eternal*, trans. I. Grunfeld, 2 vols. London, 1956.

HIRSCH, SAMUEL. *Religionsphilosophie der Juden*. Leipzig, 1842.

HOBBES, THOMAS. *Leviathan*, ed. M. Oakeshott. New York, 1962.

HOENIG, SIDNEY. *The Great Sanhedrin*. Philadelphia, 1953.

HOFFMANN, DAVID. *Die Schulchan Aruch und die Rabbinen über das Verhältnis der Juden zu Andersgläubigen*. Berlin, 1885.

—— *Die Wichtigsten Instanzen gegen die Graf-Wellhausen Hypothese*. Berlin, 1904.

HOLDHEIM, SAMUEL. *Gemischte Ehen zwischen Juden und Christen*. Berlin, 1850.

HUME, DAVID. *An Inquiry Concerning the Principles of Morals*, ed. C.W. Hendel. New York, 1957.

HUSSERL, EDMUND. *Cartesian Meditations*, trans. D. Cairns. The Hague, 1960.

—— *Phenomenology and the Crisis of Philosophy*, trans. Q. Lauer. New York, 1965.

JACOBS, LOUIS. *Principles of the Jewish Faith*. New York, 1964.

JAKOBOVITS, IMMANUEL. *Jewish Medical Ethics*. New York, 1959.

JASPERS, KARL. *Truth and Symbol*, trans. J.T. Wilde, W. Kluback and J. Kimmel. New York, 1959.

Jewish Encyclopedia, 12 vols. New York, 1901.

JOEL, MANUEL. *Beiträge zur Geschichte der Philosophie*. Breslau, 1876.

JONAS, HANS. *The Gnostic Religion*. Boston, 1958.

JUSTER, J. *Les Juifs dans L'Empire Romaine*. Paris, 1914.

JUVENAL. *Satires*, ed. and trans. G.G. Ramsey. Cambridge, MA, 1940.

KADUSHIN, MAX. *Worship and Ethics*. Evanston, IL, 1964.

KANT, IMMANUEL. *Critique of Practical Reason*, trans. L.W. Beck. Indianapolis, IN, 1956.

—— *Critique of Pure Reason*, trans. N. Kemp Smith. New York, 1929.

—— *The Fundamental Principle of the Metaphysics of Morals*, trans. T.K. Abbott. New York, 1949.

—— *Religion within the Limits of Reason Alone*, trans. J.H. Greene and H.H. Hudson. New York, 1960.

KATZ, JACOB. *Exclusiveness and Tolerance*. Oxford, 1961.

KAUFMANN, WALTER. *Hegel: A Reinterpretation*. Garden City, NY, 1965.

KAUFMANN, YEHEZKEL. *Golah ve-Nekhar*, 2 vols. Tel Aviv, 1930.

—— *The Religion of Israel*, trans. M. Greenberg. Chicago, 1960.

—— *Toldot ha-Emunah ha-Yisraelit*, 5 vols. Jerusalem, 1953.

KELSEN, HANS. *The Pure Theory of Law*, trans. M. Knight. Berkeley, CA, 1970.

KIRSCHENBAUM, AARON. *Self-Incrimination in Jewish Law*. New York, 1970.

KITTO, H.D.F. *The Greeks*, rev. edn. Baltimore, 1957.

KLATZKIN, JACOB. *Thesaurus Philosophicus*, 5 vols. Berlin, 1928.

KLAUSNER, JOSEPH. *From Jesus to Paul*, trans. W.F. Stinespring. Boston, 1961.

KOHLER, KAUFMANN. *Jewish Theology*. New York, 1918.

KOOK, ABRAHAM ISAAC. *Igrot Rayah*, vol. 1. Jerusalem, 1961.

LAUTERBACH, JACOB Z. *Rabbinic Essays*. Cincinnati, 1951.

LAZARUS, MORITZ. *The Ethics of Judaism*, trans. H. Szold, 2 vols. Philadelphia, 1900.

LEVY, ERNST. *Gesammelte Schriften*, vol. 1. Cologne, 1963.

LICHTENSTEIN, AHARON. *The Seven Laws of Noah*. New York, 1981.

LIDDELL and SCOTT. *A Greek–English Lexicon*. New York, 1927.

LIEBERMAN, SAUL. *Greek in Jewish Palestine*. New York, 1942.

—— *Hellenism in Jewish Palestine*, 2nd edn. New York, 1962.

LIST, B.W. *Graeco-italische Rechtsgeschichte*. Jena, 1884.

LONERGAN, BERNARD. *Method in Theology*. New York, 1972.

LOVEJOY, A.J. *The Great Chain of Being*. New York, 1960.

LUZZATTO, SAMUEL DAVID. *Mehkarai ha-Yahadut*, 2 vols. Warsaw, 1913.

—— *Yesodai ha-Torah*, ed. A.Z. Eshkoli. Jerusalem, 1947.

MARITAIN, JACQUES. *Man and the State*. Chicago, 1951.

MARMORSTEIN, ARTHUR. *The Old Rabbinic Doctrine of God: The Names and the Attributes of God*, vol. 1. New York, 1968.

MARTIN, E.J. *A History of the Iconoclastic Controversy*. London, 1931.

MENDELSSOHN, MOSES. *Jerusalem*, trans. M. Samuels, 2 vols. London, 1838.

—— *Jerusalem and Other Jewish Writings*, ed. and trans. A. Jospe. New York, 1969.

—— *Schriften*, ed. M. Brasch, 2 vols. Leipzig, 1880.

—— *Schriften: Jubiläumausgabe*, vols. 7, 16. Berlin, 1929, 1932.

MEYER, MICHAEL. *The Origins of the Modern Jew*. Detroit, 1967.

MOMMSEN, THEODOR. *Römisches Strafrecht*. Berlin, 1955.

MONTEFIORE, C.G., and H. LOEWE. *A Rabbinic Anthology*. New York, 1963.

MOORE, G.F. *Judaism*, 3 vols. Cambridge, MA, 1927.

MOORE, K.L. *The Developing Human*, 2nd edn. Philadelphia, 1977.

NELSON, BENJAMIN. *The Idea of Usury*, 2nd edn. Chicago, 1969.

NEUMARK, DAVID. *Toldot ha-Philosofia be-Yisrael*. New York, 1921.

NEUSNER, JACOB. *A History of the Jews in Babylonia: The Early Sassanian Period*. Leiden, 1966.

NIEBUHR, REINHOLD. *The Self and the Dramas of History*. New York, 1955.

NOVAK, DAVID. *Jewish Social Ethics*. Oxford, 1992.

—— *Law and Theology in Judaism*, 2 vols. New York, 1974, 1976.

—— *Natural Law in Judaism*. Cambridge, 1998.

—— *Suicide and Morality*. New York, 1975.

NYGREN, ANDERS. *Meaning and Method*, trans. P.S. Watson. Philadelphia, 1972.

PALLIÈRE, AIMÉ. *The Unknown Sanctuary*, trans. L.W. Wise. New York, 1928.

PEDERSEN, JOHANNES. *Israel: Its Life and Culture*. Copenhagen, 1926.

PIEPER, JOSEF. *Leisure: The Basis of Culture*. New York, 1963.

PLATO. *Euthyphro, Apology, Crito, Phaedo, Phaedrus*, ed. and trans. H.N. Fowler. Cambridge, MA, 1914.

—— *Laws*, ed. and trans. R.G. Bury, 2 vols. Cambridge, MA, 1926.

—— *Parmenides*, ed. and trans. H.N. Fowler. Cambridge, MA, 1926.

—— *Republic*, ed. and trans. P. Shorey, 2 vols. Cambridge, MA, 1930.

—— *Seventh Letter*, ed. and trans. R.G. Bury. Cambridge, MA, 1929.

—— *Statesman and Philebus*, ed. and trans. H.N. Fowler. Cambridge, MA, 1921.

—— *Timaeus*, ed. and trans. R.G. Bury. Cambridge, MA, 1929.

RAWIDOWICZ, SIMON. *Studies in Jewish Thought*. Philadelphia, 1974.

RAWLS, JOHN. *A Theory of Justice*. Cambridge, MA, 1971.

REINES, ALVIN. *Maimonides and Abravanel on Prophecy*. Cincinnati, 1970.

RICOEUR, PAUL. *The Symbolism of Evil*, trans. E. Buchanan. New York, 1967.

ROSENBLOOM, NOAH. *Luzzatto's Ethico-Psychological Interpretation of Judaism*. New York, 1965.

—— *Tradition in an Age of Reform: The Religious Philosophy of Samson Raphael Hirsch*. Philadelphia, 1976.

ROSENZWEIG, FRANZ. *Franz Rosenzweig: His Life and Thought*, trans. Nahum Glatzer, 2nd rev. edn. New York, 1961.

—— *Kleinere Schriften*. Berlin, 1937.

—— *Der Stern der Erlösung*. Frankfurt, 1921.

—— and EUGENE ROSENSTOCK-HUESSY. *Judaism despite Christianity*, trans. D. Emmet and E. Rosenstock-Huessy. New York, 1971.

ROSS, W.D. *Aristotle*. New York, 1959.

ROSTOVTZEFF, MIKAIL. *The Social and Economic History of the Hellenistic World*, 2 vols. Oxford, 1941.

ROTENSTREICH, NATHAN. *Jewish Philosophy in Modern Times: From Mendelssohn to Rosenzweig*. New York, 1968.

RUFINUS. *Summa Decretorum*, ed. H. Singer. Paderborn, 1902.

SACKS, JONATHAN. *Crisis and Covenant: Jewish Thought after the Holocaust*. Manchester, 1992.

SARTRE, JEAN-PAUL. *The Transcendence of the Ego*, trans. F. Williams and R. Kirkpatrick. New York, 1957.

SCHECHTER, SOLOMON. *Seminary Addresses and Other Papers*. Cincinnati, 1915.

—— *Studies in Judaism*, 1st series. New York, 1896.

SCHELER, MAX. *Formalism in Ethics*, trans. M.S. Frings and R.L. Funk. Evanston, IL, 1973.

SCHILLER, FRIEDRICH. *Werke*, ed. J. Mueller, vol. 1. Berlin, 1967.

SCHOCHET, ELIJAH J. *A Responsum of Surrender*. Los Angeles, 1973.

SCHOLEM, GERSHOM. *Kabbalah and its Symbolism*, trans. R. Manheim. New York, 1965.

—— *Major Trends in Jewish Mysticism*. New York, 1941.

SCHÜRER, EMIL. *Geschichte des jüdischen Volkes im Zeitalter Jesu Christi*, vol. 3. Leipzig, 1909.

SCHWEID, ELIEZER. *Sefer ha-Ikkarim le-Rabbi Yosef Albo.* Jerusalem, 1967.

SCHWEITZER, ALBERT. *The Philosophy of Civilization: Civilization and Ethics,* trans. C.T.Campion, 2nd edn. London, 1929.

SHAKESPEARE, WILLIAM. *Complete Works,* ed. W.J. Craig. London, 1945.

SHERWIN-WHITE, A.N. *Roman Society and Roman Law in the New Testament.* Oxford, 1963.

SHILO, S. *Dina de-Malkhuta Dina.* Jerusalem, 1974.

SOHM, R. *The Institutes: A Text-Book of the History and System of Roman Law,* 2nd edn., trans. J.C. Leslie. Oxford, 1901.

SOPHOCLES. *King Oedipus,* trans. T. Gould. Englewood Cliffs, NJ, 1970.

SPINOZA, BARUCH. *Opera,* vol. 3, ed. C. Gebhardt. Heidelberg, 1925.

—— *Tractatus Theologico-Politicus,* trans. R.M.H. Elwes. New York, 1951.

STEINMETZ, DEVORA. *Punishment and Freedom: The Rabbinic Construction of Criminal Law.* Philadelphia, 2008.

STRACK, HERMANN, and PAUL BILLERBECK. *Kommentar zum neuen Testament aus Talmud und Midrasch,* vol. 2. Munich, 1924.

STRAUSS, LEO. *Natural Right and History.* Chicago, 1953.

—— *Persecution and the Art of Writing.* Glencoe, IL, 1952.

—— *Philosophie und Gesetz.* Berlin, 1935.

—— *Spinoza's Critique of Religion.* New York, 1965.

SUETONIUS. *The Lives of the Caesars,* ed. and trans. J.C. Rolfe. Cambridge, MA, 1930.

TACITUS. *History,* ed. and trans. C.H. Moore, vols. 2–4. Cambridge, MA, 1925–37.

TAENZER, A. *Die Religionsphilosophie Josef Albos.* Frankfurt am Main, 1896.

TCHERNOWITZ, CHAIM. *Toldot ha-Halakhah,* 4 vols. New York, 1934–50.

THUCYDIDES. *The Peloponnesian War,* ed. and trans. C.F. Smith, 4 vols. Cambridge, MA, 1921–23.

TILLICH, PAUL. *Dynamics of Faith.* New York, 1957.

TISHBY, J. *Mishnat ha-Zohar,* 2 vols. Jerusalem, 1961.

TÖNNIES, FERDINAND. *Fundamental Concepts of Sociology,* trans. C.P. Loomis. East Lansing, MI, 1957.

TWERSKY, ISADORE. *Rabad of Posquières.* Cambridge, MA, 1962.

URBACH, E. *Ba'alei ha-Tosafot.* Jerusalem, 1955.

—— *Hazal: Emunot ve-De'ot.* Jerusalem, 1971.

VINOGRADOFF, R. *Outlines of Historical Jurisprudence.* Oxford, 1932.

WALZER, M., M. LORBERBAUM and N. ZOHAR, EDS. *The Jewish Political Tradition,* vol. 1: *Authority.* New Haven, 2000.

WEIN, BERL. *Hikrai Halakha.* Jerusalem, 1976.

WEISS, ISAAC H. *Dor Dor ve-Dorshav,* 5 vols. Jerusalem, n.d.

WELLHAUSEN, JULIUS. *Prologomena to the History of Ancient Israel,* trans. A. Menzies. New York, 1956.

WERFEL, I. *Sefer ha-Hasidut.* Tel Aviv, 1947.

WESSELY, NAFTALI HARTWIG. *Divrai Shalom v'Emet.* Warsaw, 1886.

WITTGENSTEIN, LUDWIG. *Tractatus Logico-Philosophicus*, trans. D.F. Dears and B.F. McGuiness. London, 1961.

WOLFSON, HARRY. *Philo*, 2 vols. Cambridge, MA, 1947.

—— *The Philosophy of the Church Fathers*, 3rd rev. edn. Cambridge, MA, 1970.

—— *Repercussions of Kalam in Jewish Philosophy*. Cambridge, MA, 1979.

ZUCKER, MOSES. *Hasagot al Rav Saadiah Gaon me'et Rav Mubashir, etc.* New York, 1955.

—— *Rav Saadiah Gaon's Translation of the Torah* (Heb.). New York, 1959.

Articles

Agus, Jacob. Review of Louis Finkelstein, *Pharisaism in the Making*. *Conservative Judaism* 28.3 (Spring 1974).

APTOWITZER, VIKTOR. "Zekher le-Zekhut ha'Em bi-Sifrut Yisrael." *Ha-Mishpat ha-Ivri*, vol. 2. 1927.

BEN-SASSON, H.H. "*De'ot*, etc." In *Salo W. Baron Jubilee Volume*, vol. 3. Jerusalem, 1974.

BERGMAN, S.H. "Israel and the Oikoumen." In *Studies in Rationalism, Judaism and Universalism: In Memory of Leon Roth*, ed. R. Loewe. London, 1966.

BIBERFELD, PHILIP. "Judaism and International Law." In *Israel of Tomorrow*, ed. L. Jung. New York, 1946.

—— "Das Noachische Urrecht." *Nachalat Z'vi*, vols. 6–7, 1936–37.

BLEICH, J. DAVID. "Survey of Recent Halakhic Literature." *Tradition* 16.5 (1977).

—— "Teaching Torah to Non-Jews." *Tradition* 18.2 (1980).

BOKSER, B.Z. "Morality and Religion in the Theology of Maimonides." In *Essays on Jewish Life and Thought: Presented to Salo Wittmayer Baron*. New York, 1959.

COBB, W.F. "Blasphemy." In *Encyclopedia of Religion and Ethics*, vol. 2.

COHN, H.H. and L.H. RABINOWITZ. "Capital Punishment." *Encyclopedia Judaica*, vol. 5.

DAUBE, DAVID. "The Peregrine Praetor." *The Journal of Roman Studies* 41.1–2 (1951).

DIESENDRUCK, ZVI. "Ha-Takhlit ve-ha-Te'arim be-Torat ha-Rambam." *Tarbiz* 1.3 (1930).

—— "Die Teleologie bei Maimonides." *HUCA*, 6 (1928).

DIETRICH, W.S. "The Function of the Idea of Messianic Mankind in Hermann Cohen's Later Thought." *Journal of American Academy of Religion* 48.2 (1980).

FAUR, JOSÉ. "Mekor Hiyyuvan shel ha-Mitzvot le-Da'at ha-Rambam." *Tarbiz* 38 (1968).

—— "The Origin of the Distinction between Rational and Divine Commandments in Medieval Jewish Philosophy." *Augustinianum* 9 (1969).

—— "Understanding the Covenant." *Tradition* 9.4 (Spring 1968).

FOX, MARVIN. "Maimonides and Aquinas on Natural Law." *Dine Israel* 3 (1972).

—— "Prologomenon" to A. Cohen, *The Teachings of Maimonides*. New York, 1968.

GORDIS, ROBERT. "A Dynamic Halakhah: Principles and Procedures of Jewish Law." *Judaism* 28.3 (1980).

——"Studies in Hebrew Roots of Contrasted Meanings." *Jewish Quarterly Review* 27.1 (1936).

GREENBAUM, A. "Thirty Commandments according to R. Samuel b. Hofni" (Heb.). *Sinai* 72.4–5 (1973).

GREENBERG, MOSHE. "Rabbinic Reflections on Defying Illegal Orders: Amasa, Abner and Joab." *Judaism* 19.1 (1970).

GUTTMANN, JULIUS. "An Investigation of the Sources of *Sefer ha-Ikkarim*." In *Sefer ha-Ikkarim*, 2 vols. Jerusalem, n.d.

GUTTMANN, MICHAEL. "Maimonide sur l'universalité de la morale religieuse." *Revue des Études Juives* 99 (1935).

HALIVNI, DAVID W. "Can a Religious Law Be Immoral?" In *Perspectives on Jews and Judaism: Essays in Honor of Wolfe Kelman*. New York, 1978.

HEINEMANN, ISAAK. "Die Lehre vom ungeschriebenem Gesetz in jüdischen Schriften." *HUCA* 4 (1928).

HRUBY, KURT. "La Révélation dans la théologie rabbinique." *L'Orient Syrien* 11.1 (1966).

HUSIK, ISAAC. "The Law of Nature, Hugo Grotius and the Bible." *HUCA* 1 (1925).

——"The Philosophy of Maimonides." In *Maimonides Octocentennial Series* 4. New York, 1935.

ISRAELI, S. "Exemptions from Noahide Law" (Heb.). *Ha-Torah ve-ha-Medinah* 7–8 (1954–57).

JACKSON, BERNARD. "Maimonides' Definitions of *Tam* and *Mu'ad*." *The Jewish Law Annual* 1 (1978).

KATZ, JACOB. "Soblanut Datit be-Shitato shel Rabbi Menachem ha-Meiri." *Zion* 18 (1953).

KIRSCHENBAUM, AARON. "Ha-Berit im Bnei Noah." *Dine Israel* 6 (1975).

KOHLER, KAUFMANN. "Book of Jubilees." In *Jewish Encyclopedia*, vol. 7.

KRAUSS, SAMUEL. "The Jews in the Works of the Church Fathers." *Jewish Quarterly Review* os 4 (1894).

——"Les Préceptes des Noachides." *Revue des Études Juives* 47 (1903).

LANDMAN, L., "Law and Conscience," *Judaism* 18.1 (Winter 1969).

LERNER, RALPH. "Natural Law in Albo's *Book of Roots*." In *Ancients and Moderns*, ed. J. Cropsey. New York, 1964.

LEVY, E. "Natural Law in Roman Thought." In *Gesammelte Schriften*. Cologne, 1963.

LICHTENSTEIN, AHARON. "Does Jewish Tradition Recognize an Ethic Independent of Halakha?" In *Modern Jewish Ethics*, ed. M. Fox. Columbus, OH, 1975.

LOEWE, RAPHAEL. "Potentialities and Limitations of Universalism in the Halakhah." In *Studies in Rationalism, Judaism and Universalism: In Memory of Leon Roth*, ed. R. Loewe. London, 1966.

MARX, ALEXANDER. "Texts by and about Maimonides." *Jewish Quarterly Review* 25.4 (1935).

MEEK, T.J. "The Translation of *Ger* in the Hexateuch." *Journal of Biblical Literature* 49 (1930).

NOVAK, DAVID. "Annulment in Lieu of Divorce in Jewish Law." *The Jewish Law Annual* 4 (1981).

——"A Foundation for Jewish Philosophy: Preliminary Sketch." *Journal of Reform Judaism* (1979).

——"Judaism and Contemporary Bioethics." *Journal of Medicine and Philosophy* 4.4 (1979).

——"The Origin of the Noahide Laws." In *Perspectives on Jews and Judaism: Essays in Honor of Wolfe Kelman*. New York, 1978.

——"Rayon Dat Tivit be-Mahshevet Rav Yosef Albo." *Hadoar* 62.2 (1982).

——Review of "Freedom and Punishment." *Journal of Religion* 90.1 (Jan. 2010), 93–94.

——"Universal Moral Law in the Theology of Hermann Cohen." *Modern Judaism* 1.1 (1981).

PERLES, FELIX. "Die Autonomie der Sittlichkeit im jüdischen Schriftum." In *Judaica Festschrift zu Hermann Cohens siebzigstem Geburtstage*. Berlin, 1912.

REINES, ALVIN. "Maimonides' Concept of Mosaic Prophecy." *HUCA* 40–41 (1969–70).

ROSENTHAL, ERWIN. "Torah and Nomos in Jewish Philosophy." In *Studies in Judaism, Rationalism and Universalism: In Memory of Leon Roth*, ed. R. Loewe. London, 1966.

SCHMIEDL, ADOLF. "Comparisons between Roman and Talmudic Law" (Heb.). *Ha-Schachar* 10 (1880).

SCHWARZCHILD, STEVEN. "Do Noachites Have to Believe in Revelation?" *Jewish Quarterly Review* 52.4–53.1 (1962).

——"Moral Radicalism and 'Middlingness' in the Ethics of Maimonides." *Studies in Medieval Culture* 11 (1977).

SELIGMANN, I.L. "Ger." In *Encyclopedia Mikra'it*, vol. 2.

SIMON, ERNST. "The Neighbor (*Re'a*) whom We Shall Love." In *Modern Jewish Ethics*, ed. M. Fox. Columbus, OH, 1975.

SOLOVEITCHIK, JOSEPH. "Ish ha-Halakhah." *Talpiot* 1.3–4 (1944).

TWERSKY, ISADORE. "Some Non-Halakhic Aspects of the *Mishneh Torah*." In *Jewish Medieval and Renaissance Studies*, ed. A. Altmann. Cambridge, MA, 1967.

WEISS, RAYMOND. Introduction to *Ethical Writings of Maimonides*. New York, 1975.

YOVEL, YIRMIYAHU. "The Highest Good and History in Kant's Thought." *Archiv für Geschichte der Philosophie* 54 (1972).

ZUCKER, MOSES. "Towards a Solution to the Problem of the 32 Exegetical Principles, etc." (Heb.). In *Proceedings of the American Academy for Jewish Research* 23 (1954).

INDEX